The Science of Behavior
and the Image of Man

The Science of Behavior
and the Image of Man

ISIDOR CHEIN

TAVISTOCK PUBLICATIONS

First published in Great Britain in 1972
by Tavistock Publications Limited
11 New Fetter Lane, London EC4
Printed in Great Britain
by photolithography by
Butler & Tanner Ltd, Frome and London
© 1972 by Basic Books, Inc., New York
SBN 422 74130 2
DESIGNED BY THE INKWELL STUDIO

TO THE MEMORY OF

MY MOTHER AND FATHER

WHO, BEYOND MEASURE,

HELPED ME BECOME

WHAT I AM

AND

TO MY WIFE

WHO, ALSO BEYOND MEASURE,

MADE THE BECOMING

SEEM WORTHWHILE

PREFACE

I have attempted in this book to present a systematic account of the way I have come to see the field of psychology, at least insofar as it pertains to the human subject. Because my view is unorthodox with respect to what I take to be the prevailing views in this field, I have also had to deal with fundamental issues of the nature of the scientific enterprise and other traditionally philosophical issues, such as the nature of reality and the relationships of body and mind.

I have written freely in first person to emphasize that it is my views I am presenting and to remind the reader that I am not uninvolved. For the same reason, I have occasionally indulged in irony and sarcasm, though I realize that they often backfire both in the sense of being taken literally and in the sense of arousing unnecessary resistance. I do not believe that it is possible to write on these matters without subjectivity and personal involvement—though it is, of course, possible to try to conceal subjectivity and involvement under the guise of a pseudoobjective scholarly style. I see no reason why anyone else should adopt my views unless, indeed, my argument is convincing, and I do not want to be convincing as a result of the successful use of rhetorical devices, but only, if at all, on the substantive strength of the argument. If, therefore, at times, I seem to pontificate (and past experience has taught me that, unfortunately, I often do sound that way), I apologize in advance and explain that it is not my conscious intention to do so.

The personal style, I am afraid, has not prevented a pedantic note from creeping into my writing, resulting from my compulsion to enter qualifications to my statements when I feel they should be made and my complexly structured thought processes. In one instance, I counted eighty-three words in what I hope is an otherwise clear sentence. I have, however, throughout, conscientiously striven to say what I felt I had to say as simply and as lucidly as I knew how.

I have not been able to find a satisfactory solution to one problem that is posed in the presentation of a highly integrated system of thought. At almost any point, one feels a need to say many different things at the same time—and this, of course, is impossible. I have coped as best I could by the liberal use of cross-references, footnotes, parenthesized remarks, labeled digressions, and, where I thought clarity of presentation would be advanced, repetition. If my use of these devices should jar on the reader, I can again only apologize in advance and humbly plead that I did not know how to do better.

Matters of style aside, there is at least one way in which this book will strike some readers as most unscholarly. I deliberately refrained from discussing similarities (and associated differences) between my own lines of thought and those of other writers save where I felt that it would advance the clarity of my own exposition. I have not here attempted to write a textbook or an encyclopedic monograph. I am presenting an argument, and it is complicated enough without cluttering it up with a comprehensive coverage of the literature. I did refer to the work of others where I felt it would help me to make some point and/or where I was myself conscious of a direct intellectual obligation. For the same reason, I have held documenting references to a bare minimum. If, through my unwitting sins of omission, I have done an injustice to other writers, I am truly sorry—and by way of atonement, if not restitution, I have carefully refrained from the luxury of referring to my own prior publications even though, in many instances, I borrowed liberally from them. One effect of such omissions is, from my viewpoint, all to the good. It emphasizes that this book must stand or fall on its own strengths or weaknesses; it does not borrow the pseudostrength that is implied in the tacit declaration, "Look at how many publications, those of others and my own, attest to the validity of what I am saying." That similar statements have been published elsewhere does not make anything said in this book one whit sounder or rationally more convincing.

One further point should be made in connection with scholarship. Though I am confident of my interpretations of various philosophical views and feel prepared to defend them, I am, after all, not a professional philosopher. It is entirely conceivable to me, therefore, that I have done less than justice to some of them. Though I would earnestly regret this if it should have happened, it would not really matter from the viewpoint of the limited purposes of the book. I do not recommend the book as a source of knowledge of the treasures of philosophy and do not regard myself as qualified to write such a work. That I have dared to write the present book at all—and let us face it, it is a philosophical work—is due to the fact that, as I explain at some length in Chapter 15, I regard it as imperative that psychologists should examine the philosophical premises of their science for themselves and come to their own philosophical positions in terms that respect their own goals and values. If in the process I have misrepresented some philosophical position, it is in the light (or shadow) of my misapprehension that I arrived at my own view and my reference to the former is only for the purpose of the exposition of the latter, that is, in the eventuality of a misinterpretation, it is on the latter that my thinking and exposition are predicated. I do not mean to suggest that, in such an eventuality, I might not have been wiser if I had understood better; but, in the limited frame of the purpose of this book, it is the philosophical output rather than input that calls for judgment and evaluation.

Many persons have given me the benefit of their criticism of my ideas and of earlier drafts and, in many instances, have offered helpful suggestions. I have given every criticism that has come my way the most earnest attention. Many I accepted and made appropriate revisions. In some instances, I felt that some point or another I had made was misunderstood and attempted to revise my presentation to lessen the likelihood of similar misunderstanding by others. In several instances, I have dealt explicitly with the criticisms in the book because I felt that it would clarify the points at issue. In some instances, perhaps out of my own deficiencies, I must confess that I did not feel that the criticisms were cogent or worthy of the attention that I gave to them.

I am, however, particularly obligated in this respect to my brother-in-law, Mr. Samuel Schooler, and to the following, most of them present or past colleagues: the late A. R. Cohen, J. Cohen, Mary Collins, S. W. Cook, Tamara Dembo, J. de Rivera, F. Emery, J. Harding, R. R. Holt, M. Horwitz, L. Hurvich, N. Jordan, R. A. Katzell, Doris Miller, W. S. Neff, Claire Selltiz, M. Stein, M. B. Smith, J. Weitz, and W. Wilke. Among the many students who have given me the benefit of their reactions, Mr. Charles T. Sullivan is particularly noteworthy for his voluminous written comments. I have, of course, learned from many people, but among those I think of as my major teachers (directly through classroom and other personal contacts, and/or indirectly through their writings), the following have been most influential in the shaping of my lines of thought: G. W. Allport, E. G. Boring, S. Freud, H. L. Hollingworth,

PREFACE

E. B. Holt, P. Janet, K. Lewin, W. McDougall, G. Murphy, E. C. Tolman, J. B. Watson, M. Wertheimer, and R. S. Woodworth.

I owe a very special kind of debt to Professor Ernest Nagel. When, as a young undergraduate student I brashly informed him that I was much too preoccupied with the study of psychology to do more than the absolute minimum of work in his course, he gently suggested that philosophy might have something to do with psychology. Then, though it was largely peripheral to the subject matter of the course, he said he would accept as a term paper a review of two psychology books from a philosophical point of view. I think of this as a turning point in my life. I can only hope that he will not be overly disappointed in the eventual outcome.

Miss Gloria Greaves patiently typed and retyped many versions of the manuscript and, in countless other ways, proved herself most helpful. I also owe a special debt to my sister, Eva Schooler, who volunteered to work on the index.

ISIDOR CHEIN

CONTENTS

PART I

Introduction

PART II

Basic Concepts and Psychological Processes

PART III

The Problem of the Actor

CONTENTS

PART IV

The Scientific Enterprise

PART

I

Introduction

1

THE PROBLEM OF THE

IMAGE OF MAN

Sigmund Koch has remarked that "psychology has been far more concerned with being a science than with courageous and self-determining confrontation of its historical subject matter.[1] Koch pointed out how little scientific psychology has contributed to the humanities in the face of his conviction that "psychology . . . *must* be . . . that area in which the problems of the sciences, as traditionally conceived, and the humanities intersect." He traced the difficulty to the fact that "psychology (and social science) has constructed a language that renders virtually impossible" its living up to its promise.

The trouble with this account is that language is not an arbitrary construction but a reflection of how the universe has been confronted and construed. If the language of psychology is defective, this is because the psychological subject matter is being violated. The scientist's use of language is designed to reflect the order of the phenomena he observes or expects to observe. If his language is defective, this is because he has not done justice to his observations, has failed to make allowance for observations he may reasonably be expected to make, or has implied an order that violates the order of his observations.

There is no compelling reason that I know of to expect that psychological science will in some fashion replicate the work of the humanities, and Koch raises no such expectation. The domain of the humanities is far more inclusive than the domain of psychological—or, for that

[1] S. Koch, "Psychological Science versus the Science-Humanism Antimony: Intimations of a Significant Science of Man," *American Psychologist*, 16 (1961): 624, 629, 631; and generally see pp. 629–639.

matter, all of behavioral—science, and undoubtedly many concerns of psychological science are apt to be of little interest to students of the humanities. Nor is there any reason to expect a parallelism of method or approach; every discipline must be free to develop the methods and approaches most conducive to the advancement of its concerns. Given the fact that no one has unlimited time at his disposal, I can think of no compelling reason to demand of psychologists that they become well informed with regard to the humanities (no more than I can think of any compelling reason to require of every candidate for the doctoral degree in psychology some level of mastery of two—or one—foreign languages rather than of mathematics, physics, chemistry, comparative anatomy, sociology, anthropology, economics, engineering, or any or all of the humanities).

What is disturbing, however, is that scientific psychology has produced so little that is relevant to the humanities. One cannot help feeling that a science that is, *inter alia*, concerned with human behavior ought to produce much that is at least relevant. The failure must, then, become occasion for searching self-examination. The proper source of discontent, if discontent is justified, is that psychology has failed to live up to its promise to itself, not that it has failed to live up to its promise to the humanities.

My own view is that psychologists know well enough what their subject matter is, but that, in the interests of a simple-minded conception of the nature of science, they all too often proceed to ignore much of it. A striking case in point is the position taken by Miller, Galanter, and Pribram[2] that, now that machines (computers) that behave pur-

---

[2] G. A. Miller, E. Galanter, and K. H. Pribram, *Plans and the Structure of Behavior* (New York: Holt, Rinehart & Winston, 1960). Thus, "Once a teleological mechanism could be built out of metal and glass, psychologists recognized that it was scientifically respectable to admit they had known it all along" (p. 43). Similarly, in commenting on a quotation from Clark Hull, they write that, "Passages such as this suggest that nothing less than the construction of a teleological machine would convince an experimental psychologist that there is not something occult implied by the terms 'goal,' 'purpose,' 'expectation,' 'entelechy'" (p. 45). Note that the point at issue here is quite different from another point discussed by Miller, Galanter, and Pribram in the same general context and involved in their quotation from Hull and their discussion of the Türing principle, namely, whether the ability to simulate a psychological process in a machine is a necessary and sufficient test of the completeness of one's comprehension of the psychological process.

Two readers of an earlier version of this chapter, not having read the book, felt that the tone of these quotations suggests that the authors were satirizing the experimentalists. If any other readers get the same feeling, I can only urge that

posively have been built, purpose has become a legitimate scientific concept. Apart from the question that I will shortly raise as to whether they properly construe the nature of purpose, the crucial present issue is whether faithfulness in the observation of one's subject matter can be validated by any extrinsic considerations. Does one decide on the nature of behavior on the basis of one's observations of it or on the basis of what one observes a machine to do?

Koch[3] charges that "the philosophy of science still talked in psychological literature is approximately 20 years out of date." This, of course, was written more than a decade ago and, as I see it, the situation has improved somewhat. Basically, however, psychologists are psychologists and not philosophers. It is as unfair to expect them to be fully informed and up-to-date in philosophy as it is to expect philosophers (even those who write on psychological matters) to be fully informed and up-to-date in psychology. The trouble is not in the philosophical illiteracy of the psychologists but in the supineness with which they take their cues from the reigning (or at least most vocal) forms of the philosophy of science—without confronting the issue of the kind of philosophy of science their field demands and, if necessary, inventing it.

Yes, the issue runs deeper than the service of psychology to the humanities. It concerns the nature of psychology itself, and, at the heart

---

they go back to the original. A much sounder defense of the manifest absurdity is that, until the age of cybernetics, psychologists were confronted with a Hobson's choice. They could either accept the paralysis that results from utter bafflement when confronted with large masses of unassimilable data or, ignoring these data, proceed on an orderly basis with respect to data they could assimilate. The absurdity, however, remains on two counts: (1) It was up to the scientists rather than the humanists to keep reminding themselves that they were ignoring large chunks of reality. It is, after all, science that takes special pride in humility (never, for instance, allowing itself the luxury of generalizations not supported by its data, though the rejection of such phenomena as purpose along with the conclusion that there is something "occult" about the related concepts is precisely such a generalization) and in its constant search for negative instances. (2) The behavioral scientists had the option of taking their data as they found them while reminding themselves that they did not know how to fit their own sciences together with the other sciences. This option they chose to ignore, despite their primary commitment to the observables, preferring a posture of abject servility to the other sciences; and it was psychology especially that betrayed its scientific commitments in the name of scientific respectability. The most noteworthy exceptions were the *Geisteswissenschaftsleute* who, unfortunately, had their own kind of deficient grasp of the nature of intersubjective validity ("truth," if you will) so that some of their wildest conjectures were presented as revealed truths. I shall return to related issues throughout the book, but especially in the last two chapters.

[3] Koch, p. 631.

of this issue, I find the issue of the image of Man. Specifically, I suggest, we must choose between two images. The first is that of Man as an active, responsible agent, not simply a helpless, powerless reagent. Man, in the active image, is a being who actively does something with regard to some of the things that happen to him, a being who, for instance, tries to increase the likelihood that some things will happen and that others will not, a being who tries to generate circumstances that are compatible with the execution of his intentions, a being who may try to inject harmony where he finds disharmony or who may sometimes seek to generate disharmony, a being who seeks to shape his environment rather than passively permit himself to be shaped by the latter, a being, in short, who insists on injecting himself into the causal process of the world around him. If Man is said to respond to his environment, the word "response" is to be taken in the sense that it has in active dialogue rather than in the sense of an automatic consequence.

The contrasting and the prevailing image among psychologists whose careers are devoted to the advancement of the science and among astonishingly large numbers of those concerned with behavioral orthogenics (guidance, counseling, psychotherapy, and so on) is that of Man as an impotent reactor, with his responses completely determined by two distinct and separate, albeit interacting, sets of factors: (1) the forces impinging on him and (2) his constitution (including in the latter term, for present purposes, momentary physiological states). Response is at all times and at every moment an automatic consequence of the interaction of body and environment. Man, as such, plays no role in determining the outcome of the interplay between constitution and environment. He is implicitly viewed as a robot—a complicatedly constructed and programmed robot, perhaps, but a robot nevertheless.

Note well that the issue is not simply whether behavior is purposive, not at least in some usages of the word "purpose."[4] One may conceive of Man as driven by powerful instinctual drives that impel him to seek particular ends; if the environment permits, the ends will be attained and, if not, a definite something else will happen. This model, commonly thought of as a purposive one, leaves Man a passive victim of the interplay between constitution and environment no less than do the nonpurposive stimulus-response models. Man, as such, has nothing to do with the outcome. He does nothing; things happen to him.

[4] See R. R. Holt, "Freud's Mechanistic and Humanistic Images of Man" to appear in *Psychoanalysis and Contemporary Science*, Vol. I, edited by Leo Goldberger et al. (New York: The Free Press, in press).

Nor is the issue whether one can reduce a human being to a state in which he is nothing more than a helpless passive reagent. Stupefy him, for instance, and drop him down an elevator shaft; his descent will not differ from that of any other physical body of the same shape. Nor is the issue whether there may not be reactions of the human body that are aptly described in the terms of the second image. Strike the patellar tendon, for instance, and, if the appropriate segments of the nervous system are intact and functioning and there are no physical restraints, there will follow a characteristic kick. The body is a physical body and, as such, it is utterly subject to physical law. The organism is a physiological system and, as such, it is utterly subject to physiological law; I am willing to take it as axiomatic that physiological law cannot be incompatible with physical law. I am similarly ready to take it as axiomatic that psychological law cannot be incompatible with either physiological or physical law. If it could be, the world would be reduced to chaos.

These are assumptions that I am not only willing to grant, but that I think are necessary to the scientific enterprise. They are not subject to disproof. Any apparent contradiction of them would only lead me to question the adequacy of our formulations of the relevant laws or the accuracy or sufficiency of the contradictory observations. To do otherwise would only be to put an end to inquiry and investigation—an end to science. They are not metaphysical or epistemological propositions at all, they are simply motivating assumptions of scientific inquiry.

I must assume that one who behaves is utterly subject to behavioral law and that the latter is not incompatible with either physiological or physical law. It does not follow that behavioral law is reducible to physiological or physical law, or that physiological law is reducible to physical law. A boiler system is subject to thermodynamic law, and it is also subject to mechanical law; but it does not follow that thermodynamic law is reducible to mechanical law. The concurrent relevance of two domains of law to one system does not necessarily imply that the two sets of laws are necessarily reducible to one of them. I am not saying that one set of laws is not reducible to another (such a ukase, too, would only put an end to inquiry), merely that it is not necessarily so; and I would very much want to encourage any line of inquiry that offered a promise of successfully accomplishing the reduction. Nor am I in any manner averse to the pursuit of investigations the aim of which is to determine how much of what seems to be behavior can be subsumed under physiology or physics.

I am, however, and it seems to me that any scientist ought to be, very much averse to the exclusion of observables on the ground that it is not apparent that the reduction can be accomplished. We should be equally averse if it were a certainty that the reduction is impossible. Our first responsibility, one that transcends all others, is to our observables. All our other commitments as scientists are deducible from this one, and only from this one. The law of parsimony, for instance, on which we place so much stock can only be justified on the ground that an unparsimonious explanation (one that postulates unnecessary entities, factors, forces, sources or forms of energy, intervening variables, and so forth) carries us unnecessarily far away from our observables.

To my mind, and this is the issue, we can only hold the second, the robotic, image by violating our cardinal obligation as scientists—to maintain faith with our subject matter, that is, to report scrupulously that which we observe and to observe fully without willful bias.

The opening sentence of "Ethical Standards of Psychologists"[5] is "The psychologist is committed to a belief in the dignity and worth of the individual human being." But what kind of dignity can we attribute to a robot? What is there in an impotent reactor that is of such intrinsic value as to require an unconditional commitment by psychologists to a belief in its worth? Is such a belief implicit in the images of Man presented in our textbooks or represented in the pages of our scientific journals? Does it not rather derive from our extrascientific indoctrination in the spirit of such statements as "And God said: We will make man, in our image and after our likeness."[6] A Talmudic commentary[7] on the biblical narrative of the Creation remarks on a unique aspect of the creation of Man. Unlike all others, Man was created in the singular. From the contrast, the rabbis deduce that each man must justify himself in his own life; no man may derive merit from having different ancestry than another. Moreover, the rabbis caution, God is not to be mistaken for an ordinary artisan who "may stamp his seal upon one piece of gold, and upon another. All the impressions are identical. But the Creator of the universe stamped millions of pieces of clay in His image and no two human beings are alike. For this reason, each person is entitled to say, 'For my sake was the world created,'" and, the rabbis go on to infer that "He who destroys a single life is considered as if he

[5] American Psychological Association, "Ethical Standards of Psychologists," *American Psychologist*, 14 (1959): 279–282.

[6] Gen. 1:26. I am aware that the rendition "We will make" is not a familiar one, but it is a literal translation of the Hebrew text.

[7] Mishneh, *Tractate Sanhedrin*, ch. 4.

8

had destroyed the whole world, while he who saves a single life is considered as having saved the whole world."

This is the kind of poetic association that is evoked by statements of a commitment by psychologists to a belief in the dignity and worth of the individual human being. Small wonder that some self-appointed high priests of science found themselves embarrassed by their connection with the American Psychological Association and were led to organize a new society under whose auspices they hoped to be able to pursue the path of what they consider the requirements of science, without fear of contamination.[8] The real wonder is that the rest of us, perhaps unworthy of being called psychonomists rather than psychologists, have not been equally embarrassed by the manifest inconsistency of our code of ethics with the image of Man incorporated in the prevailing scientific models. It seems to me that we must either decide that the premised commitment in the code is consistent with our defined subject matter or concede that our scientific integrity demands that we abandon any pretense at such a commitment.

If there is any antimony here, it is not as Koch would have it between psychological science and the humanities, but between our professed concerns as psychologists and our dedication to scientific method. Happily, there is no real antinomy at all. The manifest contradiction stems from the invalidity of the prevailing model and not from any contradiction between our concerns and the requirements of science.

I am charging that psychologists maintain the image of Man as a passive corporeal entity governed by a thermodynamic principle because of their philosophical precommitments and in flagrant disregard of contradictory information. To avoid misunderstanding, I want to put this charge in perspective before I present my argument.

Let me distinguish between a metatheory and a theory. My criterion for making this distinction is that the former does not lead to specific predictions the confirmation or disconfirmation of which would verify or contradict it. The properties of a good metatheory are that it provides a comprehensive frame within which phenomena can be efficiently ordered and relationships among phenomena parsimoniously expressed, that it offers the opportunity for and encourages the interrelating of all phenomena that come within its scope, and that it directs attention to

[8] I am referring to the original manifesto announcing the organization of the Psychonomic Society. Many of those who were subsequently admitted to the society would scarcely meet the high standards originally set in that manifesto —in my own judgment, of course.

the possibilities of phenomena and relationships among phenomena that might otherwise be missed. Most so-called theories are actually meta-theories; if it is true, as has been claimed, that no theory has ever been abandoned because of factual contradiction, all theories are really meta-theories. With enough ingenuity, it is presumably possible to save any theory against factual contradiction by adding one or more postulates, making one or more well-chosen *ad hoc* assumptions, or, more vaguely, assuming the intrusion of some uncontrolled variables. In a sense, for instance, every bridge is a test of the principles of Newtonian mechanics, but I doubt if anyone has ever seriously questioned Newton's laws (which, incidentally, are tautologies to start with)[9] on the grounds that bridges designed by the best of engineers have been known to collapse; one assumes instead (and quite properly, too) some defect in the materials and/or some unanticipated circumstances that generate stresses and strains that the bridge was not designed to withstand. The scientific fate of competing metatheories depends on how well they achieve the properties described earlier in this paragraph, and one may regard a meta-theory as validated to the extent that it possesses these properties to a greater degree than do its competitors.

In this connection, I hasten to add that this book is concerned with the image of Man, not with a model. As used in scientific discourse, *models* are limited-purpose scientific devices that aid in exploring certain segments of the data universe and testing certain propositions. A model is, knowingly, an analogical construction that ignores the differentiating data; thus, to the extent that the nervous system is comparable to a telephone network (one model of the nervous system), known properties of such networks ought to hold for the nervous system and certain parallel outcomes ought to be demonstrable for events in the nervous system and telephonic networks. In a sense, the model is used to test how far a particular analogy can be pushed in certain directions, but no one in his senses would assume that a telephone model of the nervous system commits him to the assumption that neurones are copper wires. By the same token, the failure of a model simply indicates that a particular analogy cannot be pushed very far in certain directions; its success or failure does not demand a revolution in science or in scientific styles of thought. This, by contrast, is precisely what the Copernican and Darwinian conceptualizations accomplished. They did not substitute one model for another. They revolutionized our image of the world and of Man's place in it. The images that these and other

9 The tautology is discussed in the last chapter of the book.

revolutionaries wrought and embodied in their metatheoretical stances gave direction and meaning to much of the subsequent course of scientific development. There were also changes in our image of the world and of Man's place in it that were not rooted in any new conceptualizations at all, but in the sheer processes of discovery, for example, of the vastness of our universe and of universes beyond the up-to-then known universe.

I am quite willing to grant to the critic whose comments led me to the preceding discursus on the difference between model and image that many of the new images also led to much unproductive controversy (for instance, whether it is or is not possible to respect Man cast in the image of a glorified monkey), but must insist that the latter devolved around side issues typically involving distortions of the images and their logical implications. Controversy over the images that respects the rules of logic cannot be unproductive. The very nature of science is at stake.[10]

The present essay is unequivocally intended as a contribution to psychological metatheory. It is not concerned with trying to establish psychological fact. I know that most psychological research, my own included, is in itself indifferent to the metatheoretical issues I shall be discussing. A research finding stands regardless of the metatheoretical frame of reference to which it is referred. Any alternative metatheoretical position that can neither assimilate it nor explain it away is, on the face of the matter, a defective metatheory. I also know that the majority of psychological researchers and teachers give little thought in their workaday lives to metatheoretical issues and that, in fact, they hardly seem to be concerned about maintaining any consistent view of these matters. Apart from the fact that inconsistency is itself likely to generate considerable confusion, there are, however, two major ways in which I think we go astray.

[10] Because the critic is a keen reader, it is possible that others may have misread what I said earlier as he did when he gently chided me with the observation that "Truth, not injured feelings of self-esteem must be our criterion." I did not say that psychology ought to operate from an image of Man that can be considered worthy of respect. I merely pointed out that the robot image is not compatible with a commitment "to a belief in the dignity and worth of the individual human being" and added that such a commitment derives from extrascientific sources. I also said that, if we are to stand by such a commitment, we do need some alternative image. However, I did not argue for such a commitment. The only basis for my argument for the alternative image, in this chapter and in the rest of the book, is "truth" and consistency. It is on this basis only that my argument should be judged. At the same time, I see nothing wrong with looking at the scientific issue in a larger context of human concerns. Science is, after all, as I shall also argue, a human enterprise and serves human concerns.

The first occurs when we try to integrate the various bits of accumulating psychological information into a more comprehensive coherent whole; it is, after all, one of the major facets of the business of science to integrate knowledge into coherent larger units. Countless researchers contributing vast numbers of bits of information do not produce a body of scientific knowledge if the bits of knowledge are unrelated to one another even though they may be systematically arrayed in a master file. The Sears Roebuck catalog and the collected volumes of the telephone directory would not be mistaken by anyone as contributions to science for all that they contain more facts per page, in highly accessible array, than any scientific tome I have ever come across.[11]

A special case of going astray for lack of attention to the pattern of the integrated whole is that, since we do not derive our research problems out of a vaccum, we do have some more or less vague and tacit notion of how the bit of information we hope to contribute will fit into the totality. Hence, our individual research projects, in themselves indifferent to the metatheoretical issues, are presented in a language and conceptualized in terms that are consistent with our metatheoretical frames of reference. The individual research project thus carries within itself a tacit directive as to how it should be dealt with in a larger integration.

Consider, for instance, research on conditioning. The basic phenomena are interpretable in terms of perceived contextual relationships and relevant motivation. Typically, however, the concepts and phenomena are presented in terms that are more or less explicitly reminiscent of wired switchboards or hydraulic erosion. That is, conditioning, taken as the prototype of all learning, is presented in terms that presuppose a robotic image of Man. Even when motivation is introduced in the model, it is only to admit a factor that affects the openness of neural pathways. To be sure, the robot image implicit in conditioning theory either blandly disregards such simple facts as that the conditioned response is different from the unconditioned response or else introduces such complications into the theoretical model as to bring into serious question its greatest alleged virtue, the parsimonious explanation that it offers.

The issue of parsimony is relevant to my entire argument in a more fundamental sense. The principle states that explanatory constructs

[11] I believe that I first came across the example of the telephone directory as a nonscientific body of systematized knowledge in a lecture by Professor Morris Raphael Cohen.

should not needlessly be multiplied, that is, it tells us to stay as close as we can to available data. But how is needlessly to be assessed? Does it require the bringing to bear of all relevant data or does it apply to limited sets of data? Let me try to illustrate the point. Whatever else I know about learning, I know that cognitions play an important role in my own learning processes. For me to take noncognitive learning theories seriously, I must assume that there are, in all other creatures, learning processes that look just like my own but that are really quite different. That is, for what are manifestly quite similar processes, I must assume that different principles of learning operate: one set of principles that apply to me and another set that apply to all other creatures. Simply on the grounds of parsimony, therefore, and Lloyd Morgan's canon notwithstanding, I must assert that the burden of proof rests on the anticognitive theorists—especially so when some of the latter have privately confessed to me that they, too, sometimes operate with cognitive maps. The latter, incidentally, are not scientific scoundrels—or, at least, not exceptionally so. They justify their manifest dereliction on the basis of a sharp distinction between private knowledge and that which, on philosophical grounds, properly belongs in the domain of science. The derailment and misconstruction of the behaviorist revolution that is involved in their position is an issue to which I will return later.

Note that I have absolutely nothing against any psychologist setting out to determine whether there are dependable stimulus-response relationships when cognitive and the like processes are disregarded. The point, if any, at which my quarrel with him begins is when he starts pretending that what he has disregarded does not exist or is not a proper concern of the scientific enterprise and when he remains obtusely oblivious to the fact that, having ignored cognitive and like factors, he is in no position to say anything about the variation or lack of variation in these factors under the conditions of his observations and, hence, that he is equally in no position to judge whether and how the dependability of the relationships he discovers itself depends on the status of the variables he has ignored. The principle of parsimony was never intended as a license to achieve simplicity by ignoring the unparsimoniousness of nature. The simplicity demanded by the principle is of the explanation, not of the explicandum. Note my emphasis on needlessly in my statement of the principle and the phrase "except by necessity" in Occam's original statement.

At any rate, my immediate concern is not with the deficiency of the conditioning model *per se* but with its effect on the tone and scope of psychological thinking in general, namely, in the sanction that it gives to the image of Man as a robot.

The second major way in which we go astray is in the distribution of psychological research effort. There may be good reason for such a distribution apart from our metatheoretical frames of reference, for instance, our tendency to follow available research techniques rather than to pursue rationally derived problems. The question, however, is whether we are justified in a sense of contentment about that distribution and the course it is likely to take or whether we ought to be worried about it. In terms of the prevailing image of Man, I think we may well rest content. In terms of the active image, I think we should be worried about our failure to generate imperatives in the upcoming generation of psychologists (to bypass the issue of our own doings) to confront problems we ourselves avoid.

It follows, then, that though my charge of flagrant disregard of relevant fact may have some bearing on the work and thought of individual psychologists, it is with the totality of our scientific enterprise that I am concerned.

Now, to my argument: (1) In Chapter 2, I will ask whether the passive or the active image fits, and in doing so I will examine the issue of freedom *vs.* necessity, deal with the meaning of freedom, and examine the nature of motivation. (2) In Chapter 8, I will try to show that the contemporary emphasis on the body, which goes hand-in-glove with the passive view, is misplaced. (3) In Chapter 13,[12] I will argue that a prevailing contemporary model of motivation, which also supports the passive image, the tension-reduction concept, is false. (4) In Part III, I will deal with the nature of the being that performs the psychological act. These four arguments are, in a sense, the pivots of the book. In the course of the argument, however (in the intervening sections and occasionally in the already mentioned ones), I will further develop a variety of systematic psychological concepts that provide what I believe to be a more adequate metatheoretical framework for psychology than is provided by other current alternatives.

---

[12] Structurally, this chapter, though it is included in Part III, belongs to Part II of the book, but I have placed it in Part III because it refers to concepts first developed in the earlier chapters of this part.

Basic Concepts
and Psychological Processes

2

MAN OR ROBOT?

No man can act in terms of the image of himself as a totally impotent being. On any attempt to do so, determinism degenerates into fatalism. We cannot dispose of the issue with a "What will be, will be." The latter may well be the case, but, if this is so, it is only, in part, because of what Man will do (including, if this happens, because he adopts a fatalistic attitude and does nothing), not despite what he will do. Now, the class *Man* includes the psychologist who adopts the image of Man as an impotent being; this psychologist, like everyone else, cannot live by this image. He may try to apply it to everyone else, but he cannot apply it to himself as a basis of action. He thus professes a faith in an order of law that applies to everyone else, but, implicitly at least, he reserves to himself a special order of law. He knows that he can intervene in events, but he claims that no one else can—and this in the name of science!

Ludwig Immergluck[1] claims that the experience of freedom is a distorted percept, perhaps even an inescapable illusion as it applies to oneself, but that it implies a view of the nature of man that is incompatible with the advancement of science. Immergluck's paper amply testifies to the potency of the illusion, if illusion it is, not merely, as he claims, with respect to oneself but, also with respect to our perception of the behavior of others. He asserts, for instance, that "should a deterministic framework propel us to search ceaselessly for specific and general behavioral laws, we might some day," get to "understand" a great deal about many things and "We might even be able to use such knowledge to advantage."[2] Statements of this kind clearly impute inten-

---

[1] L. Immergluck, "Determinism-Freedom in Contemporary Psychology," *American Psychologist*, 19 (1964): 270–281.

[2] *Ibid.*, p. 280.

tionality to the plurality of us and not merely to his own self-image. When, in the cited instance, he goes on to say, "And would this alone not constitute eloquent testimony to the dignity of man?" it is clear that he is so profoundly under the influence as to have become, at least temporarily, incapable of realizing that, on his premises the "eloquent testimony" would be merely another instance of the illusion. The notion of using something to advantage is on these premises merely another instance of "an artifact, a convenient term borrowed from everyday language, and one that reflects neither philosophic tenacity nor psychological reality."[3]

Similarly, on Immergluck's premises, we can, at most only have the *illusion* of prediction, because "predicting" in normal usage implies forward-looking (that is, intentional) behavior. Thus, Immergluck's paper moved me to write the following somewhat satirical passage:

Since the illusion is so potent, it seems to me that, unless new conditioning processes intervene, the Immerglucks are doomed to continued unresolved conflict (a term that he does not perceive as inconsistent with his premises[4]) between their philosophical premises and their phenomenological experience. As I view the historical scene, it seems to me that more and more psychologists are becoming conditioned to respond to unresolved conflicts by introducing conditioning programs that have the consequence of resolving conflicts. Moreover, because of the great potency of the illusion and because it seems like an incredibly vast undertaking (more precisely, it would violate the principle of minimum expenditure of energy) to devise a conditioning program that gets human beings to perceive analytically ("unanalyzed experience . . . being a perfectly 'natural' human trait and perhaps part and parcel of the perceptual act of all organisms" and the root source of the illusion of freedom[5]), it seems only a matter of time before the Immerglucks will be subjected to conditioning programs designed to extinguish the response, "Dangerous to science" and to substitute for it the response "How wonderful for science" to stimuli implying human freedom. The Immerglucks will then be happy (a mentalistic term that I use to cover up my ignorance of the real stimuli and responses involved in "happiness") — unless, of course, the neurosurgeons and psychiatrists are stimulated by the noises that generate an illusion of anguish to beat the psychologists to the gun by lobotomizing and/or tranquilizing them first.

Like Immergluck himself, and indeed all writers, I must merely have been making ink tracks on paper as determined by "largely unknown" "antecedent conditions and variables operating upon the organism"

[3] *Ibid.*, p. 277.
[4] See *ibid.*, p. 278.
[5] *Ibid.*, p. 279.

that goes by my name and the "pushing and pulling forces in [my] present environment."[6] Note, too, that, should it develop that my ink tracks in the indented passage are congruent with a future state of affairs, no one will have been the loser. The word "loser" in the preceding sentence implies someone with a real desire to keep something, and desire is, of course, an illusion. Note, finally, that science cannot suffer since the "advancement of science" can only have meaning with respect to some human enterprise, and any human enterprise is, of course, an illusion.

If all of this sounds like unadulterated nonsense, it is only because Immergluck starts off with an egregious, but not idiosyncratic to him, error. He confuses the contrast freedom/necessity with that of chance/necessity. He interprets the notion of man as a free agent as implying that man is "propelled by self-initiated forces that defy, by their very nature, prediction or scientifically ordered description customarily applied to inanimate events."[7] Since the idea of freedom (not so much as articulated by some philosophers as in the usages of analytically philosophically naïve moralists) carries no such implication, Immergluck never does come to grips with the idea he is ostensibly discussing.

That the idea of indeterminism does not necessarily imply disorderliness and unpredictability is obvious from the following consideration. Imagine that the state of our knowledge has come to encompass the ultimate fundamental laws of the universe. Then these laws cannot themselves be determined; they just are. To assert otherwise is to assert that the laws under consideration are not the ultimate laws. Suppose that there are several such laws and that each is fully determined by the remainder of the set; but then the existence of the set of such laws cannot be determined. Or, alternatively, suppose that the basic set is the sole survivor among many once-existing sets, the others having vanished because of insoluble internal contradictions. That this was the only consistent set that entered the competition cannot have been determined[8] and, indeed, it is likely that its internal consistency

---

[6] *Ibid.*, p. 277.

[7] *Ibid.*, p. 270.

[8] This is the main point in the last chapter of Alfred North Whitehead's *Science and the Modern World* (New York: Macmillan, 1925). Whitehead takes the realization of only one among many possible sets of consistent laws as defining the concept of God. It may also be noted, in this connection, that, among the legends of the Jews, there is one according to which God had created many worlds which he destroyed before he settled on this one—apparently leaving it to Man to complete the drama.

cannot have been determined.[9] Yet, from the very nature of the example, such an absence of determination does not carry any implication of disorder or unpredictability.

In any case, if free will implies indeterminism (and I will try to show that it does not), it should nevertheless be obvious to anyone who listens to what people are saying that no ordinary free-willer intends any implication of disorderliness or unpredictability. Thus, no one believes that becoming a saint or a *tzaddik* is a matter of an extraordinary run of chance analogous to breaking the bank at Monte Carlo or that the next moral decision of such a person is unpredictable. The idea of saintliness is that such a person will predictably choose to do good and eschew evil. Nor would any free-willer believe that the individual moral decision is arrived at by a process that is analogous to flipping a coin. If philosophers have deduced that, regardless of the intentions of the free-willer, the concept inherently implies unpredictability, this is because they have imported their own premises in its explication.

The notion of freedom rests on three, and as far as I can see only three, premises: that there are volitions (desires, motivations, and so on), that volitions have behavioral consequence, and that they are not reducible to variables of the physical environment or to variables of physiological process. That volitions should exist is no more contradictory to the doctrine of determinism than that forces (or whatever are the equivalents of forces in contemporary physics) should exist That volitions should be orderly and predictable is no more contradictory to the doctrine of determinism than that the fundamental laws of physics should operate in an orderly and predictable manner. That the determinants of behavior should include volitional variables in addition to variables of the physical environment and variables of physiological process is no more contradictory of the doctrine of determinism than that they should include m varieties of environmental and n varieties of physiological variables.

Dr. Immergluck may want (*sic*) to challenge any or all of the three

[9] This is an extension, perhaps unwarranted, of Gödel's theorem in mathematics. According to this theorem, it is impossible to prove, from its assumptions, that the number system is internally consistent. In other words, the internal consistency of the set is not contained in its other assumptions. This theorem had considerable impact on the development of modern philosophy. For its background and a lucid presentation of the proof, see E. Nagel and J. R. Newman, *Gödel's Proof* (New York: New York University Press, 1958).

premises of freedomism. He will have to do so on grounds other than the requirements of the doctrine of determinism. To be at all persuasive, he will have to produce something more than the bare assertion that volition is an illusion and he will have to produce a metatheory that does not lend itself to the kinds of absurdities I generated from his views earlier in this chapter.

I suspect that what is really bugging the Immerglucks has nothing to do with the doctrine of determinism as such, but is rooted in a number of other issues. The first is that the attribution of consequence to volition seems to imply an insufficiency of physical law; thus, if a volition can result in a movement of my arm, there seems to be a non-physical force involved in the movement of a physical body. A second issue is that, whereas physical forces are apparently omnipresent, volitions do not seem to be; this raises the problem of the conditions that govern the emergence of volitions. A third issue concerns the allegation that we can apparently only specify the occurrence of volitions on a *post hoc* basis. With respect to these last two issues, one obvious response is that we can certainly never learn to know more or do better by pretending that volitions do not exist. I shall return to all three issues later.

Have I been arguing *ad hominen* in pointing out that the psychologist who denies freedom must exempt himself from his professed order of law? I think not. I would have been if I had argued (as I think is the case) that it would be a remarkable psychologist indeed who would not exempt from this professed order of deterministic law those who are near and dear to him or who would exempt from responsibility a colleague who repeatedly libels him. This would be like bringing up to one who argues for vegetarianism that you happen to know the butcher from whom he buys his meat. I am saying that, in principle, this psychologist cannot but exempt himself from his own doctrine; in principle, he cannot apply his principles to himself as actor. And, since he is not merely a psychologist but also, as actor, a psychological subject, there must be something wrong with his doctrine.

I might at this juncture simply assert that determinism, as applied to human beings, is indefensible. But, I myself start out as a determinist. What is more, I begin with the conviction that determinism is a basic working hypothesis of scientific methodology, implicit in the right that the individual scientist reserves to himself (and in the ultimate responsibility that devolves on the community of scientists) to ask, concerning any given class of events, "What are its necessary and sufficient conditions?"[10]

So, here am I, still an avowed determinist, plugging for a view of Man as an active, responsible, free agent. Obviously, I must be motivated to find no compatibility between the two positions and must have concluded that there really is none. Still, if I ever were to become convinced that the two positions actually are incompatible, I believe that it is the determinism that would have to go.

The image of Man as an impotent being rests on the false assumption that all the determinants of behavior are included in the constitution and, separately, in the environment, that is, that every determinant of behavior is either a body fact or an environment fact.

Consider an elementary case: As I write, I hold my pen. Why? Anyone who has read Lazarsfeld's analysis of the ambiguities in the question "Why?"[11] should have little difficulty in coming up with a few

[10] There are, of course, many contemporary scientists who profess to have abandoned the deterministic outlook in favor of a probabilistic model. I believe that these scientists confuse determinism with determinacy, the issue of what is within the grasp of human knowledge. The assertion of indeterminacy (that is, that something or other lies forever beyond the grasp of human knowledge), even in the celebrated case of the Heisenberg principle, rests on certain assumptions and the validity of the assertion is no greater than the validity of the assumptions on which it is based. Thus, on the assumption that our capacity to control and measure the conditions of events will always remain less than perfect and on the further assumption that we can never be certain that we have identified all the relevant varieties of determinants (a certainty that logically rests on the exhaustion of all possibilities of experience)—and subject to the validity of these assumptions—we must conclude that no humanly formulated law can rationally be expected to hold forever without apparent exception. With the confusion of two meanings of "probable" (not perfectly certain *vs.* subject to a determinate probability distribution), this suggests that laws ought to be probabilistic rather than categorical in form—except that the conclusion, in any case, holds equally well regardless of the form of the laws. That is, a probabilistic law based on a conditional analysis is as subject to deviant distributions as a categorical law is subject to deviant cases. Note that both kinds of law presuppose determining conditions. A statistical generalization unrelated to a conditional analysis (for example, the sun will rise tomorrow because it has risen every day since the beginning of recorded history) is merely a persistence forecast that does not merit the label "law," and, even so, the logically defensible basis for making a persistence forecast is that the prediction based on a past regularity assumes that the conditions responsible for the past regularity will not have changed (for example, that the earth will not have stopped rotating). Thus, the assumption of lawfulness presupposes determining conditions regardless of whether one pursues a probabilistic or a categorical model.

[11] Paul F. Lazarsfeld, "The Art of Asking Why," *National Marketing Review*, 5 (1936).

answers: First, it is a writing implement; second, the neuromuscular adjustments necessary for holding it have taken place; third, I am writing. Note that the first of these answers, that the pen is a writing implement, refers to an environmental fact; the second, that the neuro-muscular adjustments have occurred, refers to a constitutional fact; and the third, that I am writing, refers to a . . . Well, what kind of a fact is the third? It is not exclusively an environmental fact, though it implies some environmental facts, for example, a writing implement, something on which to write, the leaving of tracks on the writing sur-face, and so on. It is not exclusively a bodily fact, though it implies a sequential pattern of neuromuscular adjustments. It is a fact referring to what Woodworth[12] has described as an "activity in progress," a fact that bridges and relates environmental and constitutional events and that embraces a more than momentary span of time. No exploration of the body can show the act of writing, though it may show its physiologi-cal correlates; nor can any study of the environment do so, though it may show changes occurring in the latter such that one would have to be stupid not to infer that it is taking place.

Note that the first answer cannot be taken as a sufficient explanation of my holding my pen; my pen remains a writing implement even when I do not hold it. Nor can the second; the appropriate neuromuscular adjustments might take place when there is no pen to hold, as when holding a nonwriting implement of the same shape in the course of a quite different activity, namely, pretending to write. But the third, if taken with its implication, does offer a sufficient explanation for, if not my holding my pen, then, at least, for my holding a writing implement.

The example just given offers a paradigm of what I take to be a *motive*: A behavior is a motive of the behaviors it includes.[13] My writing behavior is a motive for my holding my pen; I cannot write without my pen or an equivalent implement. The including behavior is not *per se* a motive; it becomes a motive only if some subsidiary behavior is necessary to it, and the latter (holding the pen, in the present instance) is motivated by the former (the act of writing).

[12] Robert S. Woodworth, *Psychology,* 3d ed. (New York: Holt, 1934).

[13] In a perfectly orderly presentation, the term *behavior* would be defined before introducing the term *motive*. To facilitate the introduction of the concept of freedom, I have preferred to use *behavior* in this chapter as though it were a primitive term, that is, let the reader take it in any meaning that is consistent with the context. In Chapter 4, I shall attempt a more formally rigorous treat-ment of this and related concepts, including that of motivation.

Since the notion of a motive as behavior may be a strange one to some people, I should clarify a few points.

1. To my own satisfaction at least, I am not introducing a new usage of the term *motive*, but explicating and articulating the common one.

2. In contrast to the common view, which takes a wish or a desire as a motivational antecedent of behavior, I take such terms as referring to behavior in an early stage of its execution. In this stage, it may, but does not necessarily, take the form of imagining some state of affairs and affirming a hope or intention of achieving the latter. The fact that the behavior may not be carried beyond this stage is what leads to the common view of wish as antecedent, but this fact is not incompatible with the view of wish as the initial phase of behavior. If you wish for something, I take this to be, in some sense, the beginning of a movement toward that something; if you wish for something to be over with, I take it as the beginning of a move away from that something. It is the behavior as a whole, however, whatever its stage of execution, that defines the subsidiary behaviors that will forward it in the given situation; the behavior, having progressed beyond the stage of the wish, continues to serve as motive for subsidiary behaviors in a manner appropriate to the degree of progress in the behavior. The behaviors motivated by a fishing trip are different when one has not yet obtained bait than when one has cast a baited hook into a stream, and different still from when a fish has impaled itself on the hook. The behaviors motivated by the behavior of baking a cake are different before the ingredients have been mixed than after. By the same token, a behavior consummated in the very making of a wish involves a wish that has no motivating consequence; it is an *empty wish* (note how this phrase acquires literal meaning when the meaning of *motive* is explicated; it is empty of any behavioral implications) or else it is not a wish at all but a more or less seriously intended plea that some other agent bring about an envisioned state of affairs.

3. I do not think of a drive as a motive, *drive* being understood in the sense of, say, E. B. Holt's *appetitive drive* or Freud's formal definition of an *instinct,* that is, a bodily condition that, in more or less random fashion, produces continued excitation of the effector organs. There is nothing about such a description of a drive that suggests why the excitation should be channeled into activities that will eliminate the excitation. Why should random movement not persist even after many

recurrences?[14] The fact is, however, that the channeling does often occur; this fact becomes intelligible on the assumption that something associated with the drive state is, in some sense, distressing to the organism. From this point of view, drive is simply a physiological state and not a behavior at all. The first directed activity in the life history of the individual is the voiding of the distress associated with drives, and it is this directed activity, not the drive *per se,* that motivates the transactions with the environment that eliminate the drive.[15] Note that the distress, like the drive itself, is not *per se* a motive, but a condition of a motive; distress is not an activity, but a state of being, and as such it is not an activity that includes within itself subsidiary activities. Also note that in ordinary usage, at least, a motive is something different from the behavior that it motivates and that I have respected this usage even though I have characterized a motive as a behavior; the motive is not the same behavior as the behavior that it motivates, but a more inclusive one.

4. In speaking of a behavior as a motive, I want to emphasize that I am saying something more than that there is an interaction between organism and environment. I am saying that an ongoing interaction between organism and environment affects the outcomes of other interactions between them. In the prevailing view, organism interacts with environment, and the outcome of the interaction is the response. Either or both may be changed in the process, but the next response is again an outcome of an organism distinct from but interacting with a distinct environment. That is, in the prevailing view, every one of the determinants of the response is contained in organism or environment. By

[14] In the frame of the passive-image concept, the anwer to this question is, of course, that a neural channel is established, that is, there really is no motivation but only stimuli, and that the only relevant distinction is between stimuli of environmental and stimuli of physiological origin. In other words, to a passive imagist, a drive is also not a motive in any normal usage of the latter term. But then, taking note of the absence of any distinct motivational concept in the passive-imagist frame, I challenge any passive imagist to produce as parsimonious an explanation as presumably almost any child can give of why I hold my pen. It should become apparent as I develop my argument that a distinct motivational concept is, in principle, incompatible with the passive image. Does the elimination of a distinct concept of motivation have the virtue of parsimony? Please refer to my earlier mention of the principle of parsimony (p. 13).

[15] I shall, however, hereinafter, continue to use the term *appetitive drive,* but in the sense of the activity directed at voiding the distress associated with drive states, as contrasted with *physiological drive* (or simply *drive*), which I will use to refer to the drive states.

contrast, the interaction I am discussing, which I say affects the outcomes of other interactions between organism and environment, is not distinctly an organismic nor an environmental fact. When it becomes a condition of mediating interactions (note well, not succeeding interactions, but mediating interactions that determine the course of the primary interaction that is still ongoing while the mediating interaction occurs), we are dealing with a new class of determinants of behavior. If the primary interaction consists of organism doing something with regard to environment and, if doing this requires doing something else— not subsequently, but in order to continue or complete doing what it is doing in the first place—we have a motive.

Or, to put the issue differently, I am saying that a molar activity unit has consequences as a molar unit that are not the same as the consequences of the molecular units that it includes.[16] This contrasts with the view that, if it permits reference to molar units at all, does so only for descriptive purposes, using the molar expression as a shorthand expression for an enumeration of molecular components or as a confession of ignorance of the molecular components, and that assumes that causality can only exist on a molecular level.

To those familiar with Gestalt theory, it will also be apparent that I do not regard the unique aspects of a totality as emergents from the combination of components, since the totality plays a role in determining what the components will be. It is not true that a sequence of neuromuscular contractions and relaxations produces the act of walking, but it is the act, that is, the molar act, of walking that determines the molecular sequence of neuromuscular events; if the same neuromuscular sequence were independently produced, we would, at best, have something that looks like the act walking. Walking is a form of going to or from some place, or of whiling away time, or of distracting oneself from some unpleasant tension, and so forth; the hypothetical instance of pseudowalking is none of these things. It should be obvious that the behavior would be left quite unspecified if we were merely to

[16] Following Tolman and Broad I use *molar* to designate the fact that the unit under consideration is being taken as a totality. I differ slightly in my usage of the contrasting term, *molecular,* and use it to indicate that the unit under consideration is being regarded as a component of a more embracing whole, even though the component may not be an ultimate physiological or physical-chemical component. That *molar* and *molecular* are relative terms is also implicit in my view, the molecular with regard to one molar unit becoming molar with regard to the molecular units that it includes. See E. C. Tolman, *Purposive Behavior in Animals and Men* (New York: Century, 1932), and J. C. Broad, *The Mind and Its Place in Nature* (New York: Harcourt Brace, 1929).

indicate that a person is walking; as long as we postulate that the same neuromuscular sequence can be generated independently of going somewhere and so forth, it should be quite clear that the description of the neuromuscular sequence would not tell us whether the person is, in fact, doing anything at all.

Perhaps the point at issue may be made a bit clearer by referring again to Miller, Galanter, and Pribram's conclusion that the concept of purpose is now scientifically respectable since the construction of machines that behave purposively. You may recall that, in my earlier allusion to this conclusion, I implied that there is some question as to whether these authors properly construe the nature of purpose. The crux of the issue is contained in their confident expectation[17] that what they call a plan will turn out to be formally identical with a computer program.

Let us consider the kind of machine that is alleged to behave purposively. Such a machine is so designed that at every moment its activity is governed by the opening and closing of circuits that are built into it and the sequence of openings and closings is controlled by the input. What is uniquely special to such a machine (in contrast to other humanly constructed machines) is that the input itself depends, in part, on the consequences of the immediately preceding action. The feature of feedback, however, does not change the fact that every action is completely determined by the succession of events in the constitution of the machine and the succession of events in its environment. The machine does not engage in a nested hierarchy of activities, such that some higher level of the hierarchy, if carried to completion, temporally includes all lower levels within itself and such that the higher level helps to determine what happens at the lower levels. That is, the machine engages in no molar activities *vis à vis* the environment that, as such, play a role in the selection of their molecular components. The sequence of events is completely determined molecularly. Hence, once the machine is set into operation, there is nothing in it or in its relation to the environment that is in any sense analogous to a plan—"plan" being defined by the authors as "any hierarchical process in the organism that can control the order in which a sequence of operations is to be performed."[18] Note that Miller *et al.* assign a controlling function to the hierarchical process, as such, and that they use the word

[17] G. A. Miller, E. Galanter, and K. H. Pribram, *Plans and the Structure of Behavior* (New York: Holt, Rinehart & Winston, 1960), p. 16.
[18] *Ibid.*

"hierarchical" to refer to the simultaneous organization of behavior at several levels of complexity, from the all-inclusive molar unit to molar subunits down to the molecular units.[19] In other words, by their own conceptualization, their allegedly purposive machine does not have any plan. If there is any plan in the functioning of the computer, the plan is associated with the programmer, who must anticipate every possible contingency if the molecular processes of the machine are to continue as the programmer intends; if an unanticipated contingency arises, the machine stops functioning. The machine, at best, even if it is programmed to program, functions according to plan—the programmer's plan—and has no plan of its own; it functions according to plan in the same sense that any well-designed machine functions according to its user's plan.[20]

Why not assume that the behaving organism also functions in such a quasipurposive manner, that is, in a succession of molecular actions in accordance with a plan externally imposed on it by some rational or, for that matter, nonrational process? The answer to this question is that such an assumption is in flagrant contradiction of observation, not, mind you, in contradiction of presupposition, hypothesis, or theory, but in contradiction of observation. Behavior is hierarchically organized, and the higher hierarchical levels have observable consequences; if anyone asserts the contrary, the burden of proof rests squarely on his shoulders. What is more, the facts of observation aside, when it comes to such matters as linguistic behavior, Miller *et al.* cite proof that such behavior can only—in principle—be comprehended in terms of such hierarchically organized processes.

Let me now make one final point in my effort to clarify the relatively unfamiliar notion of a motive viewed as a behavior. I hope it will be clear that motivation, as I conceive of it, implicitly involves perception, learning, memory, inference, meaning, and all other psychological processes. The notion of one behavior motivating another would, in my terms, be nonsensical if it were not presupposed that the actor, on some basis, accepts the premise that the latter behavior advances the former.

[19] See *ibid.*, p. 15.

[20] I have no principled objection to the notion of machines that act purposively, with plans of their own. It is merely that I do not know of anyone having designed such a machine; Miller *et al.*'s discussion and citations from the literature do not suggest that they do either. In passing, it will become clear later that I must take exception to their location of plans in the organism. The molar levels of the hierarchical processes they discuss are simply not to be found inside the organism.

By the same token, motivation is to me the master integrative concept in psychology. I can, for instance, describe the conceptual properties of motivation without reference to cognition, but I cannot do the reverse without postulating two basic and independent psychological processes. That is, I can (and, later, in Chapter 4, will) describe cognition without introducing any new concepts, but I cannot describe motivation in cognitive terms alone. I can also describe any behavior without reference to its motivation or to any of the other conditions that determine it, but I cannot conceive of a complete listing of the conditions of behavior without reference to its motivation.

To recapitulate: I have located some of the determinants of behavior in the concurrent behaviors of the organism and have indicated that these determinants cannot be subsumed under the heading of constitutional conditions nor under the heading of environmental conditions. It follows that the behaver (and this is as true of the animal as of the human) is an active agent in the universe. He is not merely a passive medium for the interplay of constitution and environment; his own activities affect that interplay.

But, you ask, are not his first activities and hence, sequentially, all his activities themselves determined? I say, of course (I have already told you that I am a determinist[21]), but once the commitment to activity has been generated, something new has been added to subsequent activity—a motive. Insofar as this happens, it does not matter at all with regard to the point at issue whether the motive has been determined by constitution, environment, or their interaction or whether it was planted there at the whim of a sorcerer or a divine creator, or whether the creator designed the totality of his creation so that this must inevitably happen to this particular creature. Once a motive is there, it is there, and, through it, the organism[22] has become a partner in the causal process. The search for objects and object/relations that can eliminate the drive is neither constitution nor environment, but an active concern of the individual.

Now, let me return to the issue of "freedom." In the most general usage of the word, it signifies unconstrained or unopposed action. Thus, we speak of a freely falling body. Note that free fall is not assumed to

[21] Subject, of course, to the qualification that I regard the set of ultimate laws, whatever they may turn out to be, as givens.

[22] At this simple level of discussion, involving an isolated motive, it may be acceptable to refer to the actor as "organism," but I shall later, in Chapter 9, argue that "organism" does not adequately describe the actor who engages in behavior.

be undetermined: The basic process of falling is determined by a relatively minute mass, a relatively enormous mass, and the distance between the two masses, which is continuously diminishing as the process continues; free fall occurs when there are no other determinants present to constrain, oppose, or in any manner interfere with the thus determined process. Note also that free fall is not unpredictable.

Similarly, when Spinoza concluded that God is the only free agent, it was on the basis of his conception that the entire universe, in both its physical and mental aspects, is an expression of God and is thus contained in His being. On this conception, nothing exists outside of God, and there is thus nothing that can constrain or oppose Him. Again, however, the idea of freedom does not imply absence of determination. God's actions are determined by the nature of His being and, if they are in any degree or manner unpredictable, this is only because of human limitations in grasping the nature of God. Neither Spinoza's universe nor his God are lawless.

What is the meaning of "freedom" in the context of an assertion that the human being is free? It seems to me that no serious proponent of such a view has ever meant to imply anything other than that the individual's motivation plays some role in determining his behavior.[23] If,

[23] One reader of an earlier draft of this essay has taken exception to this point on the ground that I miss the major issue in the historical arguments about determinism and freedom. He writes that "The advocates of freedom were interested in demonstrating that there must be a class of events which were not wholly determined by natural causes." I think that my critic is in error. He, in effect, continues a historical confusion between two distinct issues: the issue of extranatural causation and the issue of freedom. To me, it seems that the way in which the second of these issues has become tied in with the first is basically as follows: Proponents of freedom have meant by "freedom" exactly what I say they have meant. They could not, however, see how to fit the freedom concept into the framework of naturalistic thought. This left them with no alternative than to reject the latter. Some, of course, may have had an extranaturalistic axe to grind for other reasons and, hence, may have been only too delighted with this state of affairs; it provided them with an additional basis for their extranaturalistic orientation. But I do not see that we have any ground for asserting that the extranaturalistic orientation was in all, or in most, cases responsible for the stand on freedom. I think that the primary responsibility rests in the manifest fact of freedom. As my critic himself noted, moreover, extranaturalism does not require the admission of freedom; there are, as he also noted, a number of extranaturalistic views that explicitly deny human freedom. I have, in this essay, attempted to show that freedom is in fact perfectly compatible with a naturalistic view of the universe and have further attempted to present a perfectly naturalistic account of its emergence. If my position is sound, the affirmation of freedom does not require the espousal of extranaturalism; as just indicated, the affirmation of extranaturalism does not require the espousal of freedom. How much more distinct can two issues be?

and insofar as, his constitution and the environmental situation coerce a particular action, he is assuredly not acting freely. If, and insofar as his constitution and the environmental situation are such as to make a particular behavior impossible (for instance, to fly from one spot to another without the aid of a mechanical contrivance), then, assuredly, he is not free to carry out this behavior. But if, and insofar as, the environmental and constitutional situations are such as neither to compel a particular action (as in a reflex response) nor to prevent a particular behavior, it is only a tautology to assert that he is free to carry out that behavior; it is no indication of any restriction on his freedom to add that, appropriately motivated, he will carry out this behavior. What, however, is the last addition but an assertion that his motivation is one of the conditions of his behavior? Thus, once we have established that the condition of motivation is not, as such, an environmental condition nor a constitutional condition and that the sufficient conditions of behavior are of three kinds—constitutional, environmental, and motivational—we have established some degree of freedom in the ordinary usage of that term. And this regardless of where the motivation came from, that is, regardless of how it was determined.

With one exception, which I will mention in a moment, no one has ever seriously attributed to a human being the degree of freedom that is generally associated with the idea of God—utter and total absence of constraint and opposition, whether God is conceived of in anthropomorphic terms or as Spinoza's super-Gestalt. Moreover, the concept of such ultraomnipotence—and ultraomnipotence it is if contrasted with what one may think of as the omnipotence of the most powerful, autocratic, dictatorial, human potentate imaginable—is paradoxical in that it entails a complete absence of motivation. A necessary condition of motivation is that an obstacle exist to the execution of a behavior; but an obstacle implies a limitation on unconditional omnipotence. To attribute motivation to God is to attribute to Him a deficiency that is inconsistent with the image of divinity. The motivationless attribute of the concept of unconditional omnipotence leads to the rather ludicrous apposition of the unconditional omnipotence of God with (the exception noted at the beginning of the paragraph) the unconditional omnipotence characteris-

---

Perhaps one other point of clarification should be mentioned. No serious writer that I can think of has ever confused freedom with unlimited freedom. Freedom is always thought of within a context of necessity and, I think, it is only possible in such a context; otherwise freedom would become synonymous with chaos.

tic of one phase of human (and, for that matter mammalian) development, namely, the foetal stage. As Ferenczi has argued[24] each human
being—or at least those who survive their prenatal existence without
damage—begins life as an unconditionally omnipotent being. The normal foetus, like God, never encounters opposition and so, in the fundamental sense of freedom, is perfectly free.[25]

Related to the idea of freedom associated with unconditional omnipotence is the concept of freedom as the recognition of necessity. This
is the notion that, if one assents to and wills the inevitable and does not
desire the impossible—if one, so to say, aligns oneself with the historical
process—then there would be no occasion to encounter opposition, and,
in the fundamental sense of freedom, one would be free. The converse
is almost certainly true, namely, that if one chronically were to dissent
to events that are not in one's sphere of influence and to desire the unattainable, one would experience oneself as imprisoned, constrained,
bound, unfree. It is obvious, however, that if there were no freedom
other than that associated with the recognition of necessity, there would
be no freedom in the sense of the consequentiality of motivation. It is
perhaps of interest to note that the conception of freedom as recognition
of necessity is particularly emphasized in Marxist doctrine, in the context of a conception of historical inevitability as conditional on what
people will be motivated to do and in the context of exhortations to line
up with the inevitabilities of history. In other words, the doctrine obviously contains a broader and self-contradictory conception of freedom
than is embodied in the slogan. It says, "Rise up and mold the history
to the inevitability of which you must submit in order to be free."

It should be clear, then, that the basic meaning of freedom—absence
of constraint or opposition—is at once both insufficient and excessive
to define the concept of freedom in the context of human behavior. One
also needs the concept of motivation, which necessarily implies the
existence of constraint or opposition to the superordinate behavior, but
not enough constraint to prevent the undertaking and/or carrying
through of subordinate, ancillary, mediating, or motivated behavior
aimed at removing or reducing the constraint on the superordinate or
motivating behavior. As a condition of carrying out most behaviors, one

[24] Sandor Ferenczi, "Stages in the Development of the Sense of Reality," in
The Selected Papers of Sandor Ferenczi. Vol. 1, *Sex in Psychoanalysis* (New
York: Basic Books, 1952), pp. 213–239.
[25] I know that I have oversimplified the theological side of the discussion.
My aim, however, is not to explicate theology. I have introduced this discussion
merely to help clarify the concept of freedom.

further needs to be able to rely on the inviolability of physical and physiological law, for instance, that solid objects will stay solid under specifiable conditions, that bones will not become rubbery on some random schedule, that the pressure differentials above and below the plane one is riding in will continue to hold the plane up, that the gravitational constant will not become arbitrarily variable, and so on; this is one basis of the assumption that people are not free to violate physical or physiological law. Both on the side of constraints and behavior supports, then, freedom of human action can be thought of only in a context of necessity; it is inherently, that is, in the very concept of it, limited.

Moreover, consider the case of a person with conflicting motivations (that is, a person engaged in two concurrent behaviors the apparent specifications for the completion of which are mutually inconsistent). Each of the motives acts as a constraint on the other and, if the person is to satisfy one, he is not simultaneously (and in some instances may never be) free to satisfy the other. Freedom of the person, then, as distinguished from the freedom of a particular behavior, presupposes an absence of a significant degree of motivational conflict. A person can be no freer than the consistency of his motives; inconsistency of motivation sets a limit to personal freedom. I shall return to this point later, in Chapter 10. At the moment, I want to add that, except for the briefest of behaviors, the freedom of a particular behavior generally entails restrictions on the freedom of other behaviors. I think of manic excitement as an extreme instance of the loss of freedom because of failure to impose such restrictions. The manic individual begins to say something, but before he has gotten two or three words out he is responding to the words he has already uttered or to something else that he suddenly notices and starts to say something else, only to have this statement meet with the same fate. He begins to do something, and, before he gets very far, he is off on some other tack. Each new action interferes with the one preceding it so that he becomes incapable of completing, that is, has lost his freedom to complete, any action.

To recapitulate: Behavior is free to the extent that the environment and the constitution (and please remember that I am including the temporary physiological states under this term) do not dictate or preclude a particular action; the greater the range of behaviors that are possible within the limits of the constraints imposed by constitution and environment the greater the degree of freedom that exists within the limits of the imposed constraints. Within the limits of these constraints, the behavior that actually occurs is determined by the motivation of the actor. No behavior is ever completely free, some degree of freedom being lost as a consequence of the constraints of constitution and environment; but degrees of freedom are also gained from the dependabilities of constitution and environment. The gains and losses, however, do not cancel each other out because they are different in kind. In addition, with respect to any particular behavior some degree of freedom is lost to the constraints imposed by competing behaviors. A person may be free to the maximum degree that environment and constitution permit if, and to the extent that, he does not lose degrees of freedom from constraints imposed by ·motivational conflicts, sacrifices relatively trivial motives, and effectively sequences or integrates the others.

Let me now return to the subject of motivation and, specifically, to note that the generation of a motive may be in part determined by an already existing motive. Thus, I am holding my pen because I am writing, but I am writing because I am delivering a message, and I am delivering the message because——, well, maybe I had better not go into that.

I think that such a hierarchy, or nest, of motives is not beyond lower organisms, such as the rat, so that, even in the case of a rat, not all of its motives are wholly constitutionally-environmentally determined. Man can, of course, carry out such hierarchical processes to a degree that presumably cannot be matched by a rat. He can, for instance, enter into activities with extremely long-range outcomes. Thus, even relatively young humans have been known to undertake programs of study that last for four or more years. This commitment can motivate them to undertake the shorter range behaviors of doing passing work in certain courses that would otherwise not arouse a shadow of an interest, and the latter undertaking may in turn motivate them to read and report on certain books that they would otherwise rather not be caught dead with, and the latter commitment may in its turn motivate them to do a lot of other reading that will make the book intelligible and facilitate the writing of a report, and, lo, somewhere at the bottom of the hierarchy, there may come the motivation to take pen in hand.

I have obviously oversimplified the nested hierarchical structure of motivation involved in getting through college, have paid no attention to the relevance of the college situation to other and more embracing long-range motives, and have not mentioned the emergence of motivations in the college context that *per se* have nothing to do with the furtherance of the behavior of getting the coveted sheepskin. My point is, however, that when we get to deal with motives that are rooted in motives that are rooted in motives, we have come a long way indeed from actions like reflexes, which are fully determined by the interplay of constitution and environment.

There is also another point that can be drawn from the college-study situation. There undoubtedly are motives that can rather quickly be traced to the discomforts of drive states; thus, the motivation to get substances that can allay hunger and, hence, the motivation to behave in ways that will facilitate getting these substances. In the college-study case, however, if we attempt to retrace the derivational path that motivates the most circumscribed behavior mentioned, that is, the student's taking his pen in hand, we are led further and further away from immediate drive states.

A number of other motivational concepts are germane. I have already, without naming it, discussed one of these concepts, the derivation of motives, that is, the fact that carrying out a behavior may require some subsidiary behavior which in turn may require a behavior subsidiary to it, and so on. I want now to introduce two other concepts: the perpetuation of motives and the imbrication of motives.

By the *perpetuation of motives* I mean that, because of the recurrence of distressing bodily states and the difficulties in carrying out the relieving behaviors, the conditions of performing the latter become continuing concerns of the individual. The individual thus continues to act with regard to the distresses engendered by drives even while the latter do not exist. The case of many derived behaviors is similar: Difficulties in carrying out these behaviors make for continuing concern with the conditions of satisfying them so that the individual continues to act with regard to the execution of certain behaviors even while there is no immediate requirement of them. Thus, a person may be concerned with getting food even while he is not hungry, and he may be concerned with achieving recognition even while he has no immediate need for recognition. That is, hunger, recognition-seeking, and many other motives become perpetuated activities of the individual; they go on motivating other behaviors at times when they themselves do not have to be satisfied.

Note that a perpetuated motive is not to be confused with an intermittently recurring behavior. That perpetuated motives are indeed continuing concerns is evidenced by their effect on other behaviors and by the vigilance of the individual with respect to circumstances that may have bearing on them, even while he seems to be engaged in irrelevant activities.[26] I am not saying that a perpetuated motive may not seem to be interrupted, but that, if it stops being a central activity, it may be actively resumed without external reinstigation and that, even while seemingly interrupted, the person stays sensitive to data that are relevant to its again becoming a central activity.

By the *imbrication of motives* I mean the interpenetration of motives that results from the fact that behaviors are not univocally related to the motives from which they are derived or to the behaviors that they motivate. That is, the same behavior may be derived from a variety of motives and, depending on circumstances, motivate a variety of different behaviors. A particular sex behavior, for instance, may be related to the palliation of sexual hungers, to the maintenance of self-esteem, to the debasing or the glorification of the sexual object or to the fulfillment of its needs, to the achievement of economic security—to any, or to some, or simultaneously to all of these or to other motives. On the other hand, these motives (and others that, in themselves, never call for sex behavior) may require sexual restraint rather than sexual expression; the perpetuated motive to indulge may itself, depending on the circumstances, call for nonindulgence at a particular time.

In brief, as in the case of sex, any motive may become complexly interrelated with other motives and itself become profoundly modified from what it might otherwise be as it is drawn into such a complex network of relationships. A behavior may even become a motive of the behaviors that initially motivated it. Thus, because being admired may enhance a person's power so that he seeks to be admired in order to achieve power and because power may evoke admiration he may strive for power in order to be admired, admiration-seeking and power-seeking may become reciprocally motivating and both admiration- and power-seeking may motivate and be motivated by striving for achievement, efforts to attain some measure of autonomy, and so on. Some behaviors may have simultaneous bearing on so many others as to become dominant continuing concerns of the individual.

The net effect of motivational derivation, perpetuation, and imbrication is that stable, self-sustaining systems of motives develop. Such

[26] I will hereafter use *perpetuated motives* and *enduring concerns* more or less interchangeably, preferring the first as a reminder of the mode of genesis and the second as a reminder that there need be no greater activity involved, at any given time, than vigilance (that is, a monitoring of the situation for whatever may have bearing on them).

motivational systems, commonly referred to as character and personality, are a long way from the primitive distresses and pleasures associated with particular bodily states that may have started these developments. My earlier allusion to the fact that the backtracking of the motivational derivations that give rise to particular behaviors often—let me now add, most often—lead further and further away from physiological drive states may now be understood in terms of the involvement of such motivational systems and long-range continuing behaviors.

The order of freedom thus envisioned is high indeed. Among the determinants of behavior that, in principle, cannot be dealt with in purely constitutional terms or in purely environmental terms, or in terms of the interplay of purely constitutional and purely environmental factors, are motives and motives of motives and a complex personality and character structure. Man not only plays an active role in the causal complex of the world about him, but he also plays an active role in shaping himself, both as a psychological being and, need I add in these days of psychosomatic medicine, as a biological organism.

The role of the psychologist in investigating Man, so imaged, is to investigate the many degrees of freedom left over when we have discounted the purely environmental and the purely constitutional factors, that is, to discover and to order and to investigate the conditions and consequences of the third set of determinants. And, if in my exposition I have given the primary place to motivation, let me remind you that motivation, as I have expounded it, implicitly involves perception, learning, memory, inference, meaning, and any other psychological process that you may care to designate. In other words, there is no implication in anything that I have said that psychologists should stop studying perception, or learning, or whatever else may be of interest to them. I am talking about the frame within which the outcomes of such studies are to be integrated and about philosophical presuppositions that favor or disfavor theorization and derivative research which make an honest and square look at human behavior possible. I am saying that we should not permit ourselves to be seduced, as so many of us have been, by those pretentious high-order conceptualizations of psychology that would deny to Man the quality that is inalienably his—the quality of freedom—and, in the denial, make Man, as a psychological agent, inaccessible. As the distinguished neurologist Kurt Goldstein remarked to one of my former students, "Aaron," he said, "if the patient doesn't agree with the book, throw the book away. The book was written about the patient, not the patient about the book." In the same vein, I say: If the scientific conceptualizations do not agree with Man, throw the conceptualizations away; the science is about Man, not Man about science.

But I have advanced the image of Man as an active and free agent in the context of a deterministic viewpoint. Is the notion of responsibility compatible with such a viewpoint? By *responsibility*, I am merely recognizing that the activities of Man have consequences and that major determinants of these activities are to be found in Man as he has been shaped at the time he carries out these activities. I assume that the concept applies only to those activities into which he is not driven by forces beyond his control so that his motivation becomes irrelevant, and I also assume that he is in a position to anticipate, if not the precise consequences that ensue, then at least the risks of some unfavorable consequences and the probabilities of favorable ones.

There seem to be two major intellectual obstacles that stand in the way of accepting this interpretation of responsibility. The first involves an apparent paradox: A person who does something that he is motivated to do is, by any normal usage of the term, responsible for his deed, but (and, for the simplicity of exposition, let us here assume a simple two-stage process, an unmotivated motive and the derived deed) if his motive is not itself motivated, then he is not responsible for his motive; and, if he is not responsible for the motive, then how can he be held responsible for the deed? One answer to the paradox is contained in its very statement. There are two issues of responsibility involved, not one: responsibility for the motive and responsibility for the deed. The apparent paradox arises only when we cannot make up our own minds as to which issue of responsibility we are trying to assess; this state of confusion is, in my experience, typically associated with confusion as to why we are concerned with the assessment of responsibility in the first place.

For instance, if we are concerned with the justice of punishment in connection with a misdeed, and if we feel that it is not just to punish in the absence of responsibility, and if we cannot make up our minds what it is that we are considering punishment for, the deed in itself or the implemented motive, then we are destined to go around in circles. If, on the other hand, we could make up our minds whether we are considering punishment for the deed *per se* or for the implemented motive, there would be no problem: If it is the deed *per se*, then it is just to punish, for there is responsibility for the deed; if it is the implemented motive, then it is not just to punish, for there is no responsibility for the motive. A moment's consideration will show that the problem is easily compounded. For it may be held that the real issue of punishment centers neither on the deed *per se* nor on the motivation *per se*, but on the absence of sufficient restraining motivation to keep the motivation for the deed from being implemented. If we accept this issue, however, we are immediately confronted with the same problem: If the absence of restraining motivation is itself motivated, then there is responsibility for the absence and, if it is the latter *per se* for which we are considering punishment, then it is just to punish; but if we are considering punishment for the implementation of the motivation that accounts for the absence, then it may not be just to punish, for this motivation may not be motivated. Hypothetically, we could go into an infinite regress here.

The problem of the justice of punishment, at any rate, is obviously a very complex one indeed. The complexity, however, does not reside in the concept of responsibility, but rather in our difficulties in deciding what, if anything, we want to consider punishing. To deal with these difficulties would confront us with the problem of why we are considering punishment in the first place. If we were to follow through on this problem we might become clearer on the issue of what it is that we are considering punishment for; then the issue of the justice of punishment might be considerably simplified, or we might decide that the issue of justice has no bearing on our consideration of punishment. For instance, if our sole reason for punishing is to exact retribution for a deed already done, then our concern is with the deed *per se*.

I will shortly return to the relation of responsibility to punishment in connection with the second intellectual obstacle, but I want first to consider another aspect of the first. If we were to attempt to generalize the apparent paradox I have been discussing beyond the simple two-stage case, we would uncover a related but much more fundamental source of confusion, namely, the failure to distinguish between responsibility for a past process and responsibility for a current process. I have indicated that in the processes of motivational derivation, perpetuation, and imbrication, a motive may lose contact with the behavior that originally gave rise to it. Thus, I have indicated that in tracking the motivations of most behaviors we are apt to find ourselves moving further and further away from appetitive drives and more and more into a complex network of perpetuated derived imbricated motives. In other words, the factors that sustain a motive are not necessarily the same as those that gave rise to it in the first place, and this is true of every motive in the character structure. Thus, once an individual has developed

39

beyond the initial emergence of motivation (and with the exception of some motivation that continues to be rooted in physiological states), the historical determinants of motivation are just that, that is, they belong to the no-longer-existing past, and the current determinants are themselves largely motivational. Thus, though it may make sense to say that the individual cannot be held responsible for his early motivations, it does not follow that he may not be held responsible for his current motivations.

The second intellectual obstacle to the acceptance of my interpretation of responsibility is tied up with the question of what it means to "hold someone responsible." For some reason, it is commonly assumed that the statement that "So-and-so is responsible" refers only to some misdeed, as though one may not be said to be responsible for a beneficence. Consequently, the attribution of responsibility is taken to imply a punitive attitude—and such an attitude is somehow repugnant to many liberal intellectuals, as it is to me. To say that a person may be held accountable for his sins of commission and of omission is, however, not necessarily to say that he must be punished for them. It is rather to say that he is expected to attempt to make up for them. Compensatory suffering, whether self- or other-induced, is only one—and, to my mind, a highly inferior one—pattern of making up. Direct restitution, undoing the harm that was done, is another. Indirect restitution in the form of good deeds that would not otherwise have been undertaken is still another. And active effort to change one's behavior patterns so as to lessen the likelihood of the repetition of the wrongdoing is yet again another. There are, similarly, many patterns of response to the recognition of responsibility for a good deed.

It is obvious that questions can be raised here that transcend the realm of purely psychological considerations, for instance, whether one ought to expect someone to make up for his sins of omission and commission, and certain kinds of questions as to the relative merits of one or another pattern of making up. It is, however, a simple fact of observation that, with the possible exception of young infants, considerations of responsibility do represent important determinants of human behavior; that is, it is a simple fact of observation to almost anyone but a scientistic psychologist.

Not even so-called psychopathic characters, at least not in my own experience, are immune to such determinants. I have yet, for instance, to encounter one case of a psychopathic character who does not lament his own irresponsibilities; and, if to my own suspicious mind, it sounds like he is pleading for exoneration without any intention of making up for his misdeeds or correcting his ways, this does not change the fact that the recognition of his responsibility has some consequence for him; or even if, along with the lamentation, I sometimes seem to detect a note of pride in connection with his misdeeds (as in the case of one man who, despite the fact that I was in no position to either help or harm him and that I would have remained in utter ignorance of his doings but for his confessions, felt it incumbent on himself to expatiate on what a terrible person he was for having made a career of exploiting "attractive" women who seem to gravitate to him, "begging" to be exploited), there can still be no doubt that he cannot derive a full measure of enjoyment from his misdeeds because of his recognition of his responsibility. Obviously, psychopaths who come voluntarily to a psychologist, psychiatrist, or minister are self-selected, and those who come to attention by virtue of having gotten into trouble are not only a selected group but also have a special axe to grind in trying to generate an image of being under the control of some malign alien force that prevents them from acting responsibly. Even so, I cannot help but doubt that there actually are any "successful" psychopaths who are never troubled by the fact of responsibility.

In declaring that the psychopath is not immune to the fact of responsibility, I am not attempting to resolve the problem of Job by implying that those of us who are regulated by stricter consciences will necessarily lead happier lives in the long run than do the most successful of psychopaths. Indeed, though most psychopaths seem to be fairly miserable wretches, I cannot assert with any degree of confidence that they might not be even more miserable but for the meager enjoyment that their psychopathic ways bring them.

I am not, in this essay, urging myself and my fellow man to lead more saintly lives, free of sin; if I were tempted to do so, I would not rest the argument on the predication of happiness as the supreme value. I am here merely engaged in the psychological enterprise of identifying an important facet of our psychological subject matter, one that leaps to the eye in any dispassionate survey of human behavior, that it seems to me psychology cannot afford to ignore, and that scientistic psychologists do dispose of by the simple expedient of ignoring.

What of Man's essential dignity and worth? What greater measure of dignity and worth can be accorded to him than to recognize, in the fact of his motives helping to generate motives, his role in his own creation? Let me again refer to the first chapter of Genesis. I have already mentioned one difference between the account of the creation of Man and that of the remaining order of creation, namely, that Man was initially created in the singular. Let me now mention a few other striking differences. Each act of creation, except for the creation of Man, is introduced by a simple commandment. Thus, "And God said, let there be light." When it comes to the creation of Man, the text shifts from the imperative mood to the simple future tense. "We will make man" is the statement attributed to God. Moreover, each act of creation, again excepting the creation of Man, is accompanied by an affirmation that the commandment was implemented. Thus, "And there was light," "And it was so," or simply, "And God saw that it was good." Now, the phrase "And it was so" does occur in the context of the work of the sixth day, but this affirmation comes not with the statement of the creation of Man but in a later context of God's statement to Man (by now, in the plural, including both male and female) describing their dominion.

In brief, the creation of Man is, remarkably, stated in the future tense; there is no affirmation that the creation has in fact been completed. Add the implication of the initial statement of the creation of Man in the singular form, namely, that no man may justify his existence by appeal to his special ancestry, but must account for himself. Finally, note the implications of the plural "we" in "We will make man." If the "we" is the we of majesty, why the delay? And where else in the Bible does the we of majesty occur? Does it refer to the hosts of heaven? Why should God suddenly (and only here) need collaborators? What more sensible account is there, then, but that the we is literally a plural form that takes each individual human being into partnership with God in the act of the completion of the creation of Man? And what more magnificent creation, short of the creation of the universe itself, can be attributed to God than a self-creating being?[27]

[27] Though the development of the implication of the biblical text that Man is in partnership with God in his own creation, as here given, is perhaps a novel one, the implication itself is not merely something that I am now, in the twentieth century, reading into the text; it has been a recurrent theme in the rabbinic literature, finding support in various ways through interpretation of the biblical text and the associated Oral tradition. Thus, Joseph L. Baron, in *A Treasury of Jewish Quotations* (New York: Crown Publishers, 1956) pp. xiv, 623 includes the following excerpt from an address by Theodore Gaster: "Judaism has a central, unique, and tremendous idea that is utterly original—the idea that God and man are partners in the world, and that for the realization of His plan and the complete articulation of this glory upon earth, God *needs* a committed, dedicated group of men and women." I shall return to the theme in Chapter 11, with

Whether you take the Bible text as divine revelation or as a humanly inspired allegory which nevertheless expresses one of mankind's greatest and most influential aspirations, the point of my little bit of biblical exegesis has been to show that a central theme of the coupling of the image of Man with the image of God is the role assigned to Man with respect to his own creation. In any case, however you prefer to take the Bible and whatever you may make of my exposition of its first chapter, the image, I suggest, is a true one. I further suggest that any psychological science that does not face up to the aspects of the image that I have tried to develop runs the risk of concerning itself with psychological trivia arbitrarily torn out of the context of their natural setting; such a science can certainly justify no commitment of psychologists to a belief in the dignity and worth of the individual human being.

---

some further documentation. As a minor addendum here: When I first realized the above cited oddities of the biblical text and their implication, I took my discovery to my father. I had barely gotten started when he interrupted me and, with an indulgent smile, said: "You are going to tell me about the partnership between man and God." Then he heard me out, and was pleased, but the idea was obviously old hat.

3

DEFINITION, SCIENCE,

AND REALITY[1]

In the preceding chapter, I treated "behavior" as though its meaning were obvious. This is certainly not the case. It is often used as a synonym of activity and is applied to inanimate objects as well as to the activities of living beings; for instance, we may talk of the behavior of molecules or of the planets. When applied to the actions of living beings, the term is sometimes used to include, and sometimes to exclude, tropisms and reflexes. There are psychologists who define their discipline as the science of behavior and who experience no inconsistency when they conduct experiments in which the dependent variables are changes in blood or brain-tissue chemistry. I am inclined to doubt, however, that any psychologist would consider it within the bounds of psychological usage to apply the term to any kind of change in blood or brain-tissue chemistry, regardless of the instigating conditions. Or to the case of an organism caught in the act of falling, not, that is, when the act is unintentional. But how and why does one draw the line? Why is falling less a behavior than a knee jerk? Why, if at all, is a seminal ejaculation less a behavior than a passionate declaration of love? The penetration of a sperm into an ovum less than the demonstration of a mathematical theorem? The positioning of iron filings around a magnet less than playing a chess game or planning a military campaign? The digestion of one's food less than going to work to earn a livelihood?

[1] From the viewpont of its content, this chapter belongs between Chapters 15 and 16. I have, however, placed it here as an introduction to the remaining chapters of Part II and to Part III.

There are those who would say that it makes no difference where or how we draw the line. The subject matter of psychology is what the psychologist studies. "Behavior" means whatever the psychologist wants it to mean. Call the definition operational, and it becomes scientifically respectable. And award Humpty Dumpty a posthumous honorary membership in the Psychonomic Society, and perhaps a civic medal as well for his exercise of his rights of freedom of speech and thought.

As for Humpty Dumpty, I will take second place to none in my admiration of the sterling integrity of his character—before his mishap, that is; but such admiration is hardly a valid reason to look to him for intellectual leadership.

The funny thing about this capricious approach to definition is that it often goes along with an obsession with precision of terminological use in communication. Individuals so obsessed generally demand operational definitions,[2] ostensibly because they believe that no one, especially if he is a scientistic scientist, is supposed to be capable of understanding what any one else is talking about if his concepts are not operationally defined—and the presumption underlying the obsession is that, if a concept proves obdurate to operational definition, it serves a purely syntactical function, expresses emotion, or involves nothing more than a linguistic habit, but in any case it has no reference to anything at all, and, if used in a sentence, it generally results in a meaningless statement.

The historical fact is that the idea of operational definition came as a measure of last resort. Light, in some experiments, behaved (!) like a wave phenomenon and, in other experiments, like a corpuscular phenomenon. Since no one had established that the same thing could appear as both vibration and particulate emission, these findings suggested the possibility that there might be at least two different kinds of phenomena, both referred to as light, indistinguishable from each other except by direct determination. Assuming that this is so, the physicist found himself in a peculiar position. In any experiment involving light, short of a complicated and costly direct determination, he could not tell which kind of light he was using. In this extremity, it occurred to him that he could reduce the ambiguity by always specifying the means and procedures he was using to index the light involved in his experiment, and adding that the light he was talking about is the kind of light that is observed when one indexes light in this specified manner. The opera-

[2] The generic form of an operational definition is: x is what you observe when you carry out observational operations y.

tional definition is thus an extension of the primitive measure of indicating a referent by pointing. "Look over there," one might say, "and you will see what I am talking about."

It might seem that a sounder approach to the problem of specifying the kind of light involved in an experiment would be to investigate the properties of light emanating from different light sources and then specifying the source used in the experiment. This seems to be such an obvious expedient that I must assume that it has been found that what seems to be an identical light source gives out light that appears to be a wave phenomenon when studied by certain procedures and a corpuscular phenomenon when studied by others. Such a finding would imply to me that (1) there must be an essential compatibility between vibration and particulate emission and that there is consequently no reason for postulating two kinds of light, or (2) that the experimental procedures used to determine whether light is wave or corpuscle, in some as yet undetected manner, differentiate or transform an original one-kind of light into two kinds of derivative phenomena which are then taken as evidence of two kinds of light, that is, that the seeming occurrence of the two kinds of light is an artifact of the experiments, or (3) that the procedure for producing the light has not been sufficiently specified and that there is an as yet undetected systematic difference in the light-producing procedure in the two kinds of experiment, despite the apparent identity, or (4) that light does not behave (!) lawfully.

Alternative 4 cannot be taken seriously before the first three alternatives have been eliminated; and the mere failure to demonstrate one or another of the latter cannot be taken as logically sufficient evidence that they may be eliminated. Assume for the sake of argument, however, that we do take it seriously. On this assumption, it is obvious that specifying the procedures used in observation can tell us nothing about whether the light in the experiment is behaving as wave or as corpuscle.

Assume alternative 3. If the conditions for producing the two kinds of light are so subtly different, what assurance can we have that the procedures for observing light are sufficiently powerful to discriminate the two kinds? What possible reason can we have for assuming that two photometric procedures are differentially sensitive to the two kinds of light before we can produce the two kinds at will and learn enough of their differential behaviors to justify such an assumption? In other words, on the assumption of alternative (3), the operational definition does not offer a solution of the problem for the solution of which it was designed. In general, I may add that the act of pointing is not a very precise way of designating a referent.

On the assumption of alternatives 1 or 2, of course, operationalism was offering a solution to a problem that does not exist. Yet there can be no question but that operationalism has swept much of the scientific world—and, in particular, the world of the two behavioral sciences with which I am most familiar, psychology and sociology—with a quasi-religious fervor. How did this happen?

A frequent feature of nonscientific discussion is that it seems to be impossible to determine from the discussion what it is that is being asserted or denied. Thus, people will become involved in heated arguments about God, democracy, the requirements of justice, and often no one has any clear notion of what he himself is saying, no less what anyone else means. Someone declares that it is human nature to fight. Someone else vehemently dissents. No one, however, asks for a specification of the statement. Does it mean that there can be no human being who does not fight? That a person who does not fight is not human? Is it compatible with or implied in the alleged attribute to have lulls in the fighting and, if so, how long may the lulls last without contradicting the assertion? Does the alleged attribute apply to newborn babies and, if not, at what age does this alleged attribute of human nature appear? Does it extend into old age? Does it apply equally and in the same way to females as to males? How much violence is subsumed under "fight"? Does fighting imply collective activity, as in war? Does the fellow who guards the home front violate his human nature? Is any kind of aggressive action (for example, writing anonymous poison pen letters) subsumed under fighting and, if not, when does aggressive action become fighting? Is all fighting aggressive and, if not, is nonaggressive fighting equivalent to aggressive fighting in the initial generalization? What is the meaning of aggression? If a person were fortunate enough never to be crossed or to experience frustration, would he still fight? Why the qualification "human"? Is it intended to exclude nonhuman nature, to include humans under a wider generalization, or to make an assertion about humans without any commitment as to other kinds of beings?

The chances are that, if you were to press many of these questions and the questions to which the answers lead, the discussants would soon join forces and turn some of the alleged human nature on you. Later, after the hostilities are over, someone may be kind enough to explain to you that (1) social argumentation is generally not concerned with arriving at tenable conclusions, but with reciprocal interstimulation within the limits of certain tacitly understood rules, one of which is that you must never press hard to clarify what another person has said, and (2) if you are the kind of person who has a great passion for unequivocal expression, then, by the time you began to intrude on a friendly argument with your line of specifying questions, you should have been able to translate "It is human nature to fight" into a reasonably close approximation of what must really have been intended, namely, "In the contemplation of human affairs, one may with great confidence count on—and probably forever continue to count on—the likelihood that occasions and instigations will come up that will lead people to violent interaction, pairwise, teamwise, nationwise, and/or other collectionwise.

However one may justify the looseness of the common language in ordinary social conversation and whatever may be the reasonable expectation concerning a listener's or reader's responsibilities in trying to understand communications addressed to him, there can be no doubt but that scientists do experience a need for more precise linguistic forms. This may perhaps be taken as one factor that helps to explain the remarkable spread of operationalism. Inasmuch as the scientist is concerned with as precise determination as he can achieve of relationships between phenomena, the loose language and shifting meanings of the words of ordinary conversation is, to him, a trial and a tribulation; and he waxes particularly impatient at statements that seem to have no determinate reference. Even so, this state of mind cannot be taken as a sufficient explanation of the spread of operationalism since it does not necessarily call for operational definitions. There are other disciplines (for example, the law) with needs for precision in communication that were not responsive to operationalism. Moreover, Galileo, Newton, Darwin, and a host of pre-mid-twentieth-century scientists did not know enough to offer operational definitions of the concepts they used, but somehow seemed to be capable of making significant contributions to science. One may perhaps be able to read operational definitions into their writings, but they themselves neither thought nor communicated with their contemporaries in such terms. And the vivid, mentalistic, metaphorical language in which Newton expressed some of his great discoveries did not seem to inhibit the advancement of physics. The statement that is empty of any real reference reflects a characteristic of the speaker at the moment of the utterance and is not an inherent property of the common language. Many concepts can be defined with great precision in the common language, without mention of the operations to be used in observing or detecting concrete instances, and the specific meaning of many multimeaninged terms can be brought out by the context without benefit of any formal definition at all. If there are residual ambiguities, they can be brought out and the statements clarified or revised in the course of continued interactive communication—provided, of course, that there is a will to communicate.

A second factor in the spread of operationalism, I suspect, has to do with the enormously increased degree of specialization in science as a result of which the individual research worker became more and more preoccupied with his own tiny bit of subject matter and less and less aware of the scientific requirement of the integration and systematization of knowledge. The more limited the communicational contexts, the less obvious is it that there are inherent limits to the denotative restrictions that can be imposed on a word. Hence, given a need for denotational precision, the increased degree of specialization and the consequent narrowing of communicational contexts generated in scientists a readiness to believe that the new invention—operationalism—offered a means of control over denotations. It had to be something new, of course, that would offer such a promise because these scientists already had too much, and too broad, an experience with the common language in their prescientific development and in their extracurricular activities to have much faith in the potentialities of the latter. What they did not realize was the fact that, in the constricted contexts of their technical communications, even technically undefined terms could be expected to have much more restricted denotational ranges than these same terms would be likely to have in contextually unconstricted usages.

Moreover, an ever increasing proportion of scientific research was being carried on outside of the university settings and, even within the universities, the scientifically productive professors were able to get smaller and smaller teaching loads, which took the form of more and more specialized courses. The decline and narrowing of the teaching function, however, also had the consequence of a lessened occasion for the individual scientist's concern with the big picture. This, in turn, led to an ever dimming awareness of the fact that the monoideic pursuit of new knowledge without any thought as to how the new bits will fit into the totality represents as much a perversion of the scientific spirit as would an exclusive preoccupation with the totality along with an abandonment of the persistent and ever critical reexamination of existing knowledge and the pursuit of the new. There was, as a consequence, no great degree of alertness to the threat posed by any consistent application of operationalism to the integrative function of science. For the simple fact is that operationalism, consistently applied, is virtually antithetical to noetic integration and systematization. If words have no meaning beyond the observational operations that specify them, then every concept automatically explodes into many, often scores of, others. These may sometimes be recombined by the demonstration that different observational operations are equivalent, but observational operations appropriate to different contexts often cannot be readily cross-checked; and if one insists, as is thoroughly proper to a consistent operationalism, that the specification of the observational context is necessary to the specification of the observational operations, the cross-checking and consolidation of the proliferated concepts becomes, in principle, impossible.

As a psychologist, my suspicions concerning the factors responsible for the sweep of operationalism also take a psychological turn. The scientific way of life demands an acceptance of the uncertainty of conclusions reached: No proposition is beyond question, no finding beyond challenge, no answer assuredly final. Yet there is comfort, assurance, and security in certainty; so, if one must resign oneself to the uncertainty of the scientific output, one can find compensation by demanding certainty with regard to the scientific input. The demand then goes up for rigorously defined and concretely specifiable terms. Operational definitions are neither rigorous nor precise, but this is easily overlooked in their concreteness. There is a reassuring here-and-nowness in the things one can point at.

The major factor, however, is, to my mind, the rootedness of operationalism in the idealist[3] and positivist philosophies that have played so important a role in nurturing a tradition of empiricism and liberating the modern mind from an all-embracing attitude of faith, on the one hand, or an all-consuming armchair rationalism on the other. It is not out of a lack of appreciation of the role of idealism and positivism in the shaping of the modern scientific spirit that I say that it is one of the ironies of history that these philosophical viewpoints (at least, as I understand them) should be utterly incompatible with two basic and necessary premises of the scientific enterprise. Nor would I exempt contemporary logical positivism (to which operationalism

---

[3] The word is derived from "ideal" in the sense of "having the properties of an idea," not from "ideal" in the sense of an embodiment of, a conception of, or an aspiration for perfection.

has so strong an affinity as to embrace and be embraced by it), insofar as it is a positivist philosophy, from this statement despite the many significant contributions of the logical positivists to logical, conceptual, and methodological analysis.

The two basic premises are (1) that things do exist and events do occur independently of our perceptions of them, and (2) that all such things are fully knowable, subject only to such limitations as may be imposed by the possible existence of contradictory necessary conditions of knowing. Without the first premise the scientific quest makes no sense whatever; without it no scientific issue is weightier than the proverbial one of how many angels can dance on a pinhead. Without this premise, there are merely different, but arbitrary, rules that are applied to determine which statements to call true; but no rule can be superior to any other in producing a more accurate depiction of reality because, by the denial of the first premise, there is no reality to be depicted. The second premise is necessary, at least as a tacit working hypothesis.

Idealistic philosophies[4] deny the first premise—and, of course, by implication, the second. Positivistic philosophies accept the first, but deny the second. In Chapter 8, in the context of a review of solutions of the mind-body problem, I shall attempt to show that the denial of the first premise leads to an absurd conclusion, namely, that nothing whatever (not excluding perception and the very denial itself) exists. Unless and until it can be shown that this demonstration is flawed and/ or that the affirmation of the first premise leads to an equally absurd conclusion, we may take it that the first premise is established. Let me here consider the tenability of positivism.

According to this view, though objects and events may exist independently of our perception of them, we can never have knowledge of them as such. There must forever remain a residual thing/or/event-in-itself that is beyond our ken. Rejecting any source of knowledge other than sensory data, it seems to follow that we can know only about those matters that can be sensed. Such a conclusion, however, can be quite misleading. To start with, the range of the senses has been enormously extended by means of telescopes, microscopes, electrical and electronic devices, chemical tests, and so on, so that the residual "in-itself" is not a fixed quantity and is continually being reduced. In view,

---

[4] Except in the version that anyone's perception—for example, God's—is sufficient to confer existence. As we shall see, however, this view is not consistent with the basic premise of idealism.

not merely of past success, but of the enormously accelerating rate of success in the development of auxiliary devices to expand the range of the senses, it would take something more than a mere fiat or a pessimistic outlook to establish a bound short of the "in-itself."

Moreover, it simply is not true that the limit of knowledge is at the bounds of sensory experience. Reason applied to data has often resulted in discoveries that anteceded their sensory verification. A somewhat amusing case in point may be cited from a well-known psychology textbook, which explained, in its first chapter, that science deals only with that which can be seen, heard, or touched (I do not know why the author discriminated against the other senses), and in the next chapter presented the genes as scientific fact—and this even prior to the discovery of the relation of the nucleic acids to the genes.

The argument for the unknowable thing-in-itself takes a far more subtle form, however, as in the Kantian version. The issue that is raised has to do with the nature of the mind itself. The true order of nature-in-itself, it is assumed, is not arrayed according to the way we experience it in space, time, and other categories. The notions of space, time, causality, and so on are, by this assumption, creations of the mind and imposed on the order of nature. The mind is a prisoner of its own inner nature and its inescapable propensity to impose its categorizing processes on the subject matter of its experience. It is, indeed, demonstrable that people do assimilate new data into old molds, often disregarding the obvious bad fit. A young child will push a square peg into a round hole and, especially if there is some degree of penetration and he can wedge the peg into place so that it does not topple over, act as though peg and hole were made for each other. Illusions and stereotypes are more general cases in point. Nevertheless, the view that the mind imposes its forms on the subject matter of its experience has at least three fatal flaws.

1. The assumption cannot be proven true without proving it to be false. That is, to prove it true, we must penetrate to the true order of nature and the true nature of the mind. At best, then, the assumption must forever remain as assumption and, since it serves no positive function, it seems like the kind of assumption that is best reserved for the prophetic "end of days." It states limits without positive reason for such statement and long before we have any reason to suppose that we have exhausted our efforts to test the limits.

2. Nature apparently permits itself to be forced into the mold of the categories of the mind, and this must tell something of the order of

nature. Not even the child trying to force a square peg into a round hole is wholly wrong; after all, the child is not trying to force the hole into the peg. The poorer the fit, the more glaring must we expect the lack of fit to be; and the stronger the motivation to find out where things fit (and presumably the scientific fraternity, confronting nature, is somewhat more motivated than the child toying with a pegboard) the greater is the alertness to evidence of lack of fit and the more persistent the efforts to test alternative hypotheses until the conditions of optimal fit are established. From these and similar considerations it follows that our conceptions of the order of nature cannot be grossly in error and that, insofar as they are in error, there is room for optimism that inconsistencies will appear that will lead to corrections.

3. We could take the assumption more seriously if there were reason to believe that the mind thinks in invariable categories. But this is far from the case. Even relatively unsophisticated minds, for example, seem to have relatively little difficulty with two radically different conceptions of the flow of time: the variable flow of subjective time (occasions when time flies and occasions when it drags) and the invariant flow of clock or calendar time. Similarly with regard to subjective and physical space, with regard to independent and interdependent time and space dimensions (for example, flying time and miles as distance measures so that New York and London are much closer together than they used to be even though the number of miles between them has not changed), and so on. When it comes to relatively sophisticated minds, there seems to be no foreseeable limit to the variations that can be produced. Thus, merely with regard to space: metrical and nonmetrical spaces; spaces in which parallel lines remain forever equidistant from each other, or diverge, or converge; infinite spaces that are unbounded, infinite spaces that are bounded, and finite spaces that are unbounded or bounded; continuous and discontinuous spaces; spaces varying from zero to an unlimited number of dimensions; spaces that are unaffected by the masses they contain and spaces that are shaped by these masses; and so on. In the light of such variation, what meaning can be attached to the contention that the mind forces the subject matter of experience into its own mold?

Operational definitions were invented to meet a problem of defining terms that were not otherwise specifiable. The invention was a failure, but, to shift the figure of speech, scientists were not disposed to observe that the emperor wore no clothes. From an approach to the problem of definition, operationalism quickly emerged as a major philosophy of science and merged with an independently developed approach to the philosophy of science, namely, logical positivism. Many of the logical positivists had made highly significant contributions to philosophy, logic, and sundry other areas. Their prestige, articulateness, and vigor combined with the enthusiastic support of a rather small group of highly prestigeful scientist converts generated a new scientific orthodoxy. The historical role of idealistic and positivistic philosophies in the shaping of the scientific temper, the lessened centrality of the integrative aspect of the scientific enterprise, the distrust of the common language and the felt need for precise terminology, the need for an assurance of certainty with regard to the scientific input if one could not have it with regard to the scientific output—all these combined to establish a ground hospitable to the high priests of the new messianic movement.

Especially psychology. A generation or more before the advent of operationalism, psychologists were already learning to conceal their shallowness behind such propositions as "Psychology is that which the psychologist studies" and "Intelligence is that which an intelligence test measures." Watson had already ruled consciousness out of scientific existence on the ground that consciousness is not open to public observation. Systematic thinking was all too readily anathemized as armchair psychology or as nonscience. I can, for instance, recall the time when, as a graduate student in a seminar well attended by many distinguished psychologists, I had a criticism answered by the startling observation "That is logic, not science," as though the scientist has no obligation to think straight; and the most startling thing about it was that no one in the room, but myself, seemed to be startled. A syncretistic eclecticism was, with a few exceptions, the order of the day: One lifted ideas as needed, from here, there, and everywhere, without regard to such trivial matters as consistency.

The accent was on research, and the time was rapidly coming when the most common measure of the worth of a theory would be the amount of research to which the theory led rather than its scope or integrative power or, for that matter, any concern with the question of what all the research could possibly add up to. Theories were about to return as a major fad, in the form of hypotheticodeductive models, though most psychological researchers were to remain *de facto* atheoretical and a major research movement that was self-consciously antitheoretical was about to be launched in the field of operant conditioning. The new theories, however, and the research to which they led were not, when they arrived on the scene, concerned with broad-gauge checks against reality. They were generally concerned with an arbitrarily sliced-off segment of a subject-matter field and the internal consistency of the data in the segment and the set of postulates that constituted the nucleus of the theory. If a glance beyond the delimited scope of the theory revealed manifest contradiction of the theory, the thing to do was to shrug one's shoulders and stop looking; the theory was not supposed to apply to the out there.

Reality itself, if one dared to use the word at all, achieved the status of a construct; the word referred to a convenient fiction, an as-if that is not really real.

In this kind of intellectual climate, operationalism fit. An investigator could (and did) define "fear" in rats, operationally, as the number of pellets of feces dropped by a rat in a specified time interval without any concern about the fact that what one observes as one counts pellets of feces is quite different from what is normally connoted by the word "fear." Nor did he have any need to explain why, when his interest was in "fear" as normally connoted, he should have shifted to "fear" as "number of pellets of feces" or to show any reason for investigating the relation of number of pellets or feces (whether called "fear" or by a less euphemistic Anglo-Saxon term) to something else.

If the vaunted hypotheticodeductive method leads to a predicted relationship, the latter involves the term as conceived in the deductive process, not as subsequently operationally defined in the experiment designed to test the deduction. There has to be a link between the term as "operationally" defined and the term for which the substitution is being made. Thus, it would have been quite another matter if our investigator had said that, for various reasons, it seems appropriate to take number of pellets of feces as an index of fear. This would have required, in the first place, some notion of what the referent of "fear" is, that is, some conceptual clarity, nonoperational, as to the nature of "fear" and some reason for believing that number of pellets of feces may be taken as a valid index of "fear." In the second place, it would have required a cautious attitude with respect to the interpretation of any observed relationships or lack of relationships involving this index, namely, that the observed relationships may be determined by the invalid variance in the index and, by the same token, that the failure to verify expected relationships may be due to the invalid variance in the index. But our investigator, having elected to go along with Humpty Dumpty, albeit in operationalist costume, was thereby relieved of any responsibility to discover what it is about number of pellets of feces that is related to something else; he had solved that problem by fiat: "Number of pellets of feces" means "fear." Stated differently, an operational definition, if taken seriously as the definition of a concept, carried with it no notion of any possibility of associated invalid variance. Thus, the one commendable feature of operationalism, its desire to contribute to the precision of scientific thinking, is defeated.

Actually no one can live by this kind of nonsense. It is, at best, something one can profess, a *credo quia absurdum*, and the associated rituals of which one can observe. One makes one's obeisance, especially if one happens to be writing a doctoral dissertation, to the regnant philosophy of science, asserts that science is only concerned with that which can be seen, heard, or touched, offers one's operational definitions, and proceeds from there as though one were at last free to start afresh. To be sure, there are occasional caveats about the importation of surplus meanings into operationally defined terms (as though these surplus meanings had nothing to do with the prime motivation for being concerned with these terms in the first place), but surplus meaning is what one observes only in the verbal usages of others, never in one's own.

The philosophical roots of operationalism, for all their role in opening the mind of the cultured man to the data provided by experience, are not tenable in the context of the scientific enterprise; and the operational definition is not an effective means of specifying meaning. Moreover, the importance of specifying meaning for purposes of precision in communication is exaggerated out of all reasonable proportion.

It underestimates the intelligence of the addressee, the role of context in identifying meaning, and the clarificatory powers of continued communication under the condition of a will to understand.

It misconstrues the nature of linguistic symbols, including the case of mathematical symbols. Even if one were to start with symbols of agreed-on meaning, communication needs arise for which no symbols have been established but for which old symbols almost fit or constitute apt analogies, and, often without even realizing the extension of the original convention, one makes use of the old symbol. The process of extending the area of meaning continues, often forming unrelated branches, and the original agreed-on meaning may even be lost; and, if anyone thinks that mathematical symbols are immune to such a process, he is simply unfamiliar with the history of mathematics.

Thus, to take one example, "zero" originally meant—and in many mathematical contexts still means—a null or empty class, the absence of anything, nothing. Now, consider any number and do nothing to it; it remains unchanged. One of the things you do not do to it is to divide it by anything; you divide it by nothing, by zero. You may be rocked for a moment by the obvious conclusion, which you promptly reject as you realize that, in the context of "multiply by" or "divide by," "zero" no longer means "nothing," but designates a number with certain unique numerical properties. The chances are that, in your own personal history, you learned to interpret "add or subtract zero" as "do not add or subtract anything" and did not realize until many years after you had learned to multiply by zero (possibly even not until this very moment) that "zero" had acquired a new meaning; and the likelihood is that the transitions in meaning as you learned the values of a number raised to the zero power and of factorial zero also came about without full realization. The multiple meanings of "zero," all still current, do not nullify the usefulness of either the word or the associated symbol. Nor does the extension into the phrase "He is a zero, a cipher," meaning— depending on the context—either "His properties are unknown" or "He may be dismissed from mind as utterly unimportant." No one would ever confuse either of the latter meanings with the meaning of zero in "Two plus zero equal two."

Finally, the exaggeration of the role of definition misconstrues the nature of the scientific enterprise. It takes as much knowledge to be certain of the input as of the output. The scientific definition is a summary of the state of extant knowledge. Characteristically, we progress, with many corrections along the way, from a more or less vaguely apprehended referent, a hunch as to the essential nature of the thing, to a more and more precise characterization, a greater and greater assurance concerning the essence. This, and not the requirement of precision in communication, is the reason for concern with definition. The definition, regardless of how consistently our verbal usage abides by the definition, summarizes what we know, or think we know, about the nature of what we are talking about. It is as rooted in data, and as subject to correction in the light of data, as is any hunch, hypothesis, or law concerning the functional relationship between two variables. A definition asserts that, for some purpose, all the items that meet the specifications of the definition are interchangeable and that, for this purpose, none of these items is interchangeable with items that do not meet the specifications. The purpose may be one of communication. But the paramount scientific purpose is to achieve the most efficient and orderly representation of reality. Putting into one category things or events that are not interchangeable and putting into separate categories things or events that are is to introduce a barrier to the achievement of that paramount purpose.

At issue in scientific definition is not the usage of a word, though the needs of communication make it advisable to respect the common usage as much as possible, but the categorization of things and events; contingent on the wisdom of the categorizing process is the ease with which we can achieve our primary and superordinate goal, the efficient and orderly representation of what goes on in the world. To define "behavior" as "action" is within the prerogatives of linguistic usage, but to accept this usage for psychological purposes is to give up the hope of finding distinctive psychological laws. But if we sense that the "behaviors" of falling bodies, light, randomly moving particles, and their like are different from the behaviors of paying attention, learning, and their like, we need to pursue the difference. We soon realize that a crucial factor in this pursuit are the referents of the two "and their likes" and become engaged in trying to identify the critical differences. We become engaged in the hypothesis testing operation of definition, not as a beginning of science, but as an end.

4

BEHAVIOR, MIND,

AND RELATED CONCEPTS

The definition of "behavior" as *purposive activity* is, among the familiar definitions, the one that most sharply distinguishes a psychological subject matter. This definition evokes a strong negative reaction among many scientists on the ground that the concept of purpose is said to be teleological, a characterization that is held to be sufficient to damn any concept to which it applies. What is wrong with teleology and, insofar as it represents a scientifically untenable doctrine, does it apply to the concept of purpose?

The reprehensible doctrine of teleology (that is, the doctrine in its reprehensible version) holds that the end state in the development, evolution, or history of some animate or inanimate object exercises a force—a pull from the future—on the change process and thus helps to bring itself about. A well-known example is the idea that a giraffe grows a long neck in order to be able to reach the tender foliage in the upper branches of trees. As a teleological notion, the idea is that the giraffe grows its long neck because it will eventually be eating the allegedly tender leaves at the top of the tree; the end state, the eventual event, is taken to be the cause of the growth.

Since the end state does not exist prior to its attainment, the doctrine, as I have just presented it, asserts that something that does not exist affects something that does. Such an assertion is taken by some scientists as the kind of nonsense in which philosophers delight, but with which no self-respecting scientist will have anything to do. The self-righteousness is somewhat premature since an exactly equivalent doctrine has common currency among scientists, the doctrine of causes anteceding their effects. The past, as such, is, of course, as nonexistent as is the future so that the assertion of an effect from some past event imputes as much consequentiality to the nonexistent as does an effect from the future. To be sure, the source of the effect may, in many instances, go on existing subsequently to its effective action, but this is irrelevant to the nature of the traditional concept of causality. Causation is conceived of as moving from the past to the present, and one can cite many examples in which there is manifestly no temporal overlap. In stimulus-response psychology, there is no discordance in the notion of a delayed response; and geneticists do not hesitate to attribute the characteristics of descendants to the characteristics of their ancestors.

As a matter of fact, many scientists who accept the traditional concept of causality do seem to feel quite uncomfortable with it and will, if pressed, rather quickly attempt to reduce the time gap. In essence, they will say that they had stated the causal relationship rather crudely, that the true causal relationship included events from the mentioned cause up to (but not including) the time of the mentioned effect. Thus, it is not really the mentioned stimulus (for example, ringing a bell) that causes the mentioned response (for example, retraction of a finger); what really happens is that the bell is a source of energy that does something to a sense organ that, in turn, does something to a nerve fiber that sets off a series of "discharges," each of which causes the next, and so on, until a synapse is reached where something else happens that stimulates the dendrites of the neurones in the chain, and so on, until the fibers of a muscle are caused to contract and the finger is pulled away from wherever it was resting. The more fractionated the event, the smaller is the time gap between each fractional cause and its fractional effect; the smaller the assumed time gap, the less is the embarrassment at the implied consequentiality of the nonexistent.

Let us, for the sake of argument, assume that we have succeeded in so breaking down an event into component processes that the time elapsing between any given cause and its subsequent effect is less than some minute fraction of a millisecond or, if you will, of a nanosecond. In terms of errors of measurement or in terms of the boundaries of a macrotemporal event, such a duration is doubtless of negligible significance and we may quite properly ignore it. When we distinguish the interval in principle, however, we cannot disparage it because of its minuteness; nor can we justifiably pretend that its minuteness somehow abrogates the tautology that that which does not exist can have no consequences.[1] When the time gap is assumed as a matter of principle, the issue that is raised is not the issue of the bridging of a temporal gap (action at a distance, so to say—albeit a temporal distance in the present instance—with respect to which the smallness of the gap might make a difference), but the issue of the consequentiality of the nonexistent. From the reference of the present, the events at the far side of the gap no longer (or do not yet) exist, and it makes no difference whether the gap is a millennium or a minute fraction of a nanosecond wide.

The logically consistent alternatives are, then, (1) to accept the traditional concept of causality and not to reject the above-described teleological doctrine on the stated grounds[2] or (2) to reject the traditional concept of causality along with the above-described teleological doctrine.

Scientists do have a reason for rejecting the hypothesis of action from the future that does not apply to action from the past. We can get data about the past. The assumption of the effectiveness of the past, therefore, implies no limitation, in principle, on our capacity to predict successfully. Short of resort to a crystal ball—a device in which most scientists do not have great faith—we have no access to future data until after they have arrived, and this, of course, includes determinants

[1] A tautology because having consequences is a sufficient criterion of existence. There does seem to be an exception to the tautology, but it does not withstand close inspection. Assun A and B to be real events and that A is a necessary condition of B (or, more generally, that the probability of B, given A, does not equal the probability of B, given not-A and that the probability of A is independent of the probability of B). On these assumptions, the absence of A has consequence for B. Thus, it seems that something which does not exist (the absent A) can have consequence. The apparency, however, involves a semantic confusion: It is, in fact, not the absent A that has consequence, but A's absence. Absence is as existential a fact as is presence. We can, for instance, distinguish real from imaginary absences, past, present, and future absences, probable and improbable absences, and so on.

[2] By the criterion of existence mentioned in the preceding footnote, the acceptance of the traditional concept of causality requires a revision in the concept of time such that the past continues to exist in the present. Essentially, this revision, demands, I think, the conception of time as a fourth spatial dimension. Thus, just as we are capable of apprehending one dimension more than the mythical inhabitants of Flatland, so would some being superior to us be capable of apprehending the four-dimensional manifold, including the one we call time. On this conception, however, I see no reason for denying to such a creature the possibility of simultaneously apprehending what appears to us to be past, present, and future, just as we can simultaneously apprehend above, at, and below eye level. This, I may note, is a fairly common conception of the powers of God: that past, present, and future are as simultaneously open to His inspection (n.b., *inspection*, not prediction or recall) as right, center, and left are to ours. From this point of view, there is no reason for denying action from either past or future.

from the future. The assumption of teleology, then, implies a limitation, in principle, on our capacity to predict. The assumption is one that would, if it had any consequence at all, discourage scientific initiative and would therefore be best relegated to a time when there seems to be no alternative.

As an argument against teleology, the one just presented is a weak one because the teleological hypothesis is testable, without waiting for the end of days and the exhaustion of alternatives, subject only to the technology of information gathering and processing. Here, for instance, is a paradigm of an experiment: Obtain a random selection of, say, chicken eggs and randomly divide them into a number of groups. Each group is marked for destruction a specified number of days subsequent to hatching, and all chickens that die before the specified date are eliminated from the experiment. Except for this difference, all eggs, chicks, and chickens are treated in identical manners (the handlers would be kept in ignorance of the groupings) up to the moment of destruction. Thus, every egg that is laid and retained in the experimental population has a predetermined future, the different groups having different futures, and one can even provide for systematically different postexecution futures. If their end-states have an effect on their development, there should be systematic developmental differences between the executed chickens and the survivors prior to the moment of execution. I must add that I, myself, am much too confident of the outcome of such experiments to have any interest in carrying them out.

At any rate, pending the carrying out of such experiments and the presentation of strong evidence of the effectiveness of the future, I must reject both the doctrine of teleology that I have described and the traditional concept of causation. It is by now, however, time to observe that, to my knowledge, no responsible writer, scientist, or other has seriously advanced the teleological doctrine I have described. The latter is a scientists' stereotype, triggered off by any mention of a purposive concept. I have introduced it to clarify the atmosphere and for the light that it throws on the traditional concept of causation.

The teleological concept that has been seriously advanced is not that the historical future (the actual future future) has consequences in the present, but that present events include strivings toward end-states. The giraffe is said to grow his long neck, not because he will some day become an animal with a very long neck, but because he is constantly stretching it. The statement may be factually incorrect, but it cannot be caught on the issue of implying the consequentiality of a nonexistent future—or past. The concept of purpose, whether dubbed teleological or not, cannot be shown to be, in principle, incompatible with the scientific enterprise. The issue of purpose is one of fact and every class of apparently purposive activities must be dealt with on its merits.

Now, it happens that I agree that every event that I am willing to classify as behavioral does involve purposive activity. That is, I agree that its purposiveness is, in principle, demonstrable and consider it to be a good scientific strategy to classify events on the basis of whether they do involve purposive activity. Even so, I am not willing to define "behavior" as purposive activity, and let it go at that. Experience demonstrates that "purpose" is too tricky to permit its use as a primitive term. Purpose is all too easily imputed to events that I would not accept as belonging to a common class; and it is not usually imputed to certain events that I think belong with many that I, along with most observers, would readily classify as behavioral.

The giraffe has been said to grow his long neck in order to reach the foliage at the top of the tree on the basis of no evidence other than that his long neck makes it possible to reach such foliage. The stomach has been said to pour forth its juices in order to digest the ingested food on no more evidence than that the gastric juices play a role in digestion. Adrenalin has been said to pour into the blood stream in order to prepare the organism to cope with emergencies when the available fact is that adrenalin is associated with certain other bodily changes that have survival value under some circumstances. I once had a philosophy professor who claimed that the fact that animals copulate proves that they have a philosophy of life: It was obvious to him that copulation occurs in order to beget offspring (rather than that the begetting of offspring is often an incidental consequence of copulation), a fact that implies a value that, in turn, implies a philosophy. It has been said that sperm cells seek the ovum, that rocks fall because they contain within themselves a striving to reunite with the earth from which they have been forcibly torn, and that the rain falls in order to make the earth fertile. One can go on endlessly citing other examples of simple events translated into purposes and simple outcomes translated into goals by habits of speech or perception; and one can sympathize with the revulsion that many scientists feel when the concept of purpose is introduced, though not with their willingness to toss the baby out along with the dirty bathwater. On the other hand, most people would not think of the hearing of raucous noises (excepting certain styles of music), the accidental seeing of painful sights, and so forth as the purposive activities that I think they are.

We need, therefore, some rigorously defined concept of purpose or we need some more fundamental definition of behavior from which, if we choose, we can derive the concept of purposive activity. The latter approach seems to me to be the more feasible one.

The, to my mind, most incisive definition of behavior that has been offered to date is that of E. B. Holt. Let me start with this definition: "Behavior is any process of release which is a constant function of factors external to the mechanism released."[3] Two components of the definition ("process of release" and "constant function of") require some explanation.

Action involves energy that may be imparted to the acting body from an external source or that may have been stored up in the acting body and is released in the course of the action. Behavior, according to Holt, belongs to the class of actions in which the energy is released energy. The stimulus does not impart the energy of the action; it merely touches off the process, in the same sense that the flame of a match sets off a charge of gunpowder, and the explosion is also a process of release. Simple reflex actions are set off by appropriate stimuli, but the actions depend on the availability of energy that has been stored away. There are, thus, many varieties of action, not merely behavior, that involve a process of release; but every action that is acknowledged as behavioral involves such a process.

The just cited examples of nonbehavioral processes of release, once they are set off, proceed solely according to the internal conditions of the released mechanism, for instance, the state of the nerves and muscles in the reflex arc. There are, however, actions (whether their energy is transmitted or released) in which the course of the action is a constant function of something external to the acting body. Thus, the action of a physical body in free fall is adequately described as a function of the two masses involved (that of the falling body and that of the earth which is external to it) and the distance between them, and this function is constant. Similarly, a river always flows to the next lower accessible level of the earth's surface, an invariant relation between the flow

[3] E. B. Holt, "Response and Cognition," *The Freudian Wish and Its Place in Ethics* (New York: Holt, 1915), pp. 153–208, p. 167. The word "constant" is not actually included in the definition cited, but it was clearly Holt's intention to do so. The related discussion implies it and it is explicitly introduced and explained in the chapter on "The Physiology of Wishes," pp. 47–99.

of the river and the center of the earth. Holt asserts that every behavior involves such a constant function. Again, as in the instance of process of release, there are many nonbehavioral actions that manifest the constant function, but every instance of action acknowledged as behavioral has this property.

Holt's definition thus asserts that every action to be classified as behavior has both properties: It is a process of release and the course of the action may be described as a constant function of something external to the actor. Moreover, it asserts that any action that lacks one or both of these properties is not to be classified as behavior.

In passing, it may be noted that Holt explicitly denies that it is necessary to specify that a behavior is an action of a living organism, on the ground that behavior, as defined, only occurs in living beings and, at that, first appears in the evolutionary scale somewhat later than life itself. To this, I would add that the issue of adding what now appears to be a redundant specification need not be confronted unless and until a situation arises in which it is no longer redundant. Holt offered his definition in a precybernetic era and I know of no adequate reason for denying *a priori* the possibility of constructing machines capable of actions that meet the specifications of his definition or of the one that I will shortly be urging as a substitute. The addition of the living-organism specification to the definition would have the consequence of precluding any actions of such machines (subject, of course, to the semantic ambiguity of "living organism") from the realm of behavior, but I am not sure, at this stage of the game and without the opportunity to examine such actions, whether this consequence would be a virtue or a fault. I have encountered robots in the science-fiction literature whose exclusion from the human fraternity seemed to me to be arbitrary, capricious, and unprincipled. Similarly, though I am in this essay particularly concerned with Man. I would strenuously object to the arbitrary specification that only actions of human beings be considered as behaviors. Though there undoubtedly are human behaviors (for example, writing essays on the image of Man) that have no parallels among lower organisms, many human actions whose behavioral character no one has ever questioned (for example, working for money that can be used to purchase food, simple reasoning, and many others) can clearly be duplicated among subhuman forms.

One might argue that the addition of either of Holt's criteria to the other one represents an equally arbitrary restriction on the meaning of behavior. Holt's defense, and mine, is that "behavior as thus defined is in fact a striking novelty . . . in the evolutionary series. . . ."[4] In other words, with the emergence of behavior as defined, we have the emergence of a new order of natural law.

Holt proceeded from his definition to what may be described as a consolidation of the field of psychology. He tried to show that one can subsume or explain under it such notions as cognition, the content of consciousness, volition, attention, degrees of consciousness, the attribute of clearness, the distinction between consciousness and subconsciousness, *Aufgabe*, *Bewusstseinslage*, feeling, and personality. Though I would disagree with him in details, his achievement is most impressive and is a potent argument for the adequacy of his definition. Even so, and despite the fact that it will become apparent that I think he was basically on the right track, and that but for his analysis I could never have come to my alternative, I must dissent with respect to the terms that he chose to include in his definition.

To start with, I am bòthered by his "process of release." I am quite confident that every behavioral act does in fact involve a process of release—and this even with respect to behaviors like unvocalized covert reasoning that have, to the best of my knowledge, thus far evaded the direct proof of such a process. It is not, therefore, the issue of fact that bothers me. The trouble is that the term directs our attention to the history of the energies involved in behavior and it seems to me that in most instances behavioral scientists have no interest whatever in these energies as such. As far as I can tell, not even Holt himself had any interest in these energies as such. The term, therefore, misdirects our attention to an incidental correlate of behavior; it does not point to an essence. It seems to me that the property of behavior that Holt was trying to take hold of in the context of this term is something that may be identified as "spontaneity." Bear in mind that spontaneity implies action on the basis of inner energy and that the term may be applied to the actions of inanimate as well as animate objects. It is, therefore, consistent, in these respects, with Holt's "process of release." It is not, however, as sharply focused on the energic aspect of action as in Holt's term. I shall return in due course to a consideration of this property of behavior.

Much more fundamental in my dissent to the terms of Holt's definition are two objections to the idea of "constant function": (1) There is much greater certainty as to the behavioral character of certain actions than there is as to the fact of a constant-function relationship or

[4] *Ibid.*

even than there is as to the meaning of what is being asserted when one says that the course of action involves a constant function of something external. In other words, even if this property of behavior is validly identified, it cannot be as fundamental as some other property on the basis of which behavior is classified as such. (2) Taking the idea of the constant-function relationship as a criterion of behavior results in the exclusion of very brief actions as behavioral. It again seems to me that Holt was groping for a property (one that I will refer to as "directedness") that is related to, but not identical with, the one he seized on. I will shortly discuss this property in some detail, but let me first elaborate my two objections.

Consider the following behavior. A man (our subject) is sitting on the beach when there appears at the edge of his field of vision a scantily clad curvaceous female. His head turns so that she is directly in his line of sight. She proceeds to promenade along the beach, and we observe a complex series of movements on the part of our sitting subject. Part of the time, his eyes are moving; part of the time his head is turning; part of the time his torso is turning; part of the time several of these parts of our subject's body are in simultaneous motion. In the course of this series of movements there is a succession of intervals during which the eyes are motionless. During most of these pauses, the promenading lady is directly in our subject's line of sight; during some, however, the direct line of sight passes in front of the lady and during others it passes behind her. There are also some pauses, following eye-head-torso movements that carry the line of sight quite far from the lady, sometimes in the direction of the spot at which she first appeared, sometimes in the direction of her promenade. Moreover, with regard to the fixation points that are proximate to the lady, the vertical heights vary considerably, in no regular order, from the level of her bouffant coiffure, to the level of her nose, her bosom, her hips, her calves, her painted toenails.

I am sure that no one would seriously question that the activity I have just described is behavior. But, by Holt's criteria, how many behaviors? Let me try to construe the activity as comprising no more than two: the behavior of inspecting the lady (including the near misses as components of this behavior) and the behavior of looking for a possible escort, and, for the sake of discussion, let me ignore the second of these and the problem that it generates with respect to satisfying the constant function criterion with regard to the first. That is, let me limit myself to the presumed behavior of inspecting the lady. We may now reasonably say that during the time that this behavior was taking place (that is, ignoring the temporal discontinuities generated in this behavior by the intrusion of the second) our subject was constantly inspecting the lady. This "constantly," however, is not the constant function of Holt's criterion; if we ignore, as we are doing, the time when he was not looking toward the lady, it reduces to the identity "during all of the time that he was looking toward her." Holt's criterion literally demands a constant that cannot be translated as "all of the time." We might have the required constant function if the amount of time spent looking at each portion of her body were constant, if the number of items noted per second were constant, if the intensity of inspection were constant, if the rate of change in any of these functions were constant, if the rate of change in the rate of change were constant, if any of these functions varied as a constant function of the time elapsed from the onset of the behavior, and so on. Note how uncertain I am as to where to even start looking for the constancy of function that Holt's definition requires, and this, despite the fact that no one in his senses would doubt that the activity I described included the behavior of inspecting the lady. Moreover, I would be quite surprised if (on the assumption that the data were available) any of the directions I have thought of looking would actually yield the required constancy.

Consider now one of the brief pauses in the activity I have just described. The man's eyes linger for a brief moment on the lady's bosom or hip or whatever portion of her anatomy you choose. I think that most of us would—on the assumption that the man was seeing what was in the line of his regard—perceive even this brief pause as a behavior. But can we begin to dream of being able to establish the required constant function for so brief an action? I think not.

I must conclude that, for all of his noble effort, Holt has missed his objective in seizing on the idea of constancy of function as an earmark of behavior. Yet it seems to me that he was really trying to get at a much simpler notion and got into trouble in his effort to formalize it. Consider the following quotation from his essay: "*What* is this organism *doing*? . . . [The] man is walking past my window; no, I am wrong, it is not past my window that he is walking; it is *to* the theater; or am I wrong again? Perhaps the man is a journalist, and not the theater, nor yet the play, but the 'society write up' it is to which the creature's movements are adjusted; further investigation is needed."[5] In this, as in others of his examples, it would be difficult, I think, to identify the

[5] *Ibid.*, pp. 161–162.

constant-function relationship; but in this, as in every one of his examples, the action does relate the subject to something else—and the
relationship has the property of directedness, a property that should not
be confused with intentionality. Let me try a formal characterization of
this property.

But first I must explain what I mean by the term "object." I use this
term to designate any thing, event, process, situation, symbol, or what-
have-you that is referred to in a sentence by the syntactical object—
direct and/or indirect—of a transitive verb. I also use it to designate the
referent of the syntactical object of the preposition in certain adverbial
prepositional phrases.

In ordinary grammatical usage, we say that an intransitive verb does
not take an object to complete its meaning. However, limitations or
specifications of the meaning of an intransitive verb may be given by a
qualifying adverb. I am here concerned with a form of adverb, the
adverbial prepositional phrase, for example, "He walked *to the store.*"
The italicized phrase modifies the verb "walked." Still in ordinary
grammatical usage, the noun (or noun equivalent) that follows the
preposition in a prepositional phrase is said to be the object of the
preposition. As in the case for any adverb, the qualification introduced
by an adverbial prepositional phrase may specify the place of the action
("He stood in the hallway"), the time of the action ("He trembled
before knocking"), the manner of the action ("He spoke with some
trepidation"), or the degree of activation ("He advanced at an ever
slowing pace").

As far as I know, grammarians have not noted an interesting property of some adverbial prepositional phrases, namely, that they identify
the addressee of the action (the person, thing, event, process, idea,
eventuality, and the like with respect to which the action takes place);
they particularize the action as such rather than in terms of its time,
place, style, or degree; they say where the action is going rather than
where, when, how, or how much it is. In this respect, they serve exactly
the same specificatory function that the indirect object does with
respect to a transitive verb; and, in this respect, the object of the
preposition in the adverbial prepositional phrase differs from the indirect
object only as a consequence of the conventional syntactics of our
language rather than because of the different properties of what is being
talked about.

Suppose, for instance, that we had a different verb for "throw"
depending on the object thrown. Where we now say, "He threw the

ball to the pitcher," we would then say, 'He threwtheball to the pitcher."
In terms of our present syntax, "pitcher" is the indirect object of
"threw"; with the new verb, "pitcher" would be the object of the
preposition "to" in an adverbial prepositional phrase. An analogous
specialization of a verb form changes "tried to catch fish" (where "to
catch fish" is the object of the verb "tried") to "fished," an intransitive
verb. Or suppose that we had verb forms that assimilated the preposition. In this case, "walkedto" would demand an object to specify the
meaning of the verb. An analogous switch in verbs is "He addressed the
class" for "He spoke to the class."

In other words, if we concern ourselves with the semantics of a
statement rather than simply its conventional syntax, the object of the
preposition in an adverbial prepositional phrase that specifies the
course of an action may be taken as the object of a verb. At any rate,
I shall do so.

Thus, I take the word "object" to refer to the direct object of a
transitive verb, the combination of direct and indirect object, and/or
the object of the preposition in an adverbial prepositional phrase that
specifies the course of the action described by the verb.

I now point out that the particular action described by a transitive
verb cannot be specified without reference to a direct object and, often,
the specification of the action calls for reference to an indirect object
as well. The meaning of "He gave," for instance, is not clear until we
know what he gave and to whom. Similarly, as just indicated, the action
described by some intransitive verbs cannot be specified without reference to the object of the preposition in an adverbial prepositional
phrase.

With the indicated usages in mind, I define a *directed action* as an
action the course of which is, in fact, particularized with respect to an
object, regardless of the syntactical form that is used to describe it.
A directed action has not been specified if the object has not been
specified. Insofar as the course of the action under consideration can be
specified without implicit or explicit reference to an object, it is not
directed.

I do not mean *directed action* to imply any more than this. I do not
mean to imply that all of the properties or characteristics of an action,
or any of its necessary and/or sufficient conditions, have necessarily
been specified by the choice of the verb and the specification of the
object; I mean merely that the particular action has not been specified
unless the object has been specified or clearly implied. I particularly do

not mean to imply that a directed action is necessarily intentional. I have no reservation, for instance, in saying that, "The body enzymes digest the food in the alimentary tract" is a description of a directed action, even though I do not believe that the body enzymes are capable of intentional action. Similarly, the statement "A randomly moving particle struck another randomly moving particle." describes what purports to be a directed act in my meaning of the term. The statement "The book fell" also describes a directed action because, in this instance, there is an implied object ("the earth" or "the center of the earth") in an implied adverbial prepositional phrase that specifies the course of the action ("toward the earth").

The quality of action that I am defining, directedness, should not be confused with directionality except in the sense that there is an implied direction of directed action, namely, from subject to object. It is possible to describe many directional actions that are not directed, for instance, "The balloon drifted to the north." On the other hand it is possible to describe many directed actions without reference to their directionality, except in the limited implied sense of direction just explained. "The swallows flew back to Capistrano" describes a directed action, but since we have not indicated where they came from, we have not said anything about the direction of the action in the usual sense of direction.

My assertion that "The balloon drifted to the north" describes a directional, but not a directed, action may seem rather high-handed in the light of the preceding definitions. The assertion is, however, predicated on a principle that has been relatively tacit in these definitions and that I must now make fully explicit.

Grammar is indifferent to truth. The statement "The man is walking past my window," to refer back to Holt's example, is as sound grammatically as the statement "The man is walking to the theater" or the statement "The man is fulfilling his mission." Yet one or more of these statements may be factually incorrect in the sense that the window or the theater may have nothing to do with the action, and/or the man may have no mission to fulfill. My definition of directedness specified that the course of the action is in fact particularized with respect to an object. I meant, by this specification, to indicate that the object must in fact have something to do with the action.

Holt has suggested an in-principle simple test, and it is to be noted that this is a test of what I am calling directedness rather than of his required constant function, namely, to remove the presumptive object and to see if there is any consequence with respect to the course of the action.[6] For instance, to take an example from daily life, I see a man enter Grand Central Station. He is breathing hard, as though he has been running. He looks quickly about, transferring a seemingly heavy valise from one hand to the other as he does so. He fixates a distant gate that offers admission to a train scheduled for immediate departure. He begins to run in the direction of the gate. I say to myself, "The man is trying to catch that train." Fortunately, a natural test of my hypothesis occurs. The gate clangs shut, the guard locks it and walks away. My man stops running, puts his valise down, and swears under his breath. I take it that my hypothesis has been confirmed, even though, in this instance, I cannot say with what statistical level of confidence.

Another kind of test, familiar to psychologists, is to introduce a barrier between the actor and the presumed object. One pattern of action in such a test situation that supports the presumption is a detour around the barrier and a return to the object. I enter a plane marked "Flight X-13. Washington to Boston. Nonstop." Early in the flight, I notice some landmarks familiar to me from previous flights from Washington to New York City. I say to myself, "Hm. We are flying toward New York." Then I remember that I am a psychologist, not a geographer, and revert to basic principles. "No," I say to myself. "It is only incidental that New York is on our flight path. The fact that it is there has nothing to do with the course of our flight." My hypothesis would be confirmed simply by my waiting and noting that we never do land at one of the New York airports. Nature, however, intervenes and provides an additional test datum. The unusually communicative pilot informs us that there is a storm between us and New York City and that the flight will be somewhat prolonged because we will detour the storm area. It develops that the detour brings us to a point from which there is no reasonable direct flight route to Boston that passes over New York, our plane never turns toward New York, and we continue on a direct route to Boston. My hypothesis that the initial presence of New York City along our flight route had nothing to do with the latter was thus doubly confirmed. In the sense that I am using these terms,

[6] The test has serious practical and perhaps principled limitations in actual application. Thus, any marked change in a situation is apt to have consequences even though the feature that was changed had little or no bearing on the action prior to the change. For example, if a new opening is introduced in a maze wall in a segment that a practiced rat always runs past without pause, the rat will (may my stimulus-response psychologist friends please forgive me!) normally stop to investigate the new opening. My immediate concerns are not, however, with the issues of evidence but with the matters about which we would want to seek evidence.

our flight was initially in the direction of New York, but it was never directed toward that city.

It so happens that the two tests I have just described (and the third that I noted in passing, namely, that we did not land at any New York airport) are, in the main, relevant only to what have been called goal objects. There are other kinds of tests, however, relevant to other kinds of objects. I am riding in a car. The driver has been proceeding at about sixty miles per hour. Though there is no visible obstacle, my driver steps on the brake. A moment or so earlier we had passed, at the side of the road, a sign on which was printed, "Slow. Sharp Curves Ahead." In the absence of any alternative hypotheses to explain the driver's stepping on the brake just when he did and, in view of the appropriateness of this action to the message on the sign, I conclude that my driver has not only seen the sign, but has also read what was printed on it and has comprehended the message. In this conclusion, I have described three directed actions: The driver has seen the sign, he has read the printing, and he has comprehended the message. Seeing, reading, and comprehending are each actions, properly described by verbs. I would not have been describing the particular actions, however, without specifying what it was he saw, what it was he read, and what it was he comprehended: These verbs require objects. That the objects I have identified as such were the true objects seems to follow from the nature and timing of the action that is otherwise unexplained.

When the driver and I had gotten into the car, we had planned to leave that particular road at Exit 15. As we proceed, I notice a sign on which is printed, "EXIT 15—¼ mile ahead." Shortly, we are passing a sign on which is printed, "EXIT 15 and a turnoff from the road." Since I have no reason to expect a change in plan, I conclude that my driver has not seen, read, or comprehended the first of the two signs, that is, at least one of these three directed activities has failed to occur.

To be sure, my conclusion may have been wrong in either or both of the last two examples. Coincidences do occur, and my driver may have changed the plan without consulting me. If it matters very much, we can, of course, bring to bear additional information—knowledge of how other people act in such situations, the testimony of the subject, knowledge of his habits, additional reactions of the subject as the situations develop (for instance, my driver's incredulity when I said to him, "I suppose you know that we just passed Exit 15"), and so on. My present concern, however, is not with the nature and quality of the evidence that can be brought to bear on such matters, but with the nature of the concepts I am advancing. I have cited some examples of relevant lines of evidence merely to sharpen the nature of the concepts. The important point I am trying to make is that the statement "John gives Mary a cookie" describes a different behavior if it means that John gives a cookie to a nearby child who, incidentally, happens to be Mary than if it means that the fact the child is Mary is relevant to the action.

The specification of the true object is as essential to the veridical description of directed activity as is the specification of the correct verb. "He walked" does not specify a directed activity. Neither does "He walked aimlessly." In a sense, the latter sentence implies a confession of ignorance as to the directedness of the activity that was taking place—perhaps the working off of some agitation, perhaps the enjoyment of the scenery with a more or less unsystematic shift in position to change the point of view—or a denial of directedness. The choice of the verb "drifted" in "The balloon drifted to the north" clearly implies that there was no addressee. "The randomly moving particle sped toward another" describes undirected activity despite the phrase "toward another," because the qualifier "randomly" denies any real destination; but the continuation "and struck it" describes a directed activity because striking requires that something be struck.

Our language is often ambiguous with respect to the directedness of activity. Consider "The boy sat on the bench in the rotunda." The final phrase could be taken as modifying "sat," in which case it simply indicates the locus of the action. It could also be taken as modifying "bench" in which case it could be taken to designate an incidental property of the bench (its location) that is essentially irrelevant to the action; but it could also be taken as an essential property of the particular bench that is the object of the action. The phrase "on the bench" is itself also ambiguous: The relevant feature of the bench may not be its benchiness, but its sit-on-able-ness, so that any sit-on-able object would have been equally appropriate to the action being described. "On the bench" may also be construed as referring to the site of the action that continues after the boy sat down on it. The act of sitting down is unequivocally directed, though we still do not know whether the benchiness or merely the sit-on-able-ness are the relevant attributes of the object. The continuing action of sitting may, however, on the just mentioned construction, not be a directed action at all, but in this event it is likely that "sat" is not the *mot juste* to describe what the boy was doing. Most probably, the boy was resting his tired feet and/or waiting for someone or for something to happen. The very ambiguity of the language is, however, a reminder that there are factual issues in the veridical description of directed activity.

For many purposes, it may be unimportant to zero in with great precision on the true object and the most appropriate verb; but for others it may be most important. A person votes for a particular political candidate and, from the point of view of the impact of this action on the distribution of political power, it makes no difference what the precise object of the action was; we do not know or care to know the relevant combination of attributes, past history, political principles, promises, and associations of the voted candidate, or whether the voter was voting for the candidate or against the alternatives or merely fulfilling a commitment to (or following the advice of) some noncandidate, or whether the action was single- or multitargeted, conflicted (resultant of opposing actions) or unconflicted. From other points of view, albeit the question of what an unknown boy sitting on an undescribed bench in an unidentified rotunda on an unspecified occasion was actually doing may well be trivial, the question of the precise identification of subject-object transactions and their conditions is the paramount question of all. Surely the student of political behavior, whether political scientist or social psychologist, must be concerned with the different actions involved in the instance of two voters for the same candidate when one voter knows nothing about the candidate, not even his name, except for his political affiliation and the other is fully informed about the political history, ideology, and so forth of the candidate; the two voting actions, ostensibly the same, moving the identical lever, are, in fact, quite different actions because, despite the identical movements, they are directed at quite different objects.

Let me return now to my alternative, spontaneity, to Holt's first characteristic of behavior, the process of release. I have already indicated that, though I agree that all behavior does involve a process of release, I do not consider this a strategic focus for the definition of behavior. The notion of spontaneity does contain within itself, but does not focus on, the essential idea in "process of release." It also contains within itself the more salient idea of action that is to some degree innerly determined, action without sufficient external causes, stimuli, conditions, or influences. In other words, one normally ascribes spontaneity to those events for which one does not apprehend any sufficient external cause.

I am also unwilling, however, to accept this implication as a basis for a formal definition of spontaneity. There are conceptual difficulties in the concepts of inner and outer. Internal and external with respect to what? The body or organism? I shall be arguing that many "inner" determinants of behavior can not be localized in this way. The personality? This is a concept that presupposes a concept of behavior and can hardly be expected to serve as a basis for defining one of the major attributes of behavior. Moreover, to make the distinction on this basis is to arbitrarily reserve the term "spontaneity" to a psychological usage. Where is the personality of a pile of oily rags and newspapers that bursts into spontaneous combustion? Holt's point in requiring the specification of at least two attributes of behavior—and it is a point I agree with—is that there is no single attribute that will serve as a good criterion to distinguish behavior from nonbehavior. Finally, it should be noted that the concept of action without sufficient external cause, if taken literally, incorrectly presupposes the causal efficacy of external agents without regard to the properties of that which is being acted on. From this point of view, there is never any action with sufficient external cause.

Consider the instance of a pile of oily rags and paper that spontaneously bursts into flame. What has actually happened is that the contents of the pile have been oxidizing, a process that involves interaction between the pile and its contents, on the one hand, and their environs, on the other. If the environs are oxygen-free, the process cannot occur. The process of oxidation generates heat and if there are not available sufficient means to conduct the heat away—note, again, an inner-outer relationship—the amount of heat in the pile increases until the ignition temperature of some component of the pile is reached. Note, now, that the bursting into flame is itself a process that is not unrelated to the process that generated it; it is a continuation of the oxidation process under new conditions.

The entire process of spontaneous combustion is thus viewed as a single event (the oxidation of the pile of rags and papers) with two or three phases, an accumulation of heat, a bursting into flame, and a burning. The bursting into flame is a component of a more inclusive process; it is, I suggest, this containment that constitutes the real innerness of the spontaneous event. The spontaneous event is contained in a more comprehensive event. If we had touched a lit match to the pile of rags and paper, we would not have viewed the bursting into flame as spontaneous, precisely because we perceive two events, the second caused by the first; and, if the house burns down as a consequence of the spontaneous combustion, we do not view this later event as spontaneous, precisely because it is a later event, a consequence of the first, and not a component of one all-encompassing process.

By the same token, the innerness of the determination of the spontaneous event is not an innerness that is properly juxtaposed to the outerness of the acting body or of the immediate arena of action. Hence, we can retain the implication in the term "spontaneity" of some degree of inner determination and, at the same time, reject the implication that this means action without sufficient external cause. As I have already noted, there never are sufficient external causes of anything, so that, by this criterion, all events must be described as spontaneous. The differentiating criterion of spontaneity must therefore be something other than the insufficiency of external cause.

One may, of course, propose that there are indeed some spontaneous events and that such events occur without sufficient determination (as some physicists conceive of Brownian movements or quantum leaps). I have, however, committed myself to the presumption of determinism, that is, to the presumption that whatever *is*, but is itself not an ultimate law, must have a sufficiency of determination. Since I cannot conceive of any particular event as an ultimate law, I must reject the possibility of any spontaneous events on the proposed alternative characterization of "spontaneity."

I must, therefore, seek the differentiae of spontaneity elsewhere than in an alleged insufficiency of cause, whether of external cause or of cause in general. To characterize "spontaneity," I take my description of what goes on in spontaneous combustion as paradigmatic. I correspondingly define a spontaneous act as any component (phase) of a more comprehensive act of a given acting system, which component is generated, in part, by the comprehensive act; it is a continuation of the latter act under special conditions. The spontaneous act includes the more comprehensive act among its generating conditions and the latter is facilitated by—and often depends for its continuance on—the former.

Substituting "spontaneous" action for Holt's "process of release" and "directed action" for Holt's "which is a constant function of something external to the mechanism released," I offer the following as my definition of behavior: Behavior is any spontaneous directed action. There are many actions that are spontaneous, but not directed, for instance, the contractions and relaxations of muscles in the process of walking. There are many actions that are directed, but not spontaneous, for instance, the digestion of food in the alimentary tract. The latter is not a phase of a more comprehensive action that contributes to its generation; it could be thought of as a phase of living, but living as such does not contribute to its generation. There are many bodily actions that are neither spontaneous nor directed, for instance, reflex actions.[7] I cannot, however, think of any action that I would want to classify as behavior that does not possess both attributes or of any action that I would not want to so classify that does.

I have already remarked that a virtue and strength of Holt's definition is the consolidation he is able to effect with it of the field of psychology. Apart from the fact that there is no problem in the application of my definition, as there is of his, to the inclusion of very brief psychological events, can I do as well with my definition as he has done? Actually, nothing that I can see would make the substitution of my definition for his inconsistent with the entire subsequent explication of psychological concepts that he advances in his essay on "Response and Cognition." In this connection, then, I have changed nothing. I do, however, have the advantages of being able to start from where his labors ended, of having had many years of being able to test his ideas in the crucible of my own thought and experience, and of the many psychologists who have devoted themselves to similar problems since 1915. There are consequently differences in my subsequent explication of a variety of psychological concepts and some explication of concepts that he has not considered; but I will leave it to the interested reader to make specific comparisons.

I have already dealt at some length with a variety of motivational concepts in Chapter 2. I shall not repeat this discussion here. I do, however, want to clarify something I said there, to introduce a formal definition of "motive," and to make a few additional distinctions that are of systematic significance.

In Chapter 2, I said that a behavior is a motive of the behaviors it includes. I also said that the directed activity of voiding the distress associated with drives motivates the transactions with the environment that eliminate the drive. Furthermore, I implied that such distress-voiding activity is not a continuation of a more comprehensive activity; it is, therefore, not spontaneous in the framework of my definition and hence not behavior. There was, thus, a gap in my earlier presentation—motives that are not behaviors. Let me, then, offer a definition of motive that covers this case.

[7] Note, however, that reflex actions would satisfy Holt's criterion of process of release.

78

A motive is any directed act that requires a subordinate expediting act to be included in it. A motive exists whenever (1) the impelling conditions of a directed act exist and (2) the latter would be interrupted or impeded but for the occurrence of some subordinate, expediting act, for example, eliminating or detouring or vitiating the constraint. A behavior that requires the inclusion of a subordinate expediting act is *a fortiori*, a motive since, as behavior, it is itself a directed act. A number of aspects of this definition need to be spelled out:

1. Neither motive nor motivated act is necessarily a behavior. The motivated act is, however, if it occurs, spontaneous by definition. If, in addition, it is a directed act, then it is a behavior. My remarks, in Chapter 2, concerning motives as behavior still hold, therefore, but may (with the exception of my reinterpretation of "wish" and "desire") be extended to the general case of directed activity. Wishes and desires are always behaviors.

2. The motivated act that actually occurs is not necessarily the only one that could expedite the motive. In other words, the motive is not necessarily a sufficient condition of the act that it motivates. Among a variety of alternative possibilities, the one that actually occurs is selected on such bases as feasibility, simultaneous service and disservice to other motives, familiarity, and so on.

3. The impelling conditions of the motivating act may themselves be motives (that is, the motivating act may itself be motivated), involve some kind of inertial principle, and/or be intolerable states of being that are generally related to deficits of various kinds: deficits of food, drink, sleep, sexual outlets, and so on; deficits with respect to the recurrence of certain pleasurable activities; deficits of assurance of competence to cope with immediately confronting situations and/or with expected recurrences of the kinds of deficits already mentioned.[8] With respect to

---

[8] I have not included pain in the list of intolerable conditions. This is because I do not believe that pain, no matter how severe, is, as such, intolerable. The intolerable character of pain comes from the associated anxiety which I have subsumed, above, under the deficit of assurance of competence to cope. I came to this conclusion during the early 1930's, as a result of contemplating an anecdote told by one of my psychology professors, seemingly veridical accounts of stoical childbearing in novels by Hamsun, Rolvaag, and Buck, an anecdote concerning an early Stoic philosopher, the use of hypnosis as an anaesthetic (including some of my own unpublished investigations of hypnotic phenomena), an account that I read of differences in the "painlessness" of childbirth under scopalamine and ether, and my own experiences with dental work without anaesthesia. My professor's anecdote bears repeating. He had to have a tooth extracted and felt that this provided a good opportunity to introspect on pain (his was one of the earliest doctorates in American psychology). He accordingly had the ex-

some of these deficits, it is possible to specify with much greater precision than I have just what the intolerable state of being is. For instance, we know enough about thirst to be able to create conditions in which animals will die of dehydration with no evidences whatever of discomfort; hence, it is obvious that it is not the absence of fluids, as such, that accounts for thirst. There are, to my mind, some unresolved issues left in connection with the specifications of the distressing deficit states, even in connection with hunger and thirst. It is not, however, in accord with my present purposes to review the relevant literature. I shall return to the issue of what it is about these states that is distressing in Chapter 13.

4. It bears repetition that I do not regard the deficit state as a motive. It is an entirely different order of phenomenon than what is subsumed under "motive." It (or, more precisely, its elimination or replacement) is an object of activity in the same sense that an incentive is an object of activity; one may think of it as a negatively valued object, as one thinks of an incentive as a positively valued object, but an object is not a motive. Nor is the distress associated with the deficit state a motive. It is an occasion for, albeit an often compelling occasion for, activity. It has no "in order to" quality. The elimination of the distress associated with the deficit state is a motive. We do do things in order to eliminate the distress. A motive is always a superordinate event with respect to the activity that it motivates, and I have respected this usage in my definition. Though the elimination of distress associated with deficit states may itself be a motive, it is unmotivated because it is not a subordinate phase of some superordinate event. One might argue that the "in order to" quality of the elimination of distress is the achievement of

---

traction carried out without benefit of anaesthesia. His experience was that he introspected so hard that he felt no pain: Something very interesting was happening to the tooth—out there—rather than to himself. I could make sense of the story (and, knowing the man, I had no doubt of the truthfulness of the account) only on the hypothesis that his task absorption was such that he could not experience the customary anxiety. I must confess that, by contemporary standards of scientific evidence, my sweeping conclusion was not very "scientific"—not a significance test in the lot!—consisting of "data" from fiction, anecdotes, hypnosis, and a mess of personal experiences! I comfort myself with the thought that I nevertheless seem to have been right and continue to hold the conclusion with undiminished fervor. I reflect with some amusement at how some of my nulliparous female students would castigate me as a male chauvinist in the comfortable position of never having to bear children when I argued that the intractable pain of childbirth is really anxiety. I have since been partially vindicated (only partially because the techniques involved include exercises that may have the effect of reducing pain and because the lessening of anxiety may eliminate maladaptive responses that increase pain) by the sweep of so-called natural childbirth, a major feature of which is the reduction of anxiety.

quiescence, but this is equivalent to saying that one is impelled to eliminate distress in order to eliminate distress. I have no profound objection
to such statements (not even if one were to add a third "in order to
eliminate distress"), but I do not think we should confuse them with
statements of a different order such as that "John brought Mary a five
pound box of candy in the course of a campaign to make her more
compliant with his wishes," a statement that may be more familiarly
rendered, "John brought Mary the candy in order to (or, because he
wanted to) soften her up." In any of these renditions, John's motive is
the, as yet unfinished, activity of changing Mary's attitude.

From the definitions of behavior and of motivation, it follows that
every behavior is motivated. We are also in a position to define the
concept "purpose." The purpose of a behavior is the completion of the
action of the superordinate behavior in which it is included; this is
the "in order to" aspect of the behavior.[9] The difference between motive
and purpose is one of focus. Motive emphasizes the dynamic effect of
the superordinate on the subordinate act. Purpose emphasizes the service
or function of the subordinate with respect to the superordinate act.
Another term in the same semantic family, "intention," is frequently used
as a synonym of purpose, but is generally likely to have either or both
of the following connotations: Intention antecedes the execution of the
action (in my conceptualization, this would be put: It occurs in the
earliest stages of, in the period of mobilization for, the action; it bears
the same relation to wish or desire that purpose bears to motive), and/or
it refers to the actor's cognition (which may or may not be veridical)
of the purpose of the action. Thus, purposivists will describe the behavior of animals as purposive, but will rarely, if ever, talk of the intentions of animals.

There are, of course, a great many other terms in the same semantic
family (aim, conation, deliberation, design, determination, end, goal,
intent, objective, volition, will, and so on). It is not my purpose, however, to discriminate these terms one from another or to promote sensitive discriminating usage. My concern is with the explication of certain
basic psychological concepts. I have, of course, already expounded, in
Chapter 2, a number of, to me, major motivational concepts, namely,

[9] In ordinary English usage, the term "purpose" is more likely to have the
more limited connotation of a relatively fixed and strong purpose (in the sense
defined above). In psychological usage, however, the semantic spectrum of "purpose" is broader than that of common usage. No purposive psychologist, for
instance, would say that all behavior is purposive in the more limited sense of
the term.

the perpetuation, derivation, and imbrication of motives. To these, I shall return in a later chapter.

Let me turn to another variety of psychological concept. Holt and numerous later behaviorists have emphasized the immanence of cognition in behavior. To put the matter differently, the data that would lead us to identify an action as behavior would also lead us to conclude that the actor is aware of the object. If a teacher asks, "When did Columbus discover America?" and a pupil calls out "1492," then I think that everyone would agree that it is a reasonable presumption that the pupil heard a question containing one or more of the key words "Columbus," "discovered," "America." There may be some debate about whether psychologists should be concerned with such issues of fact (not what Columbus did, but whether and what the boy heard), but there is not likely to be very much debate about the presumed fact.

Yet, surely, there must be something of a *tour de force* in the bland assertion that cognition is immanent in purposive activity or the relation of specific response, and so on, and letting the matter go at that, as though one has thereby solved the problem of the nature of awareness.[10] Unless one is willing to assert that behavior is awareness and is able to justify this assertion, one is obligated to indicate what it is about behavior or what kinds of behavior that constitute awareness. It is one thing to say that the appropriateness of the action with respect to the object or the differential activities of subjects with regard to various objects under specific motivational states constitutes evidence of awareness. It is another thing to assert that such action is awareness. We may be able to train a rat so that when it has been deprived of food and is placed on a platform from which we can see two placards, one marked with a cross and the other with a circle, it will, over a series of ten such trials, always jump to the cross, even though the positions of the two placards are randomly interchanged and the relative sizes of the two figures are randomly varied from trial to trial. We may declare that the jumping pattern defines the awareness of a difference between cross and circle or that it defines an intervening variable or hypothetical construct arbitrarily labeled the awareness of a difference between cross and circle. We may similarly continue our experiment and stop putting food behind the placard with the cross. With no food behind either placard,

[10] I use the term "awareness" rather than "consciousness" because, in the next chapter, I will distinguish between "conscious" and "subconscious" awareness. I must also defer until then the issues of the subjective qualities of one's own awarenesses as distinguished from our referent when we speak of the awarenesses of others.

the time is apt to arrive when the rat will be jumping to the cross only half of the time. Since the rat has already demonstrated that he can distinguish between cross and circle, we can say that we have now operationally defined a two-valued variable, "expectation of food," and call this an intervening variable or hypothetical construct.

This is a free country and, as I have already remarked in Chapter 3, we can join the Fraternity of Humpty Dumpty if we want to. But, in my part of the country, at least, these definitions simply do not correspond to familiar linguistic usage. Such notions as awareness or expectation do not refer to our experiments and their referents quite clearly do not include the jumping activities of rats. The experiments and the rat's pattern of jumping may be taken as convincing evidence that the rat is aware of the placards and of some difference between cross and circle and that he does or does not expect to find food behind one of the placards. No arbitrary fiat, however, not even if issued by the most distinguished philosophers and scientists, can transform evidence into that which it evidences.

It seems to me that what is meant by such statements as that a rat is aware of or, more specifically, sees the cross is that you can ignore the overtly observable movements and, moreover, not concern yourself with the particulars of what is going on in the brain and neuromuscular system and still have something left over that is described as the act of seeing the cross. The referent of "sees the cross" is the something left over after the conceptual stripping I have just described of the observed action. Why should one engage in such stripping behavior? Because one assumes that the something left over can be evidenced in a variety of ways without altering its essential character and that it has distinctive consequences independently of the consequences of the overt portions of the acts in which it is imbedded.

Accordingly, I define awareness as minimal behavior, behavior conceptually stripped of all of its components save that which is barely sufficient to maintain some spontaneous directed action with respect to an object. By this definition, every behavior must include awareness since it must itself minimally, or more than minimally, satisfy the defining conditions of behavior. By this definition, too, awareness is not an intervening variable, even though we may not have identified the precise bounds of the minimum in the behavior that we observe, since it does not intervene, but is included in the observed behavior; nor is it a hypothetical construct since it must, by definition, be present in every behavior.

What about awarenesses that occur apart from behavior? I must assert that such awarenesses do not occur. Note that every awareness is inherently a directed act. I never, for instance, simply see. I see the point, or a beam or a film of light, or the color or shape of some thing, or I see a thing, an event, or what-have-you. If there is any issue, then, it concerns the spontaneity of the act of awareness. On this issue, I cannot prove that there are no unmotivated seeings, hearings, perceivings, imaginings, thinkings, and so on. I simply postulate that all awarenesses are motivated. The universal character of this postulate places it beyond empirical proof, and, as will soon become apparent, it is always possible to construe any awareness as motivated so the proposition is not susceptible to empirical disproof. The proposition is metatheoretical, as are all true postulates, and must justify itself in its consequences. It must help us to make sense of the universe, provide for a more parsimonious account and ordering of data than would otherwise be available, and so on.

The postulate is not inherently unreasonable and it has the virtue of eliminating what would otherwise be a great and apparently insoluble mystery. The area in which it is likely to occasion the most markedly lifted eyebrows is in connection with so-called sensory experiences. Yet, it seems to me that the reaction of incredulity is predicated on a postulate that is demonstrably false, namely, that the impingement of an appropriate stimulus (that is, a member of a class of energies, chemicals, and so on, within a specifiable range, that are known to be associated with a particular kind of sensory experience) on a healthy sense organ with undisturbed connections with an undamaged nervous system is a sufficient condition for an awareness of either the stimulus or its source. The very alternative in my statement of this postulate is sufficient to contradict it. A very young lady feels her swain's arm about her waist, not a pattern of pressures. Why one rather than the other? A Titchenerian might say that she is committing the stimulus error, but this is a concept that has meaning only within the context of a Titchenerian *Aufgabe*.[11] Titchener did not contend that people do not experience the objects from which the proximal stimuli emanate, but rather that, if one was engaged in the task of exploring the primal materials of consciousness one had to disregard the object and concentrate on the experience of the proximal stimulus. The very fact that subjects could learn to accept Titchener's assignment is proof that what one experiences is con-

[11] I shall return to the issue of the stimulus error in the next chapter.

tingent on the activity in which one is engaged—as neat a demonstration of the spontaneous character of at least these experiences as I could hope for.

There are great amounts of data from daily experience that point to the falsity of the pure sensory mechanism postulate. Under most circumstances, we are bombarded by stimuli, most of which we ignore. We seem to respond selectively in accordance with the nature of our concerns, that is, in accordance with our superordinate activities. There is a fair likelihood, for instance, that, until a moment ago, the reader was not aware of the pressure from the chair he is sitting on. If he is now aware of it, is it not in accordance with the transaction that is going on between us? Has anyone not had the experience of "looking through," that is, not seeing, an acquaintance or of not hearing something or other because of preoccupation with something else? One can also appeal to the general psychological literature on mental set to support the proposition that ongoing activities play a role in determining the selectivity of experience.

To be sure, the research literature on subliminal perception suggests that we become aware of much more than we think we do. There is nothing in this literature, however, to suggest that we are constantly and simultaneously aware of everything that impinges on our senses. In other words, this literature cannot be cited to provide an out for the postulate I am rejecting, not that there is much likelihood that anyone advancing this postulate would take this literature seriously.

In general, however, it is a property of the conceptualization of motivation that I am advancing that motivation is not something that exists within our bodies. Motivation involves transaction between subject and object, transaction that requires commerce with mediating and intervening objects. In other words, it is in the very nature of motivation, and particularly of complex motivational structures that one should be concerned with the world in which behavior is taking place. It seems to me to be an inevitable consequence that, given the physiological equipment with which to do so, we should be more or less continually scanning our environments, our bodies, and our selves for information relevant to the pursuit of our concerns. By my definitions, such scanning activity is motivated and every object encountered is the object of an—at least, brief directed activity—examination; the scanning activity, therefore, constitutes a series of brief behaviors, motivated directed activities. But for this basis of interest, the sounds that impinge on us would be falling on deaf ears and the light patterns on blind eyes. When an examined object is classified as irrelevant to our concerns, we become oblivious to it despite its continued impingement on our sensory equipment.

Because we are motivated—and, in this context, it makes no difference what our particular motivation happens to be—we are continually concerned with the meaning of what goes on in and about us. Semanticists, philosophers and an impressive array of psychologists notwithstanding, meaning is basically an objective fact. Children and others who take reality seriously know that they often have to find out what things (including words) mean. When someone (even an idealistic philosopher) looks up a word in a dictionary, he is tacitly agreeing that the word has a meaning independently of his knowledge of it.

The meaning of anything[12] is its place in the network of relationships[13] in which it is imbedded. In the course of our encounters with things we explore their meanings and often, in varying degrees, generate new facets of meaning as we establish special relationships to them or bring them into new relationships with one another. Meaning is as objective in its basic character as are stones, bridges, streets, flowers, parts of the body, stars, books—and this includes such facets of meaning as that a thing is a member of a class of things that are venerated by a certain class of people and despised by another—but the meaning of a thing is no more fixed than the network of relationships in which it is imbedded. Relationships change over time, and things that seem to be identical when torn from their contexts are often quite different from each other in meaning if restored to their contexts.

The subjective counterparts of objective meanings can be conceived of, figuratively, as maps of the networks of relationships in which the things are imbedded that we develop in the course of our encounters with them, maps that may include variable amounts of error and that are redrawn as our comprehension of the meaning of a thing changes. What actually happens is that the things we encounter stop being, so to speak, things-in-themselves and become things-for-us; that is, they become objects, the things we have encountered and remember encountering. The properties of an object, however, are not simply the properties of a thing receiving the action. The identity of the object is established

[12] I will use the word "thing" to designate any article, being, event, process, and so on when considered independently of any action performed with respect to it. I will reserve "object" for the object of an action.

[13] I include the attributes of things as relationships which, in fact, they always are. Weight, for instance, is not an isolated attribute but a relationship between two masses.

86

in terms of the actor's comprehension of its meaning; it is the thing-imbedded-in-a-construed-relational network. It is not necessary in each encounter to reconstruct the relational network or to consult a map of the place of the thing in a universe of other things; its place is absorbed in the identity of the object. Nor is every facet of the comprehended meaning of an object relevant in every encounter with it. One's friend, for instance, remains the same person even though, in one context, his salient attribute is his warmth, in another, it is his humor, and so on. A chair remains itself though in most contexts its relevant feature is its sit-on-able-ness and in others it is its stand-on-able-ness. Once we have discovered its stand-on-able-ness, this remains a feature of its object-character even though we may seldom have any use for this feature. But change the comprehension of the relational network itself (as distinguished from the facet of the relational network that is relevant to a given transaction), and the apparent identity of the thing changes; it becomes a different object than it was. "Joe Doaks, friend" becomes "Joe Doaks, enemy" and the "chair" becomes "kindling," "garbage," "museum exhibit," or "the thing that used to be my chair but is now...."

What I am saying is that the things that we see are normally seen not merely in terms of the presenting stimuli, but in terms of their object characters which have emerged in the course of our behavioral encounters with them, that the nature of our motivational systems requires that we establish such relationships with objects, and that the particular facets of the meaning of these objects that are salient in particular encounters are selected in terms of the specific nature of our engagement with these objects in the course of these encounters. Our normal perceptual experiences are clearly regulated by the nature of our transactions. There obviously are situations in which we disregard the object character of familiar objects, for instance, in trying to paint a scene or in serving as subjects in a Titchenerian type of experiment, and deal only with the immediate sensorially given data. I do not wish to dismiss these as the abnormal experiences, which they are, and pretend that nothing more need therefore be said about them. My point is rather that these abnormal (with no pejorative implications intended) experiences are behaviors governed by rather special superordinate behaviors.

Have I, without due acknowledgment, smuggled something into my exposition of the notion of object-identity and of the related notion of the comprehension of a relational network in which the object-thing is imbedded that is different in its nature from spontaneous directed action? If so, and to whatever extent it is so, I have failed to establish that my definition of behavior is as effective in consolidating the subject matter of psychology as I think it is. I certainly do not know of any previous effort in systematic psychological thought that has coped with the problem of the continued identity of objects despite change in their effects on sense organs and the contexts associated with particular presentations. The problem, a far more pervasive one than the included problems of the perceptual constancies of size, shape, color, and brightness, is as a rule ignored or regarded as a profound mystery.

I am not ready, however, to confess to failure. Let me approach the problem from the aspect of one of the motivational concepts advanced in Chapter 2, the notion of perpetuated motives. The idea is that there are recurrent behaviors that encounter conditions that need to be satisfied if the behaviors are to progress and that such recurrences of hindering conditions are distressing. As a consequence, we develop continuing concerns about being able to carry on these behaviors when they recur. That is, we become involved in the continuing enterprise of preparing for recurrences. Such continuing enterprises obviously fulfill the definitional conditions of spontaneity and directedness; they are, therefore, themselves behaviors and, as such, sources of motivation. I refer to these continuing enterprises as perpetuated motives. I mean perpetuated quite literally, even though, at any given time, they may not be very obvious in the course of the ongoing activity. Their continuance at such times can be evidenced in two ways: through a continued alertness to factors that have bearing on them (the sleeping mother who remains alert to the activities of her baby would be a dramatic example) and through constraining effects on manifestly ongoing activity so that the latter is not permitted to take forms and directions that endanger these enterprises and is, in fact, constrained to take forms and directions that facilitate them.

Thus, in our encounters with things, our actions with respect to them are not merely the actions (or apparent inactions) relevant to the manifestly ongoing activity, but also actions in the context of the perpetuated enterprises. The latter activities may involve facets of meaning of the things that are quite different from the facets of meaning relevant to the salient manifest activity. Moreover, to refer again to another of the notions referred to in Chapter 2, the perpetuated motives do not occur in isolation, but in complexly imbricated structures. Hence, once a thing has become an object for us and is encountered again and again in a variety of contexts, it acquires an identity that transcends its limited relevance to any immediate salient ongoing activity. In all encounters with it, we are concerned with its relevancies to all of our enduring enterprises and simultaneously act toward it in terms of all of them. We appreciate the identities of things because, in all our encounters with them—and often, in the absence of direct encounters, when the need for them arises to protect or advance our enterprises—we are concerned with their total identities for us, identities that must, perforce, within limits respect their objective identities and their objective meanings.

I think that, in this account of the subjective meaning of things and of the psychological identity and transformation of objects, I have not introduced or smuggled in any psychological processes that are not translatable into spontaneous directed activities. I think it will be obvious that much of what I have described must go on subconsciously, if at all. I shall analyze the concept of subconscious processes in the next chapter. Before turning to such issues, however, I do want to present another reason for my postulate that there are no awarenesses that are not behaviors.

The act of looking at something involves an orientation of the head with corresponding tensions in neck and/or trunk muscles, orientation of the eyes with appropriate tensions in the eye muscles, adjustment of the pupils and the shape of the eye, and, doubtless, numerous other bodily adjustments. These bodily adjustments are not generally included in the referent of "looking at the something." That is, one has conceptually stripped these bodily adjustments from the spontaneous directed activity of looking at the something. It has commonly been assumed that one can conceptually strip away or abstract all bodily adjustments and still leave an act of "looking at the something," a totally disembodied action like the residual grin of the Cheshire cat. This assumption is probably at the root of the traditional mystery of the mind-body relationship; but it is a gratuitous assumption, and one that should not be made lightly—precisely because of the conceptual difficulties in which it lands us.

The basis of the assumption is that it is obvious that many of the postural adjustments are not necessary for the act of "looking at." Thus, by an appropriate movement of my whole body, I obviate the need for special adjustments of trunk, head, and eyes; alternatively, I can turn to look at something without moving my body as a whole, by twisting my trunk, turning my head, moving my eyes. No particular body movement is necessary to effect the act of "looking at," and so it is easy to fall into the trap of concluding that body orientation is irrelevant to the essential act of "looking at"—a conclusion that is nonsensical since some bodily orientation (albeit it may be irrelevant which one or which combination) is necessary that will align the eyes with the object.

Now consider "seeing" as distinguished from "looking at" or "imagining." It seems even easier to abstract away the whole body from "seeing" than from "looking at," as though it were possible to "see" without "looking at." There is, of course, a considerable array of evidence, such as Jacobson's[14] investigations of what he described as the electrophysiology of mental activities, of the involvement of postural adjustments even in imagining, and the detectability of dream periods by evidence of quasiscanning rapid eye movements during sleep (or, much earlier, Max's[15] observation that he could tell when his deaf-mute subjects were dreaming from the muscular activities of their fingers).[16] There is also the, to me much more compelling, indirect evidence of the role of postural adjustments in seeing, in the line of investigation begun by G. M. Stratton[17] and involving the use of lenses inverting the visual field. The reader will probably have had related experiences in using a mirror to guide manipulative movements. For instance, in trying to seize a particular hair on one's face with a tweezer, the hair has an annoying way of not being where one sees it. With practice, however, one sees the hair where it is.[18] Thus, the nature of the neuromuscular adjustment changes one's seeing of the location of an object. In a much more massive way, the inverting lenses introduce radical discrepancies between where one sees objects and where one otherwise encounters them; but after a few days of continuous wearing of the lenses, the visual field is found to have become reinverted (and the removal of the lenses again inverts it). The reinversion can only be accounted for

[14] Edmund Jacobson, "The .Electrophysiology of Mental Activities," *American Journal of Psychology*, 44 (1932):677–694.

[15] Lewis Max, "An Experimental Study of the Motor Theory of Consciousness. III. Action-Current Responses in Deaf-Mutes During Sleep," *Journal of Comparative Psychology*, 19 (1935):469–486.

[16] Lest the reader who is unfamiliar with these studies suspect the evidence to be tautological—taking the muscular activity as evidence of dreaming—it should be pointed out that the relevant evidence involves waking the subjects at times when such muscular activities are or are not detectable and finding out whether a dream has been interrupted.

[17] G. M. Stratton, "Vision Without Inversion of the Retinal Image," *Psychological Review*, 4 (1897):341–360.

[18] One may describe what happens in terms of the hair being or not being where one reaches for it; the experience, however, at both the beginning and end of practice is that one reaches for it where one sees it. Hence the experience is as I have described it.

in terms of the neuromuscular adjustments. Even so, all of this evidence, in its entirety, is a long way from demonstrating the role of neuromuscular adjustments in all visual experiences. Nor am I willing to assume that a totally paralyzed person must necessarily be blind.

What does all this have to do with my postulate? If one does not assume that such mental events as seeing involve some action of the body, one is left with the mystery of how a disembodied nonmaterial mind can have physical consequences. This mystery has strongly inclined scientists to disavow mind in its entirety and to assert the manifest absurdity that all mental events are inconsequential and/or really nothing but actions of the body. If mental events are really actions of the body, we are left with the mystery of "What kinds of bodily events are mental?" The virtue of defining awareness as minimal behavior and postulating that there is nothing that could reasonably be described as awareness that is not behavior is that it (1) makes it reasonable to assume that all awareness involves some action of the body (but note, not necessarily of the motor apparatus) and, at the same time, (2) makes it possible to identify the distinctive nature of that action that makes it possible to conceptualize it as mental. I shall consider the mind-body problem at greater length in Chapter 8. In the meantime, however, I advance the claim that my definition and the associated postulate reduce a great mystery and, unless contraindications occur or someone does the same job better, I contend that this justifies me.

5

CONSCIOUSNESS, SUBCONSCIOUSNESS, AND RELATED CONCEPTS

"How," asks Jean-Paul Sartre, "can we conceive of a knowledge which is ignorant of itself?" He answers his rhetorical question with the declaration that, "all knowing is consciousness of knowing," and, earlier, he asserts as obvious that "To know is to be conscious of knowing."[1] Indeed, if most people were to reflect on such matters it would be equally obvious to them, for one cannot reflect on one's knowledge without knowing that one knows; and one would have no need of a term for "knowing" if one did not know of knowing.

So obvious is the conclusion that it is even built into the etymological structures of the words "consciousness" and "cognition." The first has the root "scio" (*scire* 'to know'), and the second "gnosis" (knowledge). Of interest, however, are the prefixes "con" and "co." Structurally, both words designate, not merely knowing, but knowing with, that is, they imply that there is an accompaniment of the knowing; and the implied accompaniment is the knowledge of the knowing or the knowledge that one knows.

Alas, one cannot always rest content with what seems to be obvious. "To know that one knows" involves two knowings: (1) the knowing of whatever it is that one knows and (2) the knowing of the first knowing. If it is generally true that "To know is to know that one knows," then it must also be true of the second knowing. That is, the

[1] Jean-Paul Sartre, *Being and Nothingness,* tr. by H. Barnes (New York: Philosophical Library, 1956), pp. 53, liv.

92

knowledge of the first knowing must itself be accompanied by still a third knowing: knowing that one knows the first knowing. And the third knowing demands a fourth, and the fourth a fifth, and so on *ad infinitum.* "To know is to know that one knows" implies an infinite regress and cannot, therefore, be generally valid. There is, in fact, no infinite regress. There are occasions when I know that I know, and I have sometimes known that I knew that I knew, perhaps even that I knew that I knew that I knew. That seems to be my limit. If I try to go further, I invariably lose the first knowing, becoming aware only of the repeated meaningless phrase "know that I" or "that I know." There may, of course, be some who can do better. But the notion of someone being able to traverse the infinite regress surpasses credulity, for, no matter how many steps may be taken, there always remain an infinite number of steps still to be taken. Thus, given at least one knowing, there must always be a knowing that is itself not known. It is, therefore, not generally true that "To know is to know that one knows." Knowing does not necessarily require a reflexive component, but one cannot (except through the deliberate exercise of trying to know that one knows . . . that one knows that . . .) establish this introspectively since one does not know the unknown knowing in the series. Thus, it appears in ordinary experience that all knowings are known and the assertion of the contrary seems to flagrantly contradict the facts of one's personal experience.

Sartre was well aware of the problem of the infinite regress and, in both of the cited contexts, explicitly rejected the formulation that "To know is to know that one knows." What, then, is he saying in his substitutes for this formulation, "All knowing is consciousness of knowing" and "To know is to be conscious of knowing"? Knowing demands a knower, and the knower is as essential an ingredient of consciousness as is the known: Just as there can be no consciousness without an object, there can be no consciousness without a subject. "Consciousness" is thus, in Sartre's usage, a technical philosophical term in the tradition of Husserlian analysis that incorporates subject, object, and subject-object relationship into one indissoluble unity. Husserl, like Descartes before him, had set out to devise a system of philosophy that would be free of error. The one indubitable given is, to Husserl, the fact of consciousness and all truth must be derived from that given by an assumptionless method. Whether Husserl's method is indeed free of assumptions is beside the point of my present concern, but it was in his analysis of consciousness that he found both object and subject; and it is, in this sense, that both object and subject are contained in consciousness.

Sartre was, however, quite clear that the subject and the relation of subject to object are not necessarily present in consciousness as objects. His assertion that "all knowing is consciousness of knowing" is the assertion that subject, object, and subject-object relation are all contained in consciousness, but not necessarily in the sense that "To know is to know that one knows." There is no implied infinite regress in the Sartrian formulations.

One of the cited contexts, however, is concerned with a critique of the psychoanalytic concepts of the unconscious and repression; and it is in this context that Sartre writes, "How can we conceive of a knowledge which is ignorant of itself? To know is to know that one knows, said Alain. Let us say rather: all knowing is consciousness of knowing."[2] Note that Alain's formulation is explicitly rejected, but the rejection is not very emphatic and one wonders why this second repetition of Alain's formulation (after the earlier rejection of it) is necessary. Sartre could not have been unaware of the oft-repeated criticism of the psychoanalytic notion of the unconscious mind as a contradiction in terms. It is as if, realizing that one cannot impose the implications of a technical usage of a term on the ordinary usage that has not confronted (and is, hence, indifferent to) the issues on which the technical usage is based, Sartre wishes to align himself with Alain's formulation so as to be able to reject "unconscious mind" as self-contradictory. It is only on the latter formulation that the criticism of self-contradiction makes sense; and, as we have seen, the latter formulation is not tenable in the face of the problem of the infinite regress.

The issue is pointed up in Sartre's own concept of the "prereflexive"[3] consciousness. The reflexive consciousness posits the consciousness reflected on as its object; it takes consciousness as object of reflection; it involves a consciousness of consciousness in the same sense that any consciousness involves an object save that the object is itself a con-

[2] *Ibid.*, p. 53. The relevant segment of *Being and Nothingness* is available in a paperback reprint, under the title *Existential Psychoanalysis* (Chicago: Regnary, 1962), p. 165. The paperback edition of *Being and Nothingness* (New York: Citadel, 1964) does not include the segment contained in *Existential Psychoanalysis*, but the two paperbacks do contain, with changes in pagination and the ordering of chapters, the entire text of the Hazel Barnes translation.

[3] The French term is ambiguous. Barnes translates it as "pre-reflective." In other discussions of Sartrian philosophy, however, one finds "prereflexive." Both translations are consistent. It is only on reflection that the reflexive character of consciousness emerges and, in Sartre's discussion, sometimes the one and sometimes the other emphasis seems most appropriate.

sciousness. In the prereflexive consciousness, "Consciousness of self is not dual. If we wish to avoid an infinite regress, there must be an immediate, *non-cognitive* relation of the self to itself."[4] There is thus consciousness in which the knowing is known by the knower and consciousness in which the knowing is not known, and the latter is not inevitably transformed into the former; and, if Sartre insists that the latter, too, is not ignorant of itself, the lack of ignorance must be taken in some noncognitive sense.

It is in terms of these two kinds of consciousness that the issue of the psychoanalytic unconscious must be examined; but, to say the least, the terminology is confusing, and, as we shall see shortly, the terminology is further confused by Freud's insistence on using the term "unconscious" to designate two kinds of unconsciousness (not to mention the persistence of the usage of "unconscious" to designate what was later distinguished as the id, while recognizing that the ego and superego are also, at least in part, unconscious, and, even more, to designate conscious contents that are normally unconscious).

Yet the issue is basically a simple one. Let me start with a neutral word that does not contain the troublesome prefix "con," namely, "awareness." I have, in the preceding chapter, identified awareness with minimal behavior, that is, a spontaneous directed act conceptually stripped of all but that which is minimally necessary to leave a directed act. There is nothing in the concept of behavior that logically requires that a behavior become the object of another behavior by the same actor; there is also nothing in the concept that logically precludes such an event.

If the actor should spontaneously engage in an action directed at one of his minimal behaviors, then he is not merely aware of the original object, but aware of his awareness of that object; any spontaneous directed action is at least a minimal behavior. Let us call any awareness which is itself an object of a behavior of the same actor a *conscious awareness*; it is an awareness accompanied by an awareness of it. By the same token, any behavior that is itself an object of another behavior of the same actor is a *conscious behavior*; and, if it is a motivating behavior and if, as motive (that is, in terms of its motivating relationship to the motivated act), it is similarly an object of another behavior, it is a *conscious motive*. Note that to speak of conscious awareness, behavior, or motivation is linguistically quite unambiguous: It is to speak

[4] *Sartre,* pp. liv–lv. Emphasis added.

95

of awareness and so forth with knowledge (awareness) of it, whereas the traditional usage of "consciousness" designates "awareness with," but does not specify with what.

But what if a behavior does not become an object of another behavior of the same actor? Then we may say that it is *subconscious,* the prefix "sub" being used in the sense of "less than." The behavior is less than conscious; what is missing is the accompanying behavior of which it is the object. The "sub" negates the "con"; and one might accomplish the same end simply by dropping the "con" from "conscious," except that the "con" is so firmly fixed in linguistic usage and in the tacit assumptions in terms of which most people apprehend such matters that it is desirable to give greater emphasis to the negation of the "con" than would be accomplished simply by dropping it, and one might also reasonably argue that both "conscious" and "subconscious" are "scious."[5]

Note that the important issue in the use of "subconscious" is the directedness of the behavior. Thus, if I am aware of an object or motivated with respect to it or, more generally, behaving toward it, but am not aware that it is an object of my awareness, motivation, or behavior, then the latter are subconscious. I may be fully aware of some aspects of my behavioral activity, but, if I am not aware of the directedness of this activity, then the behavior is subconscious. Nor is the spontaneity of the behavioral activity at issue. That is, whether a given behavior is conscious or subconscious does not depend on the consciousness of its motivation. Thus, I may say to an ostensible friend, "I was so happy to have missed you, yesterday," and immediately become aware of having said "happy" instead of "unhappy" but remain quite subconscious of any, at least momentary, motivating malice.

It is important to note that no amount of experience or research can disprove the concept of subconscious awareness, motivation, or behavior—and all the research devoted to this issue can, in principle, only have bearing on whether such behavior can be elicited or demonstrated under the specific experimental conditions. It is conceivable, for the sake of argument, that there never has been an instance, experimental or in life experience, but this would not show the concept to be false; at most it would go to show that the concept is not worth bothering with. The issue of the concept is not an issue of fact but an

[5] We do not, however, need the word "scious," since simply speaking of awareness, behavior, or motivation leaves it unspecified whether the latter is accompanied by an awareness of it. Thus, "scious awareness" involves a redundancy.

issue of conceptualization; and, as I have developed it and related concepts, it is not a contradiction in terms. Specifically with regard to definition, every definition is a metatheoretical proposition that states a rule of classification—and a rule cannot be said to be true or false[6]— but the rule does have bearing on the facilitation or hindrance of the discovery of factual relationships and of the simplicity and unexceptionability of the relationships that are discovered when the rule is applied and, more generally, on the comprehensibility of reality. Hence, the more valid a set of definitions the closer is the approximation of nature that it entails.

Yet, every alleged instance does involve an issue of fact. Is there or is there not in this particular instance of a behavior an accompanying behavior by the same actor that has the first behavior as its object? In exactly the same fashion, there can be no issue of fact with regard to the concepts of behavior, awareness, and motivation as I have developed these concepts; but there is an issue of fact with regard to every alleged instance, namely, whether the particular instance does meet the defining conditions of spontaneity and directedness and, in the case of an alleged instance of motivation, whether there is a containing directed act on which a contained act is conditional; and, of course, whether the object of the behavior, motivation, or awareness has been correctly identified.

Are there actual demonstrable instances of subconscious behavior? Of course. Let me begin with three varieties. I have already demonstrated that, for every behavior, there must be at least one subconscious behavior—either the behavior itself, or the behavior of which it is an

---

[6] Any statement of fact can, in principle, be affirmed as true (that is, shown to pass all of the tests one has thought of that are validly implied by the statement) or denied as false (that is, shown to fail at least one such test), provided that there is at least one such test. The qualifications "one has thought of" and "validly" imply that, in principle, no issue of fact can be finally settled—that is, no statement of fact is capable of absolute verification or contradiction—a conclusion that has important bearing on the nature of the scientific enterprise. See Chapter 16. The proviso states a necessary qualification of what is an issue of fact. One can also add the qualification to the use of the word "fact" that it refers to some thing, event, and so on that can allegedly be located in at least one segment of space-time. With this restriction, it is not a "fact" that, on the Euclidian assumptions, the sum of the interior angles of a triangle equal 180 degrees, though it is a fact that the inference has been drawn and shown to be implied by the assumptions and it is also a fact that many persons can both state and prove the theorem. See Chapter 7. In the restricted usage, no issue of fact can be adjudicated in the absence of relevant empirical data. These statements bear important similarities to certain doctrines associated with logical positivism, but there are also important differences.

object or the behavior of which the latter is an object, or some final behavior in this series; an infinite series of this kind is beyond belief.

Another variety of subconscious behavior is involved in the well-known formulation of the functional psychologists concerning the drift, with habituation, from consciousness to unconsciousness. Thus, the experienced driver is often oblivious of the fact that he is shifting gears. The functional psychologists did not, of course, make the distinctions I have made and therefore assumed a total loss of awareness and, perhaps, that the habituated act is a purely neurological event. Yet it is obvious that the shifting of gears is an act contained in and conditional on the act of driving the car (that is, it is spontaneous) and there is a shifting of gears that are not contained within the nervous system (that is, the act is directed); the shifting of gears is a behavior and the gears are implicitly an object of awareness. One can similarly demonstrate that the circumstances calling for the shifting of gears must in most (allowing for an occasional, highly improbable, coincidence) instances be objects of awareness. If these acts are not conscious they are so, not in the sense of a total absence of awareness, but in the sense of an absence of conscious awareness; that is, they are subconscious behaviors.

Still a third variety of subconscious behavior, closely related to the second and perhaps a special case of it, involves higher level integrations such as are found when the learning curve for a complex skill resumes its climb following a plateau. Thus, it is commonly said that the experienced typist types words and phrases rather than letters. The statement, at best, expresses only a partial truth, namely, with respect to the conscious behavior of the typist. It is, however, perfectly apparent that the best typist in the world could not possibly type words on the standard keyboard without striking letter keys; and it seems to me to be equally obvious that striking a letter key in the course of typing a word meets the specifications of a behavior. What happens is that as a consequence of the higher integration, the component behaviors become subconscious; they are so thoroughly imbedded in the higher integration that they cease to be available as potential objects of behavior unless and until the higher integration is disrupted.

From the three preceding examples of classes of subconscious behaviors, it is evident that subconscious behavior not only occurs, but must be extremely common. Even so, it hardly seems likely that the concept of subconscious behavior and related concepts would have achieved any prominence in contemporary psychological theory were it not for certain observations made in the course of investigating psychopathological and hypnotic phenomena. Let me cite some of my favorite examples from the literature. Jung somewhere describes a patient with a peculiar visual disability. This patient had good vision except when it came to seeing people's heads; he saw all people as headless. As far as I know, no available neurological or optical theory can explain so specific a visual defect. The postulation of a specific brain center or specific neural pathways for heads does not seem consistent with anything else that we know. A far more attractive explanation of the described phenomenon is that the patient is lying. But then the lie is so bizarre and so patently incredible that one would want to know what could possibly have led to such a lie. One possibility is that the patient is generally given to bizarre lies in which case what would most demand explanation is the general propensity rather than the specific instance. If, however, the patient does not seem to have any such general propensity and if despite serious effort to find an explanation for the lie, no tenable hypothesis is found, the lie hypothesis loses its attractiveness.

Another case described by Jung involves a woman who claimed that she could not hear. Despite the claimed disability, Jung noted that she would go about her housework singing to herself, a most unusual behavior for a deaf person. One day, Jung sat down at the piano and began to accompany her. If she were truly deaf, the accompaniment could make no possible difference; but, when Jung shifted the key in which he was playing the accompaniment, the patient executed a matching shift. Again we must inquire concerning the tenability of the neurological-defect and lying hypotheses that might explain the phenomena.

Janet has described an instance involving a woman exhibiting a glove anaesthesia. He explained to her that he wanted to map out the area of insensitivity. While her gaze was averted he touched her with a point in an irregular pattern, sometimes in the "glove" area, sometimes outside. When he touched her outside, she said, "I felt that, doctor." When he touched her inside the "glove" area, she said, "I didn't feel that, doctor." How did she know when to say "I didn't feel that, doctor"?

Instances such as these can be multiplied *ad libitum*. In any of them, it may be that the neurological-defect and lying hypotheses were too quickly dismissed. But the sheer accumulation and variety impels one to seek an alternative kind of hypothesis. And one is readily available. The first patient saw heads, but did not know that he saw them and therefore honestly believed that he did not. The second patient heard the piano accompaniment, but did not know that she heard it. The third patient felt the touches in the "glove" area but believed that she did not. How are such things possible? Well, once we grant the possibility of subconscious behaviors, then we must also grant that the seemingly bizarre behaviors postulated by the third kind of hypothesis are not, in principle, impossible. The question then is, what happens when we explore the hypothesis that, with respect to the kind of symptom I have described, the disability is not in the area of direct sensory-perceptual experience but rather in the area of responding to sensory-perceptual awareness? If, having failed to authenticate[7] the neurological-defect and lying hypotheses, the exploration of the third hypothesis yields plausible concrete explanations, then the third hypothesis must be taken seriously; and the hypothesis increases in weight as well as becomes more specified and articulated if there are regularities to be noted in the plausible explanations arrived at for large numbers of specific instances. The specified and articulated versions of the third hypothesis, then, come to serve as looking rules (see Chapter 15) as one comes across new instances; that is, they alert the investigator to look for certain kinds of factors. The more effective the looking rules turn out to be, the more and more seriously one must take them as valid generalizations. This is, in essence, the process by which and the context in which the psychoanalytic concept of the unconscious developed.

Pierre Janet, a sadly neglected genius,[8] recognized that the symptoms of hysteria (both of the sensory-perceptual variety described above[9] and of the motor variety exemplified by paralyses and convulsive seizures)

---

[7] I am here using this term to designate a much weaker form of supporting consideration than confirmation. I mean by "authenticate" the establishment that there is available a plausible possibility in some concrete detail as contrasted with some highly abstract hypothesis the specific application of which remains completely inexplicated. Thus neither "It must be due to some bodily process" nor "There must be some reason for the lie" can be taken as authentic explanations.

[8] Almost any psychologist will, of course, recognize the name, but few will be able to add any more than the association with Charcot, the identification as a predecessor of psychoanalysis, a characterization that is unfair to both Freud and Janet, and a notion of psychic energy. Only a fraction of Janet's writings has been translated into English. Actually, Janet was a systematic psychologist of remarkable scope and penetration within a framework of purposive behaviorism and response psychology, before either of these movements had developed, though he took his data from the phenomena of psychopathology. His concept of mental energy was, for instance, defined in physicalistic terms of the extent, intensity, and duration of movement.

[9] The symptom of seeing people as headless has some qualities of a schizophrenic process, but this is not germane to my immediate concerns.

were tied up with continued preoccupation with unfinished business from the past and was able to identify some generic features common to these symptoms, for instance, the marked constriction of the behavioral field within which the symptoms are manifested.[10] In essence, he saw such symptoms as behaviors, but subconscious behaviors, because the patients were unaware of the relation of the symptoms to their objects.

It was Freud's genius, however (after a start in which he too recognized the relation of such symptoms to the unfinished business of the past, but in terms of what strikes me as a far less sophisticated theory than that of Janet) that realized that the essential key to the hysterical symptom lay in the factor of motivation. It was Freud who expressly realized that the problem of the hysterical disability was not one of "cannot" but of "will not." And, once he undertook the task of unraveling the relevant motivations, he began to discover that hitherto incomprehensible phenomena such as dreams, slips of the tongue, momentary forgettings, and the like became comprehensible in terms of motivations similar to those relevant to the comprehension of symptoms—and, further, that the first clues to the motivation of the symptom might be derived from the analysis of dreams and parapraxes.

It is not my purpose, here, to review the development of psychoanalytic theory, for example, the realization that what were later called transference phenomena could not be sufficiently explained in terms of the peculiar properties of the hypnotic method, the charming and other properties of the therapist, or the therapist-patient relationship, and the consequent search for the motivation of these phenomena or to consider in any detail the nature and structure of psychoanalytic evidence. My immediate concern is with another development in Freud's thinking. He realized that it is not enough to assert that the subject is not conscious of some of his motives. For, even with regard to those objects, behaviors, and motives of which we may be said to be conscious, it may not truthfully be said that they are in consciousness all the time; that is, in my terms, they are not themselves constantly objects of awareness. This implied that there must be a variety of subconscious phenomena that quite easily become conscious and that must be distinguished from those subconscious phenomena of which the subject can apparently only become conscious under special conditions, typically involving considerably specialized devious effort and struggle; and further, with

[10] See especially Pierre Janet, *Psychological Healing,* 2 vols. (New York: Macmillan, 1925), and *The Major Symptoms of Hysteria* (New York: Macmillan, 1920).

regard to the first variety of subconscious phenomena, that it does not matter that, at any given moment, they are in fact subconscious, that is, that they belong functionally with the phenomena that we call conscious.

Hence, Freud distinguished two varieties of subconscious phenomena, preconscious (the "pre" designating "close to the threshold, on the verge of"), abbreviated Pcs, and unconscious (the "un" designating a strong negation, not of awareness, behavior, or motivation *per se,* but of the accompanying *con*sciousness), abbreviated as Ucs; and he proceeded to speak of the Cs-Pcs system *vs.* the Ucs. Even so, and despite the dichotomy implied in his terminology, Freud realized that there is no sharply demarcated boundary between the Pcs and the Ucs and that there are continua of difficulty (with respect to the introduction of the accompanying awareness that transforms subconscious phenomena into conscious ones) both within the Pcs and Ucs "regions" and in the area of transition between them. On this basis, though much of the Pcs is not significantly different in a functional sense from the Cs, the systematic difference of the Pcs-Ucs from the Cs becomes important. One needs a term to cover Pcs-Ucs when the differences between the latter are not contextually significant. For this purpose, Freud elected to use the term "unconscious"; that is, he was using the latter term with two basic meanings: to designate collectively all preconscious and unconscious phenomena and to designate only those phenomena that qualified under the restricted usage. Needless to say, such a dual usage invites confusion and can hardly be justified when there is a perfectly good term, "subconscious," available to carry the broader meaning. Freud, however, explicitly rejected the latter term, on no stronger basis than the expression of a bias. Perhaps he wanted to separate himself from the users of the latter term, particularly Janet, who did not accept what he regarded as his most important discovery, the unconscious proper. I have no corresponding separation need and consequently use the term "subconscious" to designate any awareness, behavior, or motive that is not itself an object of awareness whenever I am unconcerned with the reasons for the lack.

Freud also recognized that there is a sense in which one may say, without self-contradiction, that a person may be aware of an unconscious motive. He may accurately diagnose the presence of a motive, but if the person does so on the basis of knowledge about the manifestations of such motivation rather than on the basis of directly taking his motivation as object, his motivation is not truly conscious; the consequences of such indirect knowledge about his own motivation are not the same as the consequence of direct knowledge of it.[11] In other words, the specification is added that the accompanying awareness must be direct to justify speaking of consciousness; the subject must be aware of his awareness, behavior, or motivation, as such, and not merely of some consequence from which he infers its presence.

An analogous case may be cited in the behavior of one of Kurt Goldstein's patients. This patient could successfully sort the Holmgren woolens despite the fact that he suffered from an impairment of abstract behavior, a condition that Goldstein took to be incompatible with the successful accomplishment of such a task. Asked whether the skeins of wool sorted into the various piles really belonged together, the patient shrugged his shoulders, pointed to another physician, and said, "He says they do." He himself could not perceive the color relationship among less than perfectly matched skeins of wool, but could nevertheless obey a rule predicated on someone else's perception of the relationship. Similarly, many a student has learned to solve certain classes of arithmetic reasoning problems by recognizing that certain rules apply, but is unable to perceive the relationships that justify the rules. In the same fashion, individuals may learn to apply rules for translating manifest behaviors into their unconscious equivalents without ever perceiving the corresponding unconscious behaviors at all. By the same token, psychoanalysts have learned to regard with profound suspicion the too facile offering of a textbook interpretation by the patient or too ready acceptance of an interpretation offered by the analyst. In such instances, they have learned to suspect that the patient is using the facile translation to hide something, from himself as well as from the analyst. They, thereby, also give the lie to the familiar canard on the nature of psychoanalytic evidence, namely, that psychoanalysts get you coming and going; if you agree with them, they are right and, if you do not, your resistance proves that they are right.

There is a logical problem involved in the psychoanalytic concept of the unconscious, and it is one that is particularly emphasized by Sartre

[11] The most important publication by Freud on the concept of the unconscious in his "The Unconscious (1915)." See, Sigmund Freud, *Collected Papers,* vol. 4 (New York: Basic Books, 1959) or *The Complete Works of Sigmund Freud,* vol. 14 (London: Hogarth Press, 1957). It may be noted that, in this paper, written long before John B. Watson equated the psychoanalytic unconscious with the unverbalized, Freud pointed out that that which is unconscious is unverbalized, but that this is not an appropriate basis for distinguishing between the conscious and the unconscious.

in the previously cited critique. Consider the case of the young man who could not see heads. What makes us so certain that he, in fact, did see heads is the high degree of discrimination involved; to so carefully select out heads for "not seeing" implies a highly directed act, and the only basis we can think of for such an act is that it be motivated. Consider now the behavior of selecting out heads for "not seeing." Does the failure to respond to this behavior similarly imply selective inattention? Not necessarily, for, as we have already seen, not all behavior is necessarily itself an object of a behavior.

We must, however, examine the conditions under which behaviors themselves become objects of behavior. One such condition, emphasized both by Freud and the functionalists, is the occurrence of a snag in the smooth progress of a behavior. The reason why increasing skill is associated with an increasing likelihood of subconscious execution is precisely that the greater the skill, other conditions remaining the same, the less the likelihood of a snag. When we encounter a snag, our attention is drawn to, among other things, the snagged behavior. Nothing can be more rational, for sufficient conditions for eliminating the snag may inhere in the way we are carrying out the behavior; when we hit a snag, we cast about for ways of eliminating it, and this calls for an examination of what we are doing in the given situation. Similarly, the incorporation of a skilled act into a new motivational context may be sufficient to counter its normal execution. A young man is a superb social dancer, but suddenly becomes acutely aware of his body movements when he dances with a girl who arouses impulses in him that have not afflicted him before. His new project of making headway with this girl gives his dancing a new importance. The new project is fraught with difficulties that demand attention to what he is doing, and his most immediate action in line with the project involves the dance. That attention to his movements is maladaptive with respect to the dance (and perhaps, therefore, to the project) is beside the point. The initial snag is not in the dance, as such, but in the very placement of his arm around the girl in a behavioral context in which he is not skilled; and the cutaneous and pressure sensations he induces and receives as a consequence of his movements have a direct bearing on the project, independently of the dance, and again in a context in which he is unskilled. If now the smooth flow of the dance is disrupted, the dancing as such also demands attention, despite the prior high level of skill.

A second circumstance in which one becomes aware of behaviors that one might otherwise ignore is when one undertakes to observe them in the interests of some larger enterprise such as scientific inquiry. A related circumstance occurs when someone else draws attention to one of our behaviors that was flowing smoothly without any attention to it. The lecturer says, "Stop taking notes for a while and just listen to me," and immediately even the skilled note-takers who can carry on this activity without attending to it become aware of the activity.

Finally, we must recall the nonmotivational limiting conditions for becoming aware of one's behavior. We have already noted two such conditions. One involves the limit in becoming aware that one is aware, that one is doing something. An information theorist might say that one has exhausted the available information channels; one can only attend to so many things at one time. A related limiting condition is that one is so completely absorbed in an activity that one's threshold of responsiveness to anything else, including the fact of one's absorption, is markedly raised; this is, of course, an extreme of task-oriented activity. We have also noted the difficulty of responding to a behavior that is imbedded in a complex integration of activity. A related limiting condition is the imbeddedness of the behavior in any setting that obscures it. Thus, I may be engaged in a heated argument. At some point, someone says to me, "Stop shouting." My adaptation level for noise has, however, been shifting with the increasing volume of the voices involved in the argument and I shout, "I am not shouting," and remain unaware of the fact that I am shouting. The fact of the shouting is obscured by the general noise level achieved in the course of the argument.

Let us now return to the patient who would not see heads. To argue that the discriminatory behavior against heads is itself not singled out as something to be ignored, one would have to assume that it (and the behavior of which it is a component) proceeds without serious snags, that it is imbedded in a sufficiently obscuring context, that it is so all-absorbing an activity as to leave little room for attention to anything else, including itself, and/or that attention to it would overload the information-processing channel capacity of the patient. Somehow, none of these assumptions seems very compelling to me. The last assumption, by itself, would, for instance, imply that this patient's channel capacity is so low that he virtually never does anything consciously. The one before the last would imply that the patient is unresponsive to any other stimulation, but the symptom is not described as appearing while the patient is in a state of monoideic somnambulism. The others would be expected to give way to the statement, "Look at what you are doing. You must be seeing heads to discriminate against them so effectively." Experience suggests that such a symptom would not yield to so direct a challenge.

Moreover, in terms of the channel-capacity hypothesis, the case I have been considering is not typical. In this case, there are two critical conditions that must be fulfilled for the behavior to be carried out effectively: (1) The patient must not become consciously aware of the primary object (heads), not even as an object of an inspection behavior, and (2) he must not become aware of any behavior with respect to this object, for, if he were to become aware of any such behavior, he would be consciously aware of the object. In the more typical case of psychoanalytic concern, only one of these conditions needs to be satisfied. Thus, subject loves (or hates) object and, though he may not become aware of this behavior with respect to the object, he may nevertheless be consciously aware of the object by, for instance, inspecting it and becoming aware of his inspection. That is, in the typical case, the number of, so to speak, channels that need to be controlled is less than in the case we have been considering.

This brings us to the logical problem in the psychoanalytic concept of the unconscious, referred to some paragraphs back. In the domain of psychoanalytic concern,[12] the apparent absence of awareness of certain behaviors is not a mere absence but a consequence of positive actions (avoidance behaviors) taken with respect to them. Thus, the behaviors in question are themselves objects of behavior and must, therefore, be conscious. Thus, unconscious behaviors are, by definition, conscious;

---

[12] The most noteworthy exception is to be found in the area of symbolism and, more generally, primary-process thinking. In dreaming, in drowsy states, under conditions of stress, and in nonfocal behaviors, classificatory processes are markedly altered from what they are like in the context of alert focal behaviors. In effect, rules for establishing equivalence classes are markedly relaxed. Objects that are related in any way (by similarity, by contrast, by physiognomic properties, by relationships of super-subordination, for example, whole-part, or by figures of speech), are dealt with as though they were exactly equivalent, without reference to their distinguishing features, and complex thoughts tend to be expressed as simple images. Thus, the thought "How I envy her" may be expressed in an image of oneself wearing "her" shoes, a play on the figure of speech, "being in someone else's shoes," and "want to be" is reduced, by an equivalence relationship to "being." To secondary-process thinking, characteristic of alert focal behavior and operating under much more stringent rules of classification, such a behavior is inaccessible, save in its manifest content ("I dreamt I was wearing her shoes"), without considerable elaboration—and this regardless of any motivation to conceal the "latent" content.

and, whatever may be true of subconscious behaviors, generally, it seems that the psychoanalytic concept of the unconscious (at least in my interpretation of it) is, after all, self-contradictory.

There are, however, several considerations that resolve the apparent contradiction. The first has to do with a property of avoidance behavior. I can avoid object *A,* by avoiding anything that leads to object *A.* Thus, if I were to come on a sign, "Detour. Danger Ahead," I would normally take the detour and never learn what danger it was that I was avoiding. By the same token, if, at the slightest cue to the presence of a particular behavior, I abort any further inspection in that direction, then I never do come into full confrontation with my behavior. I have, so to say, started on my detour before I have had a chance to find out what the danger is that I am avoiding. And if the cue has acquired aversive properties, I do not have to spell out what it cues to start my avoidance reaction at that point.

In the second place, anxiety has a marked constrictive effect on one's ability to survey the presenting situation. Consequently, the closer I come to a source of paramount danger, the more limited does my ability to observe become; my channel capacity is, if you will, markedly reduced.

Finally, if strong motivation is denied any avenue of direct expression, it will seek whatever channels are open to it; that is, it will motivate behaviors that advance it and, if necessary, through the most devious of channels that make sense only in primary-process terms. But, primary-process terms do not make sense under conditions that favor secondary process.[13] Consequently, even though subject examines his executed behaviors, he will, of course, be aware of them, but will not normally be aware of the relation of the behavior to its motivating source or be able to comprehend the latter from the data available to him. If, for instance, one operates under rules in terms of which desire and aversion are opposites, it is difficult to comprehend aversion as an equivalent of desire or vice versa, not unless one begins to take note of the paradoxes that appear. Thus, the young adolescent may seemingly despise a girl and do everything possible to annoy her and one would not suspect anything unless one noted that (1) the experienced affect (aversion, not hatred) does not seem to justify such behavior and (2) that, somehow, he manages to maintain bodily and other intimate contact with her, pulling her hair, pinching her, interposing his body to impede her movements, making disparaging remarks about her appearance and personal habits, and so on. Aversion and contempt call for

13 See note 12.

avoidance, and nothing more, certainly not seeking out and maximizing proximity. There is more sense in primary process than we can normally credit.[14]

In terms of the considerations raised in the preceding three paragraphs, the apparent self-contradiction in the concept of unconscious behavior vanishes. If the fact that he is engaged in a particular behavior arouses anxiety, then a person can not only avoid confronting this fact, but can be strongly resistant to such a confrontation without becoming aware of it or its anxiety arousing aspects. Thus, in a particular instance of hysterical anaesthesia, a person may unconsciously continue to glory in having touched something prohibited to him by simultaneously providing himself with punishment for his offense (the manifest disability) and engaging in a ritual of preserving the prohibited touch by preventing any "overlay" of conscious cutaneous experience. Sartre's reinterpretation of the psychoanalytic unconscious as acting in bad faith has its own validity, but it does not strike me as a valid critique of the Freudian concept.

Let me recapitulate briefly. I have suggested that consciousness involves a dual behavior: a primary behavior and a behavior that takes the primary behavior as its object. I have argued that, given a primary behavior, the second behavior is not necessarily present, its major condition being a snag or difficulty in the smooth flow of the primary behavior. For those instances in which the secondary behavior does not occur, I have suggested that we refer to the primary behavior as "subconscious." With respect to subconscious behaviors, I have tacitly recommended that we follow Freud's distinction between "preconscious," readily available as objects of a secondary behavior, and "unconscious," not readily available as objects of a secondary behavior, while recognizing that there are continua of availability within each of these classes and that there is no sharp line of demarcation between them. With respect to unconscious behaviors, I have indicated that there are subconscious behaviors that are not readily available as objects of secondary behaviors for reasons that have nothing to do with the motivation of the subject and others for reasons which do; it may be appropriate to refer to the first as primary unconscious behaviors and to the second as secondary.[15]

---

[14] I realize that there is an issue of freedom entailed in this paragraph. The behavior described hardly sounds like the activity of a free agent. I will return to the issue in a later chapter.

[15] The distinction is fairly close to the Freudian distinction between primary and secondary repression, that is, between the repression of material that was never permitted to become conscious and the repression of material that once

In the preceding discussion, I have several times used the term "attention" or one or another of its grammatical variants, a term that is also associated with the notion of degrees of awareness. I doubt that my use of the term will have given anyone any trouble, but I think that the concept involved merits closer scrutiny, both because it is often improperly used as an explanatory concept and because the term is far from ambiguous. It should also be noted that the distinction I have drawn between conscious and subconscious is not one of degree; if there are instances in which it may be difficult to decide whether a particular behavior is best described as conscious or subconscious, the difficulty stems from a source other than the conceptual basis for the distinction, a source that can be clarified in examining the concept of attention.

First, then, with regard to the improper use of the concept: We often say that a person is aware of something because he is attending to it when, in fact, we have no basis for speaking of attention other than that he is aware of it. Similarly, we often say that a person is not aware of something because of his inattention when, in fact, we have no basis for speaking of the inattention other than the fact that he is not aware of it or that he is aware of a variety of things other than it. Thus, if we take the "because" literally, we explain an event in terms of itself, an explanation that is exactly on a par with an explanation of rain in terms of "It rains because droplets of water come down from the sky." I have no objection to the linguistic construction, as such, if it is meant to do no more than emphasize the active role of the subject, an active role that, on my premises, is necessarily involved in all awareness, but is not necessarily always a focus of special interest.

Curiously enough, along with the notion of attention as an explanation of awareness is the conception of it as a mental faculty that is itself an impotent reactor to the stimulus world—as if to deny the active role of the subject in awareness. We speak, for instance, of capturing and holding someone's attention as if the subject had nothing to do

---

was, except, of course, that the Freudian primary repression connotes motivated unconsciousness. In actual usage, it seems to me that there is a rather casual assimilation of structural reasons for unconsciousness to the concept of repression (motivated unconsciousness), and it seems to me that the mere historical difference in whether something once was or was not conscious does not make enough of a difference with respect to anything else to demand the conceptual distinction on this basis. Note that the usage of "primary" and "secondary" in this note and the sentence to which it is appended is not the same as that earlier in the paragraph. In the earlier usage, I was referring only to position in the exposition. In the earlier usage, one may refer to a "secondary" behavior as "primary" if one's interest in it is as an object of still another behavior.

with it. Again, I have no objection to the linguistic construction if it is intended to do no more than to emphasize our role as a stimulus source or the role of the configuration of the stimulus or object field. Thus, any sudden or unexpected discriminable change is a quite dependable attention catcher. The potency of the stimulus configuration in this respect is itself contingent on the active concerns of the subject. It so happens that almost any novelty or unexpected change is, on my premises, of potential concern to the subject and, therefore, demands attention. Even a well-practiced laboratory rat running a maze will generally stop to investigate a new opening in an alley wall; the new opening offers possibilities that may be of concern to the rat. I will warrant, however, that, with the repeated recurrence of wall openings that lead nowhere, on an irregular place and run schedule, the rat will stop attending to these openings; a human in such a situation might say to himself, "Oh, that's another of those mysterious openings that are not worth looking into," and eventually stop noticing them. Similarly (though less speculatively), a lecturer can suddenly drop or raise his voice only so often as an attention-gaining device.

I should, I suppose, mention that, unlike the concept of "attention," *per se*, the notion of "attention span" does have a limited explanatory function in that it conceptualizes certain regularities that have bearing on what we need to explain. A person notes a number of tachistoscopically exposed unrelated words within the range of his established or presumed attention span, and we may say that the attention span explains this behavior, but only in the sense that we are saying that this particular behavior is a member of an already noted class of behaviors and it is the existence of the class that demands explanation rather than the particular instance as such.[16] On the other hand, a

---

[16] In similar fashion, we "explain" an instance of asocial behavior by saying that the person is an introvert. That is, we are saying that this is the way this person generally behaves so that there is no mystery about the particular instance. I refer to such explanations as *reductional* in contradistinction to those which are *conditional-genetic* or *dynamic,* that is, explanations that identify the generating conditions of an event or class of events. Ultimately, conditional-genetic explanations must themselves be understood in reductional terms (for example, the law of gravitation), but the task of science, as I see it, is to minimize the number of reductional explanations to which we must appeal. Thus, the *positivistic* doctrine that all scientific explanation is descriptive (in the sense of reducing events to classes of observed regularities) is valid as far as it goes, but it misses the point that not any reductional explanation is as valid as any other. A reductional explanation is only as valid as our conviction that the descriptive generalization to which it appeals is a member of the set of such generalizations as will eventually prove to be the minimal set. Some reductions can be said, with

performance well out of the range of the attention span would in itself demand further explanation.

The concept of attention covers three distinct kinds of processes, individually and in all combinations. The more limited the range and variety of available objects to which a subject is responsive within any given period, the more attentive, we say, is the subject to the objects included within that range; in the extreme case of attending, in this sense, the subject is not responsive to any but one of the available objects, and, bearing in mind that any discriminable aspect of anything is itself a potential object, the most extreme case of attending is one of responsiveness to only one aspect of one thing in a field of things available as objects. Note that the focus of emphasis in this usage is on the exclusion of certain things from the immediate behavioral field. Alternatively, we speak of attentiveness when the subject, during any given period, sharply discriminates between an object and its surround and is simultaneously responsive to the articulated details of that object—and this regardless of whether the subject is also responsive to other available objects. A high degree of attentiveness in this second sense of the term is unlikely to occur simultaneously with respect to more than one discrete object, but is not incompatible with a much lower degree of attentiveness in the first sense. A student may be aware of much that is going on in the classroom while attending closely to what the lecturer is saying; and the highest degree of attentiveness in the second sense is compatible with a very high degree of alertness to (attentiveness in the first sense) the possibility of certain other events the actual occurrence of which would destroy it. A hostess may be

great assurance, to be unlikely to be members of such a set. For instance, the generalization that the passage of time explains the rusting of metal or the dimming of memory is hardly likely to be as valid as generalizations in terms of other events that occur in time. The presumed minimal set of reductional laws and the logical inferences drawn therefrom constitute the nomothetic net of conditional-genetic explanations. It should also be noted in connection with reductional explanations that atypical behaviors may be concealed within a normative range. For instance, an asocial behavior by an introvert may occur in a particular instance for reasons that have nothing to do with the usual reasons for this person's introvertive behavior; the too casual reduction may conceal the fact that something highly unusual is going on. Similarly, a seemingly atypical behavior may, under atypical circumstances, really be quite typical with respect to relevant reductions. It follows that a fundamental aspiration of the scientific enterprise is to make the criteria for applying reductional explanations so unequivocal as to make such misplacements impossible. The aspiration is, however, not to be confused with present reality and, for the present and foreseeable future, attitudes of general scientific humility and of suspicion toward all our explanatory processes are called for.

highly attentive$_2$[17] to what one of her guests is saying while remaining highly attentive$_1$ to how her other guests are enjoying themselves; but note that, in this instance, a high degree of attentiveness$_{1/2}$ to her attentiveness$_1$ (that is, conscious attentiveness$_1$) is apt to interfere with the attentiveness$_2$. Finally, the more prolonged the attentiveness$_{1/2}$, the more attentive$_3$ the subject. We say, for instance, that a student is not very attentive$_3$ to a lecture if his attention$_2$ to it is not sustained over time.

The ambiguity of the term does not destroy its usefulness. Often, it is a matter of indifference which aspect of its meaning is being specified. Often the context clearly implies the nature of the usage. If greater precision is necessary, specifications can be added and, in writing, the use of subscripts does so most efficiently. We, however, need to be aware of the ambiguities in the usage of the term to avoid confusing ourselves just as we need to be aware of the uncertainties and ambiguities with regard to the identification of the objects of attention; the subject's objects are not necessarily the observer's, and his concern with an object may be in terms of its class membership and meaning or merely as a differentiated region in a sensory field.[18]

The distinctions that I have just drawn with respect to attention also point to the dimensions of degrees of awareness. We may be said to be aware of an object to the degree that we devote our behavior exclusively to it, to the degree that we sharply discriminate it from its surroundings and are concerned with the articulated details of its structure, and to the degree that our commerce with it is prolonged. On any of these counts, we must anticipate the possibility of directed activity that is barely distinguishable from nondirected activity and of highly articulated behaviors that, as objects of secondary behavior, are barely conscious. By the same token, we must admit the possibility of highly conscious bare awareness; thus, in the dark, we may be acutely conscious of seeing movement of which we are hardly aware. With the customary failure to recognize the duality of conscious behavior, such phenomena as the latter are extremely puzzling; with the recognition of its duality, they become, in principle, quite clear.

---

[17] The subscript designates the sense in which the term is being used. In a moment, I will use attentiveness$_{1/2}$ to mean attentiveness in sense I and/or in sense 2. One may similarly adopt a convention, say, attention$_{1,2}$ to designate sense one or two (but not simultaneously both) and attentiveness$_{12}$ to indicate the concurrent usage. These convenions can readily be extended to the three senses of the term, adding parentheses to indicate subgrouping. Thus, $(13)/2 \neq 1(3/2)$.

[18] The latter distinction corresponds to the Titchenerian distinction between cognitive and attributive clearness.

6

E. B. TITCHENER,

THE BEHAVIORIST

REVOLUTION, AND THE

QUALITIES OF EXPERIENCE

A number of other matters are considerably clarified by the recognition of the duality of conscious behavior. I shall shortly deal with three: (1) Titchener's concept of the stimulus error, (2) the essential nature of the behaviorist revolution against Titchenerian introspectionism, and (3) the problem of the qualities of experience.

Through Titchener's contributions and influence, the project of developing psychology as the science concerned with identifying the elements of consciousness and the laws governing their combinations reached its highest level. With his death, the kind of psychology he stood for went into a rapid decline and, by midcentury, it may be said to have suffered a total demise. For all of its one time influence, however, it seems to me that few contemporary psychologists understand the three central issues on which it stood and fell, and, failing to comprehend, have, in effect, bypassed our history rather than profited from it.

The first of these issues I deal with in passing, though it is not directly relevant to my major concerns in writing this chapter. This is the issue of elementarism. By now, it is fairly conventional for psychologists to agree that the whole is more than the sum of its parts, a statement that is neither semantically defensible (save on the assumption of the Gestalt quality as a new element in consciousness generated by the combination of the parts) nor has anything to do with the issue on which the battle was fought. John Stuart Mill and Wundt had already introduced into introspectionist psychology the equivalent notions of mental chemistry and creative synthesis, notions that imply that the properties of a synthesis of components may be quite different from (and note that "different from" is not the same as "more than") what one would expect from a mere summation of the properties of its components. Such a notion was part of Titchener's heritage and not at all alien to the psychology he advocated. He did not, for instance, demand that one should be able to discern, within the cutaneous experience of heat, the experiences of warmth and cold that would result from the separate stimulation of skin receptors that, when jointly stimulated, yield the experience of heat—no more than he would have demanded that one should find, in water, the gaseous and combustible properties of the hydrogen and oxygen that constitute it.

The heart of the issue on which the battle of elementarism was fought was that the Titchenerian approach was unfaithful to the nature of conscious experience. One can, for instance, change (by transposition) all the "elements" of a melodious phrase with barely any discernible effect on the experience and, conversely, retain all the elements with a revolutionary effect on the experience (for example, by playing the identical phrase backwards). More fundamentally, the objection was that Titchener misconstrued the nature of the whole-part relation. The Gestalt psychologists contended that the whole is frequently (perhaps typically) prior to its parts—often historically so, as the organismicists contended[1]—in that the configuration determines the components that are discernible within it and that (to revert to my own language) behavior directed to one or more of the parts is often incompatible with behavior directed to the whole; and even when parts are combined to form a new whole, the originally combined parts may cease to be discernible in the whole and a new set of parts emerge. For instance, Figure 3 can be generated by superimposing Figure 2 on Figure 1. Figures 1 and 2 are thus parts of Figure 3, but they are not simultaneously visible within it (as they easily are when separated), and within Figure 3 neither is simultaneously visible with the whole of Figure 3; and the readily visible parts of Figure 3 are the faces of a reversible box, not contained in either Figure 1 or Figure 2. The priority of the phenomenal whole is, however, incompatible with the notion that the whole is composed out of its phenomenal elements. The conscious

[1] For instance, the body is not composed of its cells, but the cells are rather the developmental products of the ontogeny of the body.

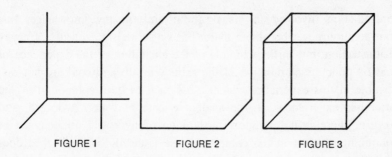

FIGURE 1   FIGURE 2   FIGURE 3

elements depend on the configurations of which they are components rather than vice versa.

It may be argued, however, that Titchener's elements of consciousness are not conscious elements in the sense implied in the preceding argument, that is, components discernible in conscious experience. With an important qualification that will be discussed in the context of the second issue, the function of the Titchenerian introspecter was to give a faithful report of his conscious experience; this function, but for the qualification, is no different from that assumed by other phenomenologists who are not introspecters in the Titchenerian sense. What divides the Titchenerian from another variety of introspecter (say, a Gestaltist) is not that one tries to discern the elements in his conscious experiences while the other does not, but the restrictions imposed on the introspective process; and these have nothing to do with elementarism, but with the issue of the stimulus error.

The Titchenerian process of discovering elements of consciousness involves two active roles (though both may, on occasion, be combined in one person): that of subject whose function it is to introspect and that of experimenter whose function it is to control the conditions of the experiences on which the subject introspects. Titchener's elements are the experiences associated with essentially simple forms of stimulation and the presumed elementary neural processes associated with such stimuli. All conscious experiences were thought by him to be of this elementary character, or complexes and compounds of such elementary experiences. These elements were conceived of as existing in the compound in the same sense that hydrogen and oxygen are considered to continue in existence when compounded in water, and it may be recalled that Titchener's psychology was called *existential psychology* long before "existential" acquired the radically different connotations that it has on the contemporary scene.

As far as I know, Titchener, himself, never recognized the internal contradiction involved in his position; and, to my knowledge, this contradiction never became a major basis of criticism. Consider, by way of illustration, my earlier example of the elicitation of the experience of heat by punctate stimulation of the skin. Warmth and cold are not discernible in this experience which is assumed to be a compound of the latter two experiences. In the analogous case of water, hydrogen, and oxygen, there is no paradox in thinking of hydrogen and oxygen as continuing to exist in the compound; the issue of their existence does not depend on their continuing to remain discernible as such (albeit in slightly modified form) while in the compounded state. The elements that Titchener was postulating are, however, elements of consciousness, not elements of stimulation or of presumed neurological process. If they are not themselves discernible in the conscious experience, they are not conscious. But, then, in what sense can they be said to continue to exist as elements of consciousness? If we were to disregard Titchener's own rejection of "mental" as anything but "conscious" (note, for instance, his stance in the imageless thought controversy) and say that they continue to exist subconsciously, we would be asserting that the subject is, in fact, aware of warmth and of cold, but not aware of these awarenesses, and also aware of heat of which awareness he is aware. Apart from the fact that I can think of no reason for making such an assertion, this is tantamount to asserting that there are three primary awarenesses involved: warmth, cold, and the compound of warmth and cold. In the analog, the parallel assertion would be that, in water, hydrogen and oxygen continue to exist in their free states while simultaneously existing in their bound states—an assertion that I feel impelled to reject. By the same token, I must reject the interpretation that warmth and cold continue to exist subconsciously in the experience of heat. It follows that warmth and cold cannot be said to continue to exist in the compound and that the compound is therefore not a compound. Thus, the Titchenerian premises do not admit any true compounds, and the only combination of elements that are logically admissible are mosaic configurations. That is, the only admissible elements are those that are discernible within conscious experience, and there is no reason for limiting the concept "element" to those experiences associated with simple stimuli. Reenter, then, the Gestalt argument, with full force. It may also, incidentally, be recalled that the Gestalt movement was launched, via Wertheimer's experiments on the phi phenomenon, in the form not of an assault on the doctrine of elements of consciousness, as such but rather of a frontal assault of the implied neurological doctrine of elementary neural processes with which the supposed elements of consciousness are associated.

The second issue on which Titchenerian psychology fell was the issue of the stimulus error. The Titchenerian introspecter was enjoined and trained to ignore all objective reference and meaning in his introspection, and, since the object in a typical Titchenerian experiment was provided in the form of experimental stimulation, the subject was enjoined against making the mistake of describing the stimulus, as any naïve subject may be expected to do, instead of his awareness of the stimulus. It was the experience that concerned Titchener, not the experienced.

The Titchenerian project was thus in sharpest contrast with the Husserlian project of a pure phenomenology. Husserl, not granting (or, more precisely, setting aside as essentially irrelevant the issue of) the independent existence of objects, could devote himself and his disciples to the study of consciousness on the basic axiom that there can be no consciousness except as consciousness of something. Within the framework of Husserlian phenomenology, there can be no stimulus error because, as far as the phenomenologist is concerned, there is no stimulus outside of consciousness and there is no consciousness apart from its object. The two radically different approaches to the investigation of consciousness did not come into direct apposition with one another, however, so that the contrast did not lead to any confrontation of the dividing issue. Phenomenology, both as philosophy and as psychology, flourished on the European continent, but remained largely unknown in the United States and had barely any impact here—except, of course, through Gestalt theory, which emphasized quite different issues, and through specific problems such as the constancy phenomena and the modes of appearance of color.

In the United States, the increasingly prevailing atmosphere of functionalism, pragmatism, and practical interests was thoroughly inhospitable to a psychology concerned with avoiding the stimulus error. The considerable influence of the latter survived the expansion of psychological horizons beyond the givens of consciousness as long as it did mainly through the personal impact of Titchener himself and a relatively small band of devoted disciples. The more interested psychologists became in such matters as animal learning, the measurement of individual differences, the acquisition of motor skills, reaction time, fatigue, child development, and the reliability of testimony, the smaller the relative emphasis in their collective effort on what the exploration of consciousness had to offer them. The fact is, however, that psychologists did not abandon introspection, though they came to prefer to refer to it as the subject's verbal report; even today, there is no dearth of psychologists who consider it important to sometimes ask the articulate human subject what he perceives and thinks and how he feels in various experimental situations. But psychologists had no use for introspection that had no bearing on the subject's relation to the world around him. In this kind of atmosphere, Titchenerian psychology had to die, and this regardless of the issue of elementarism and the impact of the behaviorist revolution.

It is, however, one thing for a line of inquiry to be abandoned because there does not happen to be anyone around interested in pursuing it and quite another to remain oblivious to what it is that is being abandoned, without any assessment of the worth of what is going by the board; and, I will warrant, most psychologists had little comprehension of what it was that Titchener had to offer. Moreover, I do not believe that the nature of Titchener's offering is fully comprehensible without the recognition of the dual awareness involved in consciousness.

Consider what the subject is saying when he tells us something like "I see red." Is he telling us about a property that seems to belong to something he is looking at or is he telling us about a quality of his experience? This is what the concept of the stimulus error is about. If the subject says, "Look at that red box," is he telling us something about his experience or is he telling us something about the box? To be sure, his directive implies that he experiences the box as having the property of redness, but does it convey any information, implied or otherwise, about the nature and properties of his experience of redness? As a psychologist, Titchener did not want to know about boxes, but about experiences. He, therefore, quite properly instructed the subject, in effect, "When you look at that box, do not tell me anything about the box and its properties. Do tell me all that you can about your experience of the box." From the point of view of the nature of the experience rather than what it is an experience of, it is entirely irrelevant that the primary object is a box, made of some particular material, capable of containing things that do not exceed a certain size, that its color signifies a special kind of content; the meaning, properties, functions, classification, and so on of the primary object are irrelevant because the object of concern is not the object of the primary awareness but the primary awareness itself. It also follows that, insofar as psychology is concerned with the study of awarenesses as such, these must be conscious awarenesses, for the Titchenerian introspecter is scrutinizing his awarenesses. The naïve subject will tell you about what he sees, not about his seeing, and thus commit the stimulus error. None of this makes any sense, however, without recognizing the dual action in conscious awareness and, by the same token, for all of Titchener's antipathy as a systematic psychologist to the concept of the subconscious, without opening the door to the latter concept. Conversely, granting the dual action in consciousness, it becomes sensible to inquire about the properties of awareness$_1$ as an object of awareness$_2$. The failure of the Titchenerians to clarify this issue, however, inevitably generated an attitude of indifference on the part of most psychologists, not only because the Titchenerian objectives did not seem to be functionally significant, but because they did not make sense.

The third issue on which Titchenerian psychology fell has to do with the question of whether there is available a method of studying what Titchener wanted to study, in effect, whether there can be any science of psychology at all if this science were to be construed as Titchener wanted to construe it.

Consider again the subject who says, "I see red." Insofar as he is referring to a property of a peripheral object, the meaning of his statement is, in principle, readily ascertainable. One needs only to determine how he uses the term with respect to the sorting of objects and how objects are sorted by others who use the term and/or how these objects vary with respect to their physical properties. In other words, we can compare the referents of the peripheral objects. Even terms describing emotion are readily understandable on this basis. Thus a term like "afraid" is initially standardized on jointly observable behavior. It is readily extended to the case in which major visible, audible, and olfactory aspects of such behavior are suppressed, but the basic relation to the object (beginning the movement to flee, narrowing the range of normal attention with associated increased attention to various bodily reactions and the nature of the separation of self from object, disarticulation of the cognitive field, expectation of imminent disaster to the self, and so forth) remains essentially unaltered and evidenced in reduced cues; to the case in which the observer has nothing whatever to go by but the word of the subject (in which case the subject's statement may be open to question, but it is nonetheless clear what he is saying); to the case in which the subject himself cannot identify what it is he is afraid of beyond a vague "something"; to the pure object-related cognitive content (as in, "This is a *fearsome* object"), which is open to intersubjective standardization on the sorting principle.

How does one, however, compare referents when the referents are, in principle, open only to one observer? How can I ever be sure that the redness of my experience of a red object is the same as the redness of your experience of the same object? How can I be sure that the fearfulness in my fear experience is the same as the fearfulness in yours, even though we are frightened by the same object? I have (with your cooperation) access to your directed activity with respect to the primary object, and you to mine. But how, with the best will in the world, can you help me to gain observational access to what you observe when you observe your experience?

The issue involved in these questions will soon be sharpened when I consider the problem of the qualities of experience. For the moment, however, let me note that John B. Watson flatly asserted that it is, in principle, impossible to standardize the usage of terms referring to experiences as objects. This is the essence of the behaviorist revolution: not the concern with behavior as psychological subject matter nor the interpretation of experience as behavior; not the project of investigating the physiological correlates of behavior, however the latter term is understood, nor the doctrine that all mental events are reducible to physiological events; not the project of learning how to predict and control responses from a knowledge of and control over the stimulus conditions; not the development of methodology that eliminates reliance on the testimony of the subject nor the insistence on restriction to such methodology; and not the emergence of a respectable language that marked the "psychological scientist," a language that freely admitted such highly ambiguous terms as "stimulus" and "response" and any other terms so long as they were declared to have been operationally defined (regardless of subsequent usage and/or whether the defining operations are sufficiently specified to satisfy the professed goal of identifying the referents unequivocally). All the latter are associated with behaviorism and perhaps, in combination, do spell out something unique; but no one of them is unique to psychologists identified as behaviorists nor represents a unique contribution of such psychologists, and none of them is shared by all psychologists who identify themselves and are identified by others as behaviorists.[2] What is special about behaviorism is the denial, as a matter of principle, of the possibility of the Titchenerian project. For, if there is no way of determining the

[2] Compare R. S. Woodworth, "Four Varieties of Behaviorism," in R. S. Woodworth, *Psychological Issues* (New York: Columbia University Press, 1939), pp. 128–135. Note also how Woodworth misses the essential issue as he professes puzzlement on pp. viii and 421 as to how to answer the question whether he himself is a behaviorist.

subject's usage of terminology, then there is no way for the subject to communicate his observations to us; our observations of our own experiences must remain forever incommunicable. Experiences, as objects, do not exist for science, not if a defining characteristic of science is the communicability of knowledge and not until we can find some way of getting to know what the subject observes as he observes his own experiences.

When, as a young student of psychology, I began to show signs of recovery from the religious fervor with which I had become suffused on reading Watson, I began to wonder how much of the new revelation consisted of nothing more substantial than a play on words. Introspection, as a method, seemed to be legitimate so long as one ignored the process and referred to the product as the subject's verbal report; mentalistic concepts like those pertaining to sensory experience were legitimized by referring to them as differential responses to various modes and patterns of stimuli; imagery, as responses to entopic stimuli; thought, as subvocal and subgestural speech; the unconscious, as unverbalized responses; and even the oedipus complex, as fixation (overlearning) due to maternal overstimulation of the infant's erogenous zones. Here was a militant movement whose war cry was that thus-and-such does not belong in scientific psychology, and this movement did not seem to be leaving anything out, only renaming. The issue of some of the questionable translations aside, the point that I was missing was that the legitimacy of primary behaviors, including primary awarenesses, was never questioned as a matter of general principle, except by confusion. What was being challenged was the possibility of investigating what these primary behaviors looked or felt like to the subject.

As a matter of fact, the situation with respect to the investigation of the properties of awarenesses is not nearly so desperate as the Watsonian behaviorists made it out to be.

For one thing, there is an issue of parsimony involved. It is conceivable that, if we could but make the comparison, it would turn out that your "redness" is exactly like my "greenness" and my "greenness" exactly like your "redness." Since, however, we both call the same objects "red" and similarly agree on calling other objects "green," it would follow that you have the experience that I would call "green" when you look at what we both agree is a red object and that I have the experience that you would call "red" when I look at what we both agree is a green object. To take such a possibility seriously, however, we would have to assume that, given (1) quite similar nervous systems in terms of gross anatomy and neurophysiological process, (2) identical or matchable discriminations, under comparable conditions, with respect to jointly available objects, and (3) identical or matchable ordering of experiences with respect to the latter, our experiences may nevertheless have quite different properties. Such an assumption violates the principle of parsimony and the burden of proof would rest on whoever asserts the differences.

It may perhaps be argued that such proof is already available, namely, that under the conditions stated in the preceding paragraph, the qualities of experience may nevertheless vary. A familiar example may be taken as typical of this line of evidence. Take a homogeneously and vividly colored yellow rectangle with a fixation point marked at its approximate center. Cover the part of the rectangle to the right of the fixation point with a gray paper. Stare fixedly at the fixation point for about one minute and then, while continuing to stare at the point, slide the gray paper away. The odds are that you will now see the color on the left-hand side of the rectangle as much less saturated than that on the right-hand side. Since the rectangle has not been altered, the change must be in your experience of it. What is most impressive about this demonstration is that the subject is not normally aware of the qualitative change in the experience and would continue to remain unaware of its having taken place, but for the evidence of his experience of the right side. Now, then, if the identical person can within an interval of one minute have a variety of qualities of his own "yellow," without awareness of the variation, does it not follow, *a fortiori*, that the yellow of one person's experience cannot be assumed to be qualitatively identical with the yellow of another's?

Far from contradicting the proposition that, under similar conditions, the similarly labeled qualities of experience must, on the grounds of parsimony, be presumed to be similar, this line of evidence offers the most telling confirmation of it. For, apart from the fact that the example violates one of the terms of the proposition (namely, the similarity of the conditions of similarly labeled experiences, and these conditions do change from the beginning to the end of the time interval) and though the example still does not tell us whether, saturation aside, the yellowness of one person matches that of another, this entire line of evidence demonstrates that the qualities of experience undergo parallel transformations under similar conditions.

If, however, we may assume that, under like conditions, the qualities of experience are alike, it follows that we can arrange for common referents in the realm of experience and can, hence, intersubjectively standardize the terminology descriptive of experience.

In the second place, we must note that much of this terminology descriptive of experience is precisely the same as the terminology appropriate to the description of things and events in the physical world.[3] The duration of an experience, for instance, can be clocked; and all terms referring to extension also have common meaning. The shape of an after-image (which is a mode of experiencing a primary object) is similar to the shape of the primary object and its size varies proportionately to the square of the distance between the subject and the surface on which the image · is projected; but the latter relationship (Emmert's law) does not hold for eidetic images and does not have any bearing on the after-image experienced with closed eyes. Similarly, there is not a term in my characterization of fear that does not lend itself to extensional definition; and, insofar as the reader is concerned, the unambiguous comprehensibility of that characterization is not contingent on whether I was describing the behavior of other persons in the context of feared objects or describing my own experience. Or, again, in the distinction, as drawn in the preceding chapter, between attributive and cognitive clearness. Or the dimensions of degrees of awareness.

There is also evidence of the communality of the meaning structure of terms that describe experience in the remarkable concurrences in judgments of physiognomic line drawings of what certain experiences feel like and in semantic differential profiles associated with such terms. Moreover, as a consequence of the confusion between perceptions and awareness of perceptions, we draw some of our terminology for object qualities from experience qualities without interfering with our intersubjective consistency in classifying objects. Thus, we do not find anything like wavelengths in our experience of color and our color words for objects are taken from our respective private sortings of our color experiences; yet we sort objects consistently and apply the same color words to them.

Finally, note that, insofar as our concern is with the discovery of relationships among events, it does not make the slightest iota of a difference whether the redness of my experience is identical with the redness of yours. For both of us, granted that neither has any deficiency of color vision, the negative after-image of a green object is red. And

---

[3] Compare Edwin G. Boring, *The Physical Dimensions of Consciousness* (New York: Century, 1933).

we both undergo the desaturation of the yellow rectangle on prolonged fixed inspection of a point in it, presumably because of the fusion of the direct percept with the negative after-image. With stuffed noses, we will both find our food tasteless. Examples can be multiplied almost endlessly.

It thus becomes apparent that the success of the Watsonian revolution against Titchenerian psychology does not rest on the validity of its central contention, namely, that conscious experience is inaccessible to scientific investigation. It capitalized on the sense of confusion generated by inadequate conceptualization and terminological inadequacy; it found a vulnerable target in the hypostatization of psychological process; it provided conceptual justification for the increasing disregard of the uncompromising restrictiveness of the Titchenerian project; it provided a rallying point for a variety of independent movements that were not necessarily mutually consistent (for example, the movement to physiologize all of psychology and the movement to build a stimulus-response psychology around the empty organism) but equally bent on robotizing the human being; it found a potent weapon in the doctrine of conditioning which, in one sense, was the old associationist doctrine in a new garb, but which did not carry the limitation of being restricted to ideas and could seemingly accommodate into one conceptual framework the accumulating knowledge of both animal and human learning; and, above all, it made up for its own conceptual limitations and the vulnerability of its own central tenet by its fervid militancy.

The fact that experience is, as such, amenable to scientific investigation does not solve a major problem posed by the qualities of experience, for it is the fact of qualities of experience that gives the mind its distinctive character *vis à vis* the physical world and is hence at the root of the mind-body problem. I may reiterate my view that mind is merely a collective term for spontaneous directed activity (or, more narrowly and traditionally construed, minimal spontaneous directed activity), and it is conceivable that I may even win over some ardent disciples. I would hope, however, that I cannot succeed in eliminating a gnawing doubt as to the sufficiency of my views so long as my disciples are capable of experiencing ardency, reverence, exaltation, satisfaction, humility, illumination, color, beauty, ugliness, darkness, and so forth, and so long as I fail to do justice to the qualities of these experiences. It is conceivable that all varieties of experience are perfectly distinguishable one from another in terms describing species and subspecies of spontaneous directed activity and, hence, definable in these terms. Yet, there is assuredly a difference between sufficiency of definition and sufficiency of characterization. My signature and my fingerprints may each be sufficient to uniquely identify me, and, for many purposes, either may be sufficient to establish correlations between my presence and certain other variables. But I submit that I am not sufficiently characterized by these attributes; nor are these necessarily the attributes that will make comprehensible the established correlations. I suspect that not even the most confirmed operationalist would be quite satisfied with the statement "Those fingerprints and signature still remember the poem they memorized in a part-whole-method-of-memorizing experiment in Psychology 1." The unique pattern of whorls and ridges that characterizes my fingerprints was there, as it is with me now, and my signature can testify to my presence on both occasions; but assuredly neither fingerprints nor signature had very much to do with the memorizing.

My point is that one can define, in the sense of providing clear and efficient criteria for separating all positive from all negative instances and, further, find that the separation facilitates the discovery of unexceptionable laws and still miss the essense of that which is defined. To be sure, I have been trying to show that the attributes I have seized on are not mere trivialities, incidental though perfect correlates of psychological process, by demonstrating that they clarify a large variety of psychological concepts. I shall also indicate in a later chapter that my conceptualization disposes of the major problem that scientists have experienced in the concept of mind. Even so, I am now saying that unless and until I can show how to cope with the qualities of experience, there remains ground for suspecting that I am somehow missing the essence. For, whatever else naïve experience may know, the outstanding property of mind is to be found precisely in the qualities, the "raw feels," of experience. So long as the raw feels persist, no account of the mind that sets them aside can be quite convincing.

It is not my intention to show why the particular qualities of experience are what they are, not even with respect to a limited number. I am, in fact, quite certain that I cannot do so with respect to the so-called secondary qualities. They are what they are—and that seems to be that, at least for the present. My aspiration is rather the more limited one of trying to set up a framework within which they can be more adequately comprehended than they would otherwise be and to dispel a number of confusions that make the problem of the qualities more intractable than it need be. Specifically, I shall deal with three issues: (1) the issue of epiphenomenalism, (2) the issue of primary *vs.* secondary qualities, and (3) the issue of the qualities of things *vs.* the qualities of experience.

When I asserted earlier that, within the context of a search for relationships, it makes no difference whether the qualities of our comparable experiences are identical, it may have seemed that I was adopting an epiphenomenalist position. Epiphenomenalism, it may be recalled, is the view that accepts the reality of mind, but excludes it from any participation in causal process, even in the realm of the mind. An idea, feeling, desire, intention—or anything else that you may think of in the realm of the mind—not only has no consequence with respect to bodily process, according to this doctrine, but has no consequence with respect to any other idea, feeling, and so forth. Every mental state, event, or process is assumed to be an incidental and inconsequential correlate of physiological process. It has no determinative bearing on, or continuity with, any other mental event; given the bodily state with which it is associated, it pops out, only to be replaced by another or by a mental gap as the bodily state changes. All continuities and determinations occur in the realm of matter, that is, in the bodily processes, in processes of the physical environment, and in the interaction of the two. Any assertion implying some consequence to the mind is merely a convenient device (justifiable only by ignorance) for referring to the as yet unknown material events within which the real causality resides.

I shall return to the issue in a later chapter. In the meantime, however, let it be noted that, insofar as my assertion smacks of epiphenomenalism, it is a far more limited epiphenomenalism than the general doctrine. At most, I am conceding that there is one (but only one) aspect of mind that must be assigned an epiphenomenal status, namely, the qualities (and probably only the secondary qualities at that) of experience. I have not backtracked at all from my contentions that all that has traditionally been identified as mental can be subsumed under the concept of behavior as I have characterized the latter, that behavior cannot be adequately characterized in terms of physiological events or in terms of separate but interacting physiological and environmental events, and that all behavior (including minimal behavior) has consequence as such. I have not asserted that every aspect of every behavior necessarily has consequence, and my maximal concession is that, with respect to some behaviors (the discrimination of the experience of color, tone, and other qualities), there is an aspect that is inconsequential. Let us examine this concession a bit more closely.

First, it should be clear that I am saying that the qualities are, at most, epiphenomena of certain behaviors and not of the physiological processes involved in these behaviors. The quality of an experience is a quality of a behavior. Since the latter cannot be adequately described in purely physiological terms, the quality of an experience cannot be taken as the quality of a merely physiological event.

Second, what I have conceded is that it makes no difference if the redness of your experience is not identical with the redness of mine, and similarly with respect to other qualities, so long as there are parallel changes in the qualities of our experiences under comparable conditions, that is, so long as the order and transformations of our experiential qualities are governed by the same laws—and the evidence is that they are.

Consider, now, an attribute of a physical thing, say, its mass or weight. The time was when it was tenable to assume that its attributes inhered in the thing. This assumption is no longer tenable, at least not in any simple fashion. The same thing will have different weights in different gravitational fields which, in turn, depends on relationships among masses; and the same thing will have different masses relative to another thing, depending on how fast it is traveling with respect to the latter. Indeed, as Whitehead has shown,[4] the very notion of location in space-time (and this, of course, subsumes within it all notions of distance, shape, rate of change, and so forth) is untenable and meaningless without the at least implicit reference of any location to all other locations. Thus, a thing cannot even be said to have a physical shape except in terms of an implied reference to the entire universe that surrounds it. My point is that the attributes of a thing do not inhere in the thing but in an infinitely complex network of relationships. Alternatively, if we must persist in thinking of things as possessing, so long as the things themselves are not changed, fixed and invariant attributes, then the attributes may not properly be thought of in terms of our usual conceptions of them, but must rather be thought of in terms of mathematical equations. Thus, the weight of a thing does not have the value W, but would have to be thought of as the property having the value X in gravitational field A, the value Y in gravitational field B, the value Z in gravitational field C, and so on. We can say that it weighs W units only to the extent that we take for granted a particular gravitational field and assume that the measure is taken from a relatively static position relative to it.

[4] Alfred North Whitehead, *Science and the Modern World* (New York: Macmillan, 1925).

What I have just described with respect to the attributes of things applies as well to the qualities of experience. That is, the qualities of experience do not inhere in the experiences themselves but in the network of relationships in which they are imbedded. The lawfulness of qualitative order and change, however, is precisely the network of relationships in which the qualities are imbedded. If we were· reasonably confident that we knew all the conditions of qualitative order and transition, we could with equal confidence determine whether your redness and my redness are in fact identical; and, if we had sufficient control over these conditions, I could display my redness to you not by giving you access to the direct observation of my experience but by duplicating this experience for you. When, therefore, I assert that, insofar as our concern is with the discovery of relationships among events, it makes no difference whether your redness and mine are identical, I am saying no more than that we do not have to await this determination before we can proceed with the investigation of the lawful conditions of the qualities.

I turn now to the issue of the distinction of primary from secondary qualities. The distinction had already been drawn by Descartes, but it was raised to the level of a doctrine by John Locke. As developed by Locke, things are invested with powers to affect other things. Among these powers are the powers to generate ideas of the things. Some of these ideas resemble actual properties of the things that generate them; others do not. The powers to generate the first kind of ideas are primary qualities; the powers to generate the second kind of ideas are secondary qualities. Note that, in Locke's conceptualization, the qualities are qualities of things and not qualities of experience. Another, and perhaps more basic distinction that he makes between primary and secondary qualities is that the former are utterly inseparable from things whereas the latter involve properties attributed to things but not inseparable from them. The primary qualities, according to Locke, are such properties as solidity, figure (shape and position), state of motion, and number. Secondary qualities involve such attributes as color, tone, and taste. No matter what you do to a thing, that which it becomes will still have the qualities of solidity, figure, motion, and number; but it will not necessarily retain color, taste, and so on. The primary qualities are thus inherent in *thingness*; the secondary qualities are not.

We may or may not be greatly impressed by the doctrine, but it would have taken a remarkable prophet to have foreseen the profound repercussions it would have in the history of philosophy, so innocuous does it seem. Yet, that is exactly what did happen. For it led George Berkeley to raise the question of how we know that the ideas of the primary qualities do, in fact, correspond to the actual properties of things and, thence, to his doctrine of *esse est percipi*, subjective idealism, Humian skepticism, objective idealism, positivism, and so on. There were, of course, other roots to these developments, including a major one in the Cartesian distinction of body and mind. (I discuss some of these developments below in this chapter and others in Chapter 8.) My immediate concern is with the fact that Berkeley's contribution to these developments, apart from some lamentable lapses in logical rigor, rested on two insidious distortions of the Lockian doctrine.

Locke had argued, in terms of an illusion that still goes by his name, that our experience of temperature cannot be taken as a valid indicator of an actual property of a thing since we can simultaneously experience the thing as being both hot and cold. The distortion implicit in the development of Berkeley's argument is that the demonstration proves that temperature is a pure fabrication of the mind and that the properties of the thing have nothing to do with the experience. Apart from Locke's implicit denial of this interpretation—the secondary qualities in his doctrine are as much powers of things as are the primary qualities—the illusion could hardly be demonstrated on Berkeley's interpretation. The demonstration requires hot, cold, and lukewarm water. How shall we go about arranging the demonstration? Wait until our minds happen to project heat, cold, and lukewarmness? Or shall we proceed to heat up some water, refrigerate another quantity of water, and, perhaps, mix equal portions of the heated and chilled water to get our lukewarm water? Clearly, there is a property of the water that is involved, and not merely our perceptual act. Nor does the dependability of the illusion itself make much sense without reference to the mechanism of sensory adaptation to surrounding temperature, that is, without a sensory apparatus to become adapted and an existing surround to which it adapts.

Having smuggled his foregone conclusion into his interpretation of secondary qualities, Berkeley proceeded to turn the argument for the distinction of the secondary qualities around in order to annihilate the primary qualities, that is, to show that there are only secondary qualities, and therein introduced his second distortion of the Lockian doctrine. In effect, he argued that, just as the same thing can be experienced as having different temperatures, it can be experienced as having different shapes and the like. Thus, a cylindrical object may be experienced as circular, elliptical, or rectangular, depending on the angle from which it is viewed. What, then, does it mean to say that our idea (perception) of the shape of the object is similar to an actual property of the object?

What Locke had contended, however, was not that our perception of the shape of the object is necessarily veridical, but of its *shapeliness,* that is, of the fact that it has shape. His argument clearly implies that he was not concerned with its particular shape. Take any thing, he said, and cut it up. Each of the parts will still have shape; and, if you cut each of the pieces into the tiniest of tiny particles, each of the latter will still have shape.

Let me note, in passing, that Berkeley, in the context of his argument concerning the primary qualities, repeated the error in his misrepresentation of the secondary qualities. The different apparent shapes of the same object are incomprehensible if the object did not have a definite shape and if light did not have the properties that it has. The projection of a circular shape on any plane surface not parallel to it is an ellipse or a rectangle; that is all that is open to view, and that is what would be recorded by a camera.[5] If there is any problem here, it is the reverse one, namely, that the apparent sizes and shapes of objects do not vary as much as they ought to in terms of the variance of the projections. The seer, in the course of his normal concerns with an object and unlike the camera, minimizes the variability in its appearances by viewing it relativistically in the context of the appearances of other objects; that is, the seer's usual concern is with the object as such and not with its projections at various loci in space.[6]

In fairness to Berkeley, it should be said that Locke invited the distortions. He treated as equivalent two notions that are quite independent of each other (the inherent attributes of formed matter—"bodies," in his terminology—and the similarity of the percept to the actual prop-

[5] Whitehead, *ibid.*, credits Berkeley with an idea that is far in advance of the latter's era; I think that Whitehead is here being overly charitable. To be sure, Berkeley did recognize that the same object has different appearances in different perspectives, but all that this meant to Berkeley was that no appearance can be taken as veridical. What Whitehead reads into Berkeley is the germ of the idea that any given shape involves not merely its measurements in its given locus, but a definite projection at any other locus, given some rules of projection; thus, the idea of shape involves not merely a definite set of measurements at the given locus but an infinity of definite sets of measurements at other loci. Whitehead is concerned with amplifying the properties of reality, independently of any observer; Berkeley is concerned with denying any reality apart from an observer.

[6] That the viewer can approximate in his seeing, if he so elects, the full variability of the projections attests to the fact that vision is not merely a matter of light striking the eyes, but an active process.

erties of the perceived body), and he did not deal with them coordinately with respect to the primary and secondary qualities. Thus, if the primary qualities refer to the inherent generic attributes of bodies, without regard to the particular statuses or values of the attributes, it is difficult to see why temperature should be excluded from among the primary attributes: After all, even though the same water may be experienced as hot and cold, hot and cold—and lukewarm, as well—reflect degrees of temperature. If, alternatively, the emphasis is on the similarity of the percept to that which is perceived, it is difficult to see why form, with its variability of appearance under different conditions, should be excluded from the secondary qualities whereas the variability of the experience of temperature under different conditions should place temperature among the secondary qualities. It seems likely to me that, if there is any validity to the distinction (and the common acceptance of the distinction, Berkeley's argument to the contrary notwithstanding, seems to attest to the fact that Locke had indeed gotten hold of something significant), Locke had first grasped it intuitively and then attempted unsuccessfully to rationalize his intuition.

Tolman[7] has suggested that the distinction that Locke was seeking has to do with the correlations of discriminanda and manipulanda. Discriminanda are the properties of objects that make it possible, given certain sensory capacities, to discriminate one object from another or the same object under different conditions. Manipulanda are the properties of objects that make it possible, given certain motor capacities, to engage in certain motor activities involving these objects. Specifically with reference to the present context, he suggests that certain kinds of discriminanda tend to be consistently correlated with particular manipulanda, whereas other kinds of discriminanda have no consistent relationship to any manipulanda. Thus, the solidity of an object is related to both discriminanda (the definiteness and stability of its shape, its bearing on experiences of touch, pressure, and kinesthesis as one comes into contact with it and as one handles it) and manipulanda (what one can do to it and the uses one can make of it); the same object may, however, also have qualities of color, temperature, smell, and so on that are not related to what one can do with it in any consistent way and that can be altered without any serious consequence for the manipulability of the object. Tolman notes that the correlational

[7] Edward C. Tolman, *Purposive Behavior in Animals and Men* (New York: Century, 1932).

differences are not absolute and categorical, but a matter of degree. An object, for instance, may be so hot as to affect what I can do with it and, when I paint something, I generally do so because I am interested in spreading the color rather than in covering the object I am painting with a mere chemical substance. Similarly, both snow and marble lend themselves to being sculpted, but I am much more likely to see my sculpture a month later if I operated with marble than with snow; or, to cite one of Tolman's examples, the seemingly bent stick semi-immersed in water violates the more common correlation of a discriminandum and manipulandum. Now, Tolman notes, the traditional primary qualities are precisely those with respect to which there are relatively dependable relationships between discriminanda and manipulanda, and the traditional secondary qualities are those with respect to which there is generally no such dependable relationship.

It is to be noted that, in Tolman's as in Locke's distinction, the qualities are located in things rather than in experience. It is a plausible speculation that the history of philosophy might have been significantly different from what it has been if Locke had thought to make his distinction on the commonsense practical basis adopted by Tolman.

Even so, it is possible to make the distinction in terms that are much closer to Locke's similarity criterion without the ensuing confusion. The point involved is one that I have already made, namely, that much of the terminology descriptive of experience is precisely the same as the terminology appropriate to the description of things. In other words, the dimensions of certain qualities of experience correspond to the dimensions of things. Thus, the dimensions of my experience of the shape of an object correspond to the dimensions of the object. When I examine the physical image of a slide transparency cast on a screen I do not merely experience the shape of the image; that is, when I examine the experience itself, it has the qualities of being more or less centered on the experienced screen, of being as large as the screen (or smaller or larger than the screen), of having properties of length and height, of containing relations of perpendicularity and other angularities, and so on. Now, then, it seems to me that, when Locke ascribed to primary qualities the condition of similarity between experience and thing, he really meant to imply nothing more than similarity with respect to *dimensionality*. On the other hand, with respect to other experiences, there are different dimensionalities involved in the experience than in the thing. The physical dimension involved in the experience of color or tone is one of frequency of vibration or wavelength, and there is nothing of these properties in the corresponding experiences;[8] moreover, the range of color experience is dimensionally a circumplex where the range of the corresponding physical events is a monotonically changing function. Similarly, the experience of heat or cold has none of the properties of rate of transmission of molecular activities. Experiences of color, tone, and temperature, then, involve secondary qualities, not merely because they are not identical with the experienced things, but because they are dimensionally different.

Finally, let me turn to the issue of the qualities of things *vs.* the qualities of experience. It has already been noted that Locke (and, in our own times, Tolman) identified the qualities with properties of things. Most contemporary usage, however, identifies the qualities with the properties of the experiences of things. The issue involved is not merely one of usage; if it were merely that, the biggest problems it would pose would be those of establishing the particular usages in concrete cases and of translation from one usage to another. The issue involved is rather one that goes to the root of an enormous amount of philosophical controversy, specifically, between realist philosophies, on the one hand, and idealist or phenomenalist philosophies, on the other. If the qualities are located in the experience rather than in the thing, then it seems that we lose any possibilities of contact with things beyond experience; that is, the only reality we can know is the reality of experience. For the experience is itself describable only in terms of its qualities, and, when we turn to the conditions of the experience, the latter are only known as they are experienced, that is, they too are located in the realm of experience. It, therefore, seems like a stratagem of desperation to locate the qualities in the things, a stratagem that converts experience into experience *of* things and thereby restores a measure of the commonsense view that we do have knowledge of things beyond experience.

Even so, when push came to shove, both Locke and Tolman lined up with the idealists. Thus, in a passage quoted by Boring,[9] Locke wrote, "Since the mind, in all its thoughts and reasonings, has no other immediate object but its own ideas, which it alone does or can contemplate, it is evident that our knowledge is only conversant about them." And Tolman, in common with all behaviorists, was thoroughly committed to the doctrines of operationalism and positivism, namely,

[8] One can, of course, experience oscillations of color or tone (as in the experiences of flicker and beat), but these are not the oscillations under discussion.
[9] Edwin G. Boring, *A History of Experimental Psychology,* 2d ed. (New York: Appleton-Century-Crofts, 1957), p. 172.

the view that, even though one assumes the existence of things beyond experience, knowledge has no way of escaping beyond the realm of experience. It is a curious paradox of our times that behaviorism that has no use at all for mentalism should itself be so thoroughly committed to imprisonment within the confines of philosophical mentalism.

The fundamental trouble traces back to the Cartesian dualism of extended substance (which is matter) and unextended substance (which is mind) and the consequent plaguing of both philosophy and science by the failure to find a satisfactory passageway between the two realms. Note how the Cartesian dualism imposes itself on the problem of the qualities: Regardless of whether the word "qualities" is assigned to the properties of things of which there are counterparts in experience or to the properties of the counterparts themselves, there are, in both cases, the things and their counterparts, and, in either case, there is no bridge between the thing and its counterpart in experience.

To anyone but a philosopher in his philosophizing moments, however (and, of course, scientists as they more or less unwittingly take a philosophical stance), it is simply unbelievable that we do not deal with things. It is unbelievable that, when I bite into an apple, I am really merely biting into my idea of an apple and that, when I turn my back on a chair to sit down on it, it is merely an image of a chair to which I am directing myself and not a solid substantial chair the existence and presence of which are independent of my perception of it. Philosophers to the contrary notwithstanding, I, at least, am convinced that I bite into real apples and not into ideas of them and that I sit on real chairs and not on images; and if some prankster were to steal the chair away even as I am engaged in the act of sitting down on it, it is still the real chair toward which my action is directed, and not my image of it, even though it is no longer where I think it is.

Suppose that I have hallucinated a chair that was never there where I have begun my act of sitting down on it. Apart from the fact that I cannot complete my act, I submit that my act is, for as long as I engage in it, directed at a real and solid chair, which I mistakenly believe to be there, and not at an image. That a real chair is involved, you will have to acknowledge in your very diagnosis that I am hallucinating a chair; for your diagnosis is predicated, in part, on the absence of the real chair; or would you prefer to interpret such an hallucinatory episode as constituted of nothing but your image of me trying to sit down on your image of a nonexisting chair? One difference between a veridical perception and an hallucination is that the former is conditional on the presence of the object; but the actual presence or absence of the object does not, up to the point where there is no longer support for continuing the action, change the nature of the transaction. One does not create hallucinated objects out of nothing; one misplaces them or generates them out of misplaced components. No one, be he philosopher or psychotic, ever tries to sit down on an image. The transaction may be aborted, but it is in its nature a transaction with a real object.

Can I not, however, imagine things that have no counterparts in reality—a man walking through a stone wall, centaurs, mermaids, and so on? Of course, I can, but only in a sense. What is involved here is that, in such imaginings, I deal with parts of real things, which I bring together in unusual juxtaposition. In principle, this is no different than the creation of new physical things and living organisms the like of which have never existed before. Experimental embryologists have, for instance, generated some pretty weird creatures. In their laboratories, cyclops, hydra-headed monsters, and creatures undreamed of in any mythology abound. Take a frog embryo, for example, at a certain point in its development and transplant tissue that normally would become a leg to a region the development of which produces the top of the skull. In time, you will have a frog with a leg growing out if its skull and, as this frog eats, the leg will wag in accompaniment.

Even so, the greater the deviation of the imaginative juxtaposition from the normal reality, the more difficult it becomes, especially without the aid of an objective representation, such as a physically real picture; and these imaginings are constrained by realistic requirements. Try to imagine a man walking through a stone wall without apparent changes in the substance of either! It is easy to word the event, words being easily manipulable objective entities, but to picture it in the imagination, that is something else again. Or even to imagine the man walking through, the wall giving way only to the exact bounds of the man's body. The best I myself can manage on that one is a series of stills.

Centaurs and mermaids are easy to imagine because we have had dealings with them in picture and story. But try to imagine a man-horse combination constructed according to the following specifications: The upper right section is hewn out of the corresponding part of a man's body along some irregular contour, the upper left section is hewn out of the matching part of a horse's body, the midsection is similarly composed out of man and horse sections but with the sides of the extractions reversed, and the lower section is similarly composed but with a return to the original sides. Even if you can lick the problems of the size differentials and irregular contours, I warrant that you will have trouble holding on to the image; and then try to imagine this creature in motion!

Or try to imagine the centaur and mermaid in sexual congress. If you are at all like me, you will have to approach the task in a problem-solving way before you can undertake the imaginative representation. You will, for instance, realize that centaurs and mermaids have different normal habitats in the reality of such creatures.[10] Where, then, shall the congress take place? Then you will discover that the relevant section of the centaur is, after all, horse; and horses (like centaurs in their relations with centaureses) mount their mares. Shall the centaur assume his normal mounting position, the mermaid presenting herself *à tergo,* or shall the mermaid face her centaur slinging the lower part of her body under him and take on the onus of the subsequent activity? Alas, the problems are not yet all solved. Mermaids are not constructed with vaults capable of receiving centaurian phalli, and you will have to invent one—as soon as you have decided where to place it. It seems clear that even in our imaginative dealings with nonexisting creatures we have to respect some kind of reality.

My point is that, in all behavior there is commerce with real objects, and, if the objects happen to be physical things, there is commerce with physical things. The object is included in the transaction that constitutes behavior; the relation of object to behavior is, therefore, not the relation of a thing to its counterpart but a relation of containment. There are no two realms (though there are two kinds of events under discussion, the thing-event as such and the including behavior-event), and there is, consequently, no need for bridges between the two realms. Moreover, if my contention is accepted that awarenesses are behaviors, then what I have just said about behaviors holds for awarenesses.

I will now contend that qualities are always qualities of objects of awareness. Thus, if the objects are physical things or aspects of physical things, the qualities are the qualities of these things or aspects. Bear in mind that the awareness of physical things are primary awarenesses that need not necessarily become the objects of secondary awarenesses; that is, they may remain subconscious. Obviously, if they remain subconscious, they do not involve any of the raw feels of consciousness;

---

[10] It may seem odd to speak of such a reality, but there is one. This will become clearer in the next chapter where I deal with the question of the meaning of reality.

and becoming conscious does not change their qualitative content. The raw feels come in only when the primary awarenesses themselves become objects of awareness, and they are the qualities of these objects; but they do not exist until, and except insofar as, the primary awarenesses become objects.

When then are the qualities of primary awarenesses? They are the discriminanda that enter into the behavioral transaction that constitutes the awareness. It is only a step from here to the raw feels of consciousness. Primary awarenesses and behaviors also have their discriminanda; that is, they have properties in terms of which they can be discriminated one from another and categorized or ordered in various ways. The qualities of the secondary awarenesses are the discriminanda (n.b.: discriminanda with which the primary awarenesses are endowed) that are utilized in the behavior of inspecting the primary awarenesses. In both cases (that is, the qualities of primary and of secondary awarenesses), the qualities are discriminanda, but discriminanda that do not become qualities unless and until they enter into behavioral transactions. I make this distinction because different qualities of the same or equivalent objects may emerge in the course of repeated encounters with them or even in the course of the development of a particular transaction.

It now becomes apparent that Locke's primary qualities refer to instances in which certain discriminanda possessed by physical things are dimensionally similar to the discriminanda possessed by primary awarenesses; and his secondary qualities refer to instances in which the dimensions of certain discriminanda of physical things are different from those of the discriminanda of primary awarenesses. Since, however, physical things taken as objects of awareness and primary awarenesses taken as objects of awareness are quite different kinds of objects, there is no *a priori* reason that I know of to expect dimensional correspondence between their discriminanda. Nor, by the same token, can the lack of dimensional correspondence be taken as evidence of the nonexistence or the inaccessibility to knowledge of either. The sources of our knowledge of each must be examined in its own terms.

7

SOME REFLECTIONS

ON REALITY

I cannot leave the preceding chapter without further comment on my proposition a few paragraphs back that in all behavior there is commerce with real objects. I was obviously not saying that the objects of behavior are necessarily realistic in all respects; for instance, I agreed that the misplacement of the hallucinated object violates the reality of the latter. Nor was it my intention to deny that one can imaginatively concoct an object the like of which never existed, never will exist, and never could exist; but the ingredients of such a concoction are drawn from transactions with real objects, and the behavior of preparing such a concoction is constrained by reality considerations and serves directed activities involving relationships to objects not in the concoction. The issue of reality is, however, sufficiently complex and sufficiently basic to many aspects of psychology to require explication. Let me then pull together a number of ideas expressed in various contexts in this book and add some further comments.

1. I take it that a necessary and sufficient condition of the reality of anything is that its existence does not depend on the cognitive activities of observers. If I observe green gremlins perched on my desk, this does not establish that they are there; and if they are not there or anywhere else save in my observation of them, then they are not real. If, however, I do observe them, then my observation of them is real because my observation of them does not depend for its existence on itself being observed or inferred by anyone, myself included. Whether there is an emission of sound waves as a result of a falling tree in an Amazonian jungle depends only on whether it occurs and not on

whether any creature hears the sound or infers the occurrence. And whether some creature does hear the sound depends only on whether it hears it and not on whether any creature observes or infers that it hears it.

2. The reality of anything may be limited in time and space. I presume that Napoleon (*the* Napoleon Bonaparte, not another with the same name) as a person did actually exist even though he is no longer around. Depending on the coordinate system that I use, I can assert the reality of his person in a number of different ways. I could say, "Napoleon *was* real in the time 1769–1821," or I could say, "It *is* a reality that Napoleon lived in the time 1769–1821," a statement that refers not only to Napoleon but also to his reality. The then present (and thenceforth, within the bounds of the time points, eternal) reality asserted in the last proposition would continue as such (that is, as having been then present), even though this planet should explode into subatomic particles and all traces of Napoleon's existence, 1769–1821, should have vanished from the universe. It is irrelevant to the reality whether anyone knows about it, or cares. Note, however, that nothing I have said implies that whatever is real must have coordinates in time and space; I shall shortly deal with time/space-transcending realities.

3. A person may act toward an object as though it were where it is not. Insofar as he does so he violates an aspect of its reality; it is not really there. Such a violation of reality, however, may or may not be irrelevant to what he is doing with respect to the object; and to the degree that it is irrelevant, the person is still acting solely with respect to the real object. If, for instance, I write a letter to a friend whose address has been changed, I am still writing to my real friend; this is so even though I know I am sending the letter to what I know to be a no longer valid address, but do so in the hope that the post office will be able to forward it. Suppose that my friend has died, but no information bearing on the latter event has reached me; I am still addressing a real person, though I have mislocated him in time, and the mislocation is irrelevant to what I am doing, though it may be relevant to the outcome. Suppose that I know of his death but nevertheless still write and mail the letter. In the latter event, one of the following must be true: (1) my friend no longer exists, but I am addressing him in his real nonexistence, that is, both his past existence and his present nonexistence are real and I have some transaction to conduct with this remarkable object, that is, with my friend in his

present nonexistence, or (2) the manifest addressee is not really the object of my action, that is, the real object is not my deceased friend. It may, of course, constitute a challenge to me or to my therapist, and perhaps to others, to discover my real object.

4. Behavior may be directed to an object that has been misplaced or whose space-time coordinates are unknown with the intention of locating it. I do not normally remember (and have by now again forgotten) the years that bounded Napoleon's earthly existence. I needed them to make a point; so I looked them up.

5. Behavior with respect to a not immediately present object may be mediated by some kind of record or a cognitive map. But unless this behavior is itself the preparation of a map (I include the formation or correction of an image or concept under the term "mapping") or a map-reading operation, the activity relation to the not present object is to the object and not to its representation on the map. When I go to the library for a book, it is for the book and not for my image of it. When I wish that my father could have read something I recently wrote, it is to my real father that I have reference and not to my image of him. I have no difficulty in imagining my father reading the item nor in imagining his approval or his challenging and probing questions. I have no need to wish for such images since I can produce them so easily. What I cannot carry beyond the stage of the wish and the imaging is the conjunction of his full and tangible presence with my writing. But, then, has his death destroyed the reality of his relation to me and mine to him? Has his real existence from, say, my earliest recollection of him to my last been diminished by an iota merely because he is no longer tangibly present? It is with him as a real person, though no longer alive, that my wish is concerned. I do not mean to imply that I cannot behave with respect to my image of him, but that is not relevant to the present context because that would involve behavior with respect to a present object.

6. Am I, incidentally, being inconsistent with the position I took in Chapter 4 where I wrote, "The past, as such, is, of course, as nonexistent as is the future so that the assertion of an effect from some past event imputes as much consequentiality to the nonexistent as does an effect from the future"? I think not, save perhaps in my usage of the phrase, "as such" (by which I there meant to convey a contrast with presently existing residues, memories, precipitates, or transformations of the past) and the word "nonexistent" (by which I intended, "nonexistent as a causal agent"). I assuredly did not mean to imply its nonexistence

in its time or the present falsity of the proposition that it did exist in its time. Nor did I intend to imply in the preceding paragraph that my father can reach out of his pastness to affect me now. What I was asserting was his reality in his time, the reality of his present pastness, the reality of my continuing relation to him as the person he was, my ability to continue to act toward him as the person he was, and the continuing consequentiality of my continuing relation to him. I can reach out to him even though I do not believe that, except figuratively speaking, he can any longer reach out to me.

7. Cognitive errors with respect to an object do not necessarily imply that the object of my behavior is the object-as-apprehended rather than the real object-as-it-is. I do not mean to preclude the former possibility; nor do I mean to deny the reality of the object-as-apprehended. But the degree of my openness to correction through feedback in the course of my commerce with it is a kind of measure of my concern with the object-as-it-is rather than with the object-as-apprehended. Much of the history of my relation to my father was (and is) constituted of my efforts to apprehend him veridically. Yet such efforts would make little sense were I not concerned with him as an independently existing person. That my fallible image of him should have guided me in my interactions with him does not mean that I was interacting with that image, no more than my use of an erroneous map implies that my intended destination is other than it is.

8. Considerations relating to future objects are somewhat different from those relating to the past. To be sure, one may, in principle, speak of a real future just as one may speak of a real past—in the two instances, respectively, in contradistinction to the presently anticipated future and the presently construed past. Just as some behaviors are directed at correcting the presently construed past so as to bring it into closer accord with the real past, so there are behaviors directed at improving the processes of anticipating the real future.

Not all behaviors aimed at changing the construction of the past are concerned with minimizing error. Indeed, it is within the compass of human enterprise to falsify the past, that is, to reconstruct "history" in ways that increase the deviations of the construction from the reality. Other concerns with the construction of the past have to do with relevance to other present concerns. That is, even in reviewing data previously available, present preoccupations may sharpen our sensitivity to aspects of past reality that might otherwise have been missed; and both the discovery of new data and changing emphases in the scrutiny of (and search for) data may imply that no final account of any past era can ever be anticipated. It is also entirely conceivable that quite different accounts of the same past events may be, apart from sins of omission, equally free of error. In any case, whether our concern with the exploration of the past is to distort the record, or to correct it, or to make it more currently relevant, it does not seem to be within the bounds of human possibility to change the real past.

The situation is, however, quite different in this respect with regard to the real future. Much of human endeavor, whether on the scale of the individual life history or on the scale of the total course of human events, is concerned with controlling and shaping the future. We are often concerned with modifying conditions so that presently justifiable predictions will be falsified—to make unlikely certain events that are highly likely on a persistence-forecast basis, and to make likely other events that are highly unlikely on the same basis. The real past is not affected by how we read it, but the actual future depends in part on what we expect it to be and what we do in the light of these expectations. The history of the future is open in a sense analogous to the sense in which behavior is free. In both cases, the complete set of determinants includes what people will do, and every phase of the future depends in part on the residues of what people will have done in an anteceding phase.

In the case of the past, we can act with respect to the real objects of the past as well as with respect to our images of them. In the case of the future, we can act only with respect to and in terms of the possibilities that we foresee, though we can try to actualize some of them and we may be oriented and guided in our actions by existing models.

9. What about imaginary objects? What is the reality of an imaginary object such as Dickens's Mr. Pickwick?[1] To be sure, an imaginary object is a product of earlier encounters with real objects: The creation of such an object borrows ingredients from past encounters and reorganizes them into a new entity. The greater the creative imagination, however, the more does the imagined object seemingly acquire a being of its own. Our question centers on the words "seemingly" and "being" in the preceding sentence.

No one, of course, would contend that Mr. Pickwick ever existed in the sense that he was a flesh and blood creature, born of woman, who

[1] I pick on Mr. Pickwick because of a 1933 symposium on imaginary objects which centered on the meaning of statements about him. Participants in the symposium were R. B. Braithwaite, G. Ryle, and G. E. Moore. See, especially, G. E. Moore, *Philosophical Papers* (New York: Collier Books, 1962), chap. 5.

could actually have been encountered in a geographically specifiable place at a specifiable hour on a specified date or at another place at another time, and who could be found on a path physically connecting the two places at any given intervening time. There never was such a real Mr. Pickwick.

Nor can anyone sensibly deny (Gilbert Ryle to the contrary notwithstanding, who contends, if I understand him, that statements about imaginary objects are not about anything) that a real portrait of the nonexisting Mr. Pickwick may be found in the pages of *Pickwick Papers*. It might be contended that statements about Mr. Pickwick are statements about the portrait, and this may well be the case for some statements. But how does this go with particular statements, such as the one Moore discusses at some length, "Mrs. Bardell had fainted in Mr. Pickwick's arms." Can we read this statement as "Mrs. Bardell had fainted in a portrait's arms"? That the sentence is a detail in Dickens's portrait of Mr. Pickwick, as in his portrait of Mrs. Bardell, goes without saying. This tells us something about what Dickens was doing, and it reminds us of our source of information concerning Mr. Pickwick. As we read *Pickwick Papers,* we may at times become aware of Dickens's doings, but the book is hardly likely to have become a classic if it did not transport thousands and thousands of its readers into direct dealings with Mr. Pickwick.

Who or what is this Mr. Pickwick besides being an imaginary person? Are his attributes limited to what Dickens explicitly says about him? The statements—or at least many of them—carry implications about values and concerns and personality traits, and the various statements tie in with one another so that a complex structure is involved. To speak of this structure as a portrait may be misleading because we ordinarily think of a portrait in terms of what is directly present to the eye, the explicit statements in the case of a literary portrait. But it is not the portrait that concerns us here; it is rather that which is portrayed. We see through the portrait to a tacitly implied complex personality, and the further we read, and as we reread, we discover new facets of that personality without ever exhausting the totality. The personality that we see through the portrait is thus richly endowed with essential human attributes, probably far more so in our awareness of it than in our awareness of the personality of the stranger to whom we are casually introduced at a cocktail party, or the historical personage about one or two or three of whose doings we may have read in a history book. This personality has not moved through space-time as real persons do, but it is a real personality in the sense described, objectively there to be discovered by those who seek it out or stumble on it. It can be meaningfully studied, interpreted, talked about, sympathized and empathized with very much as can the personalities of real persons, though certain channels of information about it are, in principle, closed off and it does not possess certain features that characterize real persons.

What I am saying is that an imagined object the conception of which is flat and static has reality only as an image, but that richly developed imaginary objects acquire a reality that goes beyond the image, including attributes that are not explicitly present in the image. Moreover, such an object can become an important part of social reality, encountered in many places. As a social object, its substance may grow beyond the dreams of its original creator. Such imaginary objects may create insoluble problems for philosophers, but I do not think they need pose problems for philosophy so long as one does not confuse them with other objects that they resemble in certain ways but not in others.

When, recently, I had occasion to pass Baker Street in London, I felt a stir of excitement that, I must confess, was greater than anything I felt as I walked over various graves in Westminster Abbey. The reality of Sherlock Holmes, though he never walked in actual space-time, haunted Baker Street in a way that some of my favorite poets did not haunt the abbey even though they were buried there; for, save for their burial, the latter had nothing of special import to do with the abbey. I do not believe I erred in thinking of Mr. Holmes as real, though I would have been in error if I had thought that he resided in the actual space-time of Baker Street.

I think it important to mention that many imaginary objects are actually media in human efforts to grasp at realities that are only dimly apprehended. Such imaginary objects—the electron, for instance—are sometimes referred to as *hypothetical constructs* or *hypothetical process variables*.[2] Now, except in philosophical and methodological discussion

[2] Or they are referred to as *intervening process variables* as distinguished from *intervening variables*. The latter are so called, I suppose, for the same reason that guinea pigs are called guinea pigs and mongolian idiots are called mongolian idiots. Intervening variables in standard usage do not intervene. Force, for example, in this usage is called an intervening variable and is said to mean nothing more than that, under certain circumstances, a physical object of specified mass is observed to move with the measured acceleration. If you think that force implies that, under these circumstances, the mass must move with that acceleration—and that the failure to do so implies that the mass or the circumstances are not what you think they are—then you do not belong to the same linguistic (and philosophical) community as those who use "intervening variable" in the standard sense described. A term like "construct" may also appear in the lan-

we have no interest in the construct "electron." Our dealings with the construct are in the service of our dealings with the reality it is designed to represent; and the construct itself changes over time, mainly as we get additional information about the reality. The construct of an atom, for instance, has gone through enormous change in the past quarter century, not to mention the transformation since the Greeks introduced it some two and one-half millennia ago. Even today, we can doubtless truthfully say that the atom is an imaginary object, but to stop at that can be extremely misleading. What is important about the construct is not that it is a product of human imagination, but that the imagination that produced it was concerned with unraveling some mysteries of the universe.

Finally, with respect to imaginary objects, it should be noted that the manifest object is not necessarily the real object to which the behavior is directed. This is so when the manifest object is being used as a symbolic equivalent of another object, as is allegedly the case in transference relationships and in dreams. Thus, a dream behavior may be concerned with one's actual father represented in the dream as an imaginary object, Father Timè. It is, I think, a tenable working hypothesis that behind every incontestably imaginary object (including Mr. Pickwick and unicorns) there lurks one or more real objects with which the behavior is concerned. The real object, in such a case, need not be the same in the original creation of the imaginary object as in subsequent dealings with that object by the original creator or by others. A working hypothesis, however, serves no function if it does not guide investigation or other conduct; and, if the work of exploration or responsiveness to feedback stops with the formation of the hypothesis, then the latter is no more than a more or less tenable (or untenable) belief or conjecture or some kind of recreational object, and it has no scientific value.

What I am suggesting is that people live their lives in a real world and that their behavior never leaves the reality even when it most seems to be doing so.

---

guage of the latter community where it refers to a pure fiction, an as-if, that implies nothing whatever concerning reality and justifies itself solely in terms of helping you to think or organize your thought. Thus, Freud—for various reasons not a person of good repute in this community—declared that he would go on talking as though Lamarckian heredity were a fact, despite the consensus to the contrary among biologists, because the construct helped him to think. From this point of view, some people who might want to join the community may be tempted to speak of a drug like LSD as a very powerful construct. This would be a mistake, however, as it would violate other conventions.

10. In the history of philosophy, one can distinguish two major views of the nature of reality, each with many variants. One of these views accepts as real physical bodies and their activities; the other, nontangible formal qualities and logical and mathematical truths. In the main, though there have been noteworthy exceptions, the proponents of either view have dismissed the other as invalid.

Triangles, say the members of one group, exist only in triangular objects, not, mind you, in any one of the latter, but as a best-fitting abstraction from many; if there were no triangular objects, there would be no triangles. Triangles, say the members of the other group, are eternally valid forms and there could be no triangular objects but for the temporary vestment of the latter with the quality of triangularity.

"So where are your triangles when they are not in triangular objects?" challenges group 1 with smug self-assurance that this is a clinching argument, but oblivious to the fact that they have begged the question in assuming that realities can only be found in space-time.

"So how is it," challenges group 2 with equally smug self-confidence that this is the clincher, "that when you destroy all the triangular objects in a room (and, in an ideal experiment, continue this mass destruction of all triangular objects in the universe), you are still left with the idea of triangularity?" Group 2 is also oblivious to the begging of the question in assuming that only eternals are real and all else is mere appearance.

I do not wish to leave the impression that these are simpletons arguing, and I have obviously enormously oversimplified the debate. For myself, however, I rather doubt that either view can be maintained consistently to the exclusion of the other, and, more fundamentally, I do not perceive any fundamental incompatibility in the two views if one discards the mutually reciprocal negations.

It seems to me entirely clear that, philosophical speculation as to the nature of reality aside, the issue as to whether something is real arises only in conjunction with the fallibility of human cognition. No one would raise the question of the reality of the sun, or a thunderstorm, or a sudden appearance or disappearance, or anything else, did he not suspect the possibility that his senses or other cognitive processes were deceiving or otherwise misleading him. It follows that a basic aspect of the meaning of "real" is "free of deception." If we start out, however, with a profound distrust of the necessary veridicality of cognitive processes, then it follows that that is *real* that is *so* independently of cognition of it. It then follows that either no things are real or that some things are as they are independently of being cognized. The first of the latter alternatives is demonstrable nonsense as I try to show in the next chapter when I deal with subjective idealism.

I have thus defined "reality" in the following two propositions: (1) Some things are as they are independently of our cognition of them, and (2) reality is the set of all things that are as they are independently of being cognized. Note that this definition, and I believe that I have captured the common meaning, says nothing about permanence, or tangibility, or having a place in space-time. Note, too, that it says nothing of the epistemological problem of knowing reality. I regard the latter as a distinct problem and have already dealt with it, in part, in Chapters 3 and 6, and will return to it in Chapter 16.

We may now deal with the compatibility of the two views of reality by defining two classes of real things: (1) Those things that occur in the fabric of space-time independently of our knowledge of them, and (2) those things that are as they are independently of our knowledge of them and independently of events in space-time. For convenience of discussion, I will designate these two classes of reality by subscripts: reality$_1$ and reality$_2$, respectively.

That realities$_1$ exist is established, I believe, in the refutation of subjective idealism in the next chapter. Note, in passing, that any psychological act, like any physical event, occurs in some time and place and, if it occurs, it does so regardless of whether anyone (including the actor) knows about it. That is, if there are any class 1 realities, there are also such psychological realities. As to realities$_2$, one has in mind mainly the issue of the reality of abstract forms and of mathematical and logical truth—eternal realities. Let me consider this issue and the relation of the second to the first class of realities.

That the sum of the angles of a triangle must equal the sum of two right angles if relevant terms are defined in a particular way and certain assumptions are made is a fact that Euclid *discovered*. The truth of the theorem, within the framework of the set of definitions and axioms, does not—and did not—depend on Euclid's discovery of it nor even on his advancement of his definitions and axioms. Before he was ever born, it was already true that if anyone would ever advance those definitions and axioms the theorem would be demonstrable, and this regardless of whether anyone would ever get around to demonstrating it. This theorem—or any other mathematical verity—describes something real. It would no doubt never have entered, as such, into human affairs if it had never been discovered; but that fact would not have invalidated the implication of the theorem in such a set of definitions and axioms.

The same holds for the "things" of mathematics. Regardless of whether anyone ever got around to doing so, the possibility existed of defining "points," "set," "equidistance," "plane" in a way that made possible the further and consistent definition of a "circle" as a set of points in a common "plane" which are equidistant from a point not in the set. The entities and relationships of mathematics exist implicatively in the context of possible sets of definitions and postulates regardless of whether anyone advances the definitions and postulates or realizes the implications. Note that not everything that one can think of must necessarily have this kind of reality. I can think of "a square circle that is compatible with the Euclidean definitions and postulates," but though the thought has a class 1 reality (I, a class 1 real being, thought it in a definite time and place), the object in question has no reality of either kind; it simply cannot exist.

Can one act toward such an object? Obviously so, but only as a symbolic substitute for some other object or as an object of search. Probably countless individuals have spent endless hours trying to square the circle (that is, to find a generally valid formula or procedure to obtain a square of exactly the same area as any given circle); but this is one aspect of exploring a reality$_2$. The generalized squared circle has not yet, as far as I know, been excluded as a possibility. It does exist for circles with radius equal to a multiple of the reciprocal of the square root of pi, and, in reality$_1$, it may be produced within any practical limits of equivalence.

Certain confusions have arisen which help to account for the beliefs that only one of the two kinds of reality is possible. Consider a circular coin. On the one hand, there are those who would argue that since the circularity is a property of the coin, it loses its reality when abstracted from the coin. I think that what they are saying is that you cannot take away the property without destroying the coin and there would be nothing left to carry the property, thus destroying the property. If something like this is what they intend, then it seems to me the statement is false (one can, for instance, obviously eliminate the property of coinness and still leave a circular object, and I have encountered coins, still in circulation, that have clearly lost their circularity), and it may take some doing to amend the statement so that it still conveys the intended meaning and remains true. More fundamentally, however, assuming that something along the indicated line of argument is intended, it is implied that it is impossible to abstract the circularity and it is obvious that "abstract" in such a sense is irrelevant to the discussion. There is, however, a sense of "abstract" (and I think what we generally mean when we use the term) in which it is possible to abstract the circularity from the coin and in which it is obvious that the abstracted circularity is as much a reality$_1$ as is the coin itself. To abstract the circularity in this sense, all we need do is disregard all other properties of the coin save that of its circularity. Note that, in doing so, we shall have done nothing to the coin, and, specifically, we shall have left it unaltered in its place in space-time. By the same token, however, we shall have done nothing to its circularity as something to be found in space-time. Nor is the presence of the circularity conditional on our abstracting it; the abstraction does not produce it, but is merely a limiting of our attention to it. The circularity of the coin is, therefore, as much an inhabitant of space-time as is the coin.

On the other hand, there are those who would argue that circularity and any other properties of the coin that you might name, individually or collectively, do not inhere in the coin (and, for the sake of simplicity of discussion and because of its irrelevance to the argument, let us ignore the bearing of the theory of relativity on such a statement). These properties—every one of them—are describable only in terms of class names; that is, they are universals, not particulars. That is, when we get down to it, there is nothing left of the coin except the logical intersection of universals; and the logical intersection of classes is itself a class, that is, a universal. Thus, there does not exist any particular coin except as a manifestation of universals, ideals in the Platonic sense.

I think that the Platonists who advance such an argument are also victims of a confusion. Even if one were to grant the validity of the argument up to the last sentence, the conclusion would not follow. For there are two kinds of universals, one a reality$_1$ and the other a class 2 reality. A collection of things in space-time itself exists in space-time.

There are also other differences between the two kinds of universals. A class of space-time realities itself (the universal, the set of all instances) in any given time period contains a larger or smaller number of independently existing members sorted together by a more or less loose test of similarity (only mathematical circles, for example, are perfect). The possibility of unequivocally sorting a set of things into a common class and excluding other things from that class depends not merely on the properties of the things but also on the properties of the sorting agency and the purposes served by the sorting; and, no matter how rigorously the class boundaries are set, they are highly likely to be arbitrary in the sense that some class members are more like some nonclass members than they are like some other class members.

Empirical taxonomies are derived from grouping operations on particulars and have no independent *a priori* existence. Any particular case may be classified by carrying out these or derived operations on it, but it is not given its existence or its existential properties by its classification. Every particular case tests, but is not tested by, the taxonomy.

Nor are the dimensions utilized in an empirical taxonomy necessarily those of an *a priori* classification; and the empirically optimal set of dimensions (in the sense of the smallest number of dimensions or criteria of classification that capture the most variance among things) may vary over time. Thus, the classification of attitudes in terms of cognitive, affective, and conative aspects has been criticized on the grounds that factor analysis does not reveal these dimensions; but it is not at all certain that the same empirical factor-analytically derived dimensions of attitudes toward a particular kind of object would be selected at different periods of history, or in different countries, or toward different kinds of attitudinal objects. Similarly, it is not at all certain that a factor analysis of characteristics of things where the measures include length, width, and depth (with some consistent criterion for deciding which measures are to be entered into the length, width, and depth columns) would reproduce these as empirically determined dimensions, or, if they are reproduced, as orthogonal dimensions; or that the same dimensions would emerge for man-made objects of different historical periods or for man-made and natural objects. Empirical taxonomies are thus time- and place-bound.

I do not mean to imply that realities$_2$ are irrelevant to empirical science.[3] They become relevant through the coordination of class 1 abstractions with class 2 concepts, a process that brings the analytic truths of reality$_2$ to bear on reality$_1$. Observe that coordination is not fusion; class 1 abstractions do not become class 2 entities, in whole or in part. Observe, too, that the possibility of such coordination speaks to the compatibility of the two kinds of reality. But the possibility of the coordination requires that there be class 1 properties of things that lend themselves to such coordination and that the appropriate reality$_2$ shall have been discovered. Also, because of expectations that the two kinds of reality are susceptible to coordination, operations with class 2 concepts may lead to search for parallels in reality$_1$; and implicative structure of reality$_2$ may lead to a situation in which the organization of knowledge and search for new knowledge of reality$_1$ may be largely governed by their coordination with class 2. Finally, a test in reality$_2$ (for example,

[3] The space dimensions are conceptual (reality$_2$) and not empirical. So are the three above-mentioned dimensions of attitude.

imagine a society in which all man-made rectangles respect Aristotle's golden mean and think of the outcome of a factor analysis of such rectangles) may reveal limitations or necessary qualifications of analyses of data in reality$_1$.

The role of the mathematician, insofar as he wishes to be of help to the empirical sciences, is to identify relevant mathematical resources to which class 1 abstractions can be coordinated, to develop relevant implications, or even to make major mathematical discoveries that can serve such a purpose. To carry out this role effectively, he must as a rule become familiar with the substantive issues and problems to which he wants to be helpful. Alternatively, empirical scientists may acquire sufficient mathematical training and acumen to develop this role for themselves.

Space and time themselves belong to reality$_2$ in that they inhere in definitions of them. It is, however, a property of reality$_1$ that, given some definitions of space and of time, there are pathways and linkages among its things that can be mapped in accord with these definitions; and this is what we mean when we say that the things of reality$_1$ exist in space-time. By the same token, however, reality$_1$ exists in reality$_2$, that is, reality$_2$ is more inclusive than and contains reality$_1$. This relation of relative inclusiveness and containment, however, does not take away from reality$_1$ its special relation to space-time; nor does it make reality$_2$ the more real of the two. If bison are four-legged mammals, it does not follow that bison are, in any sense, more or less real than are four-legged mammals.

The failure to appreciate the just-described relationships often results in great philosophical confusion. It is a fact that for many mapping operations, alternative definitions of space-time seem to be equally adequate. Nor does there seem to be any basis other than a sheer leap of faith for asserting that the entirety of reality$_1$ can only be correctly mapped in only one set of space-time concepts. But reality$_1$ must appear quite differently in different mappings. Hence, it is concluded that there is no real reality$_1$ and that it is nonsense to talk about it (or, if one rejects reality$_2$ out of hand, that it is nonsensical to talk about any kind of reality). The true case is exactly the opposite: It is not that reality$_1$ is not as described in mapping$_1$ (if it can be equally well described according to mapping$_2$) or as in mapping$_2$ (if it can be equally well described in mapping$_1$), but that, on the stated assumption, reality$_1$ has the property of being equally well mappable in more than one way. It is not the mapping or appearance of reality$_1$ that constitutes reality$_1$;

reality₁ is whatever it is regardless of how we map it or how it appears to us, save in that it lends itself to certain mappings and to certain ways of being cognized. If two or more mappings are equally valid it is wrong to assert that only one of them is; but it is only to compound the error to assert that neither is. The confusion is a special case of the confusion between the ontic and epistemic.

Most of the time, when we speak of mathematics and logic, we think of highly developed mathematical or logical systems. Far less highly developed class 2 concepts and propositions may also prove to be most valuable in the development of the empirical sciences. Presumptive possibilities, for instance, may exist only in some loosely structured reality₂. The involvement of reality₂ in the empirical sciences is, however, entirely instrumental; the sole justification of such involvement is in the facilitation of our dealings with class 1 reality.

11. There is another difference between class 1 and class 2 reality that strikes me as worthy of special mention. I have argued in Chapter 2, though I did not use this terminology, that if one were to track down all of the things of reality₁ to their determining conditions, one would wind up with one or more facts that are arbitrarily so, undetermined. Are there similar ultimate arbitrarinesses in mathematics? I think not. What of the axioms and postulates and the definitions of mathematics? Are these not ultimate arbitrarinesses? Yes, indeed, in relation to particular systems of mathematics, for example, Euclidian geometry. But, in the reality of mathematics there exist mathematical systems that go with alternative arbitrarinesses. In the time-space bound realities of the other sciences there are no existing realities that go with alternatives to the ultimate arbitrarinesses. The axioms and so on of mathematics impose no constraints on the bounds of mathematical reality save those of intrinsic implicative relationships. The ultimate arbitrarinesses of the nonmathematical sciences impose constraints on the time-space–bound realities in addition to the constraints of intrinsic implicative relationships.

It follows that no purely mathematical analysis can ever be sufficient for the purposes of nonmathematical sciences. A set of definitions, postulates, and so on may involve a contradiction of a space-time–bound arbitrariness and result in a construction that is impossible (not to mention nonexistent) in common space-time. Nor can any mathematical construction, *per se*, offer any guarantee that it is an optimal one as a guide to getting around in the realities of common space-time.

12. I must also note the existence of realities that, in a sense, bridge

the two classes of reality or, in another sense, may be said to belong to either, depending on what one is emphasizing. I have already noted examples of these. Any coordinating definition is such a bridge. Another kind of example is that any past event (for example, the existence of Napoleon or the coming into being of a quasiperson like Mr. Pickwick) has its haecceity, its here-and-now-ness, in the reality of space-time, but the fact of its pastness is from then on an eternal verity. Still a different kind of reality of this order is grasped at in the concept of possibility (and, of course, a host of related concepts, for example, potentiality, capacity, diathesis, and the like).

There are, to start with, possibilities in reality$_1$. That is, within the framework of certain semantic structures, it is obvious that whatever is must have been possible and whatever will some day actually be must today be possible. And in reality$_2$, within the framework of some conceptual system, whatever is consistent with the premises of that system is a possibility even though it may be an impossibility within the framework of another conceptual system or of reality$_1$.

Analogously, we may distinguish possibilities that have bearing on our dealings with reality$_1$: *Anything whose conditions we know and can achieve is a possibility,* and *any set of conditions of an event in reality$_1$ which does not include all of the determinants of that event leaves open the possibility of one or more alternatives to that event.* Note that the second of the immediately preceding propositions is a tautology in the framework of a determinist philosophy, and, hence, a verity in reality$_2$, the first is also a tautology because the conclusion is valid only on the assumption that we know and can achieve the conditions, something that is, at best, only demonstrable in retrospect. The propositions are nevertheless useful in our dealings with reality$_1$, because the first is a presupposition of planning and because, whenever we can think of an alternative to an event and can adduce no sufficient reason for excluding the alternative as a possibility, the second proposition serves to remind us that we have not yet comprehended the sufficient conditions of the event; it is a directive and guide to continued search. Also, in making plans for shaping the future, the second proposition serves as a directive to examine the plans for possibilities that they leave open so that the plans can be tightened or that, at the very least, we remain alert to the derailment of our efforts and can advance counteractive measures with relative speed and dispatch.

The scanning of the horizons of possibility serves an adaptive function whether it be for the scientific enterprise or the enterprise of shaping the world to our terms. Moreover, the appreciation of the existence of possibilities beyond immediately perceptible horizons serves to induce what strikes me as a rather wholesome sense of humility with respect to our place in the total scheme of things and a perpetually nagging question as to whether our terms are as good as we think they are.

Nevertheless, the notion of possibility and related concepts have had some rather mischievous consequences. They have been used as explanatory causal concepts, and, in this role, they have been used to obscure ignorance. I take this to be a cardinal scientific sin.

It has, for example, been said that one inherits certain potentialities, diatheses, or capacities (I shall use these words as synonyms for my purposes) that limit developmental possibilities. Observe that to say that potentialities *limit* possibilities is to attribute to them causal efficacy. What is the basis for such a claim? One may appeal to some kind of Mendelian principle (I am using the term in a very broad sense) that asserts on the basis of a persistence forecast (that is, if it is rational, on the assumption that relevant, but unspecified and unknown, conditions remain unaltered) that given certain traits of the ancestors there is some specifiable probability of the appearance of the trait in the offspring. Such Mendelian principles can be accounted for only on the assumption that certain materials (note well, "materials," not "potentialities" or "diatheses"), which we have come to identify as DNA molecules, are transmitted; but, since the DNA molecule is not itself and does not itself possess the trait in question, they also require the assumption of the persistence of other conditions of the appearance of the trait. The Mendelian principles are statistical and, in their very nature, do not apply to any particular case; but, given the appearance of the expected trait, we may now argue (albeit with somewhat less than perfect logic) that the appropriate DNA molecules must have been transmitted and that the relevant developmental conditions must have persisted unaltered.

All of which sounds eminently reasonable, but where do potentialities come in? Well, let us throw in another assumption, namely, that the relevant persisting conditions that are required are (1) any conditions sufficient to maintain life, or perhaps (2) any conditions sufficient to produce recognizable members of the species, or perhaps even (3) any conditions sufficient to produce nonteratological specimens of the species.[4]

---

[4] I may note parenthetically how remarkably little those who talk about the inheritance of potentialities (or, for that matter, of characteristics, as distinguished from DNA molecules) have to say about which of these assumptions they are making. And, indeed, how remarkably often they talk in terms that literally imply, for instance, that two blue-eyed parents would have blue-eyed offspring even if

At any rate, on some such assumption—and so far as I can see, only on some such assumption—one can say that the particular DNA molecules that are passed into a zygote do limit the developmental possibilities. From here, it becomes hardly more than a manner of speaking to talk about the inheritance of potentialities (rather than DNA molecules), which limit and so forth.

The trouble is that the assumption—take your pick among them—is highly questionable. Too many instances are known from casual observation (think of what has happened in the last generation to the size of young Americans relative to the size of their parents, or of what has happened to the size of American women's feet) and from experimental demonstration (for example, the Mendelian inheritance of certain wing defects in *Drosophila*, the disappearance of these defects with the systematic change of certain parameters of the developmental environment, and the reappearance of the defects in later generations in accord with the original Mendelian expectations when these environmental parameters are restored to their original values) that can be cited of the alteration of Mendelian characteristics in normal organisms in conjunction with environmental change for us to be at all comfortable with even the least extreme of the assumptions, that is, assumption 3, in relation to any characteristic.

Indeed, as a matter of principle, not even the third assumption can be defended. To justify it empirically, one would have to investigate the possible effects of every possible environmental change, in every possible combination and applied at every possible combination of times before the characteristic has set. Can it be stated as a reality$_2$ postulate? Obviously so, by incorporating it into the definition of a Mendelian trait. Thus, any trait thought to be Mendelian that turns out to be susceptible to environmental influence must be removed from the class of Mendelian traits.[5] Since no sure case can ever be adduced without exhausting all possibilities of environmental alternatives, we could never be certain on this definition that the class of Mendelian traits is not, in reality, a null

the zygotes were to be removed from the body of the mother and instantaneously transported to and abandoned on, say, the planet Venus. Some geneticists of my acquaintance have assured me that no geneticist of worth believes that characteristics are determined solely by genetic factors, independently of environmental factors, and that the whole doctrine of the purely genetic determination of characteristics is merely a manner of speaking. Perhaps so, but then one wonders about what motivates the clinging to such obviously dysfunctional and often pernicious linguistic forms.

[5] Mendel himself obviously did not intend this. Witness his care in controlling the environment of his peas.

class. The definition would thus amount to a fiat: "A good scientist must regard any trait as Mendelian unless and until someone proves the contrary."

What can possibly justify such a dictate, especially as the inversion of the normal burden of proof clearly violates the law of parsimony? The least invidious reason I can think of is that it is somehow necessary to persuade investigators that there is merit in studying the phenomena of heredity. If, for instance, the kind of people who are attracted to the scientific study of genetics are individuals whose anxiety is aroused by their tenuous grasp of reality and if they feel that only that is real which is beyond human control, they would have a strong need to persuade themselves that, once heredity is laid down, there is nothing whatsoever that can be done about it. I must confess that the reason hardly strikes me as persuasive (for example, the practical needs of animal husbandry and so on would, given the remarkable constancies of the environment under most circumstances, be sufficient to motivate the continued study of Mendelian forms of control) and the geneticists I have met do not strike me as particularly prone to psychopathology. But this leaves me without even a far-fetched nonpolitical reason that might account for the strange position assumed by hereditarians.

As long ago as 1931, E. B. Holt wrote[6] that

The contents of the germ-cell are not potential characters at all, whether bodily or mental; they are actual proteins and other substances, and to call these substances "potential" this or that is to flout the truth. . . . So that those persons who imagine that in the fertilized egg they are dealing with "potential" or "congenital" albinism, cyclopia, or lethal factor, with agoraphobia, herd instinct, or mathematical endowment, will in the end, of course, have to give place to more observant investigators who can recognize a carbohydrate or amino-acid when they see one. It is deplorable that such gross superstitions survive in modern biology and psychology. And the confusion is as disastrous for any sober study of heredity as it is for other departments of biology or psychology.

In the more than three and one-half decades that have passed since Holt wrote these words, investigators have come along who were capable of recognizing an amino acid when they see one—and they have made remarkable advances in the identification of the substances making up the chromosomes—but they seem to have clung to the "disastrous" confusion Holt discussed. If you were to scratch the surface of the concept "genetic code," so popular today, you would as a rule find yourself

[6] E. B. Holt, *Animal Drive and the Learning Process* (New York: Holt, 1931), p. 9.

right back at the potentiality doctrine and its untenable assumptions. I may not be able to explain the stubborn clinging to so indefensible a concept, but I do know that the doctrine conceals a great deal of ignorance, namely, how the genetic materials do actually become transformed into characteristics of organisms, and that anyone who uncritically absorbs and holds on to the doctrine is not likely to be motivated to eliminate the ignorance.

If the potentiality doctrine is scientifically sinful, it is socially pernicious. The placement by artibrary fiat of bounds on possibility helps to generate a self-fulfilling prophecy that stands as a barrier to the search for means of alleviating many human ills and diverts attention from necessary tasks. Nor is it only in the context of heredity doctrines that one finds such ill effects. To the underprivileged slum dweller, for instance, it makes little difference whether one denies his capacity for benefiting from educational opportunity on pseudogenetic grounds or on the grounds that the effects of early deprivations are declared to be irreversible. Nor does the alleged virtue of the great benefits ultimately to be derived by mankind from the development of genetic engineering atone for the scientific sin (stemming from the abuse of "possibility" concepts) of claiming empirical conclusions that cannot possibly be derived from empirical data. I am not, despite my obvious suspicions about the motives of many geneticists, protesting the study of genetics and genetic engineering. Far from it. What I am protesting is the distortion and falsification of reality, both reality$_1$ and reality$_2$.

It may indeed be true that we do not know how to make a silk purse out of a sow's ear, but the statement that it cannot be done is not defensible in its literal meaning; it is only interpretable as (1) a description that we do not know how to go about the task, (2) an expression of discouragement and pessimism, (3) an injunction not to try, or (4) a disparaging evaluation of one who does try.

Statements of limitations on possibility are tenable in their literal meaning only within the context of an explicit (or tacit but clearly understood) formulation of the conditions that are presumed to be necessary to remove the limitations and within the bounds of the qualifications "If these conditions are indeed necessary and so long as we cannot find a way to achieve them." Both qualifications are reminders of our ignorance and carry directives on how to go about trying to make what is believed to be impossible possible. Note that repeated failures along some particular line of effort are never conclusive because there may be involved some unidentified parameter that vitiates the effort but that is subject to change. Thus, at the time of this writing, there is some reason to believe that much of the failure in the education of under-privileged populations rests on the failure to provide them with convincing evidence of the worth and relevance of school learning and/or the nonverbal (and often verbal) communication by teachers of their conviction that their wards are ineducable. But many failures are related to some tacit premise that obscures the availability of an alternate and serviceable route to the goal. Limited possibilities of magnification through applications of optical principles were readily transcended with the shift to the electron microscope. The nontransmutability of chemical elements was transcended with the substitution of attention to the atomic nucleus for hocus pocus and primary-process–guided compounding of substances. The analysis of the chemical composition of distant astral bodies became feasible when attention was directed to the analysis of spectra and it was realized that the handy availability of samples of the substance of these bodies is not a necessary condition of such analysis.

The disastrous consequences of pronouncements of limitations on the bounds of possibility have, of course, never been so great as they might have been—and perhaps there may even have been some virtue in some of these pronouncements—but only because there always seem to be some people around who are challenged by them, or, at least, disregard them. What I am suggesting is that it would probably be well if there were more of such people, not necessarily individuals who stubbornly push ahead in blind stupidity (but note that even the alchemists made some serendipitous discoveries and laid the foundations for modern chemistry), but with a better understanding of the semantics and ontology of possibility and impossibility.

I do not foresee a time when it will become a pressing social problem to learn to convert sows' ears into silk purses, and I would not urge anyone to devote himself to this problem. If there has ever been an era in human affairs, however, when it has been vitally urgent to challenge alleged impossibilities of rescuing human resources and of social (ranging from the interpersonal to the international) problem-solving, we seem to be in its midst.

PART

III

The Problem of the Actor

8

PERSONALITY:

INTEGUMENTED OR OPEN?

I want now to turn to a second aspect of the image of Man, and I hope you will forgive me if I again refer to the first chapter of Genesis. If one were to accept that Man was created in the image of God, then it would follow that, in some sense, God exists in the form of the image of Man. Now, if you look at a Man, the most obvious thing that you see is his external physical habitus, and, on this basis, you would proceed to infer that God, too, must have a head, eyes, ears, nose, mouth, neck, trunk, arms, legs, and so on—a god that is bound by the limits of his integument just as is Man and, naturally, you endow him with the gender of the superior sex. No mature Bible scholar can, of course, take seriously any such literally anthropomorphic image of God. But, if we reject the latter image while proceeding on the notion of Man having been cast in the image of God, it would follow that, in focusing on his physical habitus, we have somehow misperceived the essential nature of Man. That is, the image of Man that is projected by the Bible cannot be taken as referring to the physical man. If the emphasis on corporeality falsifies the image of God, it by the same token falsifies the image of Man.

As in my earlier references in Chapter 2 to the first chapter of Genesis, I do not here refer to the Bible for its authority, but to pose a problem. I take the Bible, for present purposes, as an influential document that offers an image of Man that is in striking contrast with the image that prevails in contemporary scientific psychology. Contemporary psychologists, it seems to me, tend to be rather obsessed with the corporeality of Man and to be constantly diverted from the human being to the human body. This is entirely consistent with their view of Man as a robot. Conversely, the corporeal image of Man makes it somewhat easier to view him as a robot. In any case, the emphasis on corporeality puts the image of Man into a violently distorted perspective.

The emphasis on corporeality as the essential quality of Man is, of course, evident in the naïve—if persistent—effort to reduce psychological to bodily process. This is again a matter of philosophy dictating psychological theory. If one starts with the presupposition that only that which is physically palpable is real, then obviously one must either deny the reality of psychological events or reduce them to physical terms. Apart from the inherent absurdity of such a position which takes sensation (palpability) as a criterion of physical reality and then takes the latter to deny the reality of sensation, those who share this reductionist aspiration[1] carefully shut their eyes to the fact that there are manifestly no sensations (to say nothing of such matters as aspirations) in the body and that there is no unexplored space to find them in. To show that some brain damage will result in a loss of sight is no more to equate sight with the functioning of that part of the brain than a parallel operation on the eyes would equate sight with the eyes or with their functioning. Nor does what goes on in eyes, neural pathways, and brain location add up to vision. The simple logic of the matter is that these parts of the body and events occurring in them may be necessary correlates and conditions of vision, but conditions and correlates are not the same as that which they are conditions and correlates of.

Think of a complicated machine and of someone who discovers that a certain operation will not be performed if a certain part is damaged or removed. For instance, his car fails to stop when he steps on the brake pedal if the brake lining is worn out. Now, imagine that this person comes to the conclusion, not that the brake lining is a necessary condition of the braking operation, but that the braking operation is located in the lining. The pedal, the rest of the braking mechanism, the wheel itself—all these, he tells you, are peripheral to the lining and, therefore, essentially irrelevant and supernumerary appendages to the braking function, which has finally been located in the lining; and, of course, the road (the friction from which is a necessary condition of the car's stopping) is merely an external factor, part of the environment, and not a com-

---

[1] Let me emphasize that I am referring here to the particular reductionist aspiration of reducing psychological events to physical terms. This is quite different from the kind of reductionism that is implicit in the principle of parsimony, namely, the reductionism that aims at the discovery of the minimum number of ultimate arbitrarinesses, at whatever level these may be found, that collectively describe the sufficient conditions of all phenomena.

ponent of the braking function at all. Then, our imagined friend tells you that, having located the braking function, it is now clear how the braking operation works, that is, that the localization of the function explains the operation. Would you not suspect our friend of being somewhat stupid or, at least, of suffering from some kind of complex that keeps him from thinking straight when it comes to cars?

No one, in my experience, admits to this kind of thinking, not, that is, when I display its quality to him. Such thinkers hem and haw and assure me that I am taking them too literally, that they realize that the eyes and optic nerves are as necessary to vision as is the occipital lobe of the brain; and I can almost hear their subvocal parodying Galileo at the close of his recantation, "But vision *is* localized in the occipital lobe." At any rate, not too many moments after our confrontation, there they are talking again as though the recantation had never taken place. Bear in mind that the kind of people who talk this way are very likely to be numbered among those who do not admit the possibility of private meanings—at least insofar as science is concerned—and to whom the laws of science are simply laws of syntax applied to substantives the referents of which can be pointed to. In other words, they cannot appeal to common understandings of private meanings. Logical syntax does not admit common understandings of private meanings. The physical reductionists are, of course, impervious to logic; what is more important is that they are callously indifferent and faithless to their professed subject matter.

Do not misunderstand me. I do not reject physiological psychology as a legitimate field of scientific inquiry. I deem it a fine thing that there are scientists who concern themselves with the body. I cannot, however, recall having ever come across anything to encourage the hope that we are likely to learn much about the bodily conditions and concomitants of psychological processes from people who habitually confuse an aching tooth with a toothache, enzymatic deficiencies with mental retardation, the conditions of events with the events that they condition—or, for that matter, from people who industriously speculate about the physiological conditions and concomitants of psychological events long before they are clear about the nature of the psychological events whose conditions and concomitants they are seeking. Nor do I know of a single instance in which a strictly physiological inquiry, that is, one framed with the objective of casting light on the physiological conditions of psychological processes, whether such an inquiry is speculative, empirical, or experimental, has contributed to an improved description or classification of the latter or to any discoveries or improved comprehension of interrelationships among them.

The naïve reductionists do not, however, bother me. I do become bothered when I see more sophisticated and responsible psychologists falling into a similar trap. It bothers me, for instance, to see psychologists who ought to know better become blinded by a focus on the body so that they fail to observe that essentiality to biological survival is not necessarily correlated with the significance of the reduction of a particular drive in the stream of behavior. How many of the textbook writers who list thirst and hunger among the most important of human motives recognize that they have taken as their criterion of importance a biological rather than a psychological desideratum? What proportion of human behavior, for instance, is, in the ordinary course of human events, influenced by the body's dependence on the maintenance of a supply of water? Or, even within the restricted context of eating behavior, how much of such behavior is conditioned solely by states of nutritional deficiency?

There is a story, perhaps apocryphal, of Gregory Zilboorg asking a class, "What does the liver have to do with psychoneurosis?" To the reply, "Why, nothing, Dr. Zilboorg," it is said that he surveyed the class coldly, and scathingly demanded, "Can someone without a liver have a psychoneurosis?" There is doubtless as wholesome a lesson for psychologists as for psychoanalytic trainees in the anecdote, and it is just as cogent if you substitute "perception" or "learning" for "psychoneurosis." Does it follow, however, that psychologists ought to devote a major share of their teaching and research to the liver?

Let me confront the issue of corporeality in the image of Man in the case of a psychologist who, in all other respects, comes as close to a valid image of man as any psychologist I know. That this psychologist should elect to stand by the corporeal aspect of the image is a measure of the power of our deeply ingrained habits of thinking along these lines. In an important paper,[2] Gordon Allport presents the view that the person is an open system. He advances four criteria of such a system: (1) that in an open system "there is intake and output of both matter and energy"; (2) that "there is the achievement and maintenance of steady (homeostatic) states"; (3) that "there is generally an increase in complexity and differentiation of parts"; and (4) that "at least at the human

[2] G. W. Allport, "The Open System in Personality Theory," in *Personality and Social Encounter* (Boston: Beacon Press, 1960), pp. 39–54.

level, there is more than mere intake and output of matter and energy: there is extensive transactional commerce with the environment."

I call your attention to Allport's fourth criterion. It is not a distinct criterion, but merely a somewhat broadened version of the first. In fact, as stated, it is not a criterion of open systems at all because it explicitly does not apply to all open systems. If we were simply to rewrite the first criterion to say that, "in an open system there is intake and output of both matter and energy which, in some instances and particularly so at the human level, involves extensive transactional commerce with its surround," we would have incorporated what Allport wants to say in his fourth criterion without having to advance a noncriterial criterion.

So, Allport has only three criteria. What of it? Well, I think it no error that, in his combing of definitions of open systems, Allport counts four criteria. It seems clear from his discussion of his fourth criterion that he actually does have a fourth criterion in mind that is different from what he stated as the fourth criterion, but that he shies away from putting the real fourth criterion into words because his rejection of it would also compel him to reject his view of the person as an open system. The real fourth criterion, I suggest, is that an open system has no definite, clear-cut boundary with respect to its surround.

This criterion, never explicitly faced as such, Allport rejects in favor of the view of "personality as something integumented, as residing within the skin." He refers to some theorists like Kurt Lewin, Martin Buber, and Gardner Murphy who challenge this view, "considering it too closed"; but, in the main, Allport attributes the rejection of the integumented personality concept to Eastern philosophy. As Western theorists, he tells us, "most of us . . . hold the integumented view of the personality system. I myself do so."[3]

[3] Oddly enough, Allport finds one of the earliest roots of this aspect of Western thought in "the personalistic emphasis in Judeo-Christian religion." Unless I misread both the Jewish and Christian traditions, neither of these traditions can be said to lay very much emphasis on the corporeal and integumented aspects of the personality, with the Christian tradition typically denying the essentiality of the body altogether. Moreover, the personalistic emphasis in these traditions is, to say the least, subject to interpretation and hence to dispute. It certainly is questionable whether either of these traditions can be said to make "such a razor-sharp distinction between the person and all else." To take one simple case: In the traditional penitential prayer recited by Jews on the High Holy Days, each individual, in effect, accuses himself of a wide variety of crimes, from the most heinous to the relatively trivial. Whatever a psychoanalyst may make of the affect with which the prayer is recited, a traditional interpretation of the prayer is that every member of the community shares in the responsibility for all such offenses,

The Problem of the Actor

Now, it should be apparent that, whatever the personalistic and individualistic emphases of the major strands of Western traditions and thought, Professor Allport is still begging the question with regard to the fourth criterion of an open system. What is at issue is not the personalistic and individualistic emphasis, but the question of whether such an emphasis, even if accepted, necessarily requires an integumented view of the personality.

It is my opinion that neither Professor Allport nor anyone else can locate within the bounds of the integument what he thinks is to be found there. He writes that "It is the duty of psychology, I think, to study the person-system, meaning thereby the attitudes, abilities, traits, trends, motives, and pathology of the individual—his cognitive styles, his sentiments, and individual moral nature and their interrelations."[4] I submit that not one of these components of a person can be located in the interior of the integumented organism. I cannot conceive of an ability stripped of all reference to the objects to be manipulated when the ability is put to work. If to talk of an ability you must at least implicitly refer to objects not included within the bounds of the integument, then the concept of an ability has no meaning if it is restricted to something that is completely included within these bounds. If "writing" means setting down intelligible marks on paper, then the "ability to write" means that a person is capable of setting down intelligible marks on paper. But what is the meaning of "ability to write" when you eliminate the reference to paper? I can conceive of some conditions of an

regardless of what he himself may have done. Thus, Rabbi Isaac Luria (1534–1572) is quoted in Hertz's *Daily Prayer Book* (New York: Bloch, 1948, p. 906) to the following effect: "Why is the Confession couched in the plural? . . . Because all Israel is one body, and every Jew is a member of that body. Hence follows mutual responsibility among all members." And from much earlier sources, *Midrash Tanhuma,* "All of you are pledges one for the other: all of you, aye the world, exist through the merit of a single righteous man among you, and if but one man sin, the whole generation suffers." *Individualism,* to be sure, but individualism with a special meaning. Nor can such New Testament sentiments as "we being many are one body in Christ, and every one members of one another" (See Rom. 12, 1 Cor. 12, 1 Peter 2) be taken as exactly unqualified individualism.

It may be noted, in passing, that the sharpness of the boundary between organism and environment is questionable even on the purely biological level. Thus, Angyal has argued (quite convincingly, to my mind) that organism and environment are not separable as structures in space and he characterizes the statement that the individual is within the skin and the environment as outside it as "semi-jocular" and untenable. See Andras Angyal, *Foundations for a Science of Personality* (New York: Commonwealth Fund, 1941).

[4] Allport, p. 48.

ability as being within the body, but not of the objective reference. I similarly cannot conceive of any procedure that will permit us to describe or to observe an ability, a cognitive style, a sentiment without simultaneously encompassing actor and object; a trait without repeated observation of transactions between person and environment; a hallucination or a delusion without checking on the true transorganismic situation; a moral nature with no external reference.

What may seem to be impressive evidence to the contrary, that is, evidence that psychic experience is, in fact, contained within the confines of the body and, even more specifically, within the confines of the brain, is offered by observations of the effects of direct electrical stimulation of the living human brain. Penfield and his associates,[5] in the course of a diagnostic technique designed to discover specific loci of malfunction which may be said to be responsible for epileptic seizures, systematically stimulate various areas of the brain. Because the process is not painful, the patient is not anaesthetized (except, of course, for the local anaesthetic used in the preliminary operation to provide access to the brain) and can report on his experience as various points are stimulated. At certain points, patients report complex psychic experiences—vivid hallucinations that seem to be memories in some instances, dreams in others—in which familiar places and persons may be seen, songs may be heard from beginning to end, people well known to the patient may speak and act, and appropriate emotions are experienced. These hallucinations, memories, or dreams continue to unfold as the electrode is held in place and end suddenly when the electrode is withdrawn.

To Penfield and Jasper,[6] "This is a startling discovery"—and indeed it is from the viewpoint of its implications concerning the functioning of the nervous system. But, these authors continue, "It brings psychical phenomena into the field of physiology." What this statement means is not quite clear because the next sentence asserts that, "It should have profound significance also in the field of psychology provided we can interpret the facts properly," and the following sentences and paragraphs to the end of the section are all concerned with physiological matters. One would think that bringing psychic phenomena into the realm of physiology is as profoundly significant to psychology as anything could be; hence, the "should," the "also," and the "provided we can interpret the facts properly," of the last-quoted sentence seem rather puzzling.

[5] See, especially, W. Penfield and H. Jasper, *Epilepsy and the Functional Anatomy of the Human Brain* (Boston: Little, Brown, 1954).
[6] *Ibid.*, p. 143.

One must infer that "It brings psychical phenomena into the field of psychology," is not intended by Penfield and Jasper to mean what it seems to say. Perhaps they mean to imply nothing more than that here is a new, physiological approach to eliciting memories and that such elicitations may provide new insights into the organization of memories, provided we can interpret the facts properly.

Whatever they may mean by the statement, however, there is no doubt in my mind but that many psychologists will seize on these phenomena to justify their belief in the literal truth of the statement, that is, that the psychic phenomena are nothing but physiological. If so, these psychologists (and probably most physiologists as well, and, oddly, a few sociologists[7] I have encountered) simply demonstrate themselves to be incapable of distinguishing a psychological fact when they come across one.

All that happens physiologically when an electrode is applied to the brain is that some neurons are impelled to fire and, in turn, the neurons with which they are in functional contact are impelled to fire, depending on the physiological state of the latter. The situation is no different here than that noted by Penfield and Jasper in another context.[8] Noting that the stimulation of a particular point may invariably be associated with

[7] Among those sociologists who have difficulty in recognizing the integrity of the realm of psychological fact, the prevailing view is that psychological phenomena are nothing but sociological. The sociologists I have referred to in the text above actually hold both views, that is, insofar as psychological phenomena are anything but physiological, they are nothing but sociological. One must also note the existence of a large body of sociologists, however, who seem to be incapable of recognizing a sociological fact when they see one and subsume all of sociology under psychology, except that they may not accept the psychology of the psychologists they identify as psychologists. My own view of the properly sociological datum is that it cannot be described in terms that describe individual behaviors. Simple cases in point are the distribution of delinquency in the social structure and the normative system in terms of which a particular action is classified as delinquent. The sociological datum may be behaviorally and-summative, that is, a combination of individual behaviors that are not derived from it; or it may have the Gestalt quality of logical and dynamic priority to the individual behaviors it comprises. For instance, the distribution of delinquency does not explain the individual delinquent acts, though there may be other sociological facts that, at least, contribute to such an explanation; it merely takes note of them. By contrast, a social mobilization explains much of the individual behavior that it includes, though it may be conditional on an and-summation of other behaviors. An and-summative sociological datum may be consequential as a Gestalt; for instance, it is as a consensus that a consensus generates a pressure on a deviant group member to conform. But these are matters that belong to another essay.

[8] Penfield and Jasper, p. 240.

movement of the thumb, they write that, "We are entitled to conclude from the fact, not that thumb movement is represented in that point, but only that a part of neural connections involved in causing the thumb to move is to be found there." Actually, they do not note the same invariance of relationship between point stimulation and elicited psychic experience; for instance, stimulation of what seems to be the same point in the same patient may at different times evoke quite different experiences. What concerns us here, however, is that no amount of observation of physiological process can demonstrate anything but physiological process and, I submit, it cannot do so because there is nothing there but physiological process. The psychological processes reported by Penfield's patients involve relationships to objects, and generally familiar objects at that. Even in those instances where the patients report objectless fear, there is an objective relationship; something is threatening, even though the patient may not be able to identify the particular object. "Such fear causes the patient to seek protection in obvious terror although he cannot say whether he is afraid of this or of that."[9] To which I would add that if these patients could not experience the objective context implied in "to seek protection," but only some physiological state, they could, like Marañon's[10] subjects on the injection of adrenalin and with no available or suggested context to which to relate the experienced body change, properly have reported nothing more than that they felt as if they were afraid; they might, of course, infer that they were afraid and report this as their experience.

Let us assume that, in time, there will accumulate enough knowledge of the correlation between physiological and psychological processes to make it quite safe to predict the latter from data on the former. A correlation, however, cannot establish an identity, not even if the correlation is unity. This fact is easily demonstrated. Define a population of coins as follows: Take all the pennies newly minted at a given mint on a given date, all the nickels produced at a particular mint on a given date (not necessarily the same mint or the same date), and so on for dimes, quarters, and so on. In this population of coins, there will be a perfect correlation between the face that appears on the head side and the value of the coin stated on the tail side. The perfect correlation obviously does not establish that, in the defined population of coins,

[9] Ibid., p. 144.
[10] Marañon, G. "Contribution à l'étude de l'action émotive de l'adrenaline," Revue Française d'Endocrinologie Clinique, Nutrition, et Metabolisme 2 (1924): 301.

heads are tails. And, to return to the assumed psychophysiological correlation, the sheer fact of the correlation cannot be established without evidence of what is on the psychological side that is independent of the evidence of what is on the physiological side. Nor does the assumed perfect correlation imply anything about the direction of causality. In their emphasis on the familiarity of their patients with the persons and actions that appear in the evoked hallucinations, memories, and/or dreams, Penfield and Jasper tacitly assume that what is there physiologically has come about as a consequence of prior object relationships of the patients.

At this point, if not sooner, there will be those who will say that I have finally managed to hoist myself by my own petard. In suggesting that the causal process may go from the psychological to the physiological, I will have revealed myself to be a *dualist*. In the psychological-scientific climate of our time *dualist* is an epithet, and that effectively puts me in my place. Experience has taught me, however, that most psychologists who accept the assessment are quite unable to answer the question as to why dualism merits such a denigrated status. Twoness is not obviously worse than oneness. To admit distinctions between day and night, between forces and masses, between momentum and velocity, between power and energy, between organic and inorganic chemicals, between plant and animal life, and so on, is not scientifically sinful. In fact, if it is simply a distinction that defines a dualism, then, on the basis of the number of distinctions that scientists make, science is a most elaborate and complex pluralism. Why then should the distinction of body and mind occasion so much opprobrium?

It all started with the way in which Descartes set up the distinction between body and mind. It was not the distinction itself nor his doctrine of the interaction of body and mind that led to the eventual scientific disreputability of the mind. Both the distinction and the essence of the doctrine reach back into antiquity. Descartes, however, formalized the distinction by asserting that body and mind were two forms of substance, one possessing extension (matter), the other unextended (mind). Apart from the puzzle of substance without extension, the assertion of interaction between body and mind implied that extensionless substance can affect extended substance, and *vice versa*. The big issue that then arose was not whether the distinction as drawn by Descartes was sound, but how the interaction can occur. How, for instance, can extensionless substance affect extended substance? We associate mass with extension. Newtonian mechanics leaves no place for massless objects to generate mechanical forces. But if a mental phenomenon (extensionless and massless), like the idea of moving an arm (having extension and mass), can cause the arm to move, then a mechanical force is generated by a massless source; and there is nothing to receive the equal and opposite reaction. I state the puzzle of the how in Newtonian terms, but it was not necessary to wait for Newton's laws of motion for the puzzle to appear.

Descartes himself had shown that it was possible to account for the movements of a soulless body in purely mechanical terms, and he assumed that exactly the same principles apply to the human body, except that ideas could tilt the pineal gland, thereby opening and closing various valves and redistributing the play of mechanical forces. Descartes thus suggested a locus of interaction, but he still did not explain how an idea can move a body like the pineal gland. And, long before Newton's laws of motion there must have been deeply ingrained in the mind of man the idea that, apart from self-generated movement, motion can only be imparted from one body to another or induced by magic. Thus, the imparting of movement to the pineal gland by an extensionless substance could only be perceived as some mystifying magic; and this, in turn, demanded an omnipresent magician to make the adjustments.

Logically, of course, the puzzle could just as well be stated the other way—How can the movement of an extended body introduce an idea into extensionless substance?—except that there does not seem to be any backlog of experience that would set up an expectation that a psychic state can only be generated by a psychic state. The puzzle, and the challenge, of the how was therefore mainly a one-way affair. There were no, and there still are no, laws of the mind that are violated by the Cartesian distinction, but there were lots of laws of the material world (ranging from relatively primitive notions of how motion is imparted to a physical body, through the Newtonian laws of motion, to the laws of the conservation of energy and, later, of mass-energy) that would have to be declared false if the Cartesian analysis were to be accepted.[11]

11 This is not to say that the obverse of the Cartesian dualism posed no problems. In fact, insofar as philosophy has been concerned, these problems have been much more serious than the apparent violation of physical law. Given the sharp distinction between matter and mind, it seemed reasonable to assume that that which is perceived is a percept rather than a thing, that is, that the known is, as known, something mental. On this basis, however, the question arises as to how we can ever know anything beyond the mental. Descartes thus laid the foundation for the idealist philosophies. The issue of whether it is necessary to provide a bridge between the mental and physical, I have dealt with in the preceding chapter. In the present context, however, it is to be noted that Des-

At any rate, it did not take very long after the publication of Descartes's notions before philosophers (including many who identified themselves as Cartesians) became very busy demonstrating that the alleged interaction is only an illusion or that there really is no interaction because there are no two kinds of substance.

First came the occasionalists, introducing the omnipresent magician—God. Whenever an idea occurs in the mind that calls for something to happen to the body, God intervenes, declared Geulincx, and appropriately tilts the pineal gland; and whenever something occurs to the body that calls for a corresponding psychic content, God intervenes and introduces it into the mind.

Thus overburdening God with an infinite mass of petty detail did not strike philosophers like Spinoza and Leibnitz as compatible with His exalted status. They, therefore, sought different solutions to the problem.

Leibnitz realized that a great enough creator (a description that, by definition, fits God) must be assumed to be capable of producing two perfectly synchronized creations so that, without any further attention on his part, there would forever after be a perfect parallelism between the two, every change in one being paralleled (perhaps after an appropriate brief delay, we might add) by a corresponding change in the other; hence, the illusion of a causal interaction. If one identifies "mind" with "consciousness" a special problem appears in that consciousness is discontinuous so that one of the two synchronized creations keeps popping into and out of existence. I do not think it would be overtaxing the notion of a supreme creator to assume that God is quite capable of creating something that is destined to come into and out of being at preordained occasions; but Leibnitz preferred another alternative, namely, not to equate mind with consciousness, but to preserve its continuity by assuming its existence in unconscious form.

The major trouble with Leibnitz's response to the occasionalists is that it does not solve the Cartesian problem at the nontheological level. Suppose that we grant the original creation and preordained destinies of the two streams of existence, it still remains true that one of those streams seems to obey physical laws, except—and it is the question of the exception that is at issue—on such occasions as when an idea seems to move

---

cartes introduced his speculations concerning the pineal gland to provide a bridge, and not to provide a mechanism. In other words, Descartes was sensitive to the issue of the channel of interaction—an issue that he dealt with in rather primitive fashion—but he was not himself sensitive to the issue of the *modus operandi* as discussed in the text.

an arm or a leg. If one grants these exceptions, then it is not true, to take but one example, that for every action there is an equal and opposite reaction; and so on for other physical laws. In other words, if one accepts even the illusion of an apparent effect of mind on body, then one seems to be agreeing that there apparently are occasions when physical laws do not hold, and this regardless of the issues of the ultimate nature of causation or the nature of ultimate causes. If one accepts the validity of physical law, one is constrained to deny the occurrence of such occasions and to insist that there must be physical cause (however "cause" is interpreted) of every bodily change, whether of position or of state. The illusion of an idea resulting in the movement of a physical body is not a true illusion, in the sense of a false appearance, but simply a case of not knowing how or where to look.

That Leibnitz himself did not take the doctrine of psychophysical parallelism too seriously is suggested by the fact that it does not really fit—or so it seems to me—into his basic philosophical system. It seems to me that, in introducing it at all, he was betrayed by his momentary enthusiasm at having thought up the analogy of the master clockmaker and his perfectly synchronized clocks. The basic Leibnitzian doctrine, as I read it, is consistently monistic, at least insofar as the mind-matter problem is concerned. In Leibnitz's fundamental doctrine (the monadology), the ultimate elements of the universe are noninteracting, perfectly homogeneous and indivisible formal atoms or metaphysical points (monads), all perfectly synchronized in their development, existing in a preestablished harmony, and each possessing, in some sense albeit in varying degree, a certain vitality and a kind of perception, each expressing the entire universe by reflecting all the rest. Every ultimate element of the universe thus is an indivisible unity, with its material and mental aspects. Some are more highly developed in the mental aspect than others, and those most highly so developed—souls—are conjoined with aggregates of less highly developed ones—bodies. None of which resolves the issue of the challenge of the mind-matter dichotomy to the validity of physical law.

Spinoza responded to the occasionalists in his own fashion. He maintained that what we perceive as mind and what we perceive as matter are really not substantially different at all, but different modes of expression of God in whose being they are contained. God manifests himself as extended substance or as mind. It does not matter as far as the Cartesian dualism is concerned; there are no two kinds of substance to interact, but only one basic reality, the being of God. There is, hence, no problem of the how of interaction. No metaphysical problem perhaps, but still a problem when we leave the theological level of discourse. Grant, for instance, that the idea of moving an arm and the movement of the arm are both expressions of God—in Spinoza's view, the only free agent (in the sense of being unconstrained by any opposing force) in the universe—for whom it would not be inconsistent to have one followed by the other; but there is still the issue of whether the arm ever moves in the absence of physically sufficient conditions as expressed in physical law, whether there is no equal and opposite physical reaction on the source of the force that sets the arm in motion, and so on.

To this issue, Spinoza responds that physical law must be completely consistent with the physical mode of expression and, in effect, psychological law must be consistent with the mental mode of expression. Rationally, he contends, one can never assert that an idea has a physical consequence or that a physical event has a mental consequence. The chain of causes and effects must be apprehended in terms that are appropriate to the mode of expression. The idea of moving the arm cannot be thought of as resulting in an arm movement, but only as resulting in the idea that the arm has moved. The actual movement of the arm can only be apprehended as brought about by another physical event, presumably the one corresponding to the idea of moving the arm. There are, thus, two sets of causal series, and whether one pursues one or the other makes no difference; whether we conceive of nature in physical terms or in mental terms, the order that is revealed is the same since the underlying reality is the same.

Spinoza, the monist *par excellence,* turns out to be a psychophysical parallelist, just as Leibnitz, commonly held to be the prime modern example of a psychophysical parallelist, turns out on closer inspection to be a monist. This is perhaps our first intimation that the difference between monism and dualism may not be so fundamental as most people take it to be.

Spinoza's analysis is not without its difficulties. For one thing, the continuity of the mental series poses a much more serious problem to Spinoza's parallelist doctrine than to that of Leibnitz. To the latter, the parallelism is merely between body and mind, and the two sets of events need not be formally identical. A toothache, for instance, may have its bodily parallel in an abscess which need not in any manner resemble the toothache. To Spinoza, the parallelism is between the material and mental aspects of the totality of nature and, since the corresponding terms of the parallel series are two ways of conceiving an identity, they have to be formally identical. The latter requirement leads Spinoza into some egregious errors. Thus, he tells us that a circle existing in nature and the idea of that circle are one and the same thing, manifested through different attributes. Note, incidentally, that the parallelism here is not between a bodily and a corresponding mental event, but between something outside the body and a mental event. What immediately concerns us, however, is that it is manifestly untrue that a circle existing in nature and the idea of that circle are necessarily two aspects of one and the same thing. In fact, the natural and ideational circles may be separated in both time and space, as when I think of a circle I once drew; that circle no longer exists and I am now many miles from where it was when it did exist.

The extension of the psychophysical parallelism to the totality of nature requires not simply the postulation of an unconscious mind but the postulation of a coexisting mental equivalent for every physical event; otherwise there could not be the perfect parallelism of the physical and mental aspects of nature and of physical and mental law as required by Spinoza's views. On the assumption, however, that there may be some physical events unknown to anyone (as must have been the case for the applicability of physical laws to events governed by the latter prior to their discovery, for example, the all-or-none discharge of individual nerve fibers prior to the discovery of this law of neural discharge), this doctrine becomes untenable. To place the mental aspect of the workings of unknown physical events in the mind of God is to cheat on the doctrine because it involves substituting a meaning of "mental" obviously not intended by Spinoza.

Turning to another solution of the mind-body problem, though it was not offered as such, I come to Berkeley's panmentalism. On the basis of a monumental nonsequitur, Berkeley converted the proposition (itself an invalid one) that we can only know of the existence of something by perceiving it into the proposition that to be is to be perceived (*esse est percipi*). In other words, nothing exists except in perception and the Cartesian distinction is denied; there exists only the mind and there can be no mind-body interaction. It follows that physical law itself exists only in the mind; and if the mind violates the physical laws it has itself generated, who is to say it nay? Berkeley himself could not withstand the full thrust of his logic, for not only did it dispose of the body and the world of matter as an independent reality, but it was obvious that it would also dispose of the independent existence of God. A man destined to become Bishop of Cloyne in County Cork, Ireland, could not leave himself in so doctrinally vulnerable a position. He therefore argued that God exists because He is self-perceiving; and once "to be is to be perceived" is interpreted as "perceived by God," all of nature exists in the mind of God. Which brings us full circle to the issue posed by Descartes since the mind of God has generated extended substance knowledge of which is available to the unextended mind of man, also generated by God.

It remained for Hume, a disciple of Berkeley but apparently unfettered by concerns about God's existence, to try to apply Berkeley's canon of *esse est percipi* consistently—or as consistently as it can be applied.[12] The result was to wipe just about everything out of existence except as momentary sensations or images of the mind: time, causality, self, and so on. What Hume did not realize was that, by the canon, the perception that gives existence to something does itself not exist unless it is itself perceived; but this demands an infinite regress of perceptions perceiving perceptions perceiving perceptions and so on. If one ever comes, as one does, to an unperceived perception, it does not exist; and, out of nothingness, nothing can come. *Esse est percipi* leads inevitably to nothingness: Nothing whatsoever, not even the canon, exists. Panmentalism is the epitome of absurdity.

There thus seems to be only one possibility left to preserve the realm of physical law from interference by nonphysical mentalistic forces: to deny the distinctive consequential reality of the mind. Man is a machine, boldly proclaimed La Mettrie. The mind is nothing but a property of the functioning and organization of matter. Some two millennia earlier, it may be well to remember, Aristotle had also identified the soul with the form and function of matter, but with a quite different philosophical conclusion in view, the indestructibility of the soul. "Let us then conclude boldly," wrote La Mettrie, "that man is a machine, and that in the whole universe there is but a single substance variously modified."[13] Note that La Mettrie was not denying the existence of the mind or its difference from inert matter. A property of organized matter is not the same as the matter of which it is a property. What he was concerned about was the two kinds of substance postulated by Descartes. "Given the least principle of motion," he wrote, "animated bodies will have all that is necessary for moving, feeling, thinking, repenting, and in a

[12] As Holt points out in his devastating critique of the Berkeley-Hume argument, the principle cannot be applied with full consistency. See E. B. Holt, "The Argument for Sensationism as Drawn from Dr. Berkeley," *Psychological Review,* 41 (1934): 509–533.

[13] J. de La Mettrie, *l'Homme Machine.*

word for conducting themselves in the physical realm, and in the moral realm which depends upon it." While one may doubt that even La Mettrie believed that animation and the least principle of motion are sufficient for feeling, thinking, repenting, and so on, it is clear that La Mettrie was expressing his faith that these activities are consequences of physical law and consistent with it.

The nub of the issue is contained in a further development of the mechanistic doctrine, Thomas Huxley's *epiphenomenalism*. According to this view, mind is a by-product of the life processes, but has no consequences of its own. Huxley could not deny the existence of mind, and particularly of consciousness, which he identified with it, but it should by now be clear why he added the restriction of nonconsequentiality. He was preserving the laws of physics. Yet, if we follow La Mettrie, there is no reason for the restriction. If mind is the functioning and organization of the body, it is not the body, no more than the functioning of any machine is the same as the machine; and if mind is nothing more than the functioning of the body and if it is stipulated that such functioning cannot violate physical law, then, albeit repenting may involve a different kind of fuctioning than does falling down an elevator shaft, there is no reason to assume that such functioning can have no consequence. Huxley's problem is that he does not know how to fit consciousness (by which, I take it, he means what I mean by awareness) into this scheme of things. To him, awareness is essentially an extensionless substance, a shadow of the true reality, a noise generated by the friction of working parts, a phosphorescent glow produced by neural activity—a by-*product*, not a process—and, as such, it can have no consequence; but that is because of his faulty conceptualization of the nature of awareness rather than because awareness is an inconsequential action of the body. And, actually, neither Huxley nor his followers could come up with an analogy that fit what they were trying to describe. A shadow may not run the body that casts it; but shadow, noise, and glow are physical events with physical consequences.

Moreover, one must beware of converting the proposition that the mental functioning of the body cannot violate physical law into the proposition that physical law is sufficient to account for mental functioning; that is simply bad logic. Nor can one infer from the first proposition that physical law need necessarily occupy a prominent place in accounting for mental functioning. Huxley was himself a staunch advocate of Darwinian evolutionary theory. I take it that the laws of natural selection do not violate Newton's laws of motion, but, though I cannot claim to have read Huxley extensively, I rather doubt that he can have had very much occasion to refer to them.

So, the La Mettrian conception of the nature of the mind is not incompatible with the drawing of a distinction between body and mind; and, having drawn such a distinction, it is not incompatible with the proposition that they interact in the sense that structure influences function and *vice versa*. Moreover, insofar as a particular mental functioning directly involves only part of the body, there is no reason for assuming that it may not also have consequence for parts of the body that are not directly involved. The cream of the jest is that mind, so interpreted, has no extension in the sense that the body has extension; functioning and organization may be said to have a locale, an arena, a scene within which they occur, but not a locus in the sense that extended substance has a locus in space. So, except for Descartes's injudicious use of the term "substance," there is no inherent incompatibility between the Cartesian psychophysical interactionism and the La Mettrian mechanomaterialistic monism.

I have already noted the slippage of conventional tags for positions on the mind-body relationship in the instances of Leibnitz and Spinoza. To these we may add the just-cited instance of the compatibility of supposed incompatibles. Let me now cite another choice example of the slippage of these labels. Titchener[14] describes himself as a psychophysical parallelist. He explains psychophysical parallelism, however, in terms characteristic of the double-aspect view: He cites the analogy of the circle seen as concave from within and convex from without and the example of the universe as Ptolemaic when viewed from the earth as center and as Copernican when viewed from the sun as center; and he views both mind and body as abstractions from what he takes to be the real underlying unity, experience. But his self-chosen label and his explication of that label notwithstanding, he is, in fact, an epiphenomenalist: He maintains that every mental process has its source in a bodily process, but that to assert a mental effect on the body would be to contradict the law of the conservation of energy; and he explicitly counters the commonsense assumption of interactionism with an alternative epiphenomenalist construction. And, to top it all off, he regards the study of the utterly inconsequential epiphenom-

14 E. B. Titchener, *An Outline of Psychology*, revised (New York: Macmillan, 1897, 1902), pp. 360–368.

enon, consciousness, as the only subject matter (dependent variables) proper to a psychologist.

All of which adds up to the fact that it does not matter to me one whit whether I be called monist or dualist. The tags have lost all meaning, except as expletives, unless one clearly specifies the view to which they are attached. I agree with La Mettrie that the term "mental" has no meaning except in the context of some activity of the body. This does not stop me (as, in fact, it has never stopped any philosopher—disclaimers to the contrary notwithstanding—or any one else) from recognizing that mind, behavior, motivation, personality are not the same as the body.

Nor does it lead me to accept the body as the appropriate subject of the mental or behavioral act. One would be saying something quite different to one's beloved if one were to say, "My body loves you," than if one were to say, "I love you"; and the difference is not merely one of conventional language. The proper subject of the behavior sentence is the person who is acting; but I will come back to this issue in the remaining chapters of Part III.

Aristotle overgeneralized the concept of mind in identifying it with the form and function of matter. La Mettrie, similarly, did not identify which function mind is of what kind of material organization. In my own view, mind—and, more generally, behavior—is (to mention only the one of my criteria that is relevant to the present discussion) an action of a person, directed toward an object; and, as such, it always involves some activity of the body. Because every mental or behavioral act includes a bodily act, it is possible to limit one's view to the bodily inclusion or to view the whole, which makes me a double-aspecter.

Moreover, for every mental or behavioral event, there is a bodily event (the one that is included) that can in no sense be said to be generating the former; so, at least to this extent, I am a psychophysical parallelist.

I believe that what goes on in the body conditions mental and behavioral events, that the occurrence of mental and behavioral events condition what goes on in the body in addition to the direct bodily involvement, and that they may affect what goes on outside the body. It is not a peculiarity of the mind-body relationship that function (operation) influences structure and *vice versa*. Thus, when you use your car, you induce wear and tear on its parts; and if certain parts are out of order or if you run out of fuel, the car will not function. The running of the car is not the same as the car, but there is no mystery about the interaction. I am, therefore, a psychophysical interactionist.

I take it for granted that no mental or behavioral event can violate any physical, chemical, biological, or sociological laws, and I take such laws to have an objective status independent of our knowledge or mis-knowledge of them; but I also take it for granted that there is an order of law, psychological, that also applies to mental or behavioral events, and that the other orders of law must be consistent with it, and I assume that an adequate accounting of mental and behavioral events will have more occasion to refer to psychological law than to any other order of law. In admitting only one inclusive and consistent over-all order of law, I am, however, a monist.

I see no inconsistency or incompatibility in these views. I also take it for granted that the major and primary business of the psychologist, as scientist, is to seek out the psychological order of law and I do not see that he has any chance of fulfilling his mission if he does not realize that the mental and behavioral act involves something outside of the body.

I have stated that the cardinal obligation of a scientist is to maintain faith with his subject matter, and I do not know of a single psychological datum that violates the rule that it involves a relationship between an actor and an object. But psychologists do go on pretending that the datum is still complete when it has been stripped of the object. They do this, not because of what they observe, but because of what they think they should be observing.

To repeat, Allport cannot escape the fact that what he includes in the person-system is transactional in character and that the transactions involved necessarily involve objects that typically are not to be found inside the skin. Well, then, why does he not face up to this fact?

I think that there are two reasons, though Allport explicitly concerns himself only with the second, which I shall soon consider. The first is more difficult to confront, partly because the assertion that mental events are not confined to the body violates deeply ingrained habits of thought with which all of us have grown up, but partly also because this assertion contains within it an implication that seems to fly in the face of common sense. Let me try to bring out the implication.

When I assert that I see, say, an apple, I am implying that the apple is part of my perception; the apple is contained in my perception. Common sense tells us, however, that the apple is an independent entity. It remains available, for instance, for others to see. When I see it, I do not incorporate it in the sense that I would if I were to eat it. Moreover, when I see it, I only see it in some of its aspects and not in the totality that is implied in an actual incorporation of it into something else. On this basis, it seems that the apple, as such, cannot be said to be contained in my perceptual act.

What, then, is contained in my perception of the apple? Why a perceived apple. Common sense has thus landed in a phenomenalist position which it must also find untenable. It will be evident to anyone but a philosopher that it is not a perceived apple that I see, even though my seeing it establishes it as a perceived apple; it is just a plain, simple, honest-to-goodness, natural apple. If I were to perceive a perceived apple, the perceptual event would be much more complex than, and distinguishable from, the perceptual event involved in my seeing just a plain apple.

This dilemma of common sense is easily resolved since it rests on a number of invalid assumptions concerning the relation of containment. The fact of the matter is that I can cast a loop around an object without thereby destroying the status of the object as an independent entity and without preventing anyone else from also casting his own loop around the same object. Containment does not necessarily destroy the object contained; nor does it necessarily imply exclusive appropriation. Moreover, containment does not necessarily imply totality of containment. Thus, the apple that I see is a member of—contained in—the class of apples which in turn is a member of the class of fruit; but note that the class of apples does not contain the rind and core of my apple since neither rind nor core are, in themselves, apples. Stated in mathematical language, the relationship of containment is not necessarily transitive with respect to the components of that which is contained. Or, to approach the issue differently, suppose we agree that I do not see the apple in its totality, but merely an aspect of the apple. Then, it is that aspect of the apple that is contained in my perceptual act and not its unseen aspects or attributes.

But I can imagine an apple.

"How," cries common sense, "can you say that your imagining reaches out of yourself to include a nonexisting apple?"

"Do not be so pleased with yourself and your fine logic," I respond. "Bear in mind that if you best me in this argument, it will only be a pyrrhic victory for you. You will only land in the morass of phenomenalism and condemned to live out your life as a realist (because that is the only way you can conduct your life outside of an insane asylum) while professing phenomenalism. I am not trying to evade the responsibility of answering your challenge. But I do wish you would realize that your real stakes are on my side of the argument.

"Now, let me call your attention to the fact that you have just equated 'imagined' with 'nonexistent.' Where do you suppose that my imagined apple came from? Out of the beyond-time-and-space? Did I create it? Do I have a secret storehouse of images hidden somewhere in my body and, if so, how did an image of a nonexistent apple ever get into that storehouse?

"Perhaps we had better pause and examine that image. When I see the apple, I perceive it in its here-and-nowness. When I think of the apple in my fruit bin, it is not here-and-now, but in my fruit bin—or, at least, that is where it should be. It is still a plain, simple, honest-to-goodness, natural, particular apple I am thinking of—imagining, if you will. My act of imagining this apple is not, insofar as its inclusion in my mental process is concerned, very different from the case of seeing the apple. Well, then, suppose I imagine an apple—no particular apple in no particular place. It still remains true that the fact of appleness is a reality in our world, and it is to appleness that I am, in imagination, addressing myself; and the qualities of appleness, an external reality, are included in my act of imagining. I proceed to imagine a blue apple with a peach-fuzz rind and laughing green eyes. Surely, no such apple exists or has ever existed and, please God, ever will exist. Even so, I have had to reach out of myself for the existing qualities of blueness, appleness, peach fuzz, and laughing green eyes. Granted that I can combine these actualities into a nonexisting imaginative concoction, I still must include external actuality in my creation. Note that I am not saying that my imagination is limited to that which I have experienced, but that I cannot imagine anything without reaching out to and including in my imaginative acts worldly actualities outside of myself."

So much, then, for the first possible reason for rejecting the view that the person-system is itself transactional. The apparent violence to common sense turns out to be violence to naïve and unreflective common sense. When the issues are considered, there seems to be no conclusion consistent with common sense other than that psychological process is, indeed, transactional, and one gains as a by-product that one discovers that there is no need for a bridge from the world of mind to the world of matter.

Let me turn now to the second reason for rejecting the transactional view of the person system. Allport is afraid that in conceiving the personality as a transactional process he will lose the person in a series of transient transactions. "There is," he affirms, "a persistent though changing person-system in time, clearly delimited by birth and death."[15] This affirmation, I must agree, accords in the main with my own observation—except that I am not quite ready to agree that the newborn infant is already a person. Moreover, I must also agree that the person system engages in transient transactions that Allport wants to accommodate in his defective fourth criterion. Does this leave me in the paradoxical position of claiming that a persisting personality is a transactional system composed of transient transactions?

Note that Allport assumes that the only thing about a person that persists is the body. What he overlooks is the persisting system of derived, perpetuated, and imbricating motives, an issue to which I will return in Chapter 10. This system, when it finds itself in a particular situation, does engage in transactions that come to an end as new situations develop and then becomes involved in new transactions. As I write this essay, for instance, I can foresee that the writing will come to an end. Such a series of transactions does not define my personality. The enduring motivational structure that characterizes me, however, does enter into each of these transactions; and the transiency of these activities does not alter the fact that the enduring motivational system is itself transactional in character.

The enduring motivational structure, moreover, does seem to be intimately bound to the body. It moves around with the body, many of its conditions are demonstrably in the body, it is in many ways concerned with the body, and there is no critical observational evidence that it can survive the body. None of which serves to prove that it is identical with the body or that it is contained in the body.

[15] Allport, ibid., p. 48.

9

THE SELF AND ITS BODY:

FIRST INQUIRY

ABOUT THE ACTOR

There is a rather remarkable difference between the way each of us apprehends his own behaviors and those of others. The subject, that is, the one who carries out the activity, in our own behaviors is generally taken to be a self; the subject in the behaviors of others, a person. In our experience of behavior, we are primarily selves and only inferentially persons, whereas others are primarily persons and only inferentially selves.

It may, of course, be argued that, in making this distinction, I am making a mountain out of a molehill of linguistic convention and that "self" and "person" are merely two different ways of referring to the same kind of entity; and it is undoubtedly true that these terms are often used—along with a variety of others, such as "organism"—in an essentially synonymous fashion. They are so used precisely because they have in common the reference to the acting subject. I am not discussing the words, however, but the experience, and in the experience of our own behavior we apprehend an inner core of our personness as the agent whereas we have no such direct and immediate apprehension of an inner core in the case of another person.

I raise the issue not so much for its own sake as to make the point that our direct experience of behavior offers no clear identification of the subject. Self and person are not identical; but they are also not independent entities. It is not that we experience two kinds of subject, but rather that, from different perspectives, the subject seems to have somewhat different identities; not merely different aspects, but somewhat different identities. As though to underscore the fact that there are not two different kinds of subject that we apprehend while at the same time affirming the difference between self and person, there are occasions when we do apprehend the essential selfness of the other and the personness of ourselves. Thus, when the other behaves in a manner radically inconsistent with our expectations of him, we may have the compelling experience that it was not really he who acted in this way, that he (the essential he, the self) was not really in possession of himself (the person); and we may, at times, address ourselves as persons without any experience of incongruity in doing so.

Who, then, is the subject? Is he self, or person, or both? Or shall we say—as I suspect most contemporary psychologists would without hesitation do—that our experience is here utterly misleading and that the real subject is the organism?

To assert that the body is involved in the action is not the same as to assert that the organism is the subject. There are obviously a variety of ways that the body can be involved without the logical implication that the organism is the subject: (1) Certain bodily structures and processes, not necessarily the same for different behaviors, must be sufficiently unimpaired to permit a given behavior, and the criterion of sufficient unimpairment must hold for at least one way of accomplishing the behavior; that is, the body contains, or "sets," supporting and constraining conditions that determine the feasibility of given behaviors.[1] (2) I take it as axiomatic that some bodily process must be involved in any behavior.[2] I shall return to two other ways in which the body can be involved shortly.

[1] In the interests of making a relatively simple statement, I have oversimplified the first part of this sentence in two ways: (1) Alternative ways are not necessarily of equal difficulty. Thus, take away my right hand and I can still write with my left, but the greater difficulty of doing so will affect the likelihood of my engaging in writing behavior. (2) A body mechanism for engaging in a particular behavior may be unimpaired but unavailable because it is engaged in an incompatible behavior.

[2] I state the principle as an axiom, but it will be apparent from earlier discussion that I regard it as a necessary axiom: If mental events affect bodily and other physical events and if we assume physical law to be inviolable, then we must assume that the mental events must involve bodily events; parsimony then requires that we assume that mental events that have no manifest physical consequences must be similarly bound to the body. Else, we must assume that a thought that causes, say, my heart to beat faster is different in its essential character *qua* thought from one that does no such thing and, further, we must find an, as yet unproposed, solution of the mind-body problem.

The Problem of the Actor

Neither of the two preceding propositions concerning the role of the body in behavior establishes the appropriateness of substituting "organism" for "subject" in the description of behavior. For one thing, I am not at all certain just what "organism" is supposed to denote as distinguished from the living body. It is often said that behavioral activity involves the activities of the organism as a whole in contradistinction to the part activities involved in the strictly biological functions. I rather doubt, however, that more of the body is involved in, say, seeing than in digesting. Moreover, when I contemplate my hand, is my hand involved in this operation in any fashion other than as object? And what basis is there for saying that the organismic involvement is any different in the activity of contemplating my hand than in the activity of contemplating the book I hold in my hand?

It may be said that I am taking "as a whole" too literally. We may speak quite literally of the beating of my heart, of the outpouring of gastric juices in my stomach, of the activation of my brain; but we may speak of my eyes seeing, my ears hearing, my heart loving only as figures of speech. When we speak of organism-as-a-whole in the context of the latter activities, it may be argued, we mean only to indicate that the real subject has not been sufficiently identified. In this case, however, substituting "organism as a whole" for "subject" merely begs the question as to the real identity of the subject.

Alternatively, it may be argued, "organism as a whole" is merely a shorthand expression for the set (in part unknown) of bodily parts actively involved in a particular behavior. On this basis, however, there is a different subject for each behavior and the only relation between the various subjects—apart from the possible overlapping of the members of the various sets—is that the various sets of body parts happen to be components of a particular organism. On this basis, too, the subject who loves is not, in essential principle, different from the subject that digests or the complex set of bodily parts (including the heart muscle, itself) that regulates the beating of the heart. Both these inferences may be comforting to those psychologists who cannot bring themselves to accept the reality of any psychological phenomena, but, to me, they seem to belie the nature of the observed phenomena as much as the statement that it is my eyes that see.

Now, granting that my body sets some of the feasibility conditions and is actively involved in such behaviors as contemplating my hand, lifting myself, going somewhere, and so on, it is still possible that the properly descriptive relation of the body to the subject is as a vehicle;

the body carries the subject. As it happens, I am writing these lines at the time of the great transportation strike of 1965 in New York City. The events of this period serve as a vivid reminder that vehicles (subways and buses) serve to determine feasibility conditions of certain behaviors and are actively involved in the latter. My point is that the relation subject-vehicle is obviously not incompatible with the two already stated body-behavior relationships.

I am, of course, well aware that there is probably nothing I can say that is as well calculated to evoke horror among my scientist brethren as to suggest that the body serves as a vehicle for the subject in behavior. "Shades of extranatural souls!" they may exclaim, with or without awareness of the pun. Our problem, however, is precisely to identify the subject, and I can only beg of them (if they are still with me) to exercise some patience until we can properly identify the subject—and not until then decide that the relation subject-vehicle must necessarily require the invocation of an extranatural entity. Since I am confident that the properly identified subject is an entirely natural entity with respect to which the body can stand in the relation of vehicle, I do not have to answer the question of what the properly scientific course of action should be if it were to turn out that the properly identified subject is indeed an extranatural entity.

Before proceeding with my inquiry into the nature of the subject, however, let me mention still a fourth body-behavior relation that is not incompatible with any of the three already mentioned. This is the role of the body as instrument. I, for instance, use my arm to point. I have, in this connection, often carried out the following demonstration to my classes. I ask a student volunteer to point at the blackboard. When he does so, I say, "No. Do not use that arm!" He then points with his other arm. I say, "No. That is not what I want you to do. Do not use either arm!" With a more or less self-conscious grin, the student usually points with his foot or, sometimes, vigorous head and chin movements. I continue, ruthlessly, to preclude the use of the parts of the body to which the student resorts (and notice that I have just said "use"). Only a sense of delicacy leads me to refrain from mentioning the part of the body the vigorous thrusts of which are utilized to carry out an unambiguous act of pointing under the restraining conditions that I impose.

I often get a feeling of the remarkable insensitivity of some of my colleagues who are so fond of talking of the conditioning of responses to the almost unbelievable malleability of the body as an instrumentality in behavior. To emphasize the point, let me cite the thoroughly documented case of Franz Rosenzweig.[3]

Toward the end of his thirty-fourth year, in 1921, Rosenzweig first began to notice the symptoms of a disease which, a few months later, was diagnosed as "amyotrophic lateral sclerosis with progressive paralysis of the bulba." By August 1922, it had become difficult for him to write and his speech became relatively inarticulate. By December 1922, he lost all ability to write and, by the spring of 1923, he suffered a total loss of speech. By the fall of that year, there was a total loss of control of movements of limbs. After a siege of bronchopneumonia and severe fever in 1927, Rosenzweig began to suffer repeated attacks of high fever in 1928, culminating in a marked deterioration of his general health by February 1929. On December 9, 1929, Franz Rosenzweig died. It is not necessary to my point to adumbrate the details of the difficulties he experienced, and the amount of time entailed in eating and in the sheer mechanics of getting him dressed and undressed and the management of his body to relieve his intense suffering.

Those unfamiliar with the life of Rosenzweig will doubtless think of countless similar cases of prolonged debilitation and suffering, and will wonder what I am driving at. Well, Rosenzweig was a distinguished biblical scholar, essayist, and existentialist philosopher, and he continued at the height of his productive pace throughout the years I have so bleakly summarized in the preceding paragraph.

On December 9, 1929, the day of his death, he was interrupted in the "writing" of a letter to Martin Buber by a visit of his physician. In 1925, Buber had been asked to prepare a new German translation of the Bible and made his acceptance contingent on Rosenzweig's collaboration. Rosenzweig agreed, and the joint enterprise was conducted as follows: Buber would prepare a first draft which he sent to Rosenzweig, receiving in return detailed compilations of suggested changes, reservations, and references. Some of these were immediately incorporated by Buber; others were reviewed at length through an interchange of correspondence. As Buber has indicated, there were many instances in which a single word became the subject of weeks of letter writing. Whatever remained that was controversial was discussed on Buber's weekly afternoon visit. The entire process was repeated as final draft for the printer was prepared, and again with the first and second proofs. The collaborators began with the book of Genesis, worked their way through the re-

[3] See Nahum N. Glatzer, *Franz Rosenzweig: His Life and Thought* (New York: Schocken Books, 1953.)

maining four books of the Pentateuch, continued through Joshua, Judges, Samuel, Kings, and completed the translation of Isaiah in November 1929.

During the years of this collaboration, Rosenzweig composed and published numerous articles on biblical, historical, religious, and philosophical problems. He also translated many poems by the Hebrew poet, Judah ha-Levi, and in 1927 published an expanded edition of *Judah ha-Levi*, the first edition of which was completed subsequent to the onset of his virtually total paralysis. During this time, he also maintained an extensive nontrivial correspondence, managed the affairs of his household with respect to which he was both consulted and made his wishes known, received a stream of carefully selected (by himself) visitors with whom he had various matters to discuss, edited an anniversary volume in honor of Martin Buber's fiftieth birthday, listened to music, acquiring a fine collection of recordings by writing reviews of them for the *Kasseler Tageblatt*, and took great joy in watching the growth and development of his young son who was born shortly after the onset of his illness.

By now, the reader may have forgotten that Rosenzweig could neither speak nor write. How did he manage? At first, he had a special typewriter constructed on which he could tap out what he had to say. As his paralysis progressed, a system of braces and levers enabled him to point to the letters. With diminishing control, his inaccuracies increased and his helpers (mainly a heroic wife) had to guess at his intentions, testing their interpretations out by repeating them to him, watching his facial expression for approval or disapproval; and on numerous occasions, the helper simply had to resort to reciting the alphabet over and over, with the same kind of feedback to determine his desired succession of letters. I have mentioned the heroism of his wife. As for himself, in a letter of March 16, 1927, Rosenzweig denied any heroism, pointing out that it is a great deal to be able to maintain one's morale "somewhat" in the face of misfortune and that he would become terribly bored if he could not go on working.

How can one possibly interpret such a life as anything but a utilization of one's body, or what is left of it, toward a larger purpose? An extraordinary life, no doubt. But Franz Rosenzweig was a human being, a man. The order of law that governed his behavior was not, in any essential principle, different from that which governs the behaviors of the rest of us. And it is our task as scientists to be able to do justice to such extraordinary occurrences. In the case of Rosenzweig, as in the case of the rest of us, the key question is how we can identify the essential nature of the being who carries on its various enterprises. Surely, it does not help very much to describe it as a biological organism, dependent as it may be on the life and functioning of such an organism.

As alternatives to the organism, we are left with such concepts as self, ego, personality, and person. It remains, then, to examine these concepts, how they relate to one another and to the organism, how their referents fit the role of actor, and, in general, how they fit into the scheme of things.

Let me start with the self, a concept that has had a troubled history in the course of human thought, and let me introduce it with an anecdote, part of the folklore that developed about Morris Raphael Cohen at the City College of New York.

The tale goes back to a time when psychology courses were taught under the aegis of the Department of Philosophy, and psychologists and philosophers shared a tiny, overcrowded office. One day, a student entered the office and approached the nearest person who, as luck would have it, happened to be Professor Cohen. When the latter looked up, the student timidly said, "Sir, I have a problem."

Professor Cohen, whose mode of address was often as gruff as his heart was kind, barked, "Yes, what is it?"

Said the student, "I sometimes get a feeling that I don't exist."

"Who," snapped Professor Cohen, "sometimes gets the feeling that you don't exist?"

"Why, I . . . ," said the student; then, with a very sheepish expression, he turned around and walked out.

Accepting the story as true, I have been inclined to suspect that the student came into the office looking for a psychologist rather than a philosopher; and I have often wondered about what ever did happen to the student after he left. That, however, is aside from the point which is that the student had been led to discover, for himself, Descartes's proof of his own existence.

Descartes, it will be recalled, began with a determination to question everything, but soon discovered that there was one thing he could not question, namely, that he was doubting, that he was questioning, and thence arrived at the conclusion, "Cogito, ergo sum" ("I think, therefore I am").

The proof, alas, does not have the mettle that Descartes was able to develop in the proofs of his analytic geometry. The crux of the question "Do I exist?" is not whether every sentence requires a subject, but whether the subject in describing the various activities ascribed to a given individual—the "I"—is indeed throughout the same. Thus, Sartre[4] has argued that, in the very sentence "I think, therefore I am," the "I" that thinks is not the same "I" as the "I" that is. I shall return to Sartre's argument. For the moment, it is sufficient to note that it was not very long after Descartes advanced his proof before David Hume was challenging the existence of the self as a continuing entity.

"There are some philosophers," wrote Hume,[5]

who imagine we are every moment intimately conscious of what we call our SELF; that we feel its existence and its continuance in existence, and are certain, beyond the evidence of a demonstration, both of its perfect identity and simplicity. . . . For my part, when I enter most intimately into what I call *myself* I always stumble on some particular perception or other. . . . I never can catch *myself* at any time without a perception, and never can observe anything but the perception. . . . If anyone, upon serious and unprejudiced reflection, thinks he has a different notion of *himself,* I must confess I can no longer reason with him. All I can allow is that . . . we are essentially different in this particular.

Long afterwards, William James, writing of what he called "the Spiritual Self . . . a man's inner or subjective being . . . the active element in all consciousness . . . a spiritual something in him which seems to *go out* to meet these qualities and contents, whilst they seem to *come in* to be received by it . . . what welcomes or rejects . . . presides over the perception of sensations . . . that within us to which pleasure and pain . . . speak . . . the source of effort and attention, and the place from which emanate the fiats of the will,"[6] confesses that *"it is difficult for me to detect in the activity any purely spiritual element at all. Whenever my introspective glance succeeds in turning round quickly enough . . . all it can ever feel distinctly is some bodily process, for the most part taking place within the head."*[7] He concludes that in his own case, at least, *"the 'Self of selves' . . . is found to consist mainly of the collection of these peculiar motions in the head or between the head and throat."*[8] Recognizing the difficulty of introspecting on the self, he goes on, "If the dim portions which I cannot yet define should prove like unto these distinct portions in me, and I like other men, *it would follow that*

[4] Jean-Paul Sartre, *Being and Nothingness,* tr. by H. Barnes (New York: Philosophical Library, 1956).

[5] David Hume, *Treatise of Human Nature,* Book I, pt. IV.

[6] William James, *The Principles of Psychology* (New York: Holt, 1890), vol. 1, pp. 296–298. All italics in this and the following quotations are in the original.

[7] *Ibid.,* vol. 1, p. 300.

[8] *Ibid.,* vol. 1, p. 301.

*our entire feeling of spiritual activity . . . is really a feeling of bodily ac-
tivities whose exact nature is by most men overlooked.*"[9]

Titchener,[10] similarly, inquiring into the constitution of the self, as the
latter appears in consciousness, could find no more than a variety of
sensations of pressure, pain, temperature, strain, and the like, and two
additional components: visual images of the body or parts of it in some
characteristic pose and attire and the words "I" or "my." These components, he added, are typically more laden with affective tone and
swamped with feelings than is characteristic of the consciousness of
things and processes outside the body. In brief, there really is no fundamental and enduring entity that can be found in consciousness. There
is rather a variety of constituents linked together into one aggregate set
by associative processes based on the frequent concurrences of various
combinations of the components. It is this aggregate set that constitutes
the idea of self. What Titchener found in consciousness when he tried
to examine the self is thus not very different from what James and
Hume had found.

The reduction of the self to a set of varying experiences, nothing being
common to all members of the set, poses a number of difficulties. Rationally, so long as one restricts oneself to his discussion of the self,
Hume is in a stronger position than either James or Titchener. Seeking,
he is unable to find anything at all indicative of selfhood, and it is only
reasonable, in this extremity, to confess his puzzlement about what it is
that others are talking about when they speak of their selves.[11] James
and Titchener, however, do find something to relate to the experience of
self. It is not at all clear, however, why the experiences they describe
should be linked with self. Why not simply accept Hume's argument and
regard these experiences as disparate, if overlapping, subsets of experi-

[9] *Ibid.*, vol. 1, pp. 301–302.

[10] E. B. Titchener, *An Outline of Psychology*, rev. ed. (New York: Macmillan,
1902).

[11] Even so, it seems to me that Hume protests too much, that his challenge to
the reader to find a referent for the term "self" is just a bit too disingenuous,
and that his argument lacks a ring of authenticity in the sense of consistency
with his position in the world. Consider, for instance, a person who discovers
that he is utterly lacking in some apparently universal human attribute, say,
color vision or sexual desire or orgastic potency. In my own experience of such
individuals, the discovery is always accompanied by some compound of denial
of the defect, dismay, panic, defensiveness, and so on. It is precisely the absence
of any such reactions along with the note of confidence that he is assuredly not
a freak that evokes in me a feeling of the inauthenticity of Hume's argument.
His argument is part of an intellectual game and not at all a challenge to his
very existence. It does not, so to say, reach him where he lives.

ence, one kaleidoscopically giving way to another in the temporal succession of the stream of consciousness? Why, moreover, should certain experiences be more intimately linked with self than others? Why, for instance, should it be possible for me to contemplate my hand and the sensory messages that I receive from it and experience my hand as outside of myself? As I contemplate my hand, I seem to be here and my hand there. Note that James's own "Self of selves" consists mainly of the collection of peculiar experiences of movements in his head or between his head and throat, and not of the entire collection of experiences of the body. Why the distinction? Why should it be possible for a person to become so absorbed in a task-oriented activity or so enwrapped in the aesthetic appreciation of a sunset as to seem for a time to be quite selfless? It seems clear, then, that the linkage of certain experiences with the self presupposes a self to which the experiences may be linked.

James confronts the issue. He places considerable emphasis on the unifying roles of similarity and of continuity of transition.

Continuity makes us unite what dissimilarity might otherwise separate; similarity makes us unite what discontinuity might hold apart. . . . *The sense of our own personality, then, is exactly like any one of our other perceptions of sameness among phenomena.* . . . And it must not be taken to mean more than these grounds warrant. . . . The past and present selves compared are the same just so far as they *are* the same, and no farther. A uniform feeling of "warmth," of bodily existence (or an equally uniform feeling of pure psychic energy?) pervades them all; and this is what gives them a *generic* unity, and makes them the same in *kind.* . . . And similarly of the attribute of continuity; it gives its own kind of unity to the self—that of mere connectedness, or unbrokenness, a perfectly definite phenomenal thing—but it gives not a jot or tittle more.[12]

Observe that James himself does not seem quite sure of what the features of similarity are that unite the various subsets of experiences. "A uniform feeling of 'warmth,' of bodily existence, . . . of pure psychic energy" do not seem to be identical elements. Must all three, then, be present to establish sameness in kind or may it sometimes be one and sometimes another? If the latter, what is the basis of similarity between them? If the former, is James denying the possibility of a feeling of disembodied selfness such as many have, for instance, reported to have occurred in dreams and states of revery?—a denial that hardly seems consistent with so many other facets of James's thought and writing.

[12] James, vol. 1, pp. 334–335.

For my own part, I must confess that I do not experience much similarity among my experiences of my eye movements, my breathing, my subvocal speech, the clenching of my jaws, and so on, not, that is, unless I were to emphasize the "my," which would be to beg the question at issue. Indeed, if you were to ask me what is most like what I experience when I experience my eye movements or my breathing, I would be constrained to refer, not to other varieties of my experiences, but to your eye movements and your breathing. Nor can I detect anything about my experiences of my eye movements or my subvocal speech, which I can characterize as "warmth," and it seems to me that I have often had such experiences without any experience of my bodily existence as such. To be sure, we may place experiences of eye movements and of subvocal speech into a common conceptual category of experiences of bodily existence and infer the generality from the particular;[13] but James is talking not about an inference of bodily existence but about a feeling, a uniform feeling.

Continuity, as a factor unifying a succession of disparate selves, hardly fares any better than does similarity. Discontinuities in the succession of experiences of selfhood are quite common without any embarrassment to the sense of the identity of the self across the experienced discontinuity. There are, for instance, episodes of selflessness such as those to which I have referred earlier and there are experiences of amnestic gaps. Most common of all are the experienced discontinuities associated with sleep—a point to which Hume refers in challenging the continuing identity of the self. Moreover, there may be manifest discontinuities—and no obvious similarities, either—between the last Thoughts[14] prior to the beginning of the discontinuity and the first Thoughts after its end. Thus, to refer to one of James's vivid illustrations, Peter awakening in the same bed with Paul and immediately assuming his own rather than Paul's identity, one may speculate that Peter's last Thoughts before falling asleep ran along the following lines:

"I must become oblivious to Paul's presence. His body is . . . Cut that out! . . . His body is so warm—a radiator. . . . What if I . . . Stop that! . . . I must blank my mind . . . count sheep. . . . One, two.

[13] There exists an experience of eye movement; the experience of eye movement is a member of the class of experiences of bodily existence; therefore, there exists an experience of bodily existence.

[14] James adopts the convention of capitalizing the "T" in order to designate an immediately present mental state in the stream of consciousness.

... My hand. ... No, not again! ... Blank, blank. ... Darkness. ...
Darkness. ... Da ... ark ... ness. ...."

And, on awakening: "Morning. ... Light. ... Morning already? ...
Time to get up. ... Who's this? ... Oh, Paul ... That's right! We
... If I don't get up at once and run to the bathroom, I'll ...."

Where is the continuity here? And the similarity? The example is, of
course, fictitious; but the reader can check his own experience for
parallels. At any rate, James is himself not too happy with his account
to this point. "For common-sense insists that the unity of all the selves
is not a mere appearance of similarity or continuity, ascertained after
the fact. ... [There] must be a real proprietor in the case of the
selves, or else their actual accretion into a 'personal consciousness'
would never have taken place."[15]

The proprietor, James avers, is the Thought. The latter is, however,
but a momentary segment in the stream of consciousness. To maintain
the continuity, James postulates as a "patent fact of consciousness"
that each thought inherits its predecessor. "Each later Thought, knowing
and including thus the Thoughts which went before, is the final recep-
tacle—and appropriating them is the final owner—of all that they
contain and own. Each Thought is thus born an owner, and dies
owned, transmitting whatever it realized as its Self to its own later
proprietor."[16]

If we were to take literally the "all" in "all that they contain and
own," James's effort to recue the continuity of the self is a manifest
absurdity and a flagrant contradiction of James's own brilliant description of the stream of consciousness. On this basis, each of us would, in
every moment of consciousness, be conscious of his entire conscious
history—and what an awesomely burdensome state of affairs that would
be. One must conclude that James cannot possibly intend what he is
here saying, and that he must have been momentarily overwhelmed
by his Thought. The critical idea seems to be that each Thought inherits what its predecessors knew as their selves. If this were the case—
even for James—then he would hardly have the trouble that he has
in giving an account of the self. For the self would never appear in
consciousness as now this and now that; it would rather appear in
successive Thoughts as the original this plus whatever accretions appear in the intervening Thoughts. At the time of writing the chapter on

15 *Ibid.*, vol. 1, p. 337.
16 *Ibid.*, vol. 1, p. 339.

the self, James was obviously lacking in such an accrued inheritance. Moreover, if there should occur an even momentarily selfless consciousness, the entire hereditary mechanism must break down; for it is clear that James's account literally depends on the continuity of transmission.

If, then, we try to follow James as far as it is possible to do so, we must fall back on another idea that James introduces. This is the analogy of a herd of cattle each member of which carries the herd brand. "There is," James asserts, "found a *self*-brand just as there is found a herd brand. Each brand, so far, is the mark, or cause of our knowing, that certain things belong-together. But if the brand is the *ratio cognoscendi* of the belonging, the belonging, in the case of the herd, is the *ratio existendi* of the brand."[17] On this basis, we could interpret James's notion of the heritage of the Thought, not as the containment of all of its possessions, but as a set of possessions which it is able to identify as its own through its ability to recognize the identifying self-mark; and it would also be endowed with the capacity to brand its immediate contents with its unique self-mark so as to guarantee the unbroken transmission of its heritage. A momentary selfless consciousness, or a prolonged succession of such moments of selflessness, would not be incompatible with such a mechanism of inheritance. It is not necessary that each Thought contain a self-awareness; it is only necessary that it be capable of recognizing its own self-brand and of stamping its contents with that brand.

All would now be clear if James could identify the properties of the self-brand. Alas, in this respect, James fails; and, in his failure, the entire discussion comes down to a magnificently prolix begging of the question: There is a conviction of a continuous self that is capable of distinguishing its own from that of others, but no means is provided to validate the conviction or to identify the basis for making the distinction.

Still, James's failure does not imply the inevitability of continued failure. There is, in fact, a self-brand, and it is possible to say exactly what that brand is. Koffka, following an argument which he attributes to Köhler, writes:

"What is there between the last thing just in front and the behind? Is space absolutely empty there? . . . Certainly not; here, between the 'in front' and the 'behind,' is that part of the behavioural world which I call my[self]. It has a very definite place in that world, and well defined, if variable, boundaries. . . . 'In front,' 'to the left and right,' 'behind,' and 'above and

[17] *Ibid.*, vol. 1, p. 337.

below' are characteristics of space which it possesses with regard to an object which serves as the origin of the system of spatial co-ordinates. This object, then, is functionally different from all others, inasmuch as it determines fundamental space aspects."[18]

We may well add the time dimension, since the self is always found between the "already" and the "not yet."

Following this argument, we may say that *the self is that which is at the origin of perceived space-time* (origin, of course, being understood in the mathematical and not in the historical or genetic sense); or, if you will, *the self is the hereness in the thereness.* All of one's own experience, as it occurs—and, more generally, all of one's own behavior—has an implicit reference to this origin; I am here in space-time, and the objects with respect to which I act are there.[19] The implicit reference to this origin, an absolute constant of all personal experience, seems to be the self-brand that James was seeking. It is not necessary for the self, in the sense defined, to be present in awareness—and, in fact, as I will indicate in a moment, it never is—for all personal experience to be stamped with the self-brand. Every experience is associated with a particular identity because, no matter where that identity happens to be located in a time-space coordinate system that is independent of particular identities, the experienced objects are implicitly or explicitly referred to an origin that constitutes the identity and hence moves about with it. Not that I cannot experience directly the location of an object in an objective time-space coordinate system with an arbitrary and impersonal origin, for example, "the treasure is buried

[18] Kurt Koffka, *Principles of Gestalt Psychology* (New York: Harcourt Brace and Co., 1935), p. 322. The word that Koffka uses where I have inserted "self" is "ego." Since he uses "ego" in the sense in which I use "self" and since I use "ego" in another sense, I have taken the liberty of making the substitution.

[19] The same notion is implicit in Heidegger's concept of the *Dasein* (literally, "being there") as the fundamental phenomenological property of human existence. It is to be noted that there are two words for "there" in German, the word "da" having a connotation of immediately present thereness, that is, it involves an immediacy of reference of the being which is immersed in the there. The thereness of "dort" is remote, detached from any particular being. In Heidegger's thought, of course, *Dasein* is also the fundamental ontological property of human existence in the sense that the very concept of such existence is senseless without ascribing to the latter the property of *Dasein*. It seems to me that the *Dasein* refers precisely to that which I have above identified as the self. It may also be noted that all of the existentialists who have been influenced by Heidegger have adopted the *Dasein* as the actor—a practice with respect to which, as will be developed, I have some reservations and which I can only accept with an important qualification. See Martin Heidegger, *Being and Time*, tr. by J. Macquarrie and E. Robinson (New York: Harper & Row, 1962).

twelve paces north of that tree," but, when I do so, the arbitrary origin itself and the space-time system to which it refers are simultaneously located within my private space-time coordinate system.[20] Thus, I may be plotting a set of points on a graph, but the sheet of paper on which I plot the graph is before me and one point is to the right or left of another, "right" and "left" depending on my own orientation. Similarly, for purposes of communication, I can translate the location of the origin of my own space-time coordinate system into a shared coordinate system; but, in my experience of the shared coordinate system, the latter is located with respect to me.

A moment ago, I said that the self, in the sense defined, is never present in awareness. This is the point that Sartre was making, and to which I alluded early in this chapter, when I cited his criticism of Descartes's *Cogito, ergo sum*—a criticism that, incidentally, is one of the points in Sartrian philosophy that most clearly manifests the influence of Husserl. It may be recalled that Sartre contended that the I that thinks is not as the same I as the I that is. Sartre is here concerned quite literally with the I that thinks and not with the I that is observed to think; the latter does, as I will shortly indicate, belong with the I that is. Apart from the strain that such statements impose on our ordinary linguistic usages, which do not discriminate between I in one context and I in another (except when two different persons are involved), the point is a simple one. An observed I is present in an experience as object; but, to be present as an object of awareness, presupposes a subject that is aware. The moment that the latter subject is observed, it is displaced to the position of object which requires a new subject. There is thus a constant succession of subjects exactly analogous to James's constant succession of Thoughts each of which is the hereditary custodian of the self-brand. When I observe myself, there is involved an immediately present I and an I that is temporally displaced from the origin of the personal space-time coordinate system; and, even though that displacement may be so minute as to escape normal attention, it is still there, with the consequence that the seeker after the immediately present I is.engaged in the tantalizing activity of constantly almost grasping the object of his quest, only to find it eluding his

[20] To avoid misunderstanding, I must add that this private coordinate system is not one that is highly metricized. "In front," for instance, subtends a not precisely identified angle, and distance is rarely specified more precisely than "near" or "far." Some degree of metricization is however implicit in such expressions as "directly ahead" and "nearer than."

grasp. Small wonder, then, that the problem of identifying the self has proved to pose so difficult a puzzle to philosophers and psychologists alike.

I must, however, qualify my statement that the self, in the defined sense, is never present in awareness. In my usage, for anything to be present in awareness, it must be present as object; and hence my statement. To Sartre, following Husserl, the latter is not a necessary qualification of presence in awareness. The self, they would say, is transcendentally present, and, in line with the thought expressed toward the end of the preceding paragraph, one may add that it is a most tantalizing transcendental presence, indeed. The term "transcendental" comes from Kantian philosophy and refers to that which is not present in experience, but which is capable of becoming known through inferential reflective thought; in other words, it refers to those things that are not available as sensory or perceptual objects, but the existence of which can (in some acceptable sense of "existence") nevertheless be affirmed.[21]

The notion of transcendental presence (as well as the tantalizing quality of some such presences) may perhaps be more readily illustrated in another context. Köhler writes:

Before a name or another fact is actually remembered there may be a difficulty, a suspense, a delay in its appearance. Nevertheless we may know at the same time that "it is there" . . . [The] reference extends into "darkness" beyond; and yet we feel, from our side, how, over there, it rests on adequate ground. . . . Whenever we try to remember in spite of temporary difficulties, some data are given phenomenally which the thing beyond has to fit. . . . It is not reference in general which in such cases implies some transphenomenal entity; it is, rather, a particular reference which extends beyond, and its implication is that the thing outside fits the concrete phenomenal context in question.[22]

And, in this general context, Köhler quotes the following passage from James: "Suppose we try to recall a forgotten name. The state of our consciousness is peculiar. There is a gap therein; but no mere gap. It is a gap that is intensely active. A sort of wraith of the name is in it, beckoning us in a given direction, making us at moments tingle with

[21] In Kantian philosophy, the term "transcendental" is distinguished from "transcendent," the latter referring to *noumena*, unknowable things-in-themselves. The phenomenal world, in this usage, is thus constituted of transcendental and directly experienced objects and is distinguished from the noumenal world, the world of things-in-themselves.

[22] Wolfgang Köhler, *The Place of Value in a World of Facts* (New York: Liveright, 1938), pp. 117–118.

the sense of our closeness, and then letting us sink back without the longed-for term. If wrong names are proposed to us, this singularly definite gap acts immediately so as to negate them. They do not fit into its mold."[23]

It is to be noted that, in these examples, the transcendentally present object achieves its presence as an object of search. Moreover, even though one cannot for the moment identify the dimensions, attributes, or qualities of the missing object, there is also a present motive that explicitly or implicitly sets some specifications as to the object that can satisfy the motivational requirements. In the course of the search there are apt to be encounters with objects, more or less incipiently produced in the form of images or subvocal articulations, more or less attentively examined for fit, more or less quickly dismissed from further examination, and there are associated moments of greater or lesser feelings of encouragement or discouragement as to the likelihood of success. In other words, there is a great deal that is perceptually or imaginatively present that has bearing on the object of the quest, its attainability, and its proximity.

This is exactly the case as one seeks the subject I. The constancy of the reference in all experience to a common origin, the ability to follow the vectors of that reference to the point where one all but has that origin in one's perceptual grasp, and the rapidity of the onset of failure as the sought-for subject I slips into the position of object I—all of these perceptual features of the search are compelling evidences of the immediate presence of the subject I even though one cannot capture the latter in direct perception.

There are, however, genuinely selfless experiences, in the sense that there is no feeling whatever of the immediate presence of the subject I. The objects experienced still carry the self-brand of being "near" or "far" or "stretching from near to far," of being "in front" or "behind" or 'all around," and so on, but the involvement with these objects is so all-engaging as to leave no concern whatever with tracking the space-time vectors to the origin. Now, even with regard to such experiences, Sartre would say, as would Husserl before him, that the subject I must be transcendentally present. Phenomenologically, even in such experiences, space-time is generated from an origin though, in these experiences, there can be no space-time vectors pointing toward the origin. In fact, neither Sartre nor Husserl (nor, for that matter, I, myself) can

[23] James, vol. 1, p. 251.

conceive of an experience without an object and, since the objective reference ("intentionality" in the phrase of Husserl's teacher, Franz Brentano) implies that experience is an activity, there must be implicated an acting subject. Thus, to Husserl and to Sartre, subject, intentional act, and object are indissolubly linked and, together, constitute the experience. In other words, the experience is not, in their view, simply an act by which the subject relates himself to an object; it is rather the totality subject-act-object to which any description of an experience must refer.

The trouble that I experience with this formulation is that I cannot see an origin of space-time as an acting subject. I can, and do, accept it as the apparent subject, but not as the real actor. I shall return to this apparent subject, and perhaps succeed in making the apparency more palatable; but, first, I must continue with my search for the real actor.

If the self-as-subject has no observable properties other than being the origin of space-time, the situation is quite different for the self-as-object. In its many reappearances, and given its acceptancy by the subject I as the same entity, it becomes associated with a great many properties and attributes. I am not, at the moment, concerned with the actual developmental process, but with the systematic array of these properties and attributes.

To begin with, and let us face it, the ordinary (I was tempted to say, normal) person cannot be less interested in the distinction between the subject self and the object self. Whatever concept is developed from observations of the object self is assumed to hold for the self, that is, the concept assimilates the object self and the subject self into a single self-concept that extends right through past, immediate present, and future. I do not mean to preclude changes in the self-concept, but such changes are with respect to particular properties and attributes that do not challenge the fundamental identity within the limits of the temporal horizons. "I was . . ., I am . . ., I will be . . ." are all facets of a single identity. It does not have to be so, as cases of multiple personality remind us, but it normally is so.

In the second place, the self is associated with a particular body. There are experiences—somesthetic, kinesthetic, and cutaneous—associated with that body that are unique to that body. Visual experiences of visible parts of the body are paralleled by visual experiences of other bodies and auditory experiences of sounds emanating from the body are paralleled by auditory experiences of sounds emanating from other bodies,[24] but there are no parallels at all for somesthetic, kinesthetic, and cutaneous experiences in one's experience of other bodies.[25] Moreover, in a world well furnished with highly reflective surfaces, any direct confrontation of such a surface exposes a mirror image of that same body.[26]

Then, there are various limitations of the self (the apparent actor) that are associated with the body, and it seems likely that the first emergence of a self bounded in space and time occurs in this context. Finding certain states of the body intolerable, there is also a physical

[24] To be sure, the sound of one's voice has components—kinesthetic and resonating reverberations from within the skull—that are not present in hearing the vocalizations of others, but these components are assimilated into the sound of the voice. It generally comes as quite a shock to hear a high-fidelity recording of one's voice, be assured by one's familiars that that is exactly how one's voice always sounds, and nevertheless experience the played-back voice as qualitatively different from the voice one hears as one speaks. After a great many such experiences, I have learned to recognize my played-back voice as mine, but I still do not hear it as the voice that I emit.

[25] The usage of "cutaneous experiences" in this context is somewhat ambiguous and may consequently lead to a vigorous dissent. I can obviously explore a variety of objects by touch, including both my own and other bodies. In this sense, the case for touch is not different than the case for visual and auditory parallels between one's own and other bodies. In the present context, however, I am referring to one aspect of touch sensations, an aspect that has been vividly described by Erwin W. Straus ("Aesthesiology and Hallucinations," in Rollo May, Ernest Augel, and Henry F. Ellenberger, eds., *Existence* [New York: Basic Books, 1958], pp. 159–160): "Every touching is at the same time a being-touched; what I touch touches me . . . If I feel something, at the same time I feel (myself)." In passing, I may note that, in this paper and elsewhere (see, for instance, Erwin W. Straus, *Phenomenological Psychology* [New York: Basic Books, 1966]), Straus brings out many fundamental and consequential facets of sensory-perceptual experiences and related properties of the behavioral world of which our experimental psychologists of sensation and perception seem to be wholly oblivious. For my immediate purpose, however, I am only concerned with the reciprocated aspect of the touch experience. This aspect of touch reveals the integumented boundary of the body in a way that has no parallel in one's awareness of other bodies. It is in this sense that I include the cutaneous experiences among those experiences that are uniquely associated with a particular body.

[26] Again, one must recognize that there are important differences in one's perception of one's mirror image and one's perception of another's body. In a face-to-face confrontation of one's mirror image, for instance, the right hand of the imaged figure is exactly opposite one's own right hand; the right hand of a facing other person is across one's body, at one's left. As one rotates one's body toward the plane perpendicular to the mirror, keeping the mirror at one's left, one perceives the right hand as the remote one. A similar rotation with respect to another person results in the perception of his right hand as the nearer one.

and temporal separation from the objects needed to remedy this state of affairs; but the body itself offers the means of bridging the gap (initially, by emitting sounds that bring the object closer and, later, by approaching the object) and of using the object to remove the distress, displacing the intolerable body states with others that are found to be enjoyable. That is, the body offers itself as a source of hedonic value, as an instrumentality, and as a vehicle. Given these functions with respect to which the body seems to be uniquely under the control and at the service of the self, the body becomes a valued possession.

Moreover, any direction of focal attention to the body as such removes the observed part of the body from the hereness into the thereness. I am here, observing my limbs or the constriction in my chest, or the laryngeal activity, and so on. But the body is the most proximal region of the thereness. Inevitably, I must come to apprehend the body, whenever I think of it or perceive it in relation to my self, as normally surrounding the self, and, conversely, the self as contained in the body. Because, however, I can contemplate a variety of regions of the body, and these regions can be of greater or lesser magnitude and adjacency, and because I am always on the hither side of the regions I am contemplating or between separated but simultaneously contemplated parts, I have no fixed position in the body; that is, I seem to be able to move about more or less freely within it. Also, there are circumstances under which I can contemplate the body from the outside, as it were, that is, the space-time center from which the body is being contemplated is external to the body. As an inevitable consequence of these experiences, the body appears as a nonimprisoning abode of the self.

On the other hand, when the focus of attention is external to the body but not so exclusively so as to preclude any bodily awareness, the position of the origin of space-time is relative to the external object and only minimally so relative to the body or any of its parts. In such experience, therefore, given both body and external object, there can at most be only minimal differentiation of self from body. Self and body tend to become an identity in such experiences. Similarly, if the focus of attention is on the quality of a bodily experience rather than on the part of the body involved, the same lack of the self-body differentiation tends to occur. Pain, for instance, tends to be undifferentiatedly experienced as both self-pain and body pain, and undiscriminated constituents of the experience of pain tend to maximize this effect. Pain threatens the self, and it is this threatening constituent of the pain experience that endows pain with its unendurable character. But if the threat is to the self and the sensory pain experience is of the body and the threat and sensory processes are not discriminated one from another, and, further, if the concern with pain is so absorbing as to preclude the awareness of any object 'twixt self and pain, body and self are fused in the unitary experience.

One other major fact of experience tends to establish an identity of self and body; and, indeed, if the self ever seems to be constitutively inseparable from its bodily garb, it is primarily because of this fact. Thinking about anything whatever is enormously facilitated if it is imaginally represented, but one cannot think imaginally of a pure abstraction; the latter must first, in some way, be concretized and, the more fully the concretization reflects the properties of what is represented the more adequately does it serve the purposes of imaginal representation.

We may, of course, represent the self in verbal symbols and, for many purposes of thought, a word (such as "self," "myself," "I," or a proper name) may represent the self more efficiently than an imaginal representation such as the body image. Such symbols, however, are useful in thinking about the self when the focus of interest is in its actions or in what is happening to it, or in thinking about it for some analytical philosophicopsychological purpose; they do not serve the purposes of permitting one to look at or picturing oneself or any other purpose that demands a concrete imaginal representation such as a simple referent to which the words can be linked.

Moreover, the referent of the words is already compromised in that proper names and the syntactical system of pronouns normally refer to the embodied self or person. Thus, when I say "you" to you, I am not generally greatly concerned about whether I am referring to the essential "you" or, more globally, the "you" that I confront. Similarly, when you say "you" to "me," I take it that you are referring to the "me" that you confront. In both cases, a salient feature of the "you" is a visible body; or when, for instance, we are speaking to one another over the telephone, there is an at least tacitly assumed bodily presence and there are very likely to be intermittently accompanying body images; our relations to one another would be quite different if either or both of us assumed the other to be disembodied. When I address myself in second person or speak about myself in third, I am taking the viewpoint of an other, and the body image is a component of my "you" or "he" or "Isidor." When I say to you, "Hand me that hammer," I expect you, assuming your cooperation, to move the hammer to where it is convenient to my own hand; I do not expect you to transport the hammer into the essential me. Our normal linguistic usage is simply permeated with the assumption of the equivalence of body, body image, and self. This is not to gainsay that many, perhaps most, circumstances justify the usage; greater precision would smack of pedantry. It is only under special circumstances that we realize that, even though we may be invoking the body image, we may not be referring to the body at all.

The root source of the confusion (if one chooses to regard it as confusion), apart from the intimate and close relations of the self to its body, is that the subject self, being only transcendentally present in experience, exists only as pure abstraction;[27] it is never an object of experience and therefore has no proper image.[28] If there exists a "Self of selves," it is precisely this imageless subject that constitutes a link between past and future selves. To understand how that link is forged and the bearing of this on how body, body image, and self come to be regarded as an indissoluble entity at times but independent entities at others, it is necessary to examine more closely the nature of subject and object selves.

The subject self is, so to say, renewed from moment to moment so that its duration between renewals is no longer than the duration of the immediate present; that is, the subject self is a being of the present, and its renewals are concomitants of the movement of, in Eugene O'Neill's phrase, that strange interlude between the past and the future. Past and future object selves are separated from each other by at least that interlude. The effort to perceive the self, at best, introduces a renewed subject self as it reveals an immediately past or immediately anticipated object self.

The temporal gap between past and future, assuming the identity of past and future selves, may be exceedingly brief and the bridging of the gap between them poses no novel psychological problem. One may cite many examples of the perceptual erasure of discontinuities (for instance, the phi phenomenon and the motion pictures that it makes possible, the absence of holes in the visual field corresponding to retinal scotomata,

[27] Do I need to reemphasize that, when I speak of an abstraction, I am not implying unreality? The subject self is always found in a quite narrowly specifiable place at a particular time. Note, however, that the "abstraction" here refers to an extrapolation from experience and not to ignoring irrelevant features of a more complex object.

[28] The image of an origin of a system of coordinates is, to my mind, a proper image; but I have excluded it from consideration in the immediate text because it is obviously a highly advanced intellectual construction.

the continuity of heard speech despite discontinuities of sound production, and so on).

The problem is that past and future object selves acquire their identity from the intervening subject self, which, being transcendental, is so different from them in its phenomenal character and from which they derive their herd mark. The subject self is, therefore, not something that can conveniently be skipped as can a gap. The herd mark of the object selves is that they involve (or are expected to involve) actions emanating from or received at a primal origin of space-time; but, being objects, they are necessarily viewed as one views an other and, as I have already noted, an other is normally an embodied other. Hence, the object selves are embodied.

Embodiment does not necessarily require a familiar body image. The notion of transmigration of souls, for instance, explicitly affirms a change in the body along with the continuity of a self. Or, more familiar to Western modes of thinking, is the ghost image in which we picture someone as constituted of some smokelike, diaphanous, ectoplasmic substance without human form or mode of locomotion. Such a pure ghost image, however, like the image of a transmigrated self, has nothing about it, save a tag, to give it any particular identity. Hence, such images are generally reserved for individuals who do not particularly matter to us, and our images of our personal ghosts (whether of ourselves or of our significant others) generally retain a recognizable bodily form, albeit one composed of ectoplasm. But, if even one's own ghost is given its familiar embodiment, so is the object self. The body image provides the most apprehensible concrete form of the object self. The object self, therefore, which temporally surrounds and is phenomenally continuous through the subject self is apprehended as embodied in its own body. What is more natural, then, than to make the same attribution to the subject self?

So the self, object and subject, which clearly is not the body, is nevertheless garbed in the body image; and apparently we cannot picture ourselves in any clearly recognizable fashion except as so garbed. This binding of the image of the self to the body image, however, does not make the body image a constitutive part of the self, though it is a component of the self-concept. My point is that self and self-concept are not identical, no more than is any concept identical with whatever it is a concept of. In fact, that the self, an abstraction, is concretely represented by the body image is a special case of the more general principle that the imaginal representation of any concept, no matter how abstract, is always concrete, and, if an abstraction has imaginal representations, these representations are components of the concept, perhaps of its far reaches, but not of what is being conceptualized. The reality of the latter, as I have argued earlier, is independent of whether it is conceptualized.

Thus, abstract ideas are readily represented in dream imagery in the form of quasimetaphoric equivalents or other quasifigures of speech (for example, "my words" may be represented by a visual image of a dictionary, string of pearls—as in the figure of speech, "pearls of wisdom"—and so on; or "success" by an image of a ship entering a dock—as in the figurative "my ship has come in"—and so on). The imaginal representations may be far-fetched exemplifications of the concept, but they do exemplify it and thus indicate its reach or scope.

The body image is likewise used as a concrete representation of the self and is hence contained within the bounds of the concept of the self. In dreams, however, thinking normally takes place at the level of primary process, that is, abstractions are not only concretized in a way that facilitates imaginative thought, but there is also a failure or suspension of attention to differentials and concern with making distinctions;[29] things related to one another as quasimetaphors, and the like, are therefore dealt with as identities. Similarly, when we take the body image as identical with the self (and it may be worth emphasizing that it is only the body image, rarely the body itself, that is so taken), we overlook the fact that the former represents the latter and mistake the imaginal representation for that which is represented; we transform the relationship "stands for" into one of identity. Thus, when we take the self as constitutively inseparable from its bodily garb, we are, in effect, caught up in what is, from a reflective point of view, a trap of primary-process thinking; and primary process, of course, underlies (or, perhaps

---

[29] I realize that there are other characteristics of primary-process thought, for example, condensation, but I think that the preceding describes its basic characteristic. Thus, a dream image that is figuratively, but independently, related to two separate things (for example, pearls to wealth and pearls to words) may represent both simultaneously (as, "I give you my pearls" may mean, "In giving you, my psychoanalyst, my words, I am giving you of my substance and I expect an equivalent return from you" in the context of an expression of anger and disappointment at the failure of the analyst to answer questions about himself). In the dream from which the example is taken, the dreamer tries to return a string of pearls to the five-and-dime store where the clerk (note the disparagement of the analyst) accepts it but charges him an amount equal to the analytic fee. Similarly, concerns that are otherwise distinct may be simultaneously expressed as if they were identical.

better expressed, constitutes a subconscious underlay of) waking thought besides dominating sleep thought.

But even when the self is constitutively endowed with the body image and, in this version, imaginally abstracted from any particular activity or setting, it is not an inert, senseless body mass that one imagines. I can, of course, imagine my dead body; but, with such imagining, it is impossible to maintain the equation of body image and self, for, here am I, picturing a body represented as formerly mine, and it was Freud[30] who first noted that it is impossible to imagine one's own mortality. The body image that represents my self pulses not only with life but, if only latently so, with my concerns and powers; and I, at least, do not apprehend in this self-constituting body image any particular sensations in the region of the eyes, throat, chest, or anywhere else.

In any case, the self appears in experience as a something that stands at the origin of directly experienced space-time, but not as a mere *some*thing. It is a something that, in various perspectives, appears as a particular body, as resident in that body, as carried in that body, as utilizer of that body, as owner of that body, as uniquely informed of what goes on in that body, and as receiving pleasure and pain from that body. These various aspects of the self are not mutually contradictory, no more than are the varied appearances of any object when regarded in different perspectives. The "substantiality" of any object requires that it have different projections in different perspectives.

There is nothing in the preceding review of the phenomenology of the self-body relationship that is inconsistent with the proposition that there could be no cognitive processes, and hence no self, but for the existence of the body. I must again repeat, however, that a necessary condition is not the same as—nor more real than—that of which it is a condition. Nor is there any sensible reason that I know of for assuming that the most important statement a psychologist can make about the self is the assertion of the dependency of the latter on the integrity of certain bodily structures and functions. Nor is it at all evident to me that the assertion that the self cannot survive the body should surpass in psychological import Freud's observation to which I have already referred that no one can imagine his own cessation of existence when his body is destroyed. Why must my belief be behaviorally more consequential than the failure of my imaginative grasp?

[30] S. Freud, "Thoughts for the Times on War and Death. Part II: Our Attitude Towards Death" (1915), in *The Standard Edition of the Complete Psychological Works of Sigmund Freud*, vol. 14 (London: Hogarth Press, 1957).

By the same token, I cannot say that the phenomenology of the relation of the self to the body is the psychologically most significant aspect of the self-concept. I am rather inclined to doubt it, and have devoted as much space to the subject as I have only to indicate that the phenomenology of the relationship, so revolting to most contemporary scientific psychologists as mystical nonsense, is entirely amenable to naturalistic treatment.

The self-concept plays a central role in the shaping of the next candidate for the role of the actor that I want to consider, the ego. I shall continue the discussion in the next chapter.

10

WHO IS THE ACTOR?

CONTINUATION OF THE INQUIRY:

THE SELF AND THE EGO

By far the most significant aspect of the self, and far more fundamental than the issue of its location, is the appearance of the object self as actor. "Whenever my introspective glance succeeds in turning round quickly enough"—to borrow this phrase once again from William James —I find myself doing something—perceiving, thinking, loving, moving to some destination, and so on, with respect to one or another object, treating myself to some experience such as relaxing or basking in the sun, or some other reflexive act like trying to perceive myself. It is not true, as James would have it, that all that my introspective glance "can ever feel distinctly is some bodily process." What my introspective glance may reveal—if the body is experienced at all save when it is directly examined—is some blurred apprehension of the body or some bodily process or, often enough, nothing of the body at all.

Even when the revealed bodily process is focal, the salient fact about the self is not its location in that bodily process (which is not even true to the experienced fact, since I am clearly outside of that bodily process, observing it), but rather that I have apparently caught myself (my self) in the act of apprehending that bodily process. Thus, though James asserts (and I am again repeating some quotations, but omitting the italics) that "the 'Self of selves' . . . is found to consist mainly of these peculiar motions in the head or between the head and throat," he almost immediately goes on to the conclusion that "it would follow that our entire feeling of spiritual activity . . . is really a feeling of bodily activities whose exact nature is by most men overlooked." A feeling of bodily activities is not the same as the bodily activities that are felt; and James is obviously not merely aware of the bodily process, but also of the introspective act that reveals the bodily process.

Indeed, if anything establishes the spatial boundedness of the self, it is far less the data that establish the boundaries of the body than the limitations on the activities of the self. Thus, if I want to grasp a relatively but not excessively distant present perceptual object, I must use my body first as a vehicular and then as a prehensile instrument; and note that, at least in my experience of this situation, it is not my body that wants to grasp the object, but I myself. And, if there is any one thing that can be said to establish the distinctness of my identity, it is that facet of the human condition that existentialists have described as *existential solitude*, namely, the fact that I have direct perceptual access to my own experiences but none at all (that is, none that is direct) to the experiences of others as acting selves; and this fact constitutes the most impressive evidence of my boundedness, particularly when I am most strongly convinced that the experiences of the latter must be paralleling my own or that they must know their own bodies and their personal worlds as I know mine.

Observe that the premise of the nonuniqueness of the fact that one experiences is rooted in the animistic construction of the universe. With maturation, the animistic orientation to the world is, to a considerable degree, overlaid rather than displaced by a finer discrimination of sentient beings and the like. (Have you ever, as I have, sworn at some inanimate impediment—tacitly imputing intentionality to it—or, knowing full well how silly it is to do so, wondered about what it feels like to be a high-tension electric wire with powerful electrical energy coursing through it?) If a mature person can attribute to a rock the deliberate intention to trip him or, to a high-tension wire, a more intense feeling of being alive than he himself is capable of experiencing, how deeply ingrained must be his prerational conviction that all living creatures—not to mention other human beings—must be capable of cognition, feeling, and will. Thus, at the as a rule unexamined and subconscious levels of our being-in-the-world (*Dasein*), the scope of our existential solitude extends beyond the social world into the world of infrahuman creatures and inanimate things.

I may note, in passing, that existentialists are prone to emphasize the bearing of existential solitude on existential anxiety (which, of course, has other roots as well, such as the fact that one is rarely, if ever, in

the situation of being able to predict with full confidence the consequences of one's actions) in that, in an ultimate sense, one is doomed
to confront the world, and especially one's life crises, alone. Solitude is
not, however, *per se,* frightening, and there are times when one actively
seeks it or resists any infringement on it; at such times the fact of
existential solitude is an asset. Existential solitude also serves to enhance
certain other affective relationships. Thus, it is existential solitude that
gives to the experience of loving and being loved the aura of participation in a miracle.

Existentialists have, of course, also emphasized the fact that it is
within the domain of human freedom to give positive assent to the
inevitabilities of human existence within the limits of the dominion of
these inevitabilities, while at the same time denying them any power to govern behavior beyond these limits. Thus, I may give positive assent to the
inevitability of my death and the unpredictability of its moment by elect-
ing to live in a way that will always leave my affairs in as good an
order as I can give to them and, at the same time, live in all other
respects as though I expect to be an immortal, which means, among
other things, that I am free of the pressure of a self-defeating desperate
anxiety to pack in as many gratifications as my days will permit. To the
extent that I am successful in carrying out such a design for living, my
death is a positive and accepted aspect of my life in a way that I have
selected and that imposes no other constraints on my existence; and
though I were to know that I am destined to die in, say, twenty-four
hours, if this knowledge did not interfere with my design, I would live
these twenty-four hours no differently than if I did not have this
knowledge.

The same consideration applies to existential solitude. The latter may
be kept in its place by yielding any desire to directly experience another's
experience or to share with others the observation of one's own experience and accepting that no one else can have any direct observational
knowledge of one's feelings, not even in moments of crisis, but nevertheless realizing that one is not thereby precluded from mutually pro-
motive interactions with others and the warmth of comradeship and
love or for that matter from learning to comprehend the nature of
another's experience by means other than direct observation of it.

Solitude is not isolation save as one chooses to make it so. As
Rilke,[1] for instance, has described the love relationship, love consists
of "two solitudes that touch and cherish and protect each other."

[1] R. M. Rilke, *Letters to a Young Poet* (New York: Norton, 1934).

But to return to what the introspective glance reveals of the self-body relationship: If it reveals anything of this sort, it is far more likely to be a relationship of concern than of either ontological identity or the fact of conditional dependence—concern, for instance, with assessing, preserving, or improving the instrumental effectiveness of the body in relation to the activities of the self, or concern in the context of surveying the situation when one or another of these activities does not proceed smoothly, or in the context of the more or less continual scanning that goes on for matters that have bearing on one's other enduring concerns. And the concern with the instrumental effectiveness of the body is as likely as not to involve the external appearance and accouterment rather than the interior parts or processes of the body. Or the concern may be with the sheer preservation of the body as a living organism, such preservation being, even though one acts on the assumption of the immortality of the self, apprehended as a necessary or ensuring condition of being able to pursue one's thisworldly concerns in a familiar thisworldly context; in other words, the concern with the preservation of the living body is not, as a rule or ever fundamentally, a concern with preserving the existence of the self, for the nonexistence of the latter is, as already noted, unimaginable (conceivable, yes, imaginable, no), but a concern with delaying its entrance into the frightening unfamiliarity of separation from the pursuit of one's concerns and of having to function as an identity-maintaining vortex of nothingness that has lost its major general-purpose instrumentality in a new world that may contain none of the known physical and social geography and lawful thisworldly predictability. I may rationally convince myself that I will not survive my body, but, so long as I cannot imagine it, the prospect of my death continues to haunt me with the prospect of an unfathomable afterlife. Hence the degree of human effort and imagination that has gone into the production of structured images of the afterworld and the afterlife in it.

I do not mean to imply that the fear of the unknown is the sole source of the fear of dying. Quite obviously, a major source is the fear of pain and suffering associated with the causes of dying. Other sources stem from notions like that of the inevitability of a balancing of accounts in conjunction with unresolved guilt feeling and that of the uncleanness of a corpse. Note that in the latter notion (and also in others, as in our attribution of willful abandonment of ourselves to those who die and related anger against the deceased) there is an implication of sinfulness in the very act of dying, thereby adding a final debit to the account. Such attitudes, often unconscious, may coexist with contradictory beliefs; they belong in the sphere of the superego, which I will discuss in the next chapter. They may also be reinforced by and given coherent form and ritualized in various religious systems; but it is, I think, a mistake and a missing of their essential psychological relevance to dismiss them (as particularly the antireligious ones among us whose unresolved problems with respect to religion seem to me to be quite patent in their ultrasensitivity to any mention of religion are wont to do) as irrational and quasireligious superstition. These matters get into and are perpetuated in religious systems via human channels and concerns, and it seems to me that they are as common to religious agnostics, skeptics, and atheists as they are to the faithful.

At any rate, as I have already indicated, the quick turnaround glance will reveal—always, I think—some activity in which I am engaged. With an accumulation of such observations, however turnaround and retrospective, all referable to a continuing self-identity, any grasp of a recurring or continuing pattern must be apprehended as characteristic of the self. That is, they become ingredients of a complex self-concept.

The patterns which are assimilated to, and reorganized in, the self-concept are of varied kinds. Some emerge as highly abstracted evaluative concepts that contain no explicit reference to specificities of behavior, and these evaluations may refer to the roots or to the consequences of actions. Thus, I am more or less good or evil, more or less attractive or repulsive, worthy or unworthy, courageous or cowardly, dependable or undependable. Others are more literally descriptive of patterns of activity though they may also involve value-laden concepts. I am more or less quick or slow in my actions, planful or impulsive, strong or weak, autonomous or heteronomous, constant or changeable, pious or impious, consistently on time or tardy, a teacher, a student, a sports enthusiast, a golfer. Still others emerge as dispositional concepts that are taken to account for observable patterns. I have certain capabilities and certain incompetencies, certain kinds of interests and certain values; or, a step beyond these, I am more or less a conformist or rebel, egotist or altruist, brave or cowardly, an aesthete, an intellectual, undistinguished. Still others concern the proprieties and improprieties that are taken as more or less prescriptive for oneself: the kinds of things one feels called upon to do; the activities, roles, garbs, situations with which one feels comfortable and the ones that are not even thinkable for oneself; the arena of one's proper dominion and responsibility and the conditions of access by others to this arena; the domain of one's privacy and the conditions of admissible nontrespassing entry by others. Then there are the conceptualizations of the imperatives by which one lives, of one's dominant motivations and obligations, of one's control over these, of the character of one's enterprises, of the transformations that have taken place and the changes one hopes for, and perhaps of one's destiny. Finally, there are the conceptualizations of the interpenetrations and interdependencies of one's own existence and concerns with those of others, of the ways that others apprehend oneself, of one's relations to various paraindividual and supraindividual entities and affairs, and, most generally, of one's place in the world.

I have not attempted to make this listing of constituents of the self-concept exhaustive, or the various categories mutually exclusive, or to select illustrative items that can be classified only in the particular categories in which I cite them. Nor have I intended to suggest that the same set of categories will fit the self-concepts of all individuals or to imply that the structure of the self-concept is an and-summative combination of the kinds of constituents I have listed. As a matter of fact, I do not even believe that anyone can fully comprehend his own self-concept; in other words, I take it that the self-concept is largely subconscious, comprising an implicative structure the various facets of which do not become explicit or the objects of scrutiny save under appropriate and special conditions.[2] My intention in reviewing some of the constituents of the self-concept has been merely to indicate their diversity and variety.

An individual is not unassisted in developing a self-concept. Some of the constituents are intrinsically social in character. Thus, notions of one's personal status are meaningful only in social contexts and are conveyed through the weight given to one's desires and opinions, the use of symmetrical or complementary behavior forms[3] and corresponding expectations concerning the use of such forms by oneself, and the assets

[2] In this respect, let me emphasize, I do not conceive of the self-concept as being in any fundamental way different from other much simpler concepts. In any concept, there are discoverable facets and implications that may not yet have been noted or which may not be explicit in any current operation with the concept. Note, for instance, in what I have just said, the implication that a concept is an enduring entity.

[3] The distinction is Bateson's. See G. Bateson, *Naven* (Stanford, Cal.: Stanford University Press, 1958), and "Morale and National Character," in G. Watson, ed., *Civilian Morale* (Boston, Mass.: Houghton Mifflin, 1942). Behavior forms are symmetrical if and when A is expected to act toward B as B acts toward A (for example, A and B address each other by their first names); they are complementary if some difference is required (for example, B addresses A by the latter's first name, but A may only address B as Mr. Smith or Sir).

and liabilities associated with particular statuses. There are thus facets of the self-concept that are implicit in social usages. Others are conveyed by direct attribution, explicit or implicit,[4] as notions of personal worth, trustworthiness, differential abilities, and so on. One may be more or less resistant to such attributions, checking them against one's own experience and criteria or one may give them private meanings; but one is more likely than not to think of oneself as wicked (or as trustworthy, or as attractive, or courageous, or possessed of good judgment, mechanical ability, and so on) if others repeatedly characterize one in this way and act toward one in a manner appropriate to the characterization, and one may of course find support for the characterization in an examination of one's behavior patterns, which may themselves be consequent on the characterization.

There are thus, apart from one's relation to one's body, three directly relevant sources of information in the attributive construction of the self-concept: the direct observations of one's behaviors, the implicit attributions by others, and the explicit attributions by others. Data from these different sources do not have to be consistent. Those attributes are presumably most firmly grounded, however, which are most consistently supported by all three sources.

There is also an indirect and perhaps more fundamental role played by society in the attributive construction of the self-concept. In the selective emphases on certain rather than other kinds of bodily, behavioral, and social (for example, subgroup memberships) characteristics as bases of significant differentiations among persons, in the categories that are used to classify and identify behaviors, and in the expectations that are engendered as to what characteristics go with which; in what the individual encounters along these lines there are defined the fundamental dimensions and structural relationships in terms of which persons are construed. The general nature of the self-concept (that is, the categories and dimensions involved in forming it) is, of course, not different in any essential respects (save those that have to do with direct access to one's experience) from one's concept of other persons. In other words, the dimensions and categories of self-characterization are, in the main, those that apply to the characterization of others and these are borrowed from the cultures and subcultures in which one participates.

Moreover, if, as I have urged elsewhere in this book, the meaning of

4 An implicit attribution occurs when one is treated in a particular way. Thus, when I am entrusted with something there is an implicit attribution of my trustworthiness in that context.

any item is the place of the item in the network of relationships in which it is imbedded, then the meanings of the terms in which the dimensions (and positions along the dimensions) and categories of person characterization are expressed are largely contained in the languages of the individual's cultures and subcultures. In other words, though idiosyncratic facets of meaning are by no means precluded, a large portion of the tacit, unexpressed, inarticulated aspects of the self-concept (as of one's concepts of particular other persons) is socially created and maintained. I do not mean to suggest that genuine changes in the self-concept (as, again, of others) cannot occur—as when one discovers some quality of intensity of feeling of which one did not suspect oneself, or realizes that one has outgrown some feeling—but much of the process of self-discovery is a process of realizing the existence of some facet hitherto concealed in inarticulated meanings.

An intriguing paradox in these remarks concerning the role of society in establishing the dimensions and categories and the meaning structure of the self-concept of any given individual is that much of the work that goes into the creation of that individual's self-concept antedates his existence.

The self-concept construes a person—the person who is the subject in our own actions. Now, the self-concept cannot be the actor we are seeking. Is it the concept that loves, hates, aspires, hopes, plans, schemes, conserves, expends, gives, takes, locomotes, suffers, enjoys, sees, hears, tilts with windmills, and so on? Concepts may have consequences, but assuredly do not act in these ways. Is it then the construed person who is the actor we are seeking? Let us consider this question.

Does the question imply that the conceptual construction constitutes the person who engages in the action? If so, it is clear that the concept is being construed as the actor, a possibility that I have just rejected. Either the construed person exists independently of the conceptual construction or the construction has no real referent. Moreover, who has made the construction? The self? A point in space-time engages in conceptual construction? I fear I am not enough of a philosopher to buy that notion.

Neither the self nor the self-concept can be the actor. If the question implies that the self-concept refers to, but is not itself, the actor, then the concept is subject to the pitfalls of misconstruction. That is, the person whose properties are supposedly represented in the self-concept may be incorrectly or improperly represented. But, then, we still have to find our actor. My next candidate is the ego.

I use the term "ego" in the sense of a dynamic agent, a meaning that was especially imparted to it in the translation of Freud's works into English. Literally, of course, "ego" is another word for "self" and the implied relationship is not coincidental, but, as these terms are here used, the "self" is only one facet of the "ego." To clarify the usage, I must explain the origin and development of the ego. .

I have in an earlier chapter presented the notion of the development of a structured system of derived, perpetuated, and imbricated motives. I did not, however, deal with the place of the self in this system. When this is done it will become clear that this system constitutes only a part of the personality, a part that is appropriately called ego.

The key point to be noted regarding the place of the self in the systemic structure of motives is that many motives involve the self as object. In some instances, these motives are intrinsically bipolar in their objective reference, the self constituting one of the poles. Thus dependency motivation is concerned with establishing that you, an appropriate other, take care of me; dominance, that you yield to and obey me; self-assertion, that you accept my autonomy; and so on. In other instances, the self is the primary object. Thus, we may be concerned with protecting the status of the self, securing its territorial rights and properties, developing its competencies, establishing a better base of operations for it, and so on.

It may seem that some, perhaps all, of these instances involve the self-concept rather than the self *per se*. In a sense, this is undoubtedly the case; but these motives are concerned with doing something about the self, not about the self-concept. The latter is our way of apprehending the self, but it is what we apprehend that concerns us, not our mode of apprehending it. The case is, in principle, no different than the already cited instance of biting into an apple: Our perceptions and categorizing processes inform us that it is an apple, and the kind of apple with which we want to deal, but it is not our image, concept, or percept of the apple that we do (and want to) bite into; it is the apple itself. Similarly in the present case: The nature of the self-concept and/or the apprehension of its situation may occasion some action with respect to the self, but it is the self itself that is the object of the action. To be sure, it is also possible to take action with respect to the self-concept (as, for instance, when we seek disconfirmation of our belief that we are unattractive, bad, and so on), but such action is generally instrumental to doing something about the self itself.

It is probably true that most, perhaps all, motivation with regard to the self is either self-preservative, self-enhancing, or self-determining; self-preservative, not in the sense of protecting it from extinction but in the sense of preserving its status, reputation, competencies, base of operations, possessions, territorial and other rights and perquisites, and so on, and securing the conditions that make such preservations possible; self-enhancing in the sense of obtaining more of whatever is involved in self-preservation, that is, improved status, reputation, competence, powers, and so forth; and self-determining in the sense that various writers have used inner-directedness, self-actualization, growth motivation, and so on.

I do not want to draw sharp lines of demarcation between these three classes of self-motives. My immediate purpose is to delineate rather crudely the scope and variety of the motives involved. The important point to make here is that these motives are perpetuated and complexly imbricated, and I shall return to this point very shortly. But, first, I must respond to an objection that is quite likely to have occurred to the reader.

There is an important difference between an action oriented to the self and one oriented to, say, an apple. The apple is, after all, a physical thing, endowed with the kinds of attributes found among physical things. It makes some kind of sense, therefore, to say that our concerns are related to the thing itself rather than to our image of it. But the self, I have contended, is essentially a moving mathematical point; and mathematical points are not endowed with motivations, cognitions, competencies, moral qualities, rights, or reflexive activities. These properties are not attributes of the self, but attributions to it. What sense, then, does it make to say that self-preservative, self-enhancing, and self-determining motivation is directed to the self *per se* rather than to our concept or image of it?

A simple and quite proper answer to the question is that the fact that our actions toward any object are adjusted to our apprehensions of it does not imply that our actions are not directed to the object but to the apprehension. It is essentially irrelevant whether the apprehensions are correct. Thus, when I bite into my apple, I perceive it as a sound apple; if it turns out to be wormy, this does not alter the fact that my action is directed to the apple (which I take to be edible) and not to my image of it; my digestive processes can deal more or less adequately with chewed up apples, not with images of apples. In the same way, the fact that I attribute various properties to a mathematical point, validly or invalidly, does not determine whether my actions are indeed directed to doing something about or with reference to that point which I take to possess the properties I attribute to it.

There is, however, another answer to the question that contributes some perspective as to the nature of the self. A crude analogy may be helpful to its exposition. Any physical thing has a center of gravity. Actually, the center of gravity is a mathematical point which is defined with respect to the thing and moves about with it so long as the composition of the latter does not change. But it is a very special kind of point. The gravitational force is not directed to or from that point. The gravitational force is the resultant of the mutual attractions of all of the mass-possessing particles of the earth, the thing, and quite possibly all the rest of the cosmos as well. But the resultant vector has two end points, one of which we call the center of gravity of the earth and the other, the center of gravity of the thing; and, if the particulate masses of the thing are not homogeneously distributed, the center of gravity of the thing need not even necessarily be located within its spatial bounds. Yet, it is as if all of the forces involved were concentrated at the two centers of gravity. And, please note, the center of gravity of the thing (or of the earth) exists in space-time entirely independently of my knowledge of it; my cognitive processes had nothing to do with bringing it into being or locating it where it is. In other words, the center of gravity is not an intervening variable, a fiction, or a hypothetical construct; it is a reality in its own right. That I seize on this facet of the reality of the thing in order to attain my ends more effectively, and even that I may err in locating the center of gravity or otherwise misconstrue it, has nothing to do with its being.

I do not wish to push the analogy too hard, but it is obvious that the self is not any mere point in space-time. It is a hub of activity, as it were; and not only is it the object of many of the actor's major concerns, but it is as if all of the syntonic behaviors of the actor (that is, all the spontaneous directed activities in which he engages and with respect to which he at least subconsciously assents or accepts responsibility) emanate from it. My use of the expressions "as it were" and "as if" does not deny the reality of the relationships involved. The self is the center of gravity of the being of the actor, and it is only the word "gravity" that is being used somewhat figuratively in this sentence. The self is the center of grave concerns, outgoing and incoming. One could define the self in these terms, but it seems to me that a "center" needs to be locatable in space. Also, if we started with this definition, we would lose the possessive relationship that James tries to find between his

Thought and its herd of ideas, memories, and so forth. Or, to put the matter differently, in this instance (as contrasted to the instance of the physical center of gravity), the location and mark of identity is conceptually prior to the functional significance. I therefore hold to the sufficiency of my original definition of the self as the primordial origin of space-time and take its functional significance as an additional attribute not necessary to its definition.

But the functional significance of the self is basic to the existence of the entity we call the *ego*. As already noted, the self is the object of many enduring, interrelated, and interdependent concerns, that is, of imbricated perpetuated motives. Now, I submit, enduring interdependencies constitute the necessary and sufficient conditions of the definition of a structure—to be sure, not a physical structure but, nevertheless, a structure.

What is it that makes a physical structure a structure? Is it the aggregation of physical things in one place? Not at all. A structure must have some permanence, that is, its components must themselves be enduring and interacting in at least quasistationary equilibrium under a wide variety of external conditions and circumstances. The stable configuration of the structure is maintained by the interaction of the components so long as nothing enters from the outside to disrupt the stable interaction. In some physical systems (for example, a soap bubble) what would otherwise be a disruptive intrusion from the outside (for example, in the case of the soap bubble, the pressure of a blunt point) is counteracted or overwhelmed by the internal balance of forces. Engineered structures are built to withstand considerable sway, differential expansion and contraction of components under temperature change, and so on; and, of course, the introduction of feedback mechanisms increases the range and effectiveness of counteractive forces. In living structures, these counteractive, homeostatic interactions reach a high level of uncontrived development; but it is the systematic interaction that maintains the structure.

So with the ego structure. The perpetuation of concerns provides the enduring components of the structure and their imbrication provides the systematic interactive basis for preserving the structure; and it is the place of the self in this structure that justifies the application to it of the term, "ego."

In addition to the concerns devolving around the self, however, other concerns are assimilated into the structure that have no manifest direct bearing on the self-related concerns but become imbricated with the latter and with one another. At first, these nonself-related motives are simply instrumental with respect to various appetitive drives, for example, mamma's presence is a necessary condition of assurance that various discomforts will be disposed of, or to some self-related concerns in which the self, as such, is not focally involved, for example, if you take my things, they become unavailable to me. As they become perpetuated, however, they also become so imbricated with self-related concerns as to become virtually indistinguishable from the latter in their bearing on the self. Thus, to take a trivial example, my distress at observing some stranger misbehaving by my standards and my impulse to correct him may be, at least in part, generated by my investment in the continuance of a world that is stable and orderly according to my expectations of it. My own sense of security, my potential effectiveness and competence, and so on depend on this orderliness.

It must not be supposed that all the components of the ego structure are of equal importance and significance to it. Not every one of the perpetuated and enduring concerns is necessarily directly tied in with every other. There is some basis for the belief that certain concerns are directly intertwined with more of the remaining concerns in the set than are certain others. That is certain concerns, not necessarily the same ones in different cases, seem to be more central or pivotal in the structure and others to be more peripheral. It is also likely that there are varying patterns of interrelationship among concerns. As I have already indicated, which ones are central and which peripheral may vary from case to case; and there is a strong likelihood that such a differential in the positioning of, and structural interrelationships among, concerns may be found between the modal ego structures that emerge among persons raised in different cultures.

The experiential basis for the assertion of the differentiated internal positioning of various concerns and of between-cases variability comes largely from data provided by various psychotherapeutic efforts. To be sure, one may discern contending schools of psychotherapy (not to mention a large number of variations within schools and compromise positions between schools) each of which assigns universal centrality to different kinds of concern. There are, however, three points to be made in this context.

1. The possibility of taking these different positions itself speaks for a more imbricated structure than any of the schools envision. To take a simple example in which we assume only two concerns: If A says that the concern for security is basic and B contends that it is concern for

power that is basic and, further, if both A and B impress one as good observers, then the manifest contradiction is obviated if one recognizes that power may be conditional on security at the same time that security is conditional on power; both A and B are right, but the higher truth—the synthesis that neither seems to grasp—involves the interpenetration of the two concerns.

2. Among the seemingly infinite variety of human concerns, the number assigned to central positions by the various schools is very limited, a fact that I take to confirm the centrality-peripherality dimension of the ego structure.

3. It is my experience that almost any experienced therapist, no matter how committed to a particular image of man, will have encountered cases that are "classical" exemplars of his image and others that "more or less" fit; and most will have encountered at least some cases that, though they can be described in terms sacrosanct to the particular school to which the therapist is committed (a fact that I take to be a consequence of the imbrication of motives, as noted in the first point), are nevertheless more aptly and neatly described from the viewpoint of another school.

The issue between the schools is thus largely an aesthetic one, except, of course, insofar as they become doctrinaire, denying any possible validity to alternative constructions; and one may almost assert as a cardinal rule of aesthetics the ultimate incompatibility of aesthetics with an imperialism of style and approach. I do not mean to suggest that the imperialist inclinations of some of the schools are totally unjustified: A stern discipline may be a necessary condition of the full development and fruition of what the approach of a particular school may have to offer. I must also respond to those of my colleagues who would contend that the only place for aesthetics in science is as an object of study, not as a value. Apart from the fact that aesthetic considerations have often instigated and guided scientific search (for example, one encounters a lack of complementarity or symmetry that does not "feel" right), aesthetic considerations have often supplied the decisive factor in choosing between theories. Thus, if my sources are sound (I myself have no competence in the matter), Einsteinian relativity triumphed over Newtonian mechanics, not because of a better fit to the data (the Einsteinian expectancies were about as far off, in the opposite direction, as the Newtonian ones), but because of its elegant simplicity.

There is another line of argument that supports the conclusion that various ego structures must be somewhat differently centered and organized, particularly so with regard to the modal structures in culturally different societies. The argument moves from observed differences in the circumstances of human growth and development to inferred consequences. This, for instance, is the major basis on which Kardiner[5] argues for cultural differences in basic personality.

There are a variety of implications that flow from the recognition of variability in the ways that different egos are structured. The very notion of the central-peripheral dimension suggests that various ego structures are more or less tightly organized, that is, the various components are more or less completely intertwined both by direct interdependencies and mediating linkages. In the extreme case, undoubtedly a hypothetical ideal, the members of every pair of concerns in the structure would be reciprocally interdependent. The tighter the organization, in the sense just indicated, the more resistant must the structure be to disruption, dismemberment, or fission under radically changed and extremely stressful circumstances. I take this to be one of the meanings of "ego strength," though the characteristic is better described as resiliency. I shall reserve the term "ego strength" for another common meaning of the term.

By the same token, there may exist subsets of concerns the members of which are more strongly intertwined with one another than they are with the members of other subsets. The occurrence of such subsets generates lines of cleavage which any process of ego disruption must follow. In extreme instances, the disruptions are manifested in what has been described as dual or multiple personalities. It is perhaps noteworthy that these "personalities" impress one as quite impoverished (and this, of course, follows from the relatively narrow range of concerns that each involves); and the larger the number of such personalities, the greater the likelihood that one or more of them will display little more than an essentially monoideic concern.

The point is that, although the ego is normally a unitary structure, it is not generally one that is free of stress. Let me take a very simple example. Financial solvency may be a condition of a good reputation, and a good reputation may be a condition of financial solvency. The concerns for reputation and for solvency are therefore mutually reinforcing; what threatens one also, to some degree, threatens the other.

[5] See, for example, Abraham Kardiner, *The Individual and His Society* (New York: Columbia University Press, 1939). See also such works as Erich Fromm's *Escape from Freedom* (New York: Farrar, Straus & Giroux, 1941), Gregory Bateson's *Naven* and "Morale and National Character," and Erik H. Erikson's *Childhood and Society* (New York: Norton, 1963).

There are, however, ways (let me refer to them as illicit) of serving one or the other of these concerns to the detriment of the other. Thus, to oversimplify what is already an oversimplification, cheating may contribute to one's solvency but is likely to be detrimental to one's reputation. Moreover, the counterposition of concerns need not be evenly balanced under all circumstances. Thus, to return to the example, recent financial setbacks, the anticipation of heavy financial drains, and an opportunity to restore the balance by cheating may all combine to bring the concern over solvency to a peak of arousal. The concern over reputation, on the other hand, is itself divided by the advantages of solvency as against the risks of detection.

The dynamic of the ego, that is, the interplay of motivational forces involved in the ego structure, is thus one of counterbalancing relevant considerations and finding paths of action that maximize the potential gain for the entire system of interlocking concerns and minimize the potential risk. This, I take it, is what is meant when reference is made to the controlling function of the ego, a "function" that is inherent in the nature of the ego structure; that is, it is the constitutively determined mode of functioning that is involved rather than function in the sense of being functional to some articulated intentions.

Forgive me if I now start a rather lengthy digression, but I have to lay a foundation for what I want to say next about the ego. It is in the nature of a perpetuated motive that it is future oriented; the concern is one of being prepared for eventualities. Thus, the need for food, as a perpetuated concern, is based on the anticipation of the recurrence of hunger (to ignore, for the moment, other needs served by eating) and of the possibility of lack of access to food at that critical period. There is, however, nothing inherent in the perpetuated motive *per se* that defines the degree of concern with the conditions that can create the eventualities for which one must be prepared. The rat that hoards food is presumably acting out of a perpetuated food concern; but it does not follow that it will also do something about protecting the food it is hoarding from marauders; and it is surely just too much to expect that it may learn to direct its efforts at reducing the likelihood of an economy of scarcity. Similarly, the man who works for the money that permits him to keep his larder stocked is not necessarily concerned with the conditions that affect the purchasing power of his dollar or the economy that makes food available for purchase.

Concern with contingencies that may affect eventualities directly involved in a perpetuated motive is itself a derived motive. Thus, concern over food is one source of concern over money, but the latter concern (taken in conjunction with some sad realities) generates a need to store the money in a safe but accessible place; and direct or vicarious experience may lead one to a bank as the safest sufficiently accessible place. But then the solvency of the bank may become one of one's concerns, which, in .turn, may lead to concern over the trustworthiness and competence of the administrative agencies as well as the health of the economy, and then to the trustworthiness and effectiveness of the government structure.

Concerns over banks, officialdom, government agencies and personnel, and the structure of government may enter one's life in many other ways than via the route emanating from the need for assurance of continual access to food. They may, therefore become major perpetuated concerns. Whether they do or not, it is apparent that there are many points along the derivational pathways where the consequences of one's actions or inactions reflect back on the source motivations both from the viewpoint of facilitating or making more difficult the satisfaction of these concerns and from the viewpoint of determining the next stages of the derivational pathway. What you need to do to make your money secure is quite different if you have decided to bank it than if you have decided to sew it into your mattress. In other words, and this is the important point for my immediate purpose, there are chains of contingencies, one contingency depending on what happens with regard to an earlier link in the chain; and these chains are themselves interlaced in complex networks.

When any given motive is pressing and a concern about the recurrence of this motive is not involved, one may act efficiently in terms of a mapping[6] of the relatively immediate situation. From the viewpoint of

---

[6] In writing of "mapping" and "maps," I have, of course, been using a figure of speech. What I have been talking about is a special case of the more inclusive process of discovering the meanings of things (including among "things" not merely the physical features of the world about us but also processes, events, and actions). It may be recalled that, in my view, the meaning of any thing is the place that it occupies in a network of relationships and that there are no things-in-themselves (that is, things that ever exist outside of some relational context). Things, therefore, can only be dealt with as they are encountered or placed in some relational context, and, even if a thing has been torn out of its normal context, then at least one of its new relationships is that it is "out of place"; and, if it is found now in one relational context and again in another, its contextual motility is one of its relational properties. Its place in a map, fixed or mobile, is a property of the thing—and this, independently of whether we know of the existence of the map. When we deal with the thing, we necessarily deal at the same time with some sector of the map in which it is located; that is, we cannot separate the thing

acting effectively with reference to a perpetuated motive, however, one needs to refer to a mapping of the contingency network. When the perpetuated motive is itself part of a structure of perpetuated motives, the selection of an assuredly most effective action demands the scrutiny of a mapping of the entire infinite universe of possible contingency networks coursing through the presently possible futures; and this implicit demand character of the process of selecting the most effective action holds for any immediately pressing motive, itself perpetuated or not, with possible consequences (and which action has no such possible consequences?) that impinge on the structure of perpetuated concerns.

Needless to say, no human being can aspire to a total map of the universe; if he did have one, the effort to scrutinize it would result in a paralysis of all other action. We are thus doomed to uncertainty or perhaps challenged by its inevitability. What actually happens is that, from the time of our birth, we begin to make and more or less continually revise ever more comprehensive mappings of the segments of the universe that we encounter directly or vicariously. These are the maps that we consult when we decide to do or not to do something or when we choose among several available courses of action. The consultation of these maps is typically (and especially so when there is great urgency to act and the entailed action is both immediate and circumscribed) neither detailed nor conscious. The idea, as a rule, is not to linger over the details of the map or to plan in detail any large number of actions ahead, but to be alerted to the possibility of danger to any of our concerns that might be entailed in the intended action.

The important point, however, is that, since contingencies play so large a role in our lives, we develop a motive to scan our contingency maps and predicate our actions (and inhibition of action possibilities) accordingly. This motivation is perpetuated and itself becomes part of the ego structure. The implementation of this motivation may be referred to as ego control. The centrality of ego control in the functioning of the ego (and it seems reasonable to suppose that this is itself a function of the articulation, elaboration, and comprehensiveness of the contingency map) is properly referred to as ego strength. The diversity of the de-

---

from some facet of meaning. When we engage in mapping operations, we are identifying some facet of the meaning in which we take the thing. Our maps are implicit in our knowledge of the meaning of things and therefore implicit in our knowledge of the things. Finally, it should be recalled that actions and contingencies are included in my usage of "thing." A contingency map is, therefore, a process of identifying the meaning of actions in relation to one another and to other things over time. It is not something separate from the actions and events that are mapped.

rived-perpetuated motives that make up the ego structure and the articulation, elaboration and comprehensiveness of the associated contingency map constitute what I think is being referred to when one speaks of the maturity of the ego; the two facets of maturity (diversity and contingency-mapping) are, of course, not independent of each other.

The ego, an enduring system of motives and concerns, is properly identified as an actor; and it is tempting to accept it as the actor we are seeking. Indeed, to refer back to my earlier discussion of freedom and responsibility, it is the freedom and responsibility of this actor with which we are likely most often to be concerned. In the most significant sense of these terms, freedom and responsibility obtain when it is possible to act deliberately, that is, with a balanced consideration of all relevant concerns. This is precisely the mode of functioning of the ego. The arena within which the ego motives can harmoniously work themselves out constitutes the dominion (not to be confused with domination) of the ego, and it is only within one's dominion that one can act freely and responsibly. Any determinants of action that are not contained within the dominion of the ego constitute, at least potentially, constraints on the freedom (and hence limitations on the responsibility) of action with regard to the entire system of the most important and enduring of human motives. Within the dominion of the ego, the human being attains the highest level of freedom and responsibility of which he is capable.

There are many who treat responsibility as though it were an affliction, and this includes many who are proponents of the gospel of self-actualization or self-realization. I would agree that it is indeed burdensome to have attributed to oneself responsibility for matters outside of the dominion of the ego. But, such attribution aside, it seems to me that responsibility is something that justifies pride and, the higher the level of responsibility, the greater the justified pride. Indeed, this is quite generally recognized in the reverse case when we accuse someone of being irresponsible; and also, in the positive case, when we write letters of recommendation, extolling as a virtue that so-and-so is a "highly responsible" person. The trouble with the high priests of self-realization is that they are seduced by the notorious charm and attractiveness of some psychopaths. Thus, in his classical and, otherwise, most important paper on the "Self-Actualizing Personality," Abraham Maslow cites (I assume that this is a temporary aberration on his part) the hero of Ayn Rand's *Fountainhead*, a rapist and arsonist, all in the name of the fulfillment of an artistic nature, as an ideal example of a self-actualizer. What is being overlooked is that our commitments to, and involvements with, other persons and, indeed, impersonal causes become perpetuated concerns that come to occupy important places in the ego structure. That "No man is an island unto himself" is a basic truth of the ego. The psychopath is thus far from a self-actualizer; he is a self-defeater. In the most degenerate forms (and I do hope that my use of this term will be taken in its literal rather than in its moralistic and pejorative sense) of the gospel of self-realization, there occurs an apotheosis of the here and now with a corresponding extolling of the virtues of self-indulgence and impulse gratification. Again, this simply does violence to the nature of the ego. I shall return to these matters in the next chapter.

The ego, however, cannot be the actor we are seeking. For, not only are there impersonal factors outside of the dominion of the ego, but there are also motives that are not contained within its dominion. Our search for the actor has, therefore, not yet come to an end.

Before I go on, however, I must add a further comment on the ego as actor. Critics of Freudian psychoanalysis have protested that this theory commits the anthropomorphic fallacy, treating the id, ego, and superego as if they were homunculi contained within the personality. Let it be noted, then, that I have joined Freud in committing this fallacy, if fallacy it is in the present case, at least insofar as the ego (and I shall do the same with regard to the superego which I regard as an autonomously active entity) is concerned. Obviously, I do not concede that I have committed the fallacy. Clearly, to attribute humanoid characteristics to something is not, in itself, fallacious, as when we attribute such characteristics to another human being. The issue is not anthropomorphism, but whether the attribution is appropriate in its particular application. On this matter, the reader will have to form his own judgment.

11

EGO AND SUPEREGO

In popular presentations of psychoanalytic theory, the "superego" is usually represented as equivalent to what is generally meant by "conscience." In other discussions, it is commonly said that the "superego" is merely a fanciful way of representing the fact of culturally induced learning of standards of behavior. These translations misconstrue the natures of both the ego and the superego.

To start with, let me indicate that the ego is, in its nature, a moral system. In other words, the moral aspect of human nature is as much contained in the ego as in the superego. The difference, so far as morality is concerned, lies in the nature of the morality involved, not in the fact of its involvement.

It may not be too much of an oversimplification to say that, in the evolution of human morality, there have emerged two major, radically different from one another, conceptualizations of the nature and source of moral principles. One is predicated on authority, and its imperatives and prohibitions are unconditional (excepting authority-prescribed conditions) and categorical. The second is predicated on the comprehension of self and world as determined by direct and vicarious experience, and its rules, aphorisms, and maxims are taken as flexible pragmatic guides to proper conduct, subject to the particularities of the situations in which they are called on.

When one discovers manifest contradictions or inconsistencies in authoritative codes, there arise weighty problems of interpretation to determine the "true" meaning of the code to the observance of which one is committed. Similarly, the specification, especially in different contexts of the code, of what seem to be universal and particular versions of the same commandment poses similar problems of interpretation: Does not the redundancy imply that one of the versions is intended to qualify or explicate the meaning of the other? On the other hand, the many mutually contradictory maxims with which empirical-pragmatic codes of conduct seem to abound pose no problems of interpretation at all, at least not by virtue of the manifest inconsistencies. One simply acts according to the version that seems situationally most appropriate.

To many people, particularly when they first encounter the concept, it seems that the idea of a pragmatic code of conduct is a contradiction in terms. "That is good which works out for the best," it seems to such people, is a principle that abrogates all moral principle; expediency is in many ways the antithesis of morality, particularly if one starts with the fixed assumption that moral principle is, in its nature, externally given. The crux of the issue, however, has to do with the question, "Expediency with respect to what?"

Let me take a simple and quite trivial example. I want some jam, and there is some in the cabinet in the kitchen. Mother has warned me not to touch the jam and, though I want the jam, I also do not want to incur mother's wrath. But mother is in her own room, taking a nap, so I am safe from immediate detection; and I will take so little of the jam that she will never know the difference. The seemingly obviously expedient, and therefore "right," thing to do is to proceed to the kitchen with the utmost speed that is compatible with stealth so that the deed can be done and the evidence disposed of before mother awakens. By any standards of morality, however, can this be construed as a moral act?

A moment's reflection will show that, when the expedient falls short of what may be accepted as some appropriate moral standard, the trouble is not in the process by which the right course of action is defined on the basis of the operative premises, but in some insufficiency of the premises. That is, there are some relevant considerations that have not been taken into account; and the relevant considerations do not necessarily (as a matter of principle, that is) include the demands of a higher authority. Thus, to return to the instance of the jam, it is hardly likely to be the case that all of my own relevant concerns (forget, for the moment, abstract moral principles!) have been taken into account in the considerations cited. In the broader perspective that includes some of these concerns, I might say to myself, "But once I get into the jam, will I really be able to stop before there is a noticeable difference? And suppose I do get away with it this time, will I be able to keep the success from going to my head so that I will be less cautious and judicious next time? Moreover, will success this time and the next and the time after contribute to making me the kind of person who is constantly skirting the edge of what he can get away with? Is this the kind of person I want to be? And considerations of what may happen to my own self aside, do I want the kind of relationship with my beloved mother in which I am constantly deceiving her? Do I not want to be open to and with my beloved? Besides, what will my success do to my image of my precious mother? Can I go on adoring a woman whom I can so easily trick and deceive? Will not my success increase the risk of losing my love object, not because of her reactions to my wrongdoing (actually, she is most likely to continue to be ever-forgiving), but because of the way I act to her? And suppose she never looks at the jar of jam and I keep taking dribs and drabs out of it. At some point, she may want it, count on finding it, and discover it all gone. She might not think of blaming me and actually blame herself for not having checked before and replaced it. But, wanting it, she may be upset. I don't like it when mamma is upset. Do I want her to be upset?"

I have made a big *tsimmes* out of a jar of jam, and no child tempted by some jam is at all likely to engage in the kind of ruminations I have just described. But this is the essence of empirical-pragmatic morality: The greater and the more comprehensive the range and variety of relevant considerations that enter into determining a course of action, the higher the moral level of the act.[1] This, however, is precisely the mode of functioning of the ego system. The ego is, therefore, the individual prototype of empirical-pragmatic morality and is hence moral in its very nature (Q.E.D.).

It may be of some interest to note that the very same terms that characterize empiriopragmatic moral behavior may also be used to characterize intelligent behavior. The focus of "moral" and "intelligent" is, however, somewhat different. When we use the term "intelligent," we are likely to have in mind activity that serves some one particular motive—and a low order one, at that—like figuring out where something might be hidden, or what two things have in common, or what the examiner expects you to say when he asks for the two numbers that follow 0, 3,

---

[1] The point is well developed in E. B. Holt's *The Freudian Wish and Its Place in Ethics* (New York: Holt, 1915), a book with a most tenuous (if any) connection with the Freudian wish but with a great deal of bearing on the nature of ethics and morals. Of special interest is the section (see the chapter on "The Physiology of Wishes," which has as little to do with physiology as the book as a whole has to do with Freud) in which he conceptually traces the evolution of ethical-moral systems to its beginning in the simultaneous activation of two tropisms.

8, 15. The interest, correspondingly, tends to focus entirely on the question of whether the person has responded to the relevant features of the immediately presenting eternal situation, relevance is defined in the observer's frame of reference, and the actor's motivation tends to be overlooked entirely.

I am reminded of a very agitated mother who once called on me for advice about how to save her seven-year-old child from utter ruin. The lad had reported that "A very nice lady was in school today, and we played games." Questioning the child, the mother realized that he had been given the Stanford-Binet, but, to her horror, discovered that he had deliberately given some very wrong answers. When she protested that he certainly knew better, he looked at her with puzzlement and expostulated, "But the lady said we were playing games!"

The point of the anecdote aside, a much more fundamental issue is presented by the tendency of psychologists (amateur and professional) to reify an innate intellective "capacity" to "explain" why some people act more intelligently than others. Such reification violates the law of parsimony so long as one has not taken account and shown the insufficiency of the motivational history of a person's mode of relating to the worlds of words, numbers, mechanical relationships, and so on, his freedom to explore the possibilities of presenting situations, and the epigenetic character of such developments.

But where shall one draw the line? What if it is to a person's advantage to score low on an intelligence test without being detected as a malingerer? What are the rules (and the tests) of intelligent behavior under these circumstances? Or if your wife lets loose an irrational diatribe against your character? Is your intelligent concern with the substantive content of the insult or—given your own more enduring concerns—should you also be taking account of what instigated her emotional state, its character (for example, the possibility of a displacement of aggression), and the possible consequences of your response (including, as one of the possible alternatives, letting the insult pass by in silence), and so on? How intelligent is it not to give yourself a chance to face up to what you want of, and with, your wife in the long run? The boundary between what is morally the right thing to do and the intelligent thing to do in such a situation becomes obscure indeed. Add that exactly similar considerations apply to the evaluation of the "maturity" of behavior and (assuming that balance is a major criterion of aesthetics) to the aesthetics of human action. The differences, if any, are matters of focus and emphasis. But maybe the ancients had a point after all when they affirmed the convergence of the good, the true, and the beautiful.

At any rate, so much with respect to the moral character of the ego. What of the superego? The basic error that most writers on the subject (apart from the Freudian psychoanalysts) fall into is that they regard the superego as a moral code. This it, basically, is not. There are two major facets of the superego: (1) the acceptance of an external authority as the arbiter of what one may and should properly do and (2) the concept (in enormous measure, implicit) of what the authority requires. Note that, in the psychoanalytic writings, the superego is formed with the introjection of the father imago (the image, not, the frequent use of unqualified "father" notwithstanding, the actual physical father) and to this image are assimilated (that is, the image is reconstructed in terms of, though the reconstruction or reinterpretation remains, to some degree, layered) the other authority figures that one encounters. Note, however, that the object of the introjected image, the actual father, remains an external person, albeit the person as he was during a particular period of his and the child's lives. The commitment is to the authority of this person and not to the authority of an image of the person. Obedience and rebellion take place with reference to this person and not with respect to an image of him. The reconstruction of the imago is, of course, not a reconstruction of the father, but a revision of the image of what he stood for and demanded. The superego is thus basically predicated on a person and, if there is a code involved, it is inherently tacit and evolving (corresponding to the evolution of the image); and the code emerges in one's view of what the authority requires of one as occasions arise. A boy of six may grasp that it is wrong to handle his genitals unnecessarily or to view the nakedness of another, and he might even arrive at the tacit generalization that, in the eyes of his authority, there is something wrong about any form of sensuous gratification; but he is hardly likely to have formed such an impression as that this authority would prescribe that sexual relations with an aunt are unconditionally prohibited whereas, under the sanctions of matrimony, they are permitted with a niece. When, later, he learns that such a distinction is made in his culture, he attributes the difference in the gravity of violations to his personal authority; and the point is not that, if caught, there are greater prescribed penalties for one violation than for the other, but that the gravity of the challenge to authority is greater in the one case than the other. Since all illicit sexual relations are strongly proscribed, the practical difference in deterrent effect is likely to be negligible, but the difference will be felt in reactions to violations;[2] and it is basically the authority person, his possessions, his rights, and his prerogatives that are violated.

It is not my purpose here to enter into the detailed psychoanalytic conceptualization of the superego and, especially, of its mode of development. What is entirely clear, or so it seems to me, is that the two kinds of morality coexist side by side, and that the second imposes constraints on the first. There are many occasions when all of our background of experience (consideration of the superego aside) tells us that it is all right, and perhaps even required, to fulfill our motivations in certain ways, but we nevertheless remain inhibited or, doing the deed, experience shame, guilt, a need to exact punishment on ourselves or carry out some other act of expiation or atonement, or a simple loss of the pleasure that would otherwise be expected.

There are also differences in reactions to violations of the two kinds of moral requirements. There is no reason for shame, guilt, and the like in the violation of the requirements of ego morality, plain and simple. The appropriate response to such a violation is, in substance, some version of "Now, let's see what needs to be done to minimize the damage and, since the deed has already been done, is there some way to turn the outcome to advantage? It would have been better not to have gotten into this spot in the first place; but, now that I am here, this is the spot from which I have to map my next course of action." Or, at worst, some reassessment of the self such as "That was stupid

---

[2] It may be noteworthy that traditional Judaism, which accepts the aunt-niece distinction, also draws a distinction between adultery (at least one of the partners being married) and fornication (neither of the partners being a married person). The interesting point is that the Bible, which prescribes the strongest of punishments for adultery (and any progeny resulting from such a union are, at least in the heavenly book of accounts, cut off from their people through all their generations), prescribes none at all for fornication (and the children of such unions are accorded the same status as children born under the sanction of matrimony; they are not "bastards"). The difference in the gravity and consequences of the two offenses cannot be said to have made of fornication a popular pastime among traditional Jews; for the latter, it was enough of a deterrent that the practice was clearly and explicitly prohibited. Why should a prohibition with no formally prescribed sanctions against violations and relatively minor informal social sanctions have acquired such force? From a psychoanalytic point of view, the answer lies in the nature of one's commitment to one's personal primal source of authority—the father.

(or childish) of me. How could I have been so stupid (childish)?" with an at least tacit injunction to the self to be more careful and to act more wisely in the future.

Similarly with regard to the misdeeds of others so long as the superego is not involved. To the extent that the misdeeds have already been carried out, they are taken in one's stride as facts of reality, no different in principle than the facts of physical geography. To the extent that it becomes important to prevent future occurrences or recurrences, the problem that is posed is essentially one of social engineering, namely, how to educate and train people so that they take into account the full panoply of their motivations before committing themselves to overt action, how to clear away obstacles that impede the free and easy locomotion so that those who have not yet turned to wrongdoing as a means of need-satisfaction can find legitimate channels to their socially approved desired ends, how to produce open paths of action that nevertheless reduce the availability of socially undesirable byways and the temptations to resort to them, how to introduce deterrents and countervaluants into socially undesirable acts, how to shape the paths of action (for example, the embankment of roadways in the physical case or, more generally, to introduce the generation of moments of force at appropriate points) to reduce the risks that travelers along these paths will be carried off them by their own momentum, and so on. If it appears that individually desired ends are socially undesirable, bear in mind that desire is itself behavior. That is, exactly the same kind of considerations arise in conjunction with desire as in conjunction with behaviors that are overtly implemented. The point is that the prevention of violations of ego morality is no different, in principle, than any other problem the solutions to which can only be found in rational terms.

Not so in the case of violations of superego principles, whether by self or others; and evidence of irrationality in the ways of dealings with any violation offers reasonable ground for suspecting that there is a superego principle involved. Such violations (and the very temptation to commit them) are experienced as if they penetrate to and contaminate the very substance of which world and self are constituted;[3] so

[3] Compare the image of the prophet (Jer. 3:1), in my own translation and with italics added, "To say, that should it happen that a man divorce his wife and she go and become another man's [and] should he return to her again, why, then, *that whole land would become utterly polluted*, yet you [who] have prostituted yourself with many companions [are asked to] return to me, by the word of God." Note that it is not the person alone that becomes polluted, but the very territory

profoundly is the relationship to the authority figure a constituting principle of one's personal world. Even if the act is committed by another, the mere witnessing and toleration of it makes one a party to it, perhaps because of the implication, "If he can get away with such things, then why can't I?" Or, to some degree, because witnessing is a form of participation and because, at primary-process levels of thought, there is no distinction between passive and active participation. In any case, it is no longer a question of "Where do I go from here," and atonement (amends, restitution, regret) is not enough to set things right, for the sense of pollution remains until some act of expiation and purification is carried out.

To the extent that I understand them, those psychologists who have dubbed themselves "rational psychotherapists" see as the central task of psychotherapy the elimination of superego morality from any position of control in human affairs. "Rational," to them, means that moral judgments must be predicated on what I have called ego morality, though, I must confess, it seems to me that the range of what they take to be relevant considerations is often quite narrow indeed. Yet, it is noteworthy that Freud, who saw as the central task of psychotherapy the bringing about of a state of affairs in which "where there was id, there shall ego be," did not include the superego as coming within the desirable provenance of the ego. As early as 1910 and long before he formally introduced the concept of the superego, he commented, in his "Observations on 'Wild' Psychoanalysis"[4] on the pointlessness of attempting to disregard a person's inhibitions. Such a course, he contended, does not reduce the conflict: it merely turns it upside down, releasing the immoral impulse and repressing the moral inhibition; moreover, the original state of affairs tends to conform to the requirements of society whereas the inversion runs in the face of social requirements and is, hence, apt to aggravate the situation of the person by adding social condemnation, if not stronger measures, to his woes.

I am myself convinced that the reality of the human social situation demands the operation of a tradition-based morality moderated by an empiriopragmatic code. It seems to me to be necessary to make this point in order to properly comprehend the relationships between the

---

in which he finds himself. Note, too, that God can do what is unclean to others. The rights of the father are thus not abrogated.

[4] "Observations on 'Wild' Psychoanalysis," *The Collected Papers of Sigmund Freud,* vol. 2 (New York: Basic Books, 1959), pp. 297–304.

two kinds of morality and to do so despite the risk that is entailed of seeming to introduce a homiletic note into a scientific inquiry. Given only the empiriopragmatic code, there is too much leeway for each of us to know what he can reasonably count on from others even if he can assume that all the others predicate their actions on all relevant considerations. The very arbitrariness (from the viewpoint of individual experience) of tradition adds structure to an otherwise overly unstructured world, and its inherent conservatism helps to protect us from unanticipated effects of too rapid change, no matter how rational the latter may seem when it is instituted. Traditional morality has at least the demonstrated virtue of viability (else it would not have become traditional); and, if at times it seems to us that the world has been changing too rapidly for tradition to be relevant, changes in the essential character of human relationships and interdependencies seem to pursue a far more leisurely pace. To be sure, it would do us (individually and collectively) little good if the role of "inherited" morality were limited to the exacerbation of guilt feelings and the denial of pleasure from activities that ought to be pleasurable and each person went about acting entirely on his own reckoning as to what is or is not permissible and what is or is not required of him. The proper function of morality is to regulate conduct rather than feelings that do not find socially significant expression; and, whether or not individual superegos continue to exact their tolls in terms of feeling, an eventuality in which each person acts solely on his own limited judgment can only result in a degree of anarchy that must underscore the importance of reinstituting an abandoned traditional morality (or the generation of a new one) to act as an effective supraindividual regulator of conduct.

It is perhaps of some interest to note that many of the social circles that pride themselves on having become liberated from traditional morality have, in large measure, merely narrowed down its range of applicability. Within this restricted range, the moral judgments and moral categories may be found to be no different than they were in the abandoned morality though some of the moral principles may be the old ones turned upside-down; and the new moralists are often as tradition-bound (with or without the inversions) as the old, their new morality being as little rooted in rational reflection and the interchange of individual experience as the old. By the same token, one may also find social circles in which the standards of moral behavior are no different than the ones just described, but in which the point of pride is that they are the only ones who are really "true" to the essential principles of the traditional morality. I am not, here, arguing against one or another form of new morality. I am merely pointing out that the "new" is often not quite as new as its adherents think and that, despite the manifest intentions to change, there seems to be a need to cling to the old, in one form or another and to some degree or another.

The conservation and rigidity of tradition is, of course, often maladaptive, though, ideally, it does have the "give" of amenability to reinterpretation along with the option of referring back to the original givens to reestablish one's orientation and rootedness. There are times when tradition simply has no guidance to offer and, since Man must come to terms with the world as he encounters it, there are times when he must accept the responsibility of declaring that the traditional answers are not appropriate. As the poet[5] put the matter, even

> God fulfills himself in many ways,
> Lest one good custom should corrupt the world.

And to refer once again to the first biblical account of the Creation, all the translations I have seen ignore the presence of one word which simply does not fit the interpretation of the translators. Yet the text[6] is perfectly lucid and clear when the word is included though the meaning is radically altered. The text literally reads (I have italicized the translation of the generally omitted word):

"And God blessed the seventh day and sanctified it, for in it he rested from all of his work that God has created *to do*." What is the subject of "to do"? *His work!* And what had God created? *God's work to do.* What did God rest from? *His earlier work in the creation of the world.* What, then, is God's work? *The creation of the world.*[7]

[5] Alfred Lord Tennyson, *Idylls of the King.*

[6] Gen. 2:3. My attention was called to the discrepancy by a student who referred to a lecture he had attended, given by Rabbi Chaim Soleveitchik, one of the leading contemporary Judaic scholars. In the course of the lecture Rabbi Soleveitchik called attention to the sadly neglected word and (though he did not reinterpret the entire verse) drew from it essentially the same inference, emphasizing its bearing on the concept of Man's partnership with God in the work of creation.

[7] See also the following from *The Zohar*, the fourteenth-century font of the Kabbalah: "The Creation came out perfectly from God only inasmuch as it would find its emendation in man's labor of completion." Numerous rabbinic sayings testify to the subsumption of the more familiar narrower conception of "God's work" under the work of creation. Thus, Rabbi Tanhuma, in the tractate Sabbath of the *Talmud*: "Who worships on Sabbath eve is as God's partner in creation." Thus also Rashi (Rabbi Shlomo Itzhaki, 1040–1105), commonly regarded as the greatest of the commentators on the Bible and the Talmud, wrote that a judge who renders a true verdict is in partnership with God in the doings of the creation.

And what is left for Man to do? *To continue God's work; that is, to continue the work of creating the world.* At any rate, with or without biblical sanction, Man seems destined to continue to *remake* his world, not merely to relive it; and the imperialism of tradition, *per se*, hampers creativity. But tradition also provides the ground against which creativity becomes meaningful. What the human condition seems to require is a perpetual dynamic tension between the two kinds of morality.

These reflections on the functionality of tradition, in general, and of traditional morality, in particular, aside, whether we approve of the existence of the superego remains a matter of irrelevance. Like it or not, we seem to be stuck with it. It does no good to ignore it any more than it does to deny the existence and conformation of the ground on which we walk. As in the case of the ground, the problem of the ego is to cope with it. And the existence of the superego adds a major dimension to the personal identity. Literally or figuratively, I am the son of my father and, in fealty and in rebellion, I am committed to him.

The superego has systemic properties. A change in any of its components must, in some degree, change the character of the whole; but the whole also defines the limits of possible change and it gives meaning to and regulates its components. It is an enduring system and, hence, like the ego, may be conceptualized as a structure. Given the commitment of the ego to the authority the image of which is the heart of the superego structure, the regulations attributed to the authority generate many derived motives. It is, therefore, a motivational structure. Its character, however, and the motivational demands that it generates do not come within the dominion of the ego; only the commitment of the ego to it does so. In relation to the ego, the superego is like any other omnipresent environmental fact, such as the law of gravity. Its motivational demands, however, command the same bodily motor apparatus that is available to the execution of the demands of the ego motives and, to this extent, the dominions of ego and superego overlap and interpenetrate.

Kenneth Burke[8] has taken me to task for ignoring the passive side of the human being, and, though the issue involved goes beyond the question of the relation of the ego to the superego, it may contribute some perspective to take up his criticism at this point. I must confess that I

---

[8] Kenneth Burke, *Language as Symbolic Action* (Berkeley: University of California Press, 1966), pp. 58 *et seq.* He is not, in his criticism, referring to the present book but to an earlier article of mine in which the basic theses of the book were first presented.

am not at all sure that I quite comprehend his point of view, and, surely, he misconstrues mine when he writes that I "must" present my "cause *antithetically* to deterministic theories." I thought I had made it clear that I espouse a deterministic view and protest only against certain simpleminded conceptions of what determinism implies; specifically, my protest is that determinants of behavior which are neither simply environmental nor simply physiological are typically overlooked by those who espouse determinism. Stated in quite different terms, with the recognition that there is an innerness to behavior and motivation that is not the same as the innerness of the body, the simpleminded determinists overlook the first kind of inner determinants, that is, they recognize only the second kind of inner determinants (inner to the body) along with the outer (environmental) determinants. The issue is especially appropriate to the present context of the relation of the ego to the superego since, as I shall shortly suggest, the inner-outer distinction is involved in the relationship despite the fact that both ego and superego are components of the personality.

At any rate, to return to the passivity issue, it seems to me that, whatever Burke may precisely have in mind, two cases of "passivity" have to be distinguished. The first is that there are many things beyond human control to which human beings are subject, for instance, the operation of physical law, natural catastrophes, and so on. Since he had nothing to do with bringing these things about, it may be argued that Man is the passive recipient of them; he is a being to whom these things happen. If this were the clearly delimited meaning of "passive," I would not only not deny such passivity, but I have actively affirmed it; these external things and events set conditions of human behavior, as supports, as constraints, and as conditions of motivational derivation.

But "passive" has other connotations than "being the recipient of," and I would have to clarify the statement by declaring that Man is not necessarily a passively passive recipient of these external givens. That is, Man may be the recipient of the external givens, but it does not necessarily follow that he can do nothing about them. At the very least, he can accept them as givens; that is, he takes them as conditions of getting to where he wants to go or of achieving what he wants to achieve, as conditions contributing to the definition of his next steps, as guidemarks in helping him to decide how to spend his time, and so on. He can also, for whatever emotional gratification he may get out of doing this, rail against the givens for the limitations that they impose. Or he can try to pretend that they do not exist, that is, to try to so conduct his life as to be able to ignore particular limitations and unpleasant-nesses imposed by the givens.

In fact, however, if not always in affect, Man always accepts what he truly believes to be beyond his control, though the acceptance may not be of the active variety envisioned in the preceding paragraph, but only tacitly implied in the course of his activity. Even the latter kind of acceptance—a true passivity, if you will—leaves something to be said about it. If the things that happen to him are actually things that he could not have foreseen and that he cannot control or otherwise adapt to his own purposes, he is still a participant in the aftermath. In any case, such givens are properties of the human situation and do not go to the heart of the nature of the human being. On the other hand, Man is often wrong in his acceptance, implicit or explicit, of his helplessness, just as he is if he denies the truly givens. In such an event, however, he bears some measure of responsibility for his errors of perception and inference and his failure to take into account what is there to be taken account of. It thus appears that, some readings of the Greek tragedians to the contrary notwithstanding, Man has a role to play in the shaping of his fate. The tragedy of Oedipus was not that he suffered a terrible fate, but that he actively helped to bring his fate about. It should, how-ever, be clear that my "cause" would not be at all damaged by reckon-ing with the fact that Man is an entity that, like a stone, is a recipient of action (and I think, and have always thought, that we must reckon with it), but passivity, in this grammatical sense, hardly distinguishes a man from a stone.

Let me now turn briefly to the second case of passivity that needs to be distinguished. This case involves passivity as an active adaptation. Its most dramatic form is passive resistance; but, whereas the form is passive, passive resistance is an actively adopted device calculated to be an effective means of achieving one's ends. Passive resistance is, of course, merely one end of a continuum of forms of passivity assumed as active adaptations. At the other end (and it verges on certain aspects of the first case discussed above) is the decision not to invest the time and effort needed to prevent or control some event or to modify its aftermath. This decision need not be consciously articulated and ex-pressed, and as a rule it is not. It may be implicitly contained in the decision to do something other than dealing with what one has decided to accept. Active adaptations, however, are not genuine passivities no matter how passive their forms may be. When Burke speaks of "our constant temptation to become sheer automata," he surely overlooks that temptation is not compulsion and that the very arousal of temptation is not independent of human doings.

The interesting point, in the primary context of the present chapter, is that everything that I have said in response to Burke on the issue of the alleged passive aspect of Man holds also for that active substructure called the ego in relation to external authority. Surely, what has been construed as the fall of the first man in Genesis—and Burke, by some intellectual process that I have not been able to fathom, equates the fall to passivity—was not outside of the bounds of responsibility of the first human ego. The ego has to respond to the demands emanating from the image of the authority just as it does to other features of its environment, and particularly so because of the joint control of the bodily motor apparatus. Inevitably, perpetuated motives develop with regard to the requirements of the superego, and these motives are incorporated into the ego system. The requirements of superego morality thus enter as relevant considerations in the balancing of ego motivations; and superego motives have two channels of expression—one, directly on derived behaviors and, the other, via their influence in determining the resultant course of action that emerges out of the ego. This proposition involves a considerable theoretical deviation from the Freudian construction, which places executive control completely in the, so to speak, hands of the ego. My own construction, however, seems to me the only possible one if motives are interpreted as behaviors; and the alternative not only violates the principle of parsimony (by postulating motives as a distinct kind of entity) but also lands us back in the muddle of mysterious mental stuff. Moreover, even the Freudian construction gives the superego some executive powers since the latter exercises pressure on the ego.

12

THE ID

Between them, ego and superego do not exhaust the agencies of control over the bodily apparatus that is involved in behavior. Not to more than mention the constraints imposed by the physiological mechanisms themselves, we still have to take account of the id.

In Freud's writings on the subject, both before and after the introduction of the term, there are clearly discernible two conceptually relatively independent streams of thought: one involving the theory of the instincts (what I have earlier referred to as appetitive drives) and the other involving what I like to call "unfinished business." I shall consider these in reverse order.

Patients (and nonpatients, of course, as well, but I emphasize patients because it is in their case histories and fragments of their case histories that these difficulties are most vividly expressed in the literature) seem to suffer from a compulsion to relive certain memories and/or to continue to occupy themselves with concerns whose only realistic foundation is in relation to certain experiences stemming from no longer current situations. Thus, at the very beginnings and during the early years of psychoanalytic development—and, again, in conjunction with the traumatic neuroses of war—the patients seemed to be suffering from the anhedonic compulsion to relive experiences associated with memories of painful experiences. Anna O's symptoms, for instance (Breuer's first case of this kind), seemed to consist (as did Irène's, in Janet's independently developing experience) of a direct reenactment of certain experiences associated with the death of her father. Such patients were relieved of their symptoms apparently by their discharge of affect in the process of explicit recall, in the case of Breuer's and Freud's administrations, or by the more complete somnambulistic reenactment, in the case of Janet's. Both Freud and Janet, each in his own way, interpreted these phenomena as evidence of patients' hangups (in the contemporary American idiom) on the traumatic experiences and took the success of the treatment to mean that the blockages that kept the patients hung up had been removed (by adequate and appropriate emotional discharge or catharsis, in Freud's interpretation, or the demobilization of converged action tendencies, in Janet's).

In time, Freud came to realize that the specific traumatic episodes were not nearly so important as he had taken them to be. For one thing, there were too many patients with otherwise similar manifestations, but in whose lives one could not find parallel emotional traumata. Mainly, however, the traumatic explanation left one with a perplexing sense of insufficiency. Why did the patients not give vent to their feelings at the time of the critical episode and get it over with? After all, many women have tended their dying fathers without becoming hysterics; they went through their periods of mourning and did not develop hysterical paralyses, strabismus, amblyopia, and so on. Why could Anna O not have done likewise? The answer came to Freud when he began to investigate the emotional reactions of his patients to him as symptoms of the illness.

It may seem strange, but this man, so often described as full of arrogant pride (or is it proud arrogance?), could not accept his patients' expressions of love as occasioned and justified by his own august presence. To be sure, Breuer, who first encountered the phenomenon, also did not make the seemingly obvious interpretation; he took it to be caused by the use of hypnosis. But Freud gave up hypnosis, adopting the method of free association as a more effective method of reconstructing the past (not to mention its usefulness in revealing what the patient was doing in the present, in the context of dreams, parapraxes, and so forth). The radical change in technique and the associated change in the nature of the relationship between doctor and patient did not bring to an end the disturbing manifestations of the patient's love for the doctor (disturbing to Freud, given his task absorption, rather than frightening as it was to Breuer). If, however, neither Freud's presence (and his underlying humility, at least in this context, it seems to me, has to be accepted) nor his ministrations could account for the phenomenon, then it followed that these feelings represented something that, like his other symptoms, the patient brought with him. Moreover, diverse as the obvious symptomatology may have been—free-floating anxiety, one or more of a great variety of phobias or of an innumerable catalogue of conversion symptoms, compulsions, obsessions, and so on—the propensity to emotional entanglement with the doctor seemed to be omnipresent.

It did not take a very large inductive leap to conclude that these emotional reactions were symptomatic of the underlying and generic disturbance in psychoneurosis. But wait! Many persons were undertaking psychoanalytic treatment for didactic purposes rather than for reasons of alleviating suffering. They, too, brought with them the same "symptom." And, as the circle of practitioners grew, each with his own quota of "normal" trainees, it began to seem as though the underlying disturbance, or psychoneurosis, or both, were humanly universal.

At any rate, the "symptom" demanded examination. How do you examine symptoms? You look at them as closely as you can to comprehend their properties and you try to track them to their origins.

Close examination soon reveals that the love that patients and trainees (and, for a long while, an increasingly large number of "normal" persons who began to undertake a course of psychoanalytic treatment because it had become the fashionable thing to do) brought with them was extraordinarily childish: overdemanding at times, oversubmissive at times, petulant, timid, aggressive, sly, artful, treated as a commodity purchasable and sellable in a currency of favors, and liberally intermixed with hostility and hatred.

The etiological tracking was, at first, concentrated on trying to identify a specific traumatic experience; and, for a while, this effort seemed to be meeting with success. Patient after patient produced evidences of incestuous relations with the mother and associated anxieties about retaliation by a jealous and vengeful father. For a while, Freud thought he had discovered the specific prime cause of psychoneurosis—actual incestuous episodes in early childhood—but then the same kind of evidence began to come in from supposed normals. Even if one assumed the normals to be latent psychoneurotics with no more than a normal quota of psychopathology of everyday life, it was just too much to believe. The analysands had to be confabulating! But why? If the memories were not of real events, they had to be taken at least as fantasies, fantasies that, in the childish imagination, were not distinguished from real events and that, therefore, had consequences just as if they had been real events.[1] If so, however, they had to reflect char-

---

[1] There was, of course, the possibility that there were adult confabulations, perhaps induced by the patients' readiness (a gift of love!) to tell the analyst what the latter wanted to hear. But then it is not a normal adult trait to confuse reality

acteristics of the period of childhood rather than specific episodes. In this way, there arose the idea that the unfinished business of the past included, not merely inadequately resolved traumatic episodes, but, far more importantly, the inadequately resolved interpersonal relationships of childhood.

Few psychologists will think of Freud as an exemplar of devotion to the principle of parsimony; but this is only because, in the case of some, they themselves dislike the intellectual discipline that the principle demands or because, in the case of others, what they accept as the ultimate arbitrarinesses are different from what Freud accepted as the ultimate arbitrarinesses. It seems clear to me, however, and I find it impossible to imagine how any adequate review of his intellectual development can find otherwise,[2] that the principle must have been one of

---

with fantasy and, apart from their dreams, the normal patients did not show evidence of such confusion except in matters pertaining to early childhood. Moreover, these memories were not produced without pain (at least, not until psychoanalytic theories were sufficiently publicized for some patients to, so to say, have their oedipus and castration complexes at the tip of their tongues, and analysts soon learned to reject such facile, conflict-free, and painless productions as forms of resistance that had to be dealt with as such before any further movement could take place). Most important is the fact that, during the early days of analyzing presumptive normals, such memories cut directly against the grain of Freud's thought and his ideological investment in what seemed to be a revolutionary but simple and clear-cut theory of the etiology of psychoneurosis. He had every reason not to find, to say nothing of not encouraging the production of, such phenomena in his normal analysands. At any rate, Freud, himself, dealt extensively in his monograph on the so-called Wolf-Man case (See Sigmund Freud, "The Case of the Wolf-Man" in Muriel Gardiner, ed., *The Wolf-Man* [New York: Basic Books, 1971], pp. 153–262), with the possibility that his adult patients were projecting their adult constructions back to their childhoods, particularly with regard to the sexual content. Wolf-Man, far from normal by a long shot, but probably psychotic rather than psychoneurotic, had been traumatized by witnessing his parents at intercourse. A major part of the monograph is concerned with the adduction of strong evidence that the witnessing had actually taken place at an early date in Wolf-Man's life.

[2] The principle of overdetermination, namely, that there are alternative sets of sufficient conditions of almost anything and that generally there are to be found more than one sufficient explanation of any phenomenon, frequently appealed to by Freud (though never in as precise a form as I have just stated it and, hence, inviting many confusions, especially as Freud had no clear conception as to what constitutes a logically sufficient explanation), may seem to be a clear-cut contradiction of what I am saying in the text. It is not. What I am saying in the text is that Freud had a clear thrust to reduce a diversity of phenomena to the operation of a minimal number of basic principles. The principle of overdetermination is a generalization about the prolixity and extravagance of nature; and it is generally explicitly appealed to as a device to avoid dealing with an alternative explanation (for example, of the origins of man's control over fire) that is of no psychoanalytic

his intellectual ruling passions, so deeply ingrained in his ways of thinking that, so far as I know, it never occurred to him to discuss the issue explicitly.

I have already indicated that the explanation of neuroses in terms of fixations on traumatic episodes—even in those cases where specific symptom-related traumatic episodes could be identified—were never very satisfying from the viewpoint of the sufficiency of the explanation. With the recognition of the difficult problems of the oedipal period, its deep conflicts between unsanctioned desires and the associated anxieties, Freud believed that he had come to a foundation in terms of which one could explain, not only the psychoneuroses, but the transference phenomena of supposed normals. The specific traumata still had a role to play, particularly the traumata of later life, in determining the choice of symptoms; and they could also contribute to the precipitation of neuroses by exacerbating the residual concerns of the early childhood period. The main difference between normals and neurotics, however, lay in the severity of the conflicts in the oedipal period and the individual's ability to cope with them; and both the severity and coping ability were, themselves, determined during the critical period, in part by the particulars of the child-parent relationships (punishment, threats, quasiseductive relationships, the treatment of sexuality, and so on), and in part by the character of still earlier experiences beginning with the process of being born (the birth trauma) and going on through the periods of nursing, weaning, and toilet-training. Differences between the compulsional-obsessional and hysterical neuroses were, for instance, clarified in terms of concerns emanating from the period of toilet-training, and between the psychoneuroses and psychoses in terms of the concerns emanating from the nursing period.

I have not gone into the process by which Freud came to his conceptualization of the role of oral and anal concerns. For my purposes, it is sufficient to have briefly reviewed the development of the conceptualization of the oedipal period. In general, however, the key prin-

---

interest. Within psychoanalytic contexts proper, the corresponding principle is actually quite different (and is confused with overdetermination only because of a failure to comprehend the logical distinctions between sufficient, necessary, and contributing conditions, a "contributing" condition being one of a set of conditions which, together, are sufficient), namely, a principle of multiple determination. Thus, when a symptom is said to have different, often opposite meanings, this is simply saying that each of the meanings is defined by a different contributing condition, but the particular symptom (the "choice" of the symptom) is the resultant of the joint operation of the entire set.

ciples that emerged in Freud's efforts to comprehend the human psyche are that (1) in both normalcy and psychopathology, there are disruptive effects of the continuation of concerns that were appropriate only, if ever, in earlier eras of one's life, (2) in some individuals, such concerns are stronger and more disruptive than they are in others, and (3) however dormant some of these concerns may be, they can become aroused and reintensified if one is placed or finds oneself in situations on which they have bearing. Thus, whatever the ultimate outcomes of the psychoanalytic treatment of adults may be, its potential effects are contingent on the degree to which the analyst-analysand relationship arouses and reintensifies these archaic anachronistic concerns and on their subsequent fate; so, even normals who enter psychoanalytic treatment for didactic or irrelevant reasons, but with no complaints will become temporarily affected by a special neurosis of the psychoanalytic passage, the transference neurosis.

Then came Freud's encounter with the neuroses of World War I; and, out of this encounter, emerged one of the ultimate arbitrarinesses that Freud had been so assiduously seeking all his life. War neurotics are no different from other persons insofar as they are encumbered by archaic concerns. The trouble was that Freud could not discover any relationship between the symptoms of the war neurosis and these concerns. Nor could he discern any other benefits or gratifications that these patients gained from their haunted and painful reliving of traumatic experiences. The impulsion to relive the terrifying experiences in recurrent nightmares, in recurrent fugue states, and so on, seemed to have become self-motivating.[3] This observation provided the rational

[3] From the bleak account of this development in Freud's "Beyond the Pleasure Principle" (*Standard Edition,* vol. 18), one cannot tell that Freud really looked very hard—and there is at least one observation (one of many instances that can be cited that indicate that his faithfulness to his data of observation transcended his theorizing) that suggests that he did not. Freud noted that one does not encounter war neuroses in cases that had suffered actual physical trauma, the bodily injury serving the functions of the psychic symptoms. It is hard to see how such physical symptoms serve the function of the sheer repetition of the experience. It follows then that there are functions served by the neurotic symptoms other than the autonomy of reliving experience. I suspect, therefore, that Freud's openness to the repetition-compulsion principle was derived from the priority of the conclusion (the notion of a death instinct) to which the principle led Freud, if one follows his presentation of his argument. Long before this, he had severely criticized Alfred Adler for putting aggressiveness on a par with erotic impulses, but, in the meantime, he had become impressed by the destructiveness (self- and altero-directed) of the human animal. This led him to accept aggressiveness as one of the basic givens of human nature so that, for instance, where earlier he conceived of aggression as a consequence of frustration, he now conceived

basis for a great—great, in the sense of magnitude, not necessarily magnificence—inductive leap to what he called the repetition-compulsion principle: There is a fundamental impulsion in living creatures to repeat their past, even unto their preliving state (that is, even into death, so that the will to die is, until its inevitable triumph in the individual case, a matched adversary of the will to live).

Unquestionably, the repetition-compulsion principle offered Freud an ultimate arbitrariness that explained (that is, under which could be subsumed) a large array of earlier observations and conclusions, and it had the added virtue of providing a platform for Freud's growing pessimism about the malleability of human nature and the possibility of finding solutions for the increasingly complex tangle of human affairs.

Unfortunately, in its unqualified statement (apart from the qualification in terms of the assertion of simultaneously existing counterposed principles), the principle led Freud straight into conceptual disaster. I am not here referring to manifest lapses in logic (which presumably can be redeemed by identifying the connecting premises) such as the identification of killing (doing something to bring about the death of some living creature, including oneself) as an unmediated transform of dying (that is, as dying turned outward, where dying means transition to a nonliving state) or the nonsequitur involved in the leap from an impulsion to repeat past experience to an impulsion to repeat the past, including preexperience. I am speaking of the disaster of the explosion of the conceptual structure at the erection of which one has been laboring all of one's life, with the consequent inability to gather the shreds together in some alternative structure. That, except for the problem (to which he could find no satisfactory solution and to which I will return in Chapter 13) of the formal identity of the pleasure and nirvana principles (the impulsion to return to a stimulus-free state), Freud did not recognize his disaster is beside the point or makes the disaster all the worse.

---

of aggression as released by frustration. But whereas, before, he could apprehend eroticism as biologically grounded in the procreative instincts, he now needed a biological ground for aggression. To be sure, it could be placed in relation to the self-preservative or "ego" instincts (which, though he had relatively little to say about them, he had from the very beginning placed on a par with the sexual instincts), but any such placement would make aggression into a derivative whereas Freud's mood demanded that it be given a primary position. Hence, Freud's need for the repetition-compulsion principle in a form that implied the Nirvana principle from which Freud could deduce a basic need to die (and, turned outward, to destroy) in addition to the need to live. I shall return to the paradox of the nirvana *vs.* pleasure principles in Chapter 13.

For instance, a keystone of Freudian conceptualization was his definition of an instinct which he advanced in his earliest writings and
repeatedly reaffirmed throughout the rest of his life. Instinct, defined
essentially as appetitive drive, is basic (1) to Freud's notions of the
prime movers of human action (the ego, for example, is said to draw
its energies from the instinctual reservoirs of the id), (2) to his conceptualization of pleasure (the aim of an instinct), (3) to the theory of
the libido, (4) to the concept of cathexis (involving the object of an
instinct), (5) to the concepts of psychosexual stages, fixation, and
regression (involving both the sources and objects of instincts), (6) to
the concepts of defense mechanisms such as sublimation (involving the
aim of an instinct), and (7) to the entire economic aspect of psychoanalytic theory (which is concerned neither with finances nor utilities,
but with the sources, quantities, deployment, and management of psychic energies). The basic conceptualization of the nature of an instinct,
however, simply does not fit the notions of the life and death instincts.
What, for instance, are the energy sources of these instincts; what, in
their conceptualization is the nature of the excitation, the continuing
stimulation, that produces the energies, according to the basic definition
of "instinct"? What are their respective aims (the elimination of excitation, in the basic definition)? And what are the different objects with
which they are respectively embroiled as means of reaching their aims?
An "instinct," in the sense of the contrast between the life and death
instincts must be something other than what Freud defined as an instinct. But what, and how does it get its sway over human affairs?

The "life instinct," *per se,* poses no special problems. Taken by
itself, it is simply a collective term for the "self-preservative" (hunger,
thirst, and so on) and sexual instincts and bears the same relation to
the members of the collection that the sexual instinct (in the singular)
bears to the so-called part instincts—orality, anality, genitality, the erotic
involvements of skin sensitivity and of body movement, and so forth.
The usage of "instinct" for a collection of what must be the actual
instincts according to the basic definition (and one should not lose
sight of the possible occurrence of a common source, as when vague
restlessness may be channeled into either sexual or eating behaviors,
either of which may prove to be, at least temporarily, equally soothing
to the unrest) may deviate from the basic definition, but is a not
unreasonable extension from it.

The trouble arises from the notion of the death instinct and the
counterposition of life instinct to the latter. But the idea of the death

instinct flows from the unqualified statement of the repetition-compulsion principle and, in turn, lends its weight and significance to the latter. Taken by itself, even if one stops it before the issue of death is introduced, the unqualified repetition-compulsion principle is simply untrue. There are too many life experiences with respect to which there is no discernible tension whatever toward repetition, not even in memory. To take the unqualified principle at all seriously, one has to postulate some counterposed principle (such as is offered by the life instinct in the undefined sense of its contrast with the death instinct) to erase the tension to repeat. The unqualified principle, then, does demand its extension into the death instinct so that it can find its counterpart in the province of the life instinct. And the whole thing is one grand mess.

The alternative is to qualify the statement of the principle: There are some problems, events, and circumstances of the past with which people continue to be concerned and, to some degree, preoccupied. Then, however, it stops being a principle—certainly not the ultimate arbitrariness that Freud was seeking—and, at best, is simply a name for the fact. Its maximum explanatory function is to soothe puzzlement with the message "Don't be surprised at this (some particular) puzzling phenomenon; there are many others like it."

So one must regard Freud's statement of the repetition-compulsion principle and the notions he derived therefrom as an abortion. But the facts remain. People do have hang-ups in relation to past events and problems. I shall shortly return to the issue of the explanation of the phenomenon. For the moment, however, let me tie the issue to the concept of the id.

Though the pithiest description of the id generally characterizes it as the "reservoir of the instincts," the id-related material in the case histories is generally concerned with the oedipal relationships, both in their prephallic and phallic[4] phases. One must then immediately raise

---

[4] That is, involving a life period in which the central concern is with the pleasures that may be derived from the genitalia and whatever threatens these pleasures (and in which the child apprehends human relationships in terms of transactions the principal "currency" of which is genital gratification), but in which the anatomical differentiation of the sexes has not yet impressed itself on the child as one of the significant facts of the constitution of the world. All people—including females—are regarded as equipped with phalli, that is, genital members that can reach out to make contact with other phalli; and, in the case of a female child, she, too, experiences herself as capable of such reaching-out. The desire for sexual congress with the mother (shared for boys and girls alike) cannot, therefore, be comprehended in adult terms. All relevant perceptions are on a primary-process level, that is, attention to differential is not materially

the question of the degree to which the unfinished business of these early childhood periods can be regarded as instinctual, that is, rooted in appetitive drives. On the face of it, it is not at all obvious that oedipal concerns must constitute appetitive drives. The one connection that one can find in Freud (namely, that the oedipal drama is determined by heredity[5]) must, at best, be dismissed as tenuous since, by

relevant, and an equivalence of value may be sufficient to define an identity. Such primary-process identifications of one thing with another are, however, as a rule, not symmetrical. Thus, to a phallic child, a threat to take away his nose is taken as a threat to take away a cherished possession, that is, his phallus; but a threat to take away his phallus is not equivalent to a threat to take away his nose, since the latter is not, *per se*, a particularly valued member.

[5] There is nothing in Freud's basic definition of an instinct that implies that instincts are inherited. In general, Freud's treatment of heredity is most cavalier from the viewpoint of the biological sciences. Thus, in *Moses and Monotheism* (*Standard Edition*, vol. 23), he mentions his awareness of the rejection by biologists of the theory of the inheritance of acquired characteristics but casually dismisses this on the grounds that he finds it easier to think in such terms. Note that he is not seriously concerned with the issue of fact. Many writers have strongly emphasized the biological rootedness of Freud's thought, but I think they grossly exaggerate the importance of biology to Freud. It makes most sense to me to interpret his apparent preoccupation with these matters as a gesture in the direction of the scientific fads of his day. Once launched on his psychoanalytic career, he, at no point, deals seriously with physiological or genetic issues; his biologism is strictly in the context of evolutionary thought but, even so, he never deals seriously with any of the problems of the theory of evolution. I have already cited his casual acceptance of the fiction of the inheritance of acquired characteristics and the fact that his basic definition of an instinct is indifferent to the issue of heredity. His often-cited use of the phrase "anatomy is destiny" is clearly not concerned with anatomy *per se*, but with the psychological consequences of the fact of the anatomical differentiation of the two sexes. When he does refer to phylogenetic determination, it is with a belittling counterreference to the role of ontogeny; his reference to phylogeny is an appeal to the principle of overdetermination, which I have already indicated is typically his way of saying that he does not want to deal with some alternative explanation. Thus, when, in his *General Introduction to Psychoanalysis,* ("Introductory Lectures on Psychoanalysis," *Standard Edition*, vol. 16, p. 354), he refers to the phylogenetic origins of oedipal and related phenomena, he adds that it is most difficult to demonstrate the phylogenetic factor since a sufficient explanation can be found in the ontogeny of the individual. In the one paper ("The Passing of the Oedipus Complex," *The Collected Papers of Sigmund Freud*, vol. 2 [New York: Basic Books, 1959], pp. 269–276) where he explicitly confronts the heredity-environment problem, he blandly asserts that both heredity and environment contribute sufficient explanations of oedipal phenomena. But then he goes on to say that, taking for granted the sufficiency of the hereditary explanation, we may still ask how heredity works itself out, and, from there on, he talks only of such factors as the birth, weaning, and sphincter-training traumas and threats of castration. If there be any clearer way of demonstrating, short of an explicit statement, that he does not really take the sufficiency of the heredity explanation seriously, I cannot imagine what it is.

any definition of "heredity," not all that is inherited constitutes an appetitive drive.

Be that as it may, it seems clear that the oedipal and other perpetuated concerns of childhood are not assimilated into the ego structure, as I have portrayed the latter. These concerns have a different dynamic of perpetuation than do the ego concerns. The former dynamic is the dynamic of unfinished business and is backward oriented, whereas the dynamic of the latter is based on the anticipated recurrence of critical situations and is, hence, forward-looking. Moreover, the perpetuated concerns of unfinished business do not have any strong derivational implications with regard to the ego motives, and they have no foundation in the realities of the current situation and the anticipatable future. Nor do the ego motives have any derivational implications with respect to the focus of past-oriented concerns. Thus, increasing my power is of no avail in coping with the no-longer present father of my childhood and cannot alter my then-existing powerlessness; nor can the success or failure of the doomed-to-failure continuing struggle with my then-existing father have any bearing (short, of course, of the realization of the science-fiction fantasy of backward time travel with a resulting substitution of an alternate time track for the one along which I have traveled and continue to travel) on the realities of my present and future. The two kinds of perpetuated motives do not, therefore, interpenetrate as do the motives of the ego structure.

In the life space of the ego, then, the unfinished and unfinishable business of the past is a fact of the ego's environment, something to be dealt with. And it must be dealt with, for the thrust of the unfinished-business motivation has consequences for the ego. Like the superego motives, unfinished-business motives share in the ego's dominion over the body; and the working out of these motives can bring about situations that are of dire consequence to the ego motives.

Let me, now, before returning to the question of the dynamic of unfinished-business motivation, consider the other aspect of the id: the instinctual (appetitive-drive) and impulsive aspects. An appetitive drive is, in its very nature, a phenomenon of the immediate present. It is concerned with neither the past nor the future, but only with the immediate voiding of an intolerable state. It is not concerned with pleasure, gratification, or satisfaction in any ordinary sense of these terms; such concerns would imply some object over and above, or in addition to, the voidance of the intolerable state, and it is noteworthy that Freud's formulation of the pleasure principle mentions only a continued impulsion to activity until the elimination of excitation. Nor is it derived from any other motives in the sense of being a means to achieving the ends of other motives. Though it gives rise to derivative behaviors, the latter have the immediacy of the appetitive drive itself. Finally, the appetitive drive *per se* is never perpetuated (though I have found it convenient to express myself earlier as if it were); the corresponding perpetuated motive is predicated on the anticipated recurrence of the intolerable state. There is nothing, then, about the appetitive drive that brings it—or even permits it to come—into the ego structure. Appetitive drives must, in their nature, remain ego alien.

It seems to me that there is a third category of behaviors that need to be entered under "the id," and it is clear that Freud so thought of these behaviors though he never tried to conceptualize them separately or give them any clear systematic treatment. There are obviously impulsive acts that result from the impulsions of appetitive drives (and Freud simply took it for granted that all impulsive acts were of this character); but there are also impulsive acts dominated by ego motives but that, for either or both of two reasons, escape from the ego balance and control.

The initiation of any specific act demands a mobilization of effort sufficient to overcome inertia. Such a mobilization of effort is not under the control of a computer specifically programmed for this purpose, so that it is relatively easy to overshoot the mark. But the more the mark is overshot, the more difficult it is for normal controls to operate effectively. Thus, many an act that would otherwise be, so to say, nipped in the bud is carried into effect, and this is particularly true of relatively brief acts. For instance, one may say "no" where the net balance of motivation and the conscious intention demand "yes"—or *vice versa*. Many errors involving displacements of words and contaminations in which two words are merged (as in unplanned puns) are of this type.

It would be difficult indeed to show that most such occurrences (including many instances that can be found in Freud's writings) are expressions of either appetitive drives or the unfinished business of childhood, even in instances involving sex and aggression. Not every behavior that is overtly sexual or aggressive is motivated by sexual and aggressive drives. And much that is described as "regression in the service of the ego" is not in the least regressive. Thus, it is difficult for me to imagine that the writer (S. D. Schmalhausen), who first perpetrated such puns as "our contemporary syphilization" and "the younger degeneration," and who was very much occupied with the rational critique of contemporary morality, was in the least impelled by appetitive or regressive motivation when he first produced these puns, even on the assumption that they emerged unplanned and unbidden. That they proved to be adaptive in this instance is beside the point; the point is that they were (on my assumption) impulsive expressions (and therefore, to some degree, uncontrolled) of ego motivation. In the manuscript copy of the preceding paragraph, I wrote, "relatively true of relatively brief acts" and quickly realized that I intended to write "particularly true." I was already thinking "relatively brief" as I was writing what should have come out "particularly true." The impulse to write "relatively" was already strong as I started to write the word preceding "true" and took command of my intention. The error was clearly maladaptive, especially if it had remained undiscovered, but what appetitive drive and childhood concerns lurked behind it?

The second factor that leads to the escape of particular motives in the ego system from the controls of the ego balance is the occurrence of golden opportunities for the satisfaction of these motives. Taking advantage of these opportunities may not be to the best interests of the other motives in the system, but the temptation may be sufficient to mobilize the aberrant motives to a degree that permits them to escape as impulsive behavior.

Let me now return to the question of the dynamic of unfinished business. Janet's general theory of action[6] offers part of the answer. It may be recalled that, in Janet's view, the actual execution of any act (for example, writing a letter) requires the convergent mobilization of many action tendencies and, though the act may apparently reach its end (for example, the letter is written and signed), it is not truly completed until a demobilization takes place. Pending the demobilization, one is not free to undertake other acts; in other words, one remains hung up on the act. Though Janet does not expressly deal with the issue, it is clear that the failure to demobilize may be due to the fact that some of the intentions involved in the commission have not been satisfied (as when, in the instance of the letter, one still has a feeling that one has not quite said what one wanted to say or that the meaning will not get across) or, more generally, when the output is, for any reason, less than satisfactory; one has not actually done all of what one has set out to do despite the appearance of completion.

---

[6] Most relevant is the chapter on "Treatment by Mental Liquidation" in Pierre Janet, *Psychological Healing*, 2 vols. (New York: Macmillan, 1925), but the general theory is presented in many scattered sections of this work.

This account explains the continued preoccupation with the substance of the act and, with my addition, the tendency to resume it or to do it over. There is, however, reason to believe that there is a perseverative tendency in connection with unfinished acts even though the original intention was abandoned (as in the preferential tendency to resume playing with a particular toy without any effort to complete the particular activity that was interrupted). This is particularly evident in some of the long line of experimental investigations begun by Kurt Lewin and his students (until, that is, this line of investigation was absorbed into experiments on success and failure in which case the original intention may be presumed to remain despite the overt closure of the activity). Lewin's explanation is, in effect, that the failure to complete leaves one in a state of imbalance and the perserveration represents an effort to restore the balance. Expressed differently, incompletion is *per se* an intolerable state that generates a quasiappetitive[7] drive.

The interrupted activities of the experimental investigations are trivial events in the lives of the subjects (playing games or solving puzzles, generally outside of their normal habitat and in some such abstruse context as helping the investigator make a contribution to science, and the situations are typically obviously contrived), and the interruptions are not oft-repeated events. The effects therefore rather quickly wear off as the subject willy-nilly becomes involved in other activities. Not so the unfinished business of childhood. The child's major concerns are involved and, at least in his experience, his vital interests and very being are at stake; and his inability to bring these affairs to a satisfactory conclusion is a chronic aspect of his life. As the original instigating conditions slip away, he is still too busy trying to achieve a satisfactory outcome to notice that the conditions of his life have changed in relation to his unresolved tensions. Moreover, as he grows older, the conditions of his life never do change enough to permit these old tensions simply to dissipate. Again and again, he encounters situations sufficiently akin to the original instigating ones to keep the old tensions alive—situations of helplessness and dependency, encounters with seductive but unattainable adults, authority figures, and so on. In none of these situations can he bring the old tensions to a satisfactory resolution; but he keeps trying, and with each failure the old tensions are renewed and reinvigorated.

---

[7] I use the qualifier "quasi" because "appetite" has connotations that do not seem to be appropriate. I am not sure what function is served by "quasi" when Lewin speaks of quasineeds. I shall return to the question of the distressing character of appetitive drives in Chapter 13.

The Problem of the Actor

He can repress his awareness of the whole business, but he cannot repress the doomed-to-failure strivings. Small wonder, then, that these unresolved tensions of childhood become a major motif of his life.

This, then, is the id, as I conceive of it: the aggregate of these three kinds of motivation—motives related to unfinished business, appetitive drives, and impulses escaped from ego control. (Note: aggregate, not system.) There may be systematic aspects of unfinished business, but each arousal of an appetitive drive and each escaped impulse is a thing unto itself.

13

A QUESTION OF

ENTROPY *vs.* COMMITMENT

Probably by far the most prevalent conception of the generic character of motivation is that of drive, not in the sense of an imperative to void an intolerable state that may happen to entail a high level of tension or excitation, but in the sense of the entropy principle of thermodynamics, the inevitable progression of the redistribution of the energies in any closed system toward homogeneity.[1] The organism is, of course, not a closed but an open system and, as such, would not seem to be subject to the entropy principle. A candle, to take a physical example, may burn more and more fiercely for a while, that is, there is an apparent change in a direction opposite to entropy. The burning candle does not, however, violate the entropy principle. The burning candle is part of a larger, relatively closed, system within which the principle prevails and the growing flame is part of the most effective route—a detour, if you will, but a necessary detour—to entropy. Similarly, the organism may find itself in a situation in which the only path to quiescence demands an

[1] The conception of motivation in these terms has been challenged from time to time, and it may even be becoming somewhat more fashionable to do so, but I believe that it is still the prevailing conception. It is possible to define "tension" to mean simply that the actor is still separated from his goal. In this sense, a tension-reduction principle is tautologically implicit in any concept of motivation. I am not here using the term in this sense. The tension-reduction principle under discussion involves the notion that any excitation or stirred up state impels the organism into activity that will eliminate the excitation and restore quiescence. For earlier challenges to the prevailing conception, see S. Diamond, "A Neglected Aspect of Motivation," Sociometry 2 (1939): 77–85, and R. W. White, "Motivation Reconsidered: The Concept of Competence," *Psychological Review,* 66 (1959): 297–333.

increase in activity, but the end state to which it is impelled is entropy. Biological energy conversion processes (which, like the burning candle, do not violate the entropy principle) may produce new peaks of intra-bodily excitation which again impel the organism into a path toward entropy.

Far be it from me to challenge the validity of the second law of thermodynamics, and I assume that no psychological event can violate it. Nor do I wish to challenge the unidirectional movement of neural process across synapses. The question at issue, however, is whether the assertion of the law of entropy and the unidirectional propagation of neural impulses (with due allowance for simultaneous cross-channel propagation) toward motor outlets contribute to the comprehension of psychological events. The one thing that these notions do explain is that when an appropriate action that can eliminate the continued stimulus input is blocked, there will result a fair amount of quasirandom activity (as in the increased running of a rat in an activity cage or in an increase in the amount and vigor of restless movement even during sleep) or an increase in muscular tonus (the simultaneous innervation of opposed muscles canceling the movement but not the tonic contractions). What these notions fail to explain is why boredom (a stimulusless state) should have rather similar effects, or why the response output should ever become canalized into acts that eliminate the stimulus input. Why should the persistence in quasirandom output until the elimination of the stimulation ever become foreshortened? Because the elimination of stimulation is rewarding? But that introduces an entirely different kind of factor, and one that takes priority over both entropy and the unidirectional progression of innervation. What the reward explanation says is that certain states are intolerable, distressing, unsatisfying whereas others are satisfying, pleasing, and so forth. Which states are the one and which the other becomes a secondary issue of fact, and then it becomes important to note that some unstimulated states are also distressing and some highly stimulated states are highly satisfying.

Strict behaviorists, of course, do not like such words as "reward." Such words have too strong mentalistic connotations. It is better to say that successful actions are reinforced. No, not even that. You cannot speak of successful actions because success implies an end in view, and that is not proper. It is simply that if something happens—just anything, apparently, will do, so long as it is not nothing—when you do something then the immediately anteceding action (that is, what you did just before the something happened) is reinforced; from there on, it is simply a question of which actions are most frequently reinforced. To be sure, Tolman, long ago, showed that a rat running a maze may enter certain blind alleys far more frequently than it does the alley leading to food; and I find it hard to understand why encountering a wall should be less reinforcing than encountering food, that is, on the hypothesis that satisfaction is, at most, merely an irrelevant epiphenomenon. But then again, maybe my puzzlement demonstrates that I do not really comprehend the rules of scientific psychological research.

Apparently, under these rules, one is perfectly free to ignore whatever one chooses to ignore. I can recall an episode in which a psychologist, counted as one of the leading learning theorists of our day, responded to a challenge with the rather astonishing (to me, that is, not, so far as I could tell, to my colleagues who were present but showed no visible reaction) remark, "But I am not interested in learning theory. Not even in the learning behavior, in general, of rats. I am interested in *my* theory and in the deductions I make from it. If these deductions are supported, then my theory has proved itself. If one or more of them is contradicted, then I have to modify my theory. My theory is deliberately narrow in scope because that is how good theory is constructed. You start with theories very limited in scope, hoping eventually to enlarge the scope. Your counterexample does not fall within the bounds of this narrow scope." (I cannot swear to the words, but I believe that I have faithfully reported the substance of his remarks.) And another who responded to my remark that, though one may argue about rats, one thing about which I am utterly certain is that I use cognitive maps all the time, "So do I. But what does that have to do with science?" Another, not a behaviorist, who responded to the challenge that there were available simpler and less dramatic explanations of certain phenomena than were offered by his theory, "But I am only interested in *my* theory and in how well it fits the facts." Another who started a lecture with the unsolicited announcement that he had a great joke to tell about himself, namely, that he knew perfectly well that his research was trivial and nonsensical, but then "I have a list of some 200 heroes in psychology and will continue to do the kind of thing they do." Still another, less famous than any of the foregoing but nonetheless a reputable researcher, who said to me, "I cannot answer your criticisms and will not even try. I simply know that I and the people I respect will go on doing the kinds of things we have been doing. That's the way we like it." And, of course, the psychologist who devastated me with, "That's logic, not science."

Perhaps there is something about the way I advance criticism or question what I hear that provokes an effort to dispose of me rather than of my criticism. Or, perhaps it is simply that an unanticipated obstacle evokes quasirandom verbal activity which is not representative of their normal patterns of thought. One of the foregoing examples does not seem to fit these explanations, but perhaps this psychologist was seeking to dispose of me in advance or anticipating hostility from the audience. (One of his colleagues once said to me, with an air of relief, as we were chatting after the discussion period following one of his lectures, "Well, you were not so terrible." I said, "What do you mean?" Said he, "I was warned to be on the lookout for you.") But then, why cannot a man of unassailable status and scientific prestige simply say, "That sounds like a good point, but I want to think about it before I commit myself," or "I know that I can answer that, but I would need some time to pull my thoughts together," or "I could answer that, but the issue you raise is complicated and it would probably take too long and take us too far afield," or make some other cogent but noncommittal response? The issue is not the immediate response. Who, including myself, has not had to field questions to which he had no immediate answer or to which he could not, in the aftermath, think of a better answer? The issue is that these people were telling me, in effect, "I don't want to think about that and my scientific commitments do not obligate me to think about what I don't want to think about." So I come back to the possibility that I simply do not understand some of the unwritten rules of scientific conduct.

At any rate, I have no reason to believe that behaviorists are unaware that consummatory responses—typically, highly stirred up states—and the crescendo of activities that often lead up to them can be intensely pleasurable. It is simply that, by the rules of scientific behavior that they have adopted, it is scientifically illegitimate to mention such a fact. That a rule can wipe out a fact is not surprising from people who make a virtue out of being more concerned with their observational operations than with phenomena which these operations are designed to help them observe. At any rate, they would have us believe that since it does not exist insofar as science is concerned, pleasure does not signify that the activity is rewarding, but that the reward is the aftermath, the reduction of excitation or tension.

Contrast such a view with the following summary of observations by Freud. He wrote that the erogenous zones

are all used to provide a certain amount of pleasure by *being stimulated* in a way appropriate to them. This pleasure then leads to an increase in tension which in its turn is responsible for producing the necessary energy for the conclusion of the sexual act. The penultimate stage of that act is once again the appropriate *stimulation* of an erotogenic zone . . . by the appropriate object . . . ; and from the *pleasure yielded by this excitation* the motor energy is obtained . . . which brings about the discharge of the sexual substances. This last pleasure is the highest in intensity . . . it is wholly a pleasure of satisfaction and with it the tension of the libido is for the time being extinguished. . . .

This distinction between the one kind of pleasure due to the *excitation* of erotogenic zones and the other kind due to the discharge of the sexual substances deserves . . . a difference in nomenclature. The former may be suitably described as "forepleasure" in contrast to the "end-pleasure . . ." (italics added).[2]

Alas, even if we are disposed to disregard Freud's overlooking of the pleasure of the orgasm *per se* (a highly stirred up state and properly described as "end pleasure" so that Freud's "end pleasure" would have to be described as "after pleasure") Freud's conceptualization is no better than that of other psychologists impressed by the entropy principle. He writes that "I must insist that a feeling of tension necessarily involves unpleasure. What seems to me decisive is the fact that a feeling of this kind is accompanied by an impulsion to make a change in the psychological situation, that it operates in an urgent way which is wholly alien to the nature of the feeling of pleasure."[3] Immediately, he notes a paradox: "If, however, the tension of sexual excitement is counted as unpleasurable feeling, we are at once brought up against the fact that it is also undoubtedly felt as pleasurable. . . . How then are this unpleasurable tension and this feeling of pleasure to be reconciled?"[4]

One might think to resolve the paradox by assuming that the first kind necessarily gives rise to excitations in other parts of the body—thereby withdrawing the excitation from the parts first aroused and fulfilling the tension-reduction condition of pleasure—and so on until the final climax when all tension disappears. Not only is the assumption of a necessary progression demonstrably false, as is the further assumption that such pleasure necessarily, as Freud suggests, "soon passes over into the most obvious unpleasure if it cannot be met by a further accession of pleasure,"[5] but Freud himself notes that "In every case in which tension is produced by sexual processes it is accompanied by pleasure; even in

[2] S. Freud, "Three Essays on Sexuality (1905)," in *The Standard Edition of the Complete Psychological Works of Sigmund Freud,* vol. 7 (London: Hogarth Press, 1953).
[3] *Ibid.,* p. 209.
[4] *Ibid.,* p. 209.
[5] *Ibid.,* p. 210.

the preparatory changes in the genitals a feeling of satisfaction of some kind is plainly to be observed."[6] That is, Freud agrees that some states of excitation are *per se* pleasurable.

In the "Three Essays," Freud disclaims any intention to deal with the problem of the paradox other than to learn as much as possible from the sexual instance. In 1924, however, he added a footnote indicating that he had attempted to solve the problem in "The Economic Problem of Masochism."[7] The footnote gives no indication of repentance with regard to a former error, so that it seems fair to conclude that, subsequent to the latter publication, Freud still took seriously the views just quoted. Unfortunately, from the viewpoint of a consistent position, he does little more in the relevant section of the latter than to state the problem in what is for him its most critical form, namely, that the pleasure and nirvana principles, serving the life and death instincts, respectively, have been stated in identical terms, that is, the reduction of excitation. Having stated the problem and noted that excitation may be pleasurable, he writes:

Pleasure and unpleasure, therefore, cannot be referred to an increase or decrease of a quantity (which we describe as "tension due to stimulus"), although they obviously have a great deal to do with that factor. It appears that they depend, not on this quantitative factor, but on some characteristic of it which we can only describe as a qualitative one. If we were able to say what this qualitative characteristic is, we should be much further advanced in psychology. Perhaps it is the rhythm, the temporal sequence of changes, rises and falls in the quantity of stimulus. We do not know.

In other words, Freud's effort to deal with satisfaction in terms of quantities of excitation has come to just about nought, to say nothing of utter confusion. Freud, however, has, at least, the virtue of remaining an honest observer; he remains in the state of confusion by refusing to permit his theories to dominate his observation.

Let me consider one other instance in which the tension-reduction principle looms large. Festinger,[9] explicitly accepting the meaning of "reward" as referring to the reduction of excitation and starting with the observation that, by the criterion of resistance to extinction, less adequate rewards may lead to more effective learning than more adequate

[6] *Ibid.*, p. 209.

[7] S. Freud, "The Economic Problem of Masochism" (1924), in *The Standard Edition of the Complete Psychological Works of Sigmund Freud,* vol. 19 (London: Hogarth Press, 1961).

[8] *Ibid.*, p. 160.

[9] L. Festinger, "The Psychological Effects of Insufficient Rewards," *American Psychologist,* 16(1961):1–11.

ones, argues for the need to supplement the principle that organisms learn to repeat those activities that lead to reward with a second principle which is "rather of an opposite character."

The second principle, Festinger finds in his general theory of cognitive dissonance. As applied to the paradoxes of learning behavior, Festinger's principle may be stated as follows: If an organism "exerts a great deal of effort, or endures pain, in order to reach some ordinary objective, there is a strong tendency for him to *persuade himself* that the objective is especially valuable or especially desirable."[10] Or, more fundamentally: There is a need to reduce the dissonance between the cognition that one has voluntarily committed oneself to an activity which, "all other things being equal," one would avoid doing and the cognition that the reward that has been obtained is inadequate; and, "this dissonance can be reduced if the organism *can persuade himself* that he really likes the behavior in which he is engaged or if he *enhances for himself* the value of what he has obtained as a result of his actions."[11] Four objections can be raised to the adequacy of Festinger's formulation. In presenting these objections, I hope it will be clear that I am not here discussing the general theory of cognitive dissonance, nor other applications of dissonance theory to problems of motivation, but the particular application I have just described.

1. As Festinger himself notes, one means of reducing the dissonance, and the one that "is undoubtedly the one most frequently employed by organisms," is to refuse to perform the action again, so that the formulation leaves totally unclear why an individual should ever go to the trouble of persuading himself that the activity has been worthwhile. It merely begs the question to say, as Festinger does, that he is considering "only those situations in which this means of reducing dissonance is not available to the organism," that is, that he is considering "only situations in which the organism is somehow tricked or seduced into continuing to engage in the activity, in spite of the dissonance which is introduced." For there exists no dissonance until the individual has discovered that he has been tricked or seduced, or at least that the returns are not so great as anticipated. At this point, the individual does in fact have the alternative of withdrawal, or, if he does not, then there is no dissonance since the continued participation is not voluntary. If he does elect to continue, therefore, is it not more plausible to assume that he is getting more satisfaction than the experimenter is willing to credit—

[10] Italics added.
[11] Italics added.

perhaps from the seduction itself, perhaps from other sources—and may not this extra measure of satisfaction wrap the entire situation in a rosier glow than would otherwise have been experienced?

A person may, of course, discover that he has been investing more effort and suffering more pain than is justified by the returns—and feel like a fool for not having realized this sooner. In such a case, he may well be motivated to persuade himself that his investment has indeed been worthwhile. He may stop at this, entering the "experience" as "value received" in his mental ledger or saying to himself, "That was great, but now there are other things to do." Or, to protect his rationalization, he may further persuade himself that continuing the investment is still worthwhile. Whether he stops or continues, however, what is at stake does not seem to be the reduction of dissonance, but rather the preservation of self-esteem.

2. It is questionable, in principle, whether the condition "all other things being equal" can ever be satisfied if the individual voluntarily commits himself to activity that he would avoid in other contexts. Thus, the pain encountered in the context of voluntary participation in an experiment for the advancement of science cannot be compared to a similarly induced pain in an accidental encounter with a live wire; nor a pain experienced by a teenager with his girl friend as an observer with a similarly induced pain when only his mother is present as an observer. Perhaps Festinger would agree that the phrase "all other things being equal" should be deleted from the statement of the principle, but then what would this change imply for the conditions of dissonance? If I set out to determine how much pain I can endure, is it dissonance that increases my degree of gratification with every increment of pain that I can stand?

3. If, as in Festinger's experiments, there is no voluntary commitment whatever to that portion of the activity which involves the expenditure of extra effort or the endurance of unanticipated frustration or pain, or if the degree of pain, effort, or frustration turns out to be more than anticipated, then there is no reason for the first of the two dissonant cognitions. Why should a person not say to himself, "That damned experimenter (or salesman, or whatever). He sure concealed from me what I was letting myself in for (or buying, or whatever)"?

4. The principle is stated without limit. Thus, Festinger's rats should develop more and more affection toward the delay box, the longer they are delayed; an outcome which I must, to say the least, doubt. By the same reasoning, a hostess who can count on the politeness of her guests

should serve only tough and rubbery steaks; the tougher the steak, the better—or so they will persuade themselves—it tastes. I am certain that Festinger does not mean to apply the theory without limit; but, if the theory does not contain within itself any principle that defines its limits of application, then it is no theory; for, in any new application, we have no theoretical way of anticipating whether the limit has been exceeded.

Let me recapitulate. Festinger, starting with the premises of the entropic characterization of motivation, then finds it necessary to add a complementary countervailing principle. That is, he starts with the assumption that stimulation, effort, pain, frustration, or anything that impedes the discharge of tension or that results in the building up of tension should evoke avoidance reactions and displeasure. This is, as Festinger knows and shows, not always the case. Therefore, if one is to retain the primary principle, it is necessary to introduce a complementary principle which Festinger finds in the theory of cognitive dissonance. Since principle and counterprinciple form a unit, however, then, if the primary principle is unsound, the complementary principle must also be unsound. I have argued that the counterprinciple is, in fact, unsound, that is, in terms of formal logic, I have affirmed the consequent of the immediately preceding hypothetical proposition. Affirming the consequent does not, in itself, affirm the antecedent. But, in the present instance, assuming that my argument with respect to the basic unsoundness of the theory of cognitive dissonance holds water, the failure of the consequent leaves the primary principle with all of its manifest insufficiencies and, unless and until someone comes up with a tenable counterprinciple, it must be rejected.

Apart from the difficulties that Freud got into as a result of his espousal of the entropy principle as applied to motivation and Festinger's failure to amend the principle in a satisfactory way, there are some quite commonplace observations that, it seems to me, quite flatly contradict it. A person who loses his desire for food does not typically rest content in his blessed state, one finds this an occasion to seek medical or psychotherapeutic assistance; and I suspect that even a dyed-in-the-wool stimulus-response operationalist would, *horribile dictu,* seriously contemplate going to a psychoanalyst if he finds himself without sexual libido or given to quick discharge of sexual tension by virtue of premature ejaculation. Most of us, I dare say, do not look forward with great enthusiasm to the day when we will be able to satisfy all of the nutritive needs of our bodies and to anticipate hunger by taking an appropriate pill. In matters of food, sex, and other recreational enterprises, human beings have devoted great ingenuity and planning to the development of means and devices to intensify desire and to prolong the period of gratification that precedes repletion.

I have devoted as much space as I have to the issue because, so long as one assumes the fundamental character of motivation to be encompassed in terms of a physical law, my entire argument concerning the nature of Man is undermined. The fundamental concept to which I have appealed in constructing my image of Man is that of motivation. If it were true that motivation is basically nothing but an extended manifestation of a physical law (extended, that is, only in the sense that the law holds in contexts one does not ordinarily think of in conjunction with physics), then Man, himself, is basically nothing but an extension of physical law. If such were indeed the case, I would have to come to terms with it. But the whole point of this book and, therefore, of the immediately preceding argument is that such is not the case.

Motivation implies a mission, a commitment to accomplish something—or, at least, to try. Missions, however, do not exist apart from circumstances that define the character of the activity required in order to fulfill the commitment. There are circumstances in which the commitment requires immediate, more or less vigorous action; the state or condition of motivation is acute. There are other circumstances in which the mission demands nothing more than an alertness to possible changes in circumstances that bear on the mission; the motivation is alive but latent.

When an intolerable circumstance exists, whether it be a condition of the body or not, the motivation is always acute: Some more or less vigorous action, if only blind trial-and-error, is demanded. This action may be inhibited by the requirements of other commitments, but the body is mobilized for it; it is the appropriate movement that is blocked (by the simultaneous innervation of opposed muscles), not the discharge into motor outlets, and the result may be increased muscle tonus or diffuse, quasirandom, motor discharge.

It may be recalled that, in Chapter 2, I referred to the distress associated with drive states as the occasion for the first directed activities in the life history of the individual; but I did not, at that point, indicate what it is about drive states that is distressing. Are hunger and thirst, for example, *per se* distressing?

Consider a newborn baby. With the onset of hunger, there is much diffuse and vigorous activity, including crying. Put the nipple into the infant's mouth. Immediately, the diffuse activity gives way to one concentrated activity, vigorous sucking and apparent contentment. Take the nipple away. Again diffuse activity and crying. Restore the nipple. Again contented vigorous sucking. What has happened? Has the hunger been appeased? But there was not yet time for the milk to be digested and passed into the circulatory system, to bathe the stirred-up nerves in a soothing solution. So far as I can see, the one thing that has changed is that the diffuse motor discharge has been channeled into the concentrated activity of feeding. It is a complex act, but coordinated. Interfere with any of its components (for instance, hold the infant's mouth open and introduce the same warm milk at the same rate of flow) and you will not get the same effect. It may be recalled in this connection that J. B. Watson had observed a long time ago that the sudden loss of support is a sufficient cause of the "fear" reaction in young infants, but that W. Valentine subsequently observed that the same condition in a context of play (as when the baby is repeatedly tossed up into the air and caught on the way down in the firm arms of one of the parents and given a follow-up hug) brings on expressions of joy. Similarly, with regard to Watson's observation of startle and fear reactions in response to a sudden loud noise, Valentine observed that this was not likely to occur if this happened while the infant was busily nursing, held to the mother's bosom by her firm arms. What is the difference between the Watson and Valentine situations? In the Watson situations, some action is demanded, but there is no prepared action to take. In the Valentine situations, the child can abandon itself to the ongoing activity; that is, no new action is demanded, the stimulus input being channeled into the ongoing activity.

I take this as the basic model of the distress associated with drive states. One is impelled to action, but there is no coordinated course of action to take; it is this state of affairs that is distressing. The same infant, years later, may be sitting reading an interesting book. Hunger begins to develop. For a while, the concentrated activity of reading absorbs the discharge released by the hunger, and he experiences no distress. Then he notices that he is finding it more and more difficult to concentrate and he feels vague discomfort. He puts the book down, roams around the room looking for something to latch on to, picks various things up, vaguely examines them, and puts them down. He looks out of the window in a desultory way, goes back to his chair and tries the book again. Nothing satisfies. Each activity bid eases the discomfort somewhat, but it is not enough to harness the diffuse motor discharge. Let something exciting be taking place as he looks out of the window and the absorption of watching would hold him for a while, but nothing was happening as he looked out. Eventually, he realizes that he is hungry; or, even without conscious thought, he becomes involved in the activities of getting and preparing some food. With this involvement, the distress diminishes and may even vanish entirely.

Quasi-random, diffuse motor discharge is not peculiar to drive states. When any act is started a neural process is set up. If the act is impeded or blocked before it is completed, the nervous energy must still find an outlet.[12] When a complicated course of action is embarked on, there are likely to be many beginnings of interfering acts along the way and, if the course of action entails anxiety or an urgency to "have done with it," there are recurrent impulses to withdraw from the action. Complicated and difficult behavioral activities require a discipline to inhibit interfering acts. The blocked acts, however, must find outlets, and the result is an increase in bodily tension (or, with insufficient discipline, diffuse motor discharge) for them to be completed.[13] But, if quasi-random, diffuse motor discharge is *per se* distressing, the execution of complicated and difficult acts should be facilitated by absorbing the discharge into relatively routinized minimally distracting activity, such as doodling, smoking, and stylized mannerisms; and this is, of course, the case.

Acute motivation is by no means limited to intolerable states and normally, with increasing maturation, less and less activity is devoted to the voiding of such states, or, for that matter, even to preventing their occurrence. The commitments entailed in enduring concerns also demand action to forward the latter when opportunity arises and, often

[12] The issue here is not quite the same as the issue of "unfinished business" discussed in the preceding chapter. From the viewpoint of the simple neural event, if there is no further input, the act is over and done with when the nervous energy reaches some motor output. If this were all that there is to "unfinished business," there would be no reason to resume or for continued preoccupation with the interrupted act. "Unfinished business" can produce a quasi-appetitive drive only by virtue of continued input which is related to the meaning of failure to complete. In this connection, it may be recalled that Helen Lewis has shown experimentally that a task-oriented subject has no perseverative tendency to resume or show continued concern about an act that he himself has not completed because his partner completed it. That is, an act can be completed—insofar as the issue of "unfinished business" is concerned—even though one has not completed it oneself.

[13] What I have just described is, in essence, Janet's concept of psychological tension. This concept is all too often confused with his concept of "psychological energy" which is simply his shorthand expression for the fact that every psychological act involves duration, intensity, and extension of movement, and this entails the expenditure of energy. Tics, mannerisms, etc. which he refers to as "phenomena of derivation" are instances of diffuse motor discharge.

enough, to create such opportunities when there is a possibility of doing so. At such times and, of course, whenever the situational changes are such as to threaten the enduring concerns, the latter are transformed from latency to their acute phases. Thus, the enduring concerns of the ego system, the superego, and the id (the concern with the unfinished business of the past) come to take up most of one's behavioral life.

The energies of acute motivation and the minimal energy requirements of perpetual alertness with regard to matters that may affect the enduring concerns are the energies of the body. It may be timely to remind the reader that I do not regard psychological events as something other than bodily events, but rather as special kinds of bodily events, namely, those that involve spontaneous directed activities. It is, therefore, no retreat from my position to refer to what goes on in the body when it seems useful to do so. It may be noted, however, that I have been able to say what it seemed to me important to say about what goes on in the body without going into details of the structure of the brain and nervous system, the physicochemical processes of the propagation of neural impulses, the anatomy and chemistry of the synapses, and so on.

Let me turn now to the problem of the feelings and emotions that seem to be so intimately involved in motivated activity, but that also constitute a troublesome issue in systematic psychology because it seems possible to have affectless motivated activity. Thus, some psychologists have contended that emotions are motives. But, then, whereas such emotions as fear seem to have the same urgency about them as do appetitive drives, they do not have the same basis in drive states. Are they, then, a different class of drives and, if so, what is their energic basis? Moreover, how is it that some affects—like pleasantness—seem to have no affirmative action implications whatever? Others have described affects as the conscious aspects, associates, correlates, or epiphenomena of motives. But if so, why is it that some motives are so accompanied and others not? Some contend that emotions, like motives, can be repressed; others, that to speak of repressed emotions is a contradiction in terms. And so on.

As I make my own way through the confusion,[14] I have come to some

[14] That I am able to do so at all, I owe largely to the stimulating and provocative ideas of my erstwhile colleague, now at Clark University, Dr. Joseph de Rivera. Until I came into contact with his ideas and research, I had many ideas about the affects but, when it came to trying to fit them into a systematic psychological framework, I could do little more than shrug my shoulders in bafflement. Though we are still far from seeing eye to eye on all matters, my basic

relatively simple notions. Affects[15] are the qualities[16] of what one observes when one regards one's own motivational state: feelings, when
the focus is on the condition of the doer or on the course of the action;
emotions, when the focus is on the relation of the doer to the object of
the action. When the focus is on the mission *per se*, the motivation is
apprehended as affectless. Because of what they connote, some affects
come to be positively valued, so that their achievement becomes a
motive; others, negatively valued so that their avoidance becomes a
motive. It would carry me too far afield to try to give an exhaustive
treatment of the affects here, but I will try to illustrate what I have just
said with regard to the affect pleasure.

To begin with, I distinguish between pleasure, a turbulent, stirred-up,
zestful enjoyment, and pleasantness, a relaxed, serene, calm, passive
enjoyment. Pleasure comes with the awareness that a mission is well
under way, that the enterprise is advancing without insuperable obstacles.
One's eye is on the immediate process rather than on the goal, and the
latter is relevant only in the sense that it sets a frame of reference that
defines the kind of information that will indicate progress. Often, the
information is sensory in character and, the greater the appropriate
sensory input, the greater is the pleasure. Appropriate sensory stimulation is pleasurable even in the latent phases of the mission, but it is
most intense in the active phases. Often, especially during the acute
phases, the relevant information is of a kind that indicates that difficulties have been overcome and that immediately confronting difficulties
can be overcome. Hence, the greater the sense of successful effort, the
greater the pleasure; and one often more or less deliberately introduces

indebtedness to him remains. I can only express the very sincere hope that it
will not be too long before his brilliant and massive systematic phenomenological,
semantic, and structural-linguistic investigations of emotions and interpersonal
relations are brought to a point where he feels ready to publish.

[15] It should be clear that I am speaking of affective experience, not of emotional expression. It seems to me that the dynamics of emotional expression
(facial and postural changes, inspiration-expiration ratios, electrodermal manifestations and so on) are bodily dynamics. As such they are of no psychological
interest except as they may be taken as indicators (highly fallible under many
circumstances) of affective experience. Their use for such purposes does not come
within the purview of this book. The issue of emotional expression is also complicated by the emergence of formal nonverbal languages of emotional expressions.
Conventionalized postures, facial expressions, vocal modulations, and so on are
used to convey the presence of various affects, and nonverbal languages, like
verbal ones, can be used to lie and are perhaps somewhat more facilely utilized
than are words to convey unconscious motivations, with a resulting disparity
between what is conveyed and what is consciously experienced.

[16] See the discussion of qualities in Chapter 6.

delays and other difficulties to increase the amount of necessary effort, thereby enhancing the pleasure of the action.

All this is, of course, conditional on the absence of experienced danger to one's other enterprises; and activities, which under appropriate circumstances are intensely pleasurable, may be stripped of the pleasure or even become acutely displeasurable when one experiences concurrent danger to one's other enterprises, even though one may be sufficiently committed to the immediate course of action. By the same token, the greater the number and centrality of the commitments involved in the successfully advancing action, the greater the sense of the depth of pleasure, as though, in the extreme case, the innermost fibers of one's being are involved. There are, thus, at least two dimensions of the pleasure experience—intensity and depth; and, in the middle ranges of pleasure, the two dimensions are relatively independent. On scales from zero to one, pleasure is at 0,0 in the absence of either pleasure or displeasure; and it is at 1,1 in the greatest pleasure the human being can know. But, in between, it can be quite intense without being very deep or quite deep without being very intense.

Pleasantness is the sense of all immediate missions accomplished (or, at least over with, as in the whole-hearted acceptance of failure) and of being in a situation in which there is nothing that need be done at the moment with regard to one's enduring concerns and in which nothing is likely to happen that has bearing on them, so that one can relax one's active scanning of the surround. It is enhanced by sensory input that is soothing to nerve and muscle and that emphasizes the absence of any need to take action. Under these conditions, it is at its maximum following vigorous action, especially so following intensely and deeply pleasurable activity. Note that pleasantness is not a stimulusless state. One needs feedback from the body and the surround to experience relaxation and to know that all is well and that there is no call to do anything.

Displeasure is the sense that one's mission is not going well. Like pleasure, displeasure is also a stirred-up state, but it is agitated rather than zestful. Also like pleasure, it is characterized by the two relatively independent dimensions of intensity and depth, and it is mediated by both sensory and other informational input. Though conceptual opposites, pleasure and displeasure may, in fact, be experientially intermingled if the informational input is inconsistent and contains mutually contradictory components.

Unpleasantness is associated with infringements on general relaxation, infringements on pleasantness, so to say; and the more earned the relaxation by the successful completion of effortful activity, the more unpleasant is a given infringement, for instance, raucous noise (sometimes called music) coming in from the outside when you have earned your rest. Note that the same stimulus input may at other times be a matter of indifference or even pleasurable. What makes it unpleasant is that it interferes with relaxation. Because relaxation may be actively sought and because infringements on general relaxation that simply follows effortful activity are likely to introduce relaxation as a goal object, such unpleasantness is not nearly so distinguishable from displeasure as pleasantness is from pleasure.

There are, of course, certain kinds of sensory experience—visual, auditory, olfactory, and so on—that we characterize as pleasant or unpleasant because their occurrences are highly correlated with and therefore come to be taken as signs of good or bad states of affairs (good or bad in relation to our commitments, that is)—and some of our commitments may also require that we "like" certain things and "dislike" others—or because they enhance or distract from the activities at hand. In terms of the distinctions I have drawn, these pleasantnesses and unpleasantnesses are actually more or less mild pleasures or displeasures. If there is an issue here, it has to do with the usage of terms, not with the nature of the experiences. In the popular usage, if any distinction at all is made between "pleasant" and "pleasurable" and between "unpleasant" and "displeasurable," it tends to confine pleasant-unpleasant to sensory experience and pleasurable-displeasurable to activity; but I think that this distinction is unsound—as if there were pleasurable activities without sensory aspects or sensory experiences that do not occur in the contexts of what we happen to be doing! Any sensory experience, for instance, conventionally regarded as unpleasant can be quite pleasing in an appropriate activity context. For example, continuing hunger pangs as one leaves the dinner table may be gratifying to someone committed to losing weight and pain may be gratifying in the context of a test of endurance or in the context of expiation of guilt.

It may contribute to the conceptual clarification of the relationship between affect and motivation to review the relation from a slightly different point of view. Affects play a role in motivation through their significations. In other words, affects are not motives in the sense that superordinate behaviors are motives, although they do play a role in directing behavior. It should be recalled that motives, as I have explicated the term, are not in themselves sufficient to determine their subordinate behaviors. The sufficient conditions of the latter are given by the joint operation of the regnant motivations and the apprehension of the behavioral situation as the latter bears on the motivations. Thus, the behavior of working for an "A" in a college course does not, in itself, contain a directive to write a first-rate term paper; the latter directive, given the motivation in the first place, comes from the apprehension of the extant conditions for getting an "A." By itself, the apprehension of the situation implies contingent or hypothetical directives. That is, it implies, "If you want so-and-so, you must (or, probably should) do such-and-such." A subordinate behavior (that is, one determined by the progress of superordinate behaviors and, in relation to them, the assessment of the situation) may, of course, from its position in the nested hierarchy of behaviors, operate as a motive in its own right. The assessment of situations thus plays a role in the generation of motives as well as in the generation of the lowest-order activities in the hierarchy. Now, what I am saying with regard to the relation of affect to motivation is that affect plays precisely such a role—an assessment-of-situation role—in motivation.

There are, however, two important differences between affectless and affective assessments of behavioral situations. First, in affectless assessment, contingent directives may be apprehended in the absence of motivation to act upon them. A counselor, for instance, may point out such contingent directives to his client without being motivated to accept them for himself; and any person may similarly realize with regard to his own situations that some course of action would be indicated should he desire some particular end, even though he may have no commitment to attaining that end. Affective assessments, by contrast, are always bound to the motivations of the assessor. Second, even though the motivation be present, in the affectless assessment, the situation as apprehended simply defines something to be exploited in the service of the motive. In affective assessment, by contrast, the continuance, modification, or voiding of the subject-situation relationship is itself highly relevant to the regnant motivations. In other words, there is a major focus in the affective assessment on the relationship, as such, of the motivated subject to the apprehended situation. Thus, in the affectless apprehension of danger, there is merely an implied directive to do something (if only to maintain a wary alertness) with regard to the source of the danger; that is, there is nothing but a cold-blooded appraisal of the threat and an appraisal of the action that needs to be taken. In fear, by contrast, there is a major focus of concern with one's situation as well as with the perceived source of danger. Similarly, in the case of cold-blooded hostility, there is simply a focus of concern on the object and the actions that would advance the motivation to aggress against it. In anger, there is not only the latter focus, but also an at least equally salient focus on the intolerableness of one's situation. In joy, there is a keen awareness of the desirability of being in the situation.

The question of affects is further complicated by the fact that there are socially proper affects in various contexts. One might think that society would only be concerned with what people do overtly. For whatever reason, however (perhaps because of an assumption that "right" affects are conditions of proper conduct or that a person who is always affectively correct can be relied on more than one who is not), this is not the case. Society as a whole and one's social circles are very much concerned with the propriety of one's inner feelings and emotions. One is expected to like certain things and dislike others, to be angered by some things, entranced by others, to have appropriately modulated feelings with regard to various kinds of sights, sounds, tastes, smells, ideas, ideologies, actions, and what not. Ethical and religious systems enjoin us to experience certain affects such as compassion for the unfortunate and loving one's neighbors, and proscribe other affects such as jealousy and coveting. As a result we acquire an investment in claiming and persuading ourselves that we experience certain affects and do not experience others; and if we fail to persuade ourselves of the propriety of our affects when, in fact, they are not proper, we make things right by experiencing shame and guilt.

By far, more important than the effect of the normativity of affect on dissimulation is the fact that it makes it important to try to achieve the right affects by seeking out occasions in which they are likely to occur, avoiding occasions likely to promote wrong affects, and seeking to monitor one's feelings and to discipline them. That is, having right and not having wrong affects becomes an enduring concern. The normatization of affect is not the only factor to have such an effect. Affects, after all, come to signify how our affairs are going so that they provide data that are invaluable in monitoring our affairs. Moreover, the uncertainties of existence are such that we need not only to manage our affairs well, but we also need feedback to tell us that our management is as effective as we hope it to be. In time, the feedback may come to loom as large as—or even larger than—the management.

In the case of a feeling like pleasure, where it seems to be much easier to judge intensity than depth, one may, as a consequence, become preoccupied with the pursuit of (and, with respect to the future, the assurance of) relatively superficial and easily achieved pleasures and the avoidance of displeasures, including those of the latter that may be associated with our more important enterprises. The concerns with self-reassurance that one's affairs are going well, thus, so to say, divides the ego against itself. It is important (both from the viewpoint of clear and consistent theory and from the viewpoint of proper diagnosis to aid in the treatment of cases in which this kind of development comes to constitute a serious social or personal problem) to realize that this kind of pursuit of pleasure is an ego enterprise and not an expression of the id, though it does have the effect of reducing the constraints on some of the id motives.

This development is analogous to one that occurs among some of those Protestants who take the doctrines of predestination and God's grace seriously: Good deeds are not a means of winning heavenly rewards but a sign of God's grace; and some become obsessed with good deeds, not because this is what is demanded of them or to win the rewards of good deeds but only to reassure themselves that they are still in good standing. Their obsession betrays and defeats them because they become preoccupied with the form rather than the substance of the good deeds, missing the compassion, charity, and love of fellow man that mark the good Christian.

The development of a passionate pursuit of intense but relatively superficial pleasures is especially likely during periods of social crisis when the uncertainties and ambiguities of existence are intensified; it is especially likely to strike the adolescent youth whose futures are, under the best of circumstances, uncertain and unclear.[17]

Strict behaviorists may avoid the phenomena of inner feeling and emotion as mentalistic poison. The price they pay is that they lose much of the human being and what makes him do what he does.

[17] See, especially, Nathan Adler, "The Antinomian Personality: The Hippie Character Type," *Psychiatry*, 31, no. 4 (1968): 325–338.

14

ECCE HOMO!

Ego, superego, and id are interrelated in a variety of ways.

From a purely formal point of view, each of the pairs has something in common and something in difference. Ego and superego are both moral systems, but they represent different kinds of morality: the ego, implying a pragmatic moral approach to the world, predicated on taking into account the long-run and wide-ranging consequences of behavioral actions; the superego, an internalized moral authority, accepting as binding the obligations and prohibitions that are implied in the concept of the primal authority figure and in the modifications of this concept through the assimilation into it of the apprehension of later sources of authority. Ego and id are both concerned with gratification, the fulfillment of motives and commitments (including, in the case of the ego, as one of its many commitments, the commitment to the primal authority figure), but they differ in their approach to gratification: id, an impulsion to the immediate gratification of individual motives as they become acute and opportunity affords, without regard to consequences in the next moment or to other motives; ego, a concern with maximizing the long-run gratification of an entire system of motives even at the cost of failure in immediate gratification. Id and superego are both essentially infantile in their character, but the motivations involved are typically opposed, the exceptions occurring when id motives fit in with the talion law, that is, when aggression also serves the ends of punishment, or, more generally, when different facets of a given neurotic symptom[1] simultaneously fit the requirements of id and superego motives on a primary-process basis.

[1] It is worth recalling that Freud's greatest discovery was that conversion symptoms are, in my terminology, behaviors—refusals to move, see, hear, and so on—that solve (at some cost and with some compromise) the problem of

I hasten to add that, in characterizing the superego as infantile, I am not making a judgment about all authoritarian codes of conduct but merely about one of the roots of commitment to them. Other commitments to authoritarian codes, if and when they come into being, are built into the ego system and are not extraneous to it. That is, they are generated in the course of the operation of the other ego motives and, in turn, qualify the latter. The commitment to the primal authority figure is itself a by-product of, and is perpetuated as, unfinished business of childhood. In this sense, the superego is a development of the id rather than of the ego, and it retains much of the character of the id in its irrational[2] mode of operation; but it, of course, also has its roots in the ego motivation current during the childhood period and perpetuated as concerns about the integrity of the self and the body.

These formal similarities, however, pale into insignificance when put up against three facts as a consequence of which the three factors are tied together into one dynamic system:

1. Motives do not exist apart from a body. If ego, superego, and id are constituted of motives, as I have argued, then they each require a body; and it is the same body to which they are tied. What happens to that body, the activities that occupy it, and its very appearance (because of social reactions to it) affect all three. The three factors are

---

contrary and contradictory id, ego, and superego motivations. Because of unclarity with regard to the mind-body relationship, such symptoms were confused with true psychosomatic symptoms and disease processes (which are by-products of how the body functions in certain behaviors) in talk of the mysterious leap from the psychic to the somatic. In the present context, an hysterical symptom may simultaneously represent the completion or preservation of an id behavior and the punishment for it. Thus, in one of Freud's famous cases, Dora's, a cough could designate an enactment of the completion of fellatio with her father (clearing her throat and spitting out of the seminal fluid) and punishment for the fantasy (illness). An hysterical anaesthesia may preserve and consecrate an illicit bodily contact while also providing punishment for the pleasure of it.

[2] One of the facets of Freud's genius was that he implicitly cast an entirely new light on the concept of rationality through his interpretations of psychoneurotic symptoms, dreams, parapraxes of everyday life, and so forth. Nothing can seem more rational than the way symptoms and the like resolve the conflicting requirements of id, ego, and superego motivations. If, nevertheless, we continue to think of such behavioral manifestations as irrational, we need to revise our concept of the meanings of "rational" and "irrational." This is that a behavior is irrational to the extent that it fails to take into account available relevant information; that is, irrationality is contained in the narrow scope of the premises on which behavior is based rather than on the bad logic by which it proceeds. H. L. Hollingworth, independently, arrived at an essentially similar notion in his concept of sagacity and reduced scope. Note that Janet also took reduced scope as one of the major (pathognomonic) symptoms of hysteria.

continually in competition for the effector mechanisms of that body in order to achieve their own effectance; and, if complete paralysis of behavioral activity is not to ensue, the three kinds of motivation, characteristically at odds with one another, have to be synchronized or compromised in some way. Motives of the three kinds impose constraints on one another and, to the degree that they find common channels of expression, they facilitate one another. They do not exist independently or autonomously.

2. The effectance of any of the three kinds of motives, and even the attempt to carry them through, has environmental consequences some of which retroflexively influence the expressibility of the three kinds of motivational factors. Both because of the common body and of the environmental reactions to behavior, ego, superego, and id exist in an interdependence of fate.

3. Subjectively, the responsible agent for all of one's apprehended behavior is the self, regardless of the source of motivation. To be sure, many id behaviors and some psychoneurotic symptomatic behaviors have an alien quality about them, as if one were possessed and compelled to carry out these behaviors as if they occurred of themselves. But it is the self that is possessed and becomes, as it were, the compulsory agent of these actions; and the very need for the alibi of compulsion or the very repression of the awareness of the action testifies to the continuing sense of responsibility. Similarly with regard to the behavior of others. It is only to the degree that we apprehend the behaviors of others as not self-initiated (that is, not initiated by the self) or as not falling within the competence of the self to prevent that we absolve others of responsibility for their actions. The self, therefore, which as object is at the core of the ego system, is as subject the common apprehended responsible agent of ego, superego, and id behaviors.

It is inescapable, therefore, that ego, superego, and id, along with the self and the body, constitute one system; it is this system that is the person, the actor whose nature and character we have been seeking. Moreover, if we choose to ignore the dependent relationship of the other components of the person on the body, then we are dealing with the personality in the sense that psychologists intend the term.

It is common, of course, to identify "personality" as an aggregate of traits. Traits, however, are patterns of behavior across time. By this usage, therefore, personality does not exist at any given moment. It does not seem to me that even the trait theorists intend so extreme an implication. They try to save themselves by assuming that the trait is not the pattern, as such, but rather a continuing disposition; but they have nothing to say about the nature of the disposition save that it manifests itself in the pattern. Semantically, therefore, "disposition" has no content in their usage other than that contained in "pattern." The disposition is defined by the pattern and is therefore a synonym for it; it cannot, except by verbal magic, explain the pattern since there is no independent basis for speaking of it. One withdraws or holds oneself aloof from interpersonal contacts because one is disposed to withdraw or hold oneself aloof from interpersonal contacts, that is, one is repeatedly observed to withdraw from or hold oneself aloof from interpersonal contacts; and it rains because the water in the sky has a disposition to fall. Add that most trait theorists are professing operationalists. To speak of traits as dispositions does not save the person (and who or what is the person in trait theory?) from a personalityless existence at any given moment.

Note that I do not object to the study of traits, along with keen attention to manifest inconsistencies in the patterns and the environmental constancies on which the traits depend, as providing cues to the nature of the personality. The trait, however, cannot be comprehended apart from its bleak and contextless (and therefore meaningless)[3] description save as one can relate it to the motives that are being served.

At any rate, the consistency of traits (in the sense of the formal identity of the behavioral output, ignoring the motivation) is grossly exaggerated. The apparency of consistency is largely achieved by ignoring data. To start with, there is a curious kind of logic involved. One starts with the assumption of consistency in the underlying disposition when one has no basis for assuming the disposition in the first place apart from the apparency of the consistency. One then reifies the "disposition" and treats it as the cause of the consistency for which it is nothing more than a synonym. Intelligence is the cause of a pattern of intelligent behavior; introversion is the cause of a pattern of introverted behavior; assertiveness and submissiveness are, respectively, the causes of assertive and submissive behaviors.

Alas, inconsistency then insists on rearing its ugly head. So, insofar as we maintain the attitudes of trait theorists, we dispose of it in a variety of characteristic ways. We take relatively low reliability coefficients of

[3] Do not confuse the meaningfulness of the words in the context of the structure of the language with the meaningfulness of the trait, the thing that the words are describing!

the order of .60, .70, or .80, and we rejoice over them; and our exhilaration soars beyond bounds when we achieve one of .90, which still leaves us with a standard error of a score that is more than two-fifths of the standard deviation of the distribution.[4] After all, very high reliabilities are not easily obtained, we say to ourselves, and we are happy with what we get, and casually overlook the fact that our low aspirations betray our initial assumption. I am not objecting to the appropriate use of tests with relatively low reliabilities; I am merely commenting on the meaning of the low reliabilities in the context of the logic of the case.

Some of us are more sophisticated. We apply the tools of factor analysis (or similar techniques, including Guttman scale analysis) and realize that we have been using too large a variety of test items. There are really a large number of different kinds of intelligence, a large number of different kinds of introversion, and so on. That is to say, what we originally took to be one underlying disposition is really very many. This does not stop us from discovering that traits like intelligence, in the original undifferentiated sense or in some half-hearted differentiated sense (ignoring most of the differentiations that our factor analyses have revealed), is really based in the genes; but that is another story that I will not go into here. What is more immediately relevant is that when we go after the finer consistencies, the differentiated dispositions, we still do not get extraordinarily high reliability coefficients; and what we do get is largely obtained by counterbalancing inconsistencies against one another, as in so-called factor-pure tests. Or, in the case of the extremely narrow-band Guttman scales, we are still satisfied with repro-

---

4 In plain English, this means that the true score, that is, the score that would have been obtained on a perfectly reliable test of whatever the test is measuring, corresponding to any given obtained score has a very good likelihood of being somewhere within the limits of a wide range of true scores. For example, in a test with a normal distribution, a mean of 50, a standard deviation of 10, and a reliability of .90, a true score of 50 may be associated with obtained scores ranging from 39 to 61—and there is still an almost one-in-twenty chance of getting an obtained score outside that range. Alternatively stated, there is a one-in-ten chance that a true score of 61 will be associated with an obtained score at least as low as 50 and a similar chance that a true score of 39 will be associated with one at least as high as 50. The corresponding range for a similar test with a reliability of zero is 25–75. On the average, however, one does considerably better with such a test than one would by blind guessing, especially if one did not want to guess that everyone has a perfectly average score. And all this, on the assumption that the test satisfies certain optimal conditions of measurement, that is, that it yields a normal distribution and satisfies conditions known as homoscedasticity and homoclisy.

ducibility coefficients[5] of the order of .90, though Carmi Schooler has shown that it is fairly easy to get reproducibilities of this order by feeding random "response" data to four or five items (the typical number of items in a Guttman scale) into a computer.

We have another way of dealing with apparent trait inconsistencies, and we use it, among other purposes, to help rationalize away our low aspirations for reliability. Having assumed the trait disposition as a basic constituent of the personality, we assume that inconsistencies are due to extraneous interfering factors. Thus, if a person shows an unevenness of performance on an intelligence test, we assume that this is due to the interference of nonintellective factors, such as motivation and affect. As if intelligence ever appears apart from motivated activity, or can be given any intelligible meaning apart from what the person takes into account in attempting to fulfill his motives; and as if whether he does or does not (habitually or otherwise) take some relevant factor (relevant to what? his purposes or the tester's?) into account can ever be comprehended without reference to the full panoply of his motivations and affects. Enough that the notion of stable and internally consistent trait dispositions has been saved.

But then another well-known fact is conveniently overlooked. It is already revealed in the fact that what impresses one as a reasonably consistent trait can be factorized and shown to be a composite of a number of relatively distinct traits. In effect, consistency appears to be a function of the narrowness of the band of concerns and interests the test items appeal to. Moreover, what is true within tests holds for the test as a whole. That is, if you try to predict behavior from psychological test scores, then, the further you go from the precise kind of material used in the test and the kind of situation involved in the testing, the less helpful are the test scores; and, at that, some part of the success is often attributable, in indeterminate measure, to the operation of self-fulfilling prophecies. The point is that trait consistencies appear in very

---

[5] The reproducibility coefficient is a measure of the degree to which a given score has an unequivocal meaning in terms of how that score was achieved (everyone achieving a given score has answered any given item in the same way) and the next higher score is obtained by giving the same "keyed" responses as the given score plus one other keyed response. Low reproducibilities obviously mean that a given score hides a good deal of response variance. The question at issue concerns the meaning of high reproducibilities. No one, apparently, ever thinks of applying reproducibility analysis to standard psychological tests because high reproducibilities are not expected; and this tells its own story.

narrow bands, and the narrowness of the bands entails narrowness of the range of observational situations as well as of relevant motivations. At the very least, this raises the question of whether it is necessary to appeal to anything other than the narrow bands of concern and situation to account for such consistencies as do appear. In other words, do not the limitations on the range of concern and situation sufficiently explain the consistencies? Why postulate additional determinants such as specific trait dispositions?

I am not challenging the premise of the lawfulness of behavior. What I am saying is that attending only to consistencies of surface activity (that is, disregarding the motivational and situational context) can only, at best, produce weak (albeit possibly useful) statistical generalizations; and this does not strike me as a good way to go about discovering laws. Add that, in trait theory, each trait, with or without an assumed genetic basis, is an ultimate; and the unparsimoniousness of the approach, even after factor analytic reduction, becomes glaring. After all, one must still conceptualize the individual psychological act and the environmental conditions of its emergence; and there remain a host of other phenomena with which a comprehensive psychology has to deal, the conceptualization of which throws no light on the meaning of traits, and to the conceptualization of which the traits contribute nothing. In brief, then, the concept of personality as an amalgam of traits is peculiarly sterile for scientific purposes.

We shall, of course, doubtless go on talking about traits and measuring them because, in the conduct of our daily affairs, stereotyping can be quite functional; so can illusions and delusions. From this point of view, the multiplication of measurable and otherwise discriminable traits can be quite dysfunctional: The seemingly simple order that stereotypes generate and that makes our lives comfortable is destroyed as their number is multiplied. And, curiously, the blurred, confused, mixed-up stereotype is more useful in a practical way than the relatively distinct and clear components into which it can be analyzed. A general purpose intelligence test in which no one can tell what goes into the determination of a score is more useful when it is only the output that counts than an assortment of measures of more finely discriminated varieties of intelligence. But it is not the way of science to set the search for useful stereotypes as its ideal—especially blurred, confused, mixed-up stereotypes.

The statement about the greater practical utility of confused trait stereotypes and similar ones that can be made about any other trait is paralleled in psychometric theory by what is known as the reliability-validity paradox. Though every psychology student learns quite early that test reliability is a necessary condition of validity, it turns out that, in a fundamental sense of reliability, the more reliable a test is beyond some minimally acceptable point, the less likely is that test to be valid (useful) for any practical purpose. In this fundamental sense, a trait is reliable to the degree that all of its items tap the same trait and only that trait, so that, among other things, every item is intercorrelated with every other item to the maximal degree that the marginal frequencies permit. But a highly reliable test, in this sense, is on an extremely narrow band whereas most behavioral outputs are complexly determined and, as a rule, differently so in different cases or in the same case at different times; that is, most behavioral outputs are on a very wide band. As noted earlier, even the same score on most tests can be achieved in many different ways. Thus, on a 100-item test, scoring each item zero or one, there are more than 17 million million conceivable ways of getting a score of exactly 90; and, if that looks like a big number, the number of conceivable ways of getting a score of 50 is astronomical. Even on a ten-item test, there are more than 250 ways of getting a score of 5. This, of course, says nothing about the different ways in which the same answer can be arrived at to a given item. For instance, think of a seven-year-old lad who answered a question about the product of nine times nine by saying, "Seven sevens are forty-nine. Then, two sevens are fourteen. That's sixty-three. Then I need two nines—eighteen. That's eighty-one. Eighty-one!" The next day, to the same question: "I don't remember." "So figure it out." "O.K. Ten times ten is 100. Take away ten, that's ninety. Then take away nine, that leaves eighty-one. Eighty-one!" Today, that lad is a professor of mathematics, but my point is that both of his exemplary ways of arriving at the answer would be scored on any ordinary test in exactly the same way as the rote and uncomprehending recall of the product.

For many purposes, it may matter little how a person gets his score especially if you are willing to bear the costs (or, even better, if you can get someone else to bear the costs) of being wrong some of the time in the inferences you draw and the predictions you make; and you may have no less damaging alternative. But,'if you are trying to figure out what a person is doing and why, it certainly does matter. A psychology that stops caring about what precisely it is that people do, why they do it, and why they do it the way they do it has simply given up on its task. This is the way of the trait conceptualization of personality. I hasten to add that not every psychologist who speaks of traits and who uses tests is of this ilk; but such psychologists do not take traits and test scores as the ultimate variables of psychology. They also need some alternate conceptualization of the nature of personality.

Let me return then to the conceptualization of person and personality that I was propounding before I entered on the digression on the alternative conceptualization which takes the trait as the basic and ultimate ingredient of the personality. Like every other psychological conceptualization that I have thus far advocated—motive, behavior, consciousness, subconsciousness, attention, and so forth—the concepts of person and personality are grounded in six basic concepts or some subset of them.

The first four of the basic concepts are spontaneity, directedness, the setting of conditions for the fulfillment of action, and the relationship of the inclusion of one act in another. The referents of these terms are, at least in principle, precisely identifiable in terms that draw on no other psychological concepts but are definable as discriminable aspects of action, itself a concept not unique to psychology. A fifth concept was introduced, that of the distressing character of drive states; and I advanced the conjecture that the distress emanates from the unavailability of a course of action coordinated to the elimination of the drive state, or, in other words, that the diffuse, random discharge of neural energy into the motor outlets of the body is *per se* distressing and that this is an ultimate psychological given. Finally, I introduced as an ultimate psychological given the concept of the self as a primal origin of space-time. From the first five of these concepts, I generated the concepts of motivation and behavior.

All other psychological concepts were dealt with in terms of discriminable varieties of behavior or aspects of behavior or in terms of interrelationships among behaviors or the interrelationships of behavior and self. A trait, for instance, is simply a regularity of an abstracted aspect of behavior (the output), the regularity depending on specifiable kinds of conditions of motivation and situation. In other words, the entire set of psychological concepts is definable in terms of six fundamental concepts, only two of which are distinctively psychological. I have, of course, also made use of other terms in the development of the concepts and in argument about them, but these terms are simply common words in our language that should pose no problems even to a strict behaviorist. From the six basic concepts, however, I have generated some concepts (such as mind) that would indeed raise the hackles on any strict behaviorist. If, occasionally (and it is indeed possible that

I have done so), I have slipped some surplus meaning into my use of terms, I would contend that these meanings are also specifiable in terms of the six basic concepts.

The personality, I have suggested, is a motivational system the interrelated constituents of which are three kinds of motives—ego, superego, and id—two of which and part of the third (the unfinished business of childhood) constitute structural subsystems. I have already noted formal pairwise similarities and differences among the three kinds of motivational factors. Let me now note certain properties that all three have in common. Each is responsible for or combines with the others to produce certain immediate motives and behaviors, and even time-extended behaviors, that are in principle capable of being completed under favorable circumstances. There is, so far as I can see, nothing distinctively significant about this characteristic of behavior. It is a common property of behaviors of all creatures capable of behaving; and, indeed, more or less tacitly, most psychologists probably assume it to be a necessary property of all motivated activity. If there is anything especially worth noting about this property, it is the reminder that not all behavioral activity deriving from, say, the ego system is itself part of the ego structure; and even this reminder needs to be qualified. There is a tendency for the ego structure to become, so to say, "wrapped around" certain long-range behaviors that can, in principle be (and often are, in fact) completed. This is why, for instance, the successful completion of a long and arduous course of study and professional preparation and the ending of an intense but prolonged courtship often result in a depressed sense of loss, emptiness, and void—essentially a form of depersonalization.[6] At that point, if the newly completed activity was indeed a central pole of one's existence, one needs a new, untried, and unexplored motivational central theme around which to wrap one's life—what seems like a total restructuring of the ego and, hence, a new personality. It may take a while to convince oneself that the change is not that catastrophic.

It is not true, however, that all motives are in principle fulfillable, and it is the unfulfillable motivation that constitutes the most distinctively human pillars of the personality. To be sure, such motives may also be discerned in creatures of a lower order, but only in relatively primitive, undifferentiated, and uninterlocking forms.

[6] Note the person concept in the negative case. What is commonly stressed in depersonalization is the loss of bodily boundaries, but there are many experiences of disembodiment that no one would think of as depersonalization. The crucial element is the sense of loss of personality that comes with the feeling that the self-image—in any of its ingredients—no longer fits.

Ego, superego, and id each include such motives. The perpetuated motives of the ego system are unfulfillable because they are essentially concerned with being prepared to meet contingencies that may yet arise. I may, for instance, have seemingly accomplished all that needs to be done to assure my continued security, but this does not bring my security motivation to an end. I still have to be concerned lest what I have already accomplished become undone and I still have to be on guard lest contingencies arise for which my preparations are insufficient. My security needs may be assuaged, but there is no consummatory act I can perform that will bring them to an end or remove them from my personal equations. Always, they continue to point into the future. Similarly, the basic motives of the superego cannot be fulfilled because they are concerned with continuing to please and appease the primal authority figure. In conformity with my superego motivation, I may virtuously refrain from some otherwise desirable act or do something that would otherwise be obnoxious to me, but this does not eliminate the imago and its requirements. As to the unfinished business of the past, it can never be truly finished because the occasion to complete it has gone by never to return.

I am not saying that personality cannot undergo major changes. This is accomplished through changes in the ego structure, via the introduction of new ego motivation or otherwise modifying the interrelations of the ego motives to one another and to the superego and the id; and, to a lesser degree, through the reconstruction of the imago. The modification of the personality does not, however, change the essentially unfulfillable character of the basic ego and superego motives.

Many writers have emphasized as the most distinctively human attributes such characteristics as the erect posture, the structure of the human hand, the prolonged period of infancy, and the possession of language. I have no desire to underplay the significance of such attributes in making the human being a distinctive creature, to whatever degree and in whatever ways he is distinct. But I see these attributes as conditions of the attainment of the defining attribute of humanity. Language, for instance, is important because it facilitates the development and operation of human enterprises. A language that did not serve such functions—if one can imagine the existence of such a language—would be notable only as an essentially trivial curiosity; and, but for some other enterprise, it would not be noted at all. The erect posture and prehensile hand make possible certain activities, but if there were no need for such activities, what would their import be? Prolonged infancy is a base for the emergence of certain self-related and interpersonal concerns, but if it had no such consequences, why, apart from a passion for classification, should one bother to note it? Similarly with regard to self-consciousness. A statue endowed with self-consciousness would (Étienne de Condillac to the contrary notwithstanding) still not be human.

The essential psychological human quality is, thus, one of commitment to a developing and continuing set of unending, interacting, interdependent, and mutually modifying long-range enterprises. The requirements of this commitment and its component commitments influence day-to-day and moment-to-moment activities. The component commitments and resulting activities may get in one another's way and the failures and inadequacies of any given activity may impede others and, indeed, endanger the entire set of enterprises. These deficiencies in the operation of the system also help to define the human quality, but in the sense of how it measures up against an abstract ideal rather than in the sense of what distinguishes it from other living creatures.

To the extent that a human organism (that is, a creature born of woman and sired by man) fails to develop such a commitment, it is not yet fully human, though it may have the potentiality of becoming so.[7] To the extent that an individual's commitment is permanently disrupted by cortical injury or other stresses, he becomes dehumanized despite the retention of a human form and despite our tendency to respond to him as he was rather than as he has become.

Abject poverty, for example, may be painful in its deprivations, but it is not dehumanizing (and the deprivations may even generate a challenging long-range project the pursuit of which adds zest and a sense of meaning to one's life), so long as it is experienced as a passable stage on the way to the betterment of one's situation. Similarly, severe relative deprivation in a socioeconomically differentiated society constitutes an insult to one's integrity only so long as one has a continuing concern about the maintenance and advancement of one's status and worth. Poverty, however, absolute or relative (and, one might add, material or spiritual), is dehumanizing precisely to the degree that one is led thereby to a surrendering of oneself to continual preoccupation with the ever-recurrent immediate miseries of a perpetuated present. That is, poverty is dehumanizing to the extent that it leads to the abandonment of one's

[7] In the Jewish religious tradition, one may grieve over the death of an infant less than one month old and one gives it decent burial, but one does not recite the prayer for the dead and one does not observe the formal days of mourning or the anniversaries of the death, a tacit acknowledgment that the one that has passed away was not yet really a person.

claims on, and one's program with regard to the relatively distant future. When and to the degree that we observe such an abandonment, we apprehend an essentially animalistic existence.

To be sure, insofar as poverty is the low pole of a highly differentiated status system, it may be a contributing factor to the generation of a sense of worthlessness (that is, of one's self as being of no account). Also, insofar as it is associated with the apparent unavailability of means of improving one's situation, it contributes to a sense of impotence, futility, and hopelessness. The latter condition contributes to the feeling of being of no account; and the sense of worthlessness helps to generate the feelings of impotence, futility, and hopelessness because, in experiencing oneself as of no account, one feels oneself to be cut off from the support and concerned involvement of one's fellow man (typically, necessary conditions of the opportunity structure). The feelings of worthlessness and powerlessness, however, though they may add to the distresses associated with poverty, do not produce in the observer the experience of contact with something less than human. But they do make it senseless to commit oneself to long-lasting enterprise, and it is the abandonment of a claim to, and program for, the relatively distant future that are so experienced.

I am obviously not saying that all or most of the extremely poor are less than human, nor that one should lose sight of the potential humanity of those of the poor who have become dehumanized (the *lumpenproletariat*, in Karl Marx's pejorative usage of this term), nor have I here concerned myself with the conditions that save so many of the poor from becoming dehumanized. What I am talking about is the meaning of the term "human"—the distinction that is implied when we take something as human or as something less than human—as the meaning is adumbrated in experience.

If the "broken" poor are often experienced as dehumanized, persons who are dying are often experienced as having achieved a transhuman quality as we observe their severing of their ties with their worldly enterprises and projects. Their very resignation to, and their acceptance of, the imminence of death clothes them in an other-than-human quality. Transhuman rather than subhuman, in this case, because we feel that, when one is truly confronted with the imminence of death, it is appropriate to terminate one's worldly affairs. That is, under these circumstances, the final serene surrender of one's human status is not only not ignoble, but is rather touched with glory, and, indeed, because of our own difficulties in any but an abstract grasp of our own mortal termination, there is something superhuman about it.

Regardless, however, of whether (depending on the circumstances) we see the dehumanization of another person as blameworthy and sinful or as praiseworthy and meritorious—or as neither—in these apprehensions of transitions from the human quality, our feelings give the lie to the familiar verbalization that to be human it is enough to be possessed of a particular kind of human form and endowed with biological life. The crucial discrimination is not the shape of the living body, but the commitment to enduring, ongoing, and, to us, comprehensible projects. By the same token, when we react to a being with a grossly distorted human form as something inhuman, we cannot do so without simultaneously attributing to it some malign, but to us, inherently lawless and not articulately comprehensible, projects.

"I," declared Terence, "am a man: nothing human is alien to me." I suspect that Terence was not referring to such things as the vermiform appendix, but to human doings; and, since whatever is incomprehensible is inherently alien, he must implicitly have been excluding, in principle, incomprehensible doings as well. On this interpretation, Terence was declaring that, implicit in the abstract concepts of what it means to be human is the inalienability of the being from those enterprises in which it might conceivably be engaged. Perhaps my interpretation (and I can think of at least two others) distorts Terence's meaning; but, no matter, it expresses mine.

Even so, it is the fact of projects and not their fathomability that constitutes the basic and profound core of the concept *human*. We ascribe various enduring concerns and enterprises to our gods; but, in the very process of doing so, we anthropomorphize, that is, humanize, the gods. We may declare the ultimate designs of the gods to be beyond human comprehension, but the very attribution to them of ultimate designs, that is, of overarching concerns, conceives of the gods in human terms, that is, as quasihuman beings.

In like manner, to the extent that a nonhuman creature, real or fictitious (like Mickey Mouse or Pogo), displays what seem to be human concerns, we tend to regard it as human. But to the extent that we apprehend an individual, real or fictitious, as lacking a complexly imbricated structure of motives or, as in the instance of the personalities in cases of multiple personality, as concerned with only some narrow segment of the range of human concern or as living only in the moment, we perceive such an individual as essentially a caricature of a human being.

Having reached the end I was seeking with regard to the image of man, it nevertheless seems to me to be somewhat incongruous to close this discussion without reverting to the beginning: the question of freedom. I have just declared that the essential psychological human quality is one of commitment to a developing and continuing set of unending, interacting, interdependent, and mutually modifying long-range projects and enterprises. It, however, makes no sense whatever to make such a statement without, at the same time, implying that the human being is, in his essential character of being human, a free agent; and, I have argued that it is the rejection of the possibility of freedom that has led so many psychologists to cast their thinking, research, and even their guidelines to the amelioration of the human condition in terms of a false and misleading image of Man. It, therefore, seems timely at this point to review and refocus the issue and to elaborate on some of the dimensions of freedom.

There are those who declare that, given the biological structure, the temporary physiological states and momentarily ongoing bodily processes (including those structures, states, and processes that have resulted from genetic givens and from prior organism-environment interactions) and given the extraorganismic environmental situation, there is one and only one action possibility at any given time. That is, these people claim that, given the organismic events, as such, and the environmental situation, as such, there are never any degrees of freedom left with respect to what may take place. Some of these people may admit the occurrence of an illusion of freedom, but they are constrained by their view to treat the illusion (as, indeed, any other mentalistic phenomenon) as an epiphenomenon, that is, as having utterly no consequence, save through its physiological correlates. As I have argued in Chapter 2, however, those who hold to such a deterministic view are doomed to present themselves as living refutations of their philosophical presupposition. They can themselves neither live by such a doctrine nor take it seriously as being always true of other persons with whom they are involved in personal interactions. That is, they hold their doctrine as true of the human being only when they regard him as an object of scientific inquiry. But, since human beings appear, more often than not, as other than objects of scientific inquiry, the proponents of the doctrine hold it (implicitly, to be sure) to be false most of the time; and, if they themselves generally reject their own doctrine, what reason can be advanced for anyone else to take it seriously? What is being asserted, in effect, is that science must necessarily be faithless to its subject matter, and I, at least, hold such a conception of science to be a contradiction in terms. Either the doctrine is false or there can be no valid science of human behavior.

There are those who hold to a variant of the view just described, though they themselves are likely to view their modification as of momentous import. In its most extreme form, the variant view is that no behavioral event is ever completely determined; that is, there is always (and it is this "always" that makes my version of the view extreme) the intrusion of a random factor in addition to the organismic and environmental determinants. When any event that has already occurred is examined retrospectively, however, it is evident that the probability of this event having occurred is unity. In other words, the random factor is itself a kind of determinant (a kind of cosmic roulette wheel that enters into the determination of all events) that, together with the organismic and environmental determinants, leaves zero degrees of freedom with respect to what may take place. It is further evident that, in the very nature of the concept, the random factor is itself not influenced (as are the organismic and environmental determinants) by the history of organism-environment interactions. In other words, the human being is, if anything, accorded even less consequence with regard to the determination of his actions by the probabilistic doctrine than is accorded to him by the deterministic doctrine of the preceding paragraph. Enter the refutation of the latter doctrine with full force as reason for rejecting its variant.

There are those who react to the palpable absurdity of either or both of the preceding doctrines by asserting that, within a framework of necessity, the human being is still left with some freedom of choice and that the foundation for the exercise of this freedom is itself not determined. I fear, however, that the identical paradox of the preceding two doctrines reappears in this doctrine, (that is, in the present case, that the human being as such has nothing to do with the determination of his actions whereas the very reason for asserting the doctrine is that, whatever philosophers may say to the contrary notwithstanding, he knows himself to be a free agent) for, either the foundation for the choice must always have been there or it has appeared for the occasion from nowhere as a *deus ex machina*.

One may seek to avoid the problem by taking no position. But that is to ignore the fact that, in the conduct of one's life apart from the scientific role, one must adopt the premise of freedom. Thus, the non-committal stance holds only for the scientific role, that is, one takes no position with regard to whether science should be faithful to its subject matter or to a doctrine that violates the subject matter. Actually, of course, such people vacillate in practice between the assumption and denial of freedom in some unprincipled, whimsical, and inconsistent fashion. One throws in a pinch of freedom here and washes it out there, all with one's hands firmly clasped behind one's back and one's eyes tightly shut.

One may take the position that man is doubtless a free agent, but that one chooses (in line with one of one's freedoms) to investigate only the organismic and environmental determinants of behavior, ignoring the arena of freedom and contenting oneself with the quite weak statistical generalizations that remain possible when one ignores a major source of variance. Some combination of, or compromise between, this and the preceding position seems to characterize much of contemporary psychology. Far be it from me to interfere with anyone who wishes to develop his skill at moving about with blinders on—and especially so if he is frightened by the vista when he takes the blinders off. I cannot help but wonder, however, to what degree the view just described is an affirmation of the holder's own humanity along with a disguised denial of humanity to the human objects of psychological study. I also cannot help but feel (and I emphasize that I do not assume that others should necessarily share my feeling) that the proponent of this view has voluntarily decided to omit from his purview the most interesting and challenging part of the field of psychology. But, my suspicions and feelings aside, I also cannot help but wonder what it is that the proponent of this view thinks he has said when he affirms that man is a free agent (does he, for instance, mean "freedom" in the sense of unpredictable or in the sense that I have rejected two paragraphs back?) and whether he would still make the same choice if he could but offer some sensible interpretation of the phrase.

All of which seems to leave but one other possibility, namely, to refer freedom to a class of determinants that are not random, not merely organismic, not merely environmental, and not merely some combination of random, organismic, and environmental factors. This is the course I have attempted to follow in the present work, namely, to associate freedom with the operation of motives and motivational structures, to show that motives and motivational structures satisfy the conditions laid down in the preceding sentence, and to show that the operation of motives and motivational structures is what people experience when they experience their own freedom and ascribe freedom to others.

Even so, there are certain sources of confusion that need to be cleared up. This becomes evident when one considers such distinctions as "outer" *vs.* "inner" freedom, Eric Fromm's "freedom from" *vs.* "freedom to,"[8] and Sir Isaiah Berlin's "negative" *vs.* "positive" liberty.[9] On the face of it, the three distinctions seem to be essentially similar; but, until I experienced some measure of insight, I found myself in great difficulty when I tried to coordinate them. The result of my insight may be summarized as Figure 4.

| | Absence of | |
	Compulsion	Constraint
Inner	freedom to	freedom to
Outer	freedom from negative liberty	positive liberty

FIGURE 4

Let it be noted that (1) the freedom under consideration is the freedom of any given action, (2) that "compulsion" refers to the generation of a force impelling one to perform that act against one's wishes or to refrain from performing it despite one's wishes to do so, (3) that "constraint" refers to the unavailability of means or the violation of conditions necessary to or facilitating, and/or to the presence of obstacles or other conditions that prevent or make difficult, the performance of the act, and (4) that "inner" and "outer" refer, respectively, to whether the compulsions or constraints emanate from within the psychological system, on the one hand, or from the physiological system or the environment, on the other. Note especially that the notion of com-

---

[8] Eric Fromm, *Escape from Freedom* (New York: Farrar & Rinehart, 1941).
[9] Sir Isaiah Berlin, *Four Essays on Liberty* (London: Oxford University Press, 1969).

pulsion implies the presence of motivation and of a force contrary to that motivation, and that the idea of constraint has to do with the possibilities of action independently of whether one is or is not motivated to carry out some act.

Each of the four cells of Figure 4 constitutes one of the dimensions of freedom with respect to a given act. Thus, given the desire to perform that act, the act may be carried out freely to the degree that there is no countering motivation to prevent it (absence of inner compulsion), to the degree that the actor possesses the necessary knowledge and skill to perform it (absence of inner constraints), to the degree that there are no external forces to prevent it (absence of outer compulsion), and to the degree that the external situation facilitates this kind of action and does not make it difficult to carry it out (absence of outer constraints). Obsessional thoughts and hallucinated threatening voices are typically associated with a high degree of inner compulsion (occurring against the person's will) and low or zero degrees of inner and outer constraints and of outer compulsion.

That the obsessional thought and hallucinated voices are also positively motivated is irrelevant to the issue of the degree of freedom not to have the thoughts or hear the voices. Thus, mutually incompatible motives generate compulsive forces and constraints with regard to one another. Outer compulsion may be directly physical (as when a current carries one away from where one wants to go), but it is also often mediated by the creation of situations that bring into play countering motivations, that is, it is mediated by the activation of inner compulsion; this is, for instance, the idea behind the use of reward and punishment as a means of influencing behavior. When there is an impulsion to activity, outer compulsion may also be implemented by the imposition of sufficient constraints on all acts but one that runs contrary to a person's desires. Finally, let me point out that any action (and this, of course, includes any compelled action) that takes over some executive apparatus (for example, walking in a particular direction, preoccupation with some line of thought, and the like) constitutes a constraint on any other action that is not coordinate with the first but that requires the same executive apparatus.

The interrelations among the four dimensions of freedom are thus not necessarily simple. I nevertheless consider it useful to distinguish them for the light that the distinction throws on the concept of freedom, for the attention it draws to the various possible sources of unfreedom, and for the help that it offers in understanding the coordinate concept of responsibility and in assessing the latter.

Returning, now, to the Figure, it will be evident that I have identified both Fromm's concept of freedom from and Berlin's concept of negative liberty with the dimension of outer compulsion. Both of these thinkers are concerned with the reduction of those coercive forces that limit human freedoms. My original difficulty in relating Berlin's and Fromm's lines of thought to one another stemmed, however, from my failure to understand that they derived their respective contrasting concepts from different concerns. What Berlin was saying is that a person is not truly free to do as he wishes, even though he has been liberated from outer compulsions, unless and until the outer means are provided that make it possible for him to act on his desires. What Fromm was saying is, in effect, that a person is not truly free to do as he wishes, even though he has been liberated from all outer compulsions, unless and until he has also been liberated from interfering inner compulsions emanating from conflicting desires and concerns. Both thinkers are right; taken together, they are even more right; but, even together, they would be still more right if they were to pay more attention to the infringement of freedom that stems from ignorance and incompetence (the inner constraints). The latter, too, have bearing on the freedom to.

We may now assert that an individual is free to the degree that his actions are free within the limits of the constraints and compulsions that are necessary to maintain his freedom, that is, within the limits of the operation of the laws of the universe and of an optimal universally accepted code of behavior. His ability to act in ways that will serve his ends is contingent on the dependability of the consequences of his actions, and these are contingent on the operation of an order of law; but, then, he has no freedom at all to violate the laws of the universe and is subject to the constraints (and, possibly, compulsions) of man-made law.

I have no reason to suppose that full knowledge of universal law and an optimal man-made code will be available in the foreseeable future, and it seems reasonable to suppose that the freedom of the freest of men will fall far short of the maximum possible. In speaking of man as a free agent, therefore, I am speaking of a quite limited freedom, yet far less limited than the statement seems to imply. For to the extent that he can coordinate and integrate his motives and develop his knowledge of the world around him and improve his competencies to cope with it, he not only reduces the inner limitations on his freedom, but increases his chances of modifying the outer ones as well. The past histories of the biological evolution of man and of his social struggles to extend the bounds of liberty, the manifest advantages to each individual of his personal freedom to the degree that he resolves his inner conflicts, and the social interdependencies of individual freedoms all suggest an ineluctable thrust toward the extension of the bounds of freedom toward their outermost limits. If I am right in this conjecture, such a thrust must transcend the particularities of individual enterprises and our image of Man should also include what Man, because of this feature of his *human* nature, is striving to become. Some individuals may, of course, fall by the wayside, yield their liberties and freedoms, and even accept some degree of slavery; but, in doing so, they violate their human nature.

At any rate, *ecce homo*! At least, as I see him. No superman, to be sure, just a *human* human being, trying to become more so.

PART

IV

The Scientific Enterprise

15

TWO SUBCULTURES OF

BEHAVIORAL SCIENCE

Again and again, throughout this book the discussion has devolved around issues of the conceptualization of the scientific enterprise. It seems appropriate at this point to focus on the central issue, the nature of knowledge and its acquisition. It may come as a surprise to some readers that there is an issue here, or at least one that is taken seriously by anyone except nonpositivistic (and, hence, obviously archaic) philosophers and college freshmen and sophomores. To such readers, it may seem foolish nonsense to spend time on such questions as "What is the nature of knowledge?" when one can be investing that time accumulating knowledge; besides, we know exactly what to do to add to knowledge (observe and experiment) and the operationalists and logical positivists have already solved all of the problems that are not, in their very nature, nonsensical.

Unfortunately, basic problems are not so easily disposed of. Willy-nilly, in our conduct as scientists, we commit ourselves to philosophical, metaphysical, ontological, epistemological, and axiological positions. If we leave the philosophical problems to the philosophers, then, depending on what "leave it to" means, there are consequences that we have to pay. If it means, "Let them adjudicate the issues and we will abide by their decisions," the consequence is that we put our scientific lives into their hands. Granted that they are far better equipped to cope with such problems than we are, and I myself have no reservations whatever in granting this, their coping still takes place on their terms and value hierarchies (and let me add, hang-ups), not necessarily ours.

Granted, moreover, that we are willing to so commit ourselves, to which philosophers shall we make the commitment? How shall we pick our philosophical doctors? How shall we pick the ones that best fit our own needs? Shall we pick one because we like his treatment? How can we be sure that it is not his bedside manner that attracts us? In any case, in selecting one standard-bearer over another, we shall have made a philosophical decision, and the question remains whether we shall have done so blindly or whether we shall have brought our own knowledge of our situation, our own awareness of possible alternatives, and our own wisdom to bear on the decision.

Alternatively, if "leave it to the philosophers" means "Let them cultivate their own gardens while we cultivate ours," this is in itself a commitment to an unthought-through philosophical position, and it carries with it the further likely consequence of vacillation between mutually incompatible philosophical positions.

I do not mean to suggest that each psychologist ought to immerse himself in problems of philosophy. If he were to do so, he would have precious little time to pursue his work as a psychologist. There are a great many things for which he has to accept on faith alone the word, competence, integrity, and authority of other psychologists, not to mention mathematical statisticians, physiologists, sociologists, and so on. In his personal agenda of things to check on for himself, philosophical issues may have the lowest of priorities.

Psychologists and other scientists are no less human than are other people. Each of us has his idiosyncratic pettinesses, generosities, aspirations, anxieties, enthusiasms, aversions, prejudices, confusions, insights, moments of glory and self-transcendence, and so on. Nor would I, even if I could, have it otherwise, not even when it comes to our individual professional lives. I do not share the idealized image of the scientist as a detached, disinterested, selfless individual engaged in the single-minded pursuit of truth. It seems to me that part of the excitement of the scientific enterprise inheres in the colorful, charismatic personalities of some of the individuals engaged in it, and their stature is in no whit diminished by their irrationalities, passionate convictions, and stubborn resistances to changes in outlook. Not only is the scientific enterprise not endangered by such unscientific personal intrusions, but it often gains therefrom. Important advances have been made through stubborn persistencies along certain lines against, both, all apparent reason and consensus as to the weight of evidence.

Nor can I conceive of science as anything other than the aggregate of the activities of more or less interdependent sets of individual scientists and teams of them whose common focus of concern joins them together, at least temporarily, in loosely constructed confederations with more or less rigorously imposed initiation rites, more or less common specialized languages, more or less stable and complicated networks of interpersonal communication, more or less stable media of formal information exchange, more or less of a shared folklore, unwritten, evolving and unfinalized, more or less diversely interpreted codes of good conduct, and more or less specialized but open economic systems that both facilitate and constrain the activities of the individual scientists. The scientists who constitute the specialized subject-matter confederations are conjoined in even more loosely structured confederations covering the respective disciplines and, beyond that, a bewildering array of cross-disciplinary groupings and the entire scientific enterprise. What generates the larger confederations is that specialized lines of inquiry have less specialized ramifications, that there are certain interdependencies of fate at every level of confederation, and that the scientists are also members of cross-secting confederations that entail less specialized activities (for example, teaching obligations). As seen from the viewpoint of a sufficiently high level of abstraction, all scientists worthy of the name have at least one characteristic in common, namely, a passionate[1] desire to know what is, has been, and will be going on in the world independently of their observation of it and a willingness to invest the effort and to abide by the discipline of finding out.

Among their activities, of course, are the processes of coming to conclusions. This leads many scientists and others, to the notion that it is the set of conclusions (and not the personal activities) that con-

[1] Note, "passionate," not "impassioned." Passion is likely to be regarded as unseemly in a scientist. The norm of a mask of utter objectivity, disinterest (willingness to accept any outcome, not lack of interest), and detachment is reserved for matters of substantive content rather than the pursuit itself. Affect flows freely over issues of how the search for knowledge should be conducted, whether these issues concern the formulation of problems for investigation or the method of pursuit. There are also scientists who would reject my description of them on the ground that it is senseless to speak of a world independent of its observation. I am myself convinced, however, on the basis of many observations that this is a philosophical veneer beneath which one does not have to scratch very far to find the passion. Why, for instance, should they be as concerned as they are with the paraphernalia of scientific method if not to protect against errors of observation and inference? What can "error" mean if there is no independent world to which it refers? Why should they place as high a premium as they do on independent replications of observations? Why if there is nothing "out there" to be observed should one expect observations to replicate one another? Why should someone else's observations which I do not myself observe be taken as more "real" than what he (and I) observes?

stitute the body of science. But the conclusions, no matter how well buttressed, are, in their very nature, tentative. Science is not an anthropomorphic godlike entity that lays down laws and serves as the arbiter of truth. Statements that begin with "According to science," or "It is a scientific fact that," or "That belief is false because it is contrary to science," profoundly distort the nature of the scientific enterprise. Science is not a gospel. It is a process, something that human beings do.

If there is any one thing that keeps the process alive, it is the maxim, generally unverbalized, that there is no conclusion or proposition whatever (and you may add, including this one, if you will) that may not, in principle, be challenged on rational or observational grounds. It is this basic openness to skepticism and disbelief that, along with the passionate desire not to permit oneself to be deceived with regard to "what's cooking when one isn't looking," that gives to science (or, more properly, to its devotees) its characteristic impetus. Without the total openness to doubt, the enterprise would degenerate into a body of dogma. This total openness, moreover, serves as the best safeguard that has yet been devised against the counterproductive idiosyncracies, prejudices, and inadequacies of the individual scientists.

Even so, scientists move in relatively tight circles and come to share various attitudes, beliefs, ways of doing things, and blind spots. The members of these circles, and indeed of the entire confederated brotherhood, are not randomly selected. Many of their idiosyncracies and prejudices are, therefore, common. The errors and distortions to which the latter lead are not counterbalanced by opposing errors and distortions. Consensuses and uniformities of willfulness, prejudice, theoretical scotomata, and stereotypic research activities emerge; and the stronger the consensus and the greater the uniformity, the greater is the social pressure to conform to the ways of the majority and the greater the resistance to change.

When convention takes command of the scientific enterprise in a relatively circumscribed arena (say, with regard to the basic modalities of color vision or the processes of linguistic acquisition), the consequences are themselves relatively circumscribed, and it is only a matter of time before a breakthrough comes. When, however, larger issues are involved, and this is most thoroughly the case with regard to philosophical issues, the character of the entire scientific enterprise is affected —and not necessarily in its best interests. Stereotyped conceptualizations of the nature of the enterprise and of the character of its operations that may have been functional in some limited arena from an heuristic point of view are uncritically transposed to other arenas where they become underlying and unexamined premises of inquiry. The effect does not always obtain. Physicists, for instance, rooted as their work is in higher mathematics, which has no commitments to the reality of space-time, seem to remain extraordinarily open to thinking the unthinkable. But, for the most part, scientific inquiry in other arenas is hampered and constrained by premature, unthought-through, and insufficiently tested quasiresolutions of its identity problems.

If the underlying stereotyped conceptualizations are themselves uncritically borrowed from professional philosophers who, in their wisdom, scan the needs of science without ever immersing themselves in its operations—or from physicists-turned-philosophers who generalize without reservations from their experiences as physicists—the hampering of the enterprise, the constraints on it, and the inadequately resolved identity problems are all very likely to become acutely exacerbated. I do not want to be misunderstood. I eagerly welcome the interest and concern of these "outsiders." At the very least, they offer us new perspectives, expand our horizons, and protect us from philosophical naïveté. What I am saying is simply that we cannot afford to put ourselves in their hands and accept their ministrations without ourselves examining our philosophical needs and coming to our own decisions. Let us, by all means, find out what these outside experts have to say and to offer, to whatever degree our time and other commitments permit. Indeed, I would say that we urgently need to have many more of us make the time to become relatively sophisticated in this outside literature and to give philosophical psychology, philosophical sociology, and so on far more prominent places in our curricula than they now enjoy. We can ill afford to permit a small number of relatively ill-read (and I unhesitatingly include myself in this number) behavioral scientists who are concerned about the nature of the scientific enterprise to define the culture of science (including the reward system) within which we must all function; and we certainly cannot afford to permit this to happen on a semiliterate borrowing basis. Let us, by all means, turn to the philosophers; but let us deal with them as with expert outside consultants, with pride in our own identity and retaining the full measure of our own autonomy. Let us not approach them as obsequious supplicants eagerly awaiting their decrees as communicated to us by self-appointed intermediaries. In the long run, I suspect they will find the change exhilarating and ourselves far more interesting and exciting clients.

From one point of view (that of preserving some measure of openness with regard to the foundation premises, but not from the point of view of the politics and sociology of our occupation), it is fortunate that the circles in which behavioral scientists move are, in the main, relatively circumscribed. This has permitted competing schools of thought to develop, each with its own subculture and foundation premises. Each subculture is rooted in a long historical tradition, and each involves its own normative patterns of behavior, its own languages, and its own value systems. As is true of all cultures that coexist in a common geographical area, most individuals manage, to a greater or lesser degree, to assimilate elements of the competing cultures and to integrate or compartmentalize the latter in a more or less satisfactory manner so as to permit unimpeded behavior. Barring total assimilation of the competing cultures to one another, however, they continue to be distinguishable and to exercise differential effects on different individuals.

Not commonly recognized as such, however, is the fact that, cutting across the subcultures of the "schools" and to some degree separating one from another, there are clearly discernable two more inclusive subcultures of behavioral science.[2] In contemporary psychology, the clearest exemplar of the one may be found in neobehaviorism and, of the

[2] The distinction I am about to draw is perhaps most familiar in terms of the distinction in the German literature between the *Naturwissenschaften* and the *Geisteswissenchaften* (natural sciences *vs.* the mental or cultural sciences). See, for instance, the two appended chapters by H. Klüver in Gardner Murphy's, *An Historical Introduction to Modern Psychology,* 2d ed. (New York: Harcourt Brace, 1939), "Contemporary German Psychology as a 'Natural Science'" and "Contemporary German Psychology as a 'Cultural Science.'" Neither the terms nor much of the substantive content of the distinction are acceptable to me, however. For one thing, there is the unacceptable implication that mind is not a natural phenomenon or a fact of nature. For another, many (perhaps all) who advocate the second approach as the appropriate one for the behavioral and historical sciences set up unverifiable intuition as the basis of "truth-finding," which would take the whole approach outside of the scientific enterprise as I understand the latter. I am not, however, prepared to take them at their word and, in fact, few, if any, of them would accept any intuition as being as good as any other. One might be cynical about it and say that, according to them, one's own intuitions are always good and alternate intuitions are always bad; but this characterization is false on both counts and entirely misses the point that one may accept as valid intuition those that one has never experienced oneself. One may also recall in this connection a statement commonly attributed to Neal Miller (as good an exemplar of the natural science approach in psychology as one can find), "Here, at Yale, we do not believe in insight, but we nevertheless try to practice it." All of which suggests that the distinction distorts the concepts of truth and verification as much for the natural sciences as for the behavioral and historical sciences. I shall of course, discuss the issue at some length below.

other, in existential psychoanalysis. I can almost see and hear the expressions of shock of some readers, including some existential psycho-analysts, at my apposition of existential psychoanalysis with science; but I hope that these readers will bear with me for a while as I strive to convince them that there are indeed two subcultures of science in-volved rather than one of science *vs.* one of antiscience. I would not object to reserving the term "science" for the one and "antiscience" for the other except for three reasons.

1. In our crazy, mixed-up civilization, there are segments in which each of these terms is affectively loaded and one or the other term is highly prized. I am, of course, addressing and include myself in the segment that highly values science. To accept the terminological dis-tinction is, therefore, to sell the second subculture short even if some of its participants would be quite happy to relinquish all claim to being scientists. Confession and self-avowal does not strike me as a sufficient basis for the distribution of justice.

2. And more fundamentally, the terminological distinction obscures the fact that, however the participants may characterize what they are doing, both subcultures are busily occupied with, and their *raison d'être*, is the systematic pursuit of knowledge of "what's cooking when one isn't looking." The distinction, therefore, confuses and deceives the public with regard to what is going on.

3. Most fundamentally, the distinction science *vs.* antiscience ob-scures to the scientists themselves the options that are open to them and inhibits them from examining their fundamental identity problems.

As a matter of convenience, I shall use the term "scientism" (and the derivative "scientismic" and "scientismist") to refer to one of the subcultures and "clinicalism" (along with "clinicalismic" and "clinical-ismist" or the simpler "clinicalist") to refer to the other.

These terms have to be watched very carefully. "Scientism" is com-monly used with pejorative connotations, especially so in those segments of our civilization to which science itself is anathema. I do not intend any of these connotations. I have accepted the term, despite the risks of misunderstanding that its use entails, because there is an "ism" in-volved and to emphasize its connection with the dominant form of the scientific enterprise. I have selected the term "clinicalism" because of the connotation of the word "clinical" that emphasizes concern with the particular case and, of course, because there is also an "ism" involved. The use of "clinicalism" entails the risk of confusion with "clinical" (as in clinical psychology and clinical medicine). In medicine, "clinical" is often used to refer to the use of laboratory tests, X-rays, and other procedures utilized in medical practice for the purpose of diagnosing the particular case; and there are those who would restrict clinical psychology itself to diagnostic activities. At any rate, there are many clinical psychologists who are scientismists; and there are many who are neither scientismists nor clinicalists, but simply practitioners of one kind or another with no scientific aspirations or pretensions. There are also clinicalists among psychologists who have nothing to do with clinical practice.

The fundamental issue separating the two subcultures has to do with the concept of truth, and I shall return to it in the next chapter. I think, however, that it will be most helpful, at this point, to try to characterize and delineate the two subcultures, even though doing so entails considerable risk of oversimplification and overidealization. As I remarked earlier with regard to the subcultures of the schools, most individuals who live in multicultural environments tend to assimilate elements of the competing cultures in various degrees and ways. The effect is that underlying differences which continue to exist side by side, often even in the same individual who vacillates from one to another in various respects, tend to become obscured. Also, as I noted in the earlier context, each subculture has its own history. It may be worth noting, for instance, that Wilhelm Wundt, commonly described as the "father of experimental psychology," found it necessary to write two kinds of psychology each of which, respectively, constitutes part of the history of one or the other subculture. Historical traditions, however, are rarely either unidimensional or unilineal. Gestalt theory, for instance, at least in Wertheimer's version, and Lewinian psychology are far closer in spirit to clinicalism than to scientism though they do not quite fit my delineation of the two subcultures in certain respects. So, I am oversimplifying; but how can one avoid oversimplification in describing a culture, or, for that matter, a personality?

The most pervasive and fundamental aspect of what I am here calling scientism is its profound commitment to what most psychologists have been taught to identify as scientific method. I shall assume familiarity with this aspect of scientism as background for my exposition of clinicalism, below. For the moment, I shall content myself with pointing up three relatively minor aspects of the subculture of scientism which (minor though they be within scientism) play a major role in the clash of the two subcultures.

The most extreme expressions of scientism involve doctrinaire views on the nature of science and on proper rules of scientific conduct and expression. By strict application of some of these rules, a considerable array of sciences, from anatomy to zoology, would be ruled out of the domain of science because they are, in the main, not experimental, not quantitative, not concerned with prediction, and/or not hypothetico-deductive in structure. A work like Darwin's *Origin of Species* would similarly not be expected to make the grade since it promulgates as a theory propositions that can only be applied on a *post hoc* basis and do not serve the ends of prediction. Most scientismists, however, would exempt those disciplines because they compensate by their highly technical vocabularies that cannot be confused with ordinary English; and Darwin is, by tradition, an exemplar of the true scientist.

The exemptions on the basis of a technical vocabulary are consistent with scientism. The scientismist is given to respectable language, respectability being far more important in practice than the rationalizing value of precision. Notoriously ambiguous terms such as "stimulus" and "response" are respectable, and others are made so by claims of operational definition, with little regard to requirements of operational definition or concern about whether the defining operations are sufficiently specified to serve their ostensible function. Indeed, that schismogenetic forces stem from linguistic usage and related styles of thinking, rather than from occupation with scientific versus applied goals, is attested to by the relatively high status among scientismists (and the self-images) of conditioning therapists; the vulnerability of the latter to scientific criticism has recently been well documented.[3] The same point can be made with respect to Skinnerian practitioners such as learning programmers and animal trainers. They are practitioners, but they speak the language, share the values, and belong to the ingroups of the scientismic subculture.

A major characteristic of scientism is its commitment to reductionism. Science itself, under the rule of parsimony, also possesses an ineluctable thrust toward reductionism in the general sense of a commitment to seek explanations of all phenomena in a minimal number of primitive terms and propositions. The reductionism that is inherent in science, however, respects the unparsimoniousness of nature and it does not have any commitment to a preselected set of fundamental

[3] L. Breger and J. L. McGaugh, "Critique and Reformation of 'Learning-Theory' Approaches to Psychotherapy and Neurosis," *Psychological Bulletin* 63 (1965): 338–358. Responses to the paper by Breger and McGaugh have appeared in the same journal.

concepts. Scientism, by contrast, tends to seize on a particular set of primitive terms and propositions (typically, but not necessarily, drawn from physics, chemistry, or physiology) and to assume it to be both optimal and sufficient. The particular set may vary from one scientismist to another, but both operate in terms of such sets, tolerate one another's sets, and dismiss anything not included in or deducible from the union of sets selected by themselves and fellow scientismists as unreal and inconsequential. The arbitrariness is not indefensible. It has the great virtue of getting the power of such limited sets thoroughly tested and offers special possibilities of serendipitous discovery.

Turning now to the contrasting subculture, I have already implied that I am not here concerned with any form of application of psychology, but with an approach to knowledge, one that has as legitimate a place in the totality of the scientific enterprise as does scientism. Even so, the clinicalist's preferred point of attack toward the advancement of knowledge is as likely as not to be some effort to do something about a human problem. Despite its widespread influence in psychology, clinicalism is so deeply submerged under the prevailing scientismic ideology that its participants are even less aware of it than scientismists are of scientism; and scientismists seem to have no comprehension whatever of its character. I shall, therefore, take more time to epitomize it.

The key to clinicalism is its urge to be able to comprehend every instance in a domain of inquiry in all of its particularity and unique individuality. The clinicalist tends to be suspicious of any fixed scheme of classification, preferring to pick the concepts that best fit the case, and hence to select from a nonsystematic array of concepts; and he may put an item into a class, or remove it from one, on the basis of a new datum that he has not previously considered as a basis for the classification. He may espouse a particular theory, but only as a helpful guide to observation; basically, he disrespects the limits and consistencies of any theory, using it flexibly and freely modifying it as needs arise. He distrusts statistical evidence because it is statistical. He rejects fiducial probabilities because the very concept abandons the uniqueness of the particular case. He may make probabilistic statements, but in the sense of level of confidence, rather than relative frequency. Evidence, to him, is constituted of the phenomenal given, itself, or, if the given needs explaining, of the subjective compellingness and fittingness of an account in terms of temporal-situational context; and the context includes the sequellae of his insight/intuition-guided or "set"-breaking interventions. Controlled observation is, for him, constituted of intensive and extensive probing and feedback from test interventions. He is not gravely concerned with precision of terminology, and freely resorts to figures of speech. He assumes that communications are given in a context and to an intelligent audience. Though he may express some generalization, he does not intend it to be taken literally and is apt to feel badgered when one persists in trying to hold him to it; the meaning is, to him, contained in the anticipated application far more than in the literal wording.

The clinicalist does not seek to discover, formulate, or prove any general laws, not even idiographic laws in the sense of statistical generalizations based on the population of behaviors of a particular individual, since he does not assume any constancy of mathematicofunctional relationships over time or situation—not even for any given individual. He assumes that determinants—inner and outer—are in continual flux, in ever-changing configurations of varying subsets, and doubts the discoverability of laws. The search for laws also presupposes confidence in a system of principles of classification and tacitly gives a seal of approval to the latter. The clinicalist is apt to take predictability of nontrivial behavior as *prima facie* evidence of constraints that distort normal behavior. Evidence of the predictability of behavior in controlled laboratory conditions evokes a suspicion that laboratory situations are so abnormal that no generalizations from them are warranted.[4]

A clinicalist may carry out experimental or statistical studies, but the payoff, to him, is not necessarily in the confirmation or rejection of the

[4] The issue of law is, of course, the one on which writers like Wertheimer and Lewin most deviate from clinicalism. It is to be noted, however, that their conception (especially Lewin's) of the nature of law differs most markedly from that of the scientismists. Scientismic laws are statistical generalizations and are, in principle, individually subject to disconfirmation. This is not true of Wertheimer's and Lewin's laws (nor, for that matter, of Isaac Newton's as I have indicated elsewhere in this book). A law like Wertheimer's *prägnanz* is not disconfirmable since any alleged disconfirmation merely raises the issue of one's conception of what constitutes "good" form. Individual laws, in this conception, or at least the fundamental ones, are basically tautologies. I shall return to the issue in the next chapter. In the meantime, note that Lewin never gave up the aspiration to be able to comprehend particular cases in their full particularity. A sufficient body of law must be capable of doing so; and note that this statement, too, is a tautology, I should perhaps add that I use "tautology" in a strictly logical sense and not in the sense that the statement of a tautology or a tautological inference may not reveal something previously known. Thus, logically, the valid conclusion of a syllogism is tautologically contained in the premises and rules of inference but, as Wertheimer has so strongly argued, may nevertheless reveal something entirely novel to the thinker. I would myself add that, in a sense, the basic scientific quest is for magnificent tautologies.

research hypotheses, and he may have lost all interest in the latter by the end of the study. The payoff is in the revealed details and in the transformation of his ways of looking at the world, a transformation that may be incidental to the fate of the hypotheses and hinge on a minor finding, on difficulties in carrying out the research design, or even on continued reflection associated with concentrated immersion in the research process or data. The decision to do the study in the first place may have been a feeling of unclarity, a practical need, conformity to the prevailing scientific culture, or what not, but the study itself is basically an occasion for a concrete encounter with the world; and, insofar as he has cognitive goals that go beyond the specific encounter, it is primarily an opportunity to increase his sophistication so that he can observe more keenly and critically in future encounters. Where the scientismist's main interest is in a precise summary of what he has learned, the clinicalist's main interest is in formulations that lead to keener observation.

The clinicalist researcher is apt to see nothing wrong in a biased test of a hypothesis, that is, one in which no research outcome will lead him to abandon the hypothesis. This attitude infuriates scientismists (though, in their own way, the latter do likewise more frequently than they realize). A hypothesis worthy of test is not one lightly to be abandoned, and one can always attribute a negative outcome to previously unsuspected special factors; what the clinicalist wants is to become alerted to such special factors. What the scientismist perceives as an *ad hoc* construction of an outcome is to the clinicalist a modified orientation to carry into the future. The research process is, however, so heavily rationalized in terms of the premises of the scientismic subculture that the clinicalist may himself not realize what he is doing. He just knows that what he is doing makes sense. Nor is the scientismist likely to become aware of or to comprehend the not uncommon reaction of incredulity by the clinicalist to the confirmation of one of his incontrovertible hypotheses—so deeply ingrained in his suspicion of patness.

The clinicalist may feel that he has more to gain from reading Dostoyevsky, Dreiser, Hamsun, Mann, Proust, and Shakespeare than from all of the pages of the *Journal of Experimental Psychology*. The very compellingness of their portraiture, despite the manifest abstraction from the totality of human existence and the tampering with the data of experience in the processes of fictional creation, establishes such authors as keen observers. They offer few generalizations about behavior. But a good example of seeing human behavior in its complexity may be worth more in developing principles of grasping particularities than scores of statistically significant generalizations about highly circumscribed behaviors occurring under laboratory conditions.

Consider a trivial example of how a clinicalist usually functions. On request, you give a friend a cigarette. After inhaling deeply, he says, "Boy but that feels good; I finished my last one about two hours ago and have not had a chance to go out and get another pack." What additional evidence do you need to infer that he must have been craving a smoke, that the word "one" in his statement referred to a cigarette, and that the phrase "of cigarettes" was elided from the end of his statement? The clinicalist, like most sensible people, would not hesitate, on the information given, to draw these inferences. The important thing to note is the transparency of the particular case from the point of view of comprehending it—and this despite the problems that may be encountered in developing a nomothetic net capable of encompassing it.

Now add some details. Your friend has been under constant observation. He has not smoked a cigarette all day and has not been known to do so since he quit smoking long before. He has a visitor and the entire scene takes place in the presence of the latter. With this additional information, the previous construction is not tenable and one needs additional information to comprehend what has occurred, especially so concerning the transactions between your friend and his visitor. But again, note that the problem of comprehending the particular event on its own terms is far simpler than the problem of developing a generally valid, highly articulated, and unambiguously denotative nomothetic net from which it can be deduced.

My trivial example contains within it the essence of the clinicalist method. The clinicalist's apperceptive background of experience, his theories, his generalizations, serve as guides in the search for relevant specifications that permit the comprehension of particular events and minimize the risks of construing them in an overly pat manner. He seeks relevant details that lead to compelling accounts; and if, in encounters with certain kinds of events, he finds details that do not fit, he looks for additional specifications that make for better fitting and compelling accounts; if adequate specifications repeatedly fall into a pattern of sorts, he formulates a rule to serve as a reminder of things to look for in later encounters with similar kinds of events. What the scientismist perceives as a vaguely formulated and largely unverified generalized proposition of fact is to the clinicalist basically a starting point, a guide to inquiry in future confrontations. Thus, a clinicalist may say, "An overreaction conceals the opposite reaction." What he means is, "When you encounter what looks like an overreaction, suspect the concealment and look for evidence of the opposite reaction"; and, though the instruction is not specific with respect to the indentification of "over" and "opposite," it is neither invalidated nor rendered meaningless by its imprecision. The clinicalist would not take it as a contradiction of his rule if it turned out that overreaction is often a role enactment that can best be comprehended on another basis; the latter outcome would suggest a qualification of "overreact." The important point to note is that it is the comprehended particularity—with all of the ambiguities of such comprehension and the consequent need to return again and again to like cases for fuller articulation—that provides the clinicalist's base for inducing looking (and expectation) rules. Clinicalist induction, however, is not a matter of counting cases. A single striking case or an unexpected insight may suggest a looking rule capable of illuminating scores of other cases.

There are clinicians and other practitioners who do take clinicalist theories literally, and dogmatically so. This happens for two main reasons: (1) They are victims of the predominance of the scientismic subculture in the universities: Since this subculture allows for only one kind of knowledge—the generalization—and only one basis of valid knowledge—controlled observation—students learn to construe the world of knowledge in these limited terms. When they later find far less relevance in their academic knowledge than in some clinicalist theory, they confuse relevance with literal validation and construe the theory as a set of precisely formulated and validated propositions of fact; this is the only construction of the nature of knowledge that they know. (2) The second reason stems from the practitioner situation. Having to render a service in the face of incomplete and inadequate knowledge, the practitioner may find relief for his own anxiety in an exaggeration of his certitude. But if the practitioner uses theory in the rigid manner that he talks it, he wins the true clinicalist's contempt for his mechanical comprehension.

Not that clinicalist theory has no factual content. No such theory could survive were it not effective in helping to comprehend particular events, and it could not be effective if it were not in reasonably close contact with matters of fact. Moreover, clinicalist theories are subject to revision to make them more effective, and, hence, tend to become ever more closely attuned to fact. The propositions of clinicalist theories are, therefore, properly stated in factual form, but they are not intended in finished form; they are still, basically, guides to looking.

The clinicalist's concern with particularity aside, scientismist and clinicalist approach generalization from opposite poles and their methods suit the angles of approach. Scientismist starts with cautiously and precisely formulated propositions to be rigorously tested, building slowly on this solid foundation, and he does not much care if they are not broadly significant. Clinicalist starts with propositions that have manifest bearing on the complexities he confronts, and revises and qualifies them on the basis of experience in their use, and he is not gravely concerned if, at any stage of his working with them, they do not yet meet the tests of precision of formulation and rigors of qualification (or, for that matter, internal consistency) that the scientismist would want to impose.

The scientismist and clinicalist differ markedly in their respective time perspectives and, consequently, in the tempos of certain aspects of their work. Recognizing that science offers no means of achieving absolute certainty, scientism is nevertheless subject to a great urgency in arriving at definitive statements even if the latter have to be sharply delimited in scope; the major desideratum in the design of an experiment is the silencing of all anticipatable debate. Clinicalism is, by contrast, quite leisurely in its confidence that continual return to particularities must, in time, provide correctives for error. The underlying mood of scientism is contained in the question "How can knowledge grow if we do not get started on knowing at least something definitively?" And, correspondingly for clinicalism, "How can knowledge grow if we keep blocking growth by prematurely freezing categories and the dimensions of inquiry into functional relationships, thereby losing contact with the primary data of all knowledge, the manifold particularities?" But with respect to practical applications, the time perspectives are commonly reversed: the scientismist adopting a long-range view and the clinicalist impelled by the urgencies of immediately presenting problems.

The scientismist works by tracking the relationships of clearly defined independent and dependent variables under specified parametric values of control variables. The clinicalist works mainly by trying to track the flux of complex events on the basis of intensive probing for relevant circumstance, and feedback from interventions the nature and timing of which cannot be preplanned in detail; and he tries to develop prin-

315

ciples of heuristic (literally, "aiding discovery") and otherwise consequential interventions.

The scientismist puts his premium on precision and certainty; the clinicalist, on comprehension and significance (nonstatistical!). To the scientismist, the content of knowledge is in its verbalization; to the clinicalist it is in the cognitive orientations of the knower. Looking rules embodied in tentative generalizations are as shareable as are statements of fact, and principles of intervention as publishable as principles of experimental design. The clinicalist, however, would rather run the risk of being misunderstood than that of being unfaithful to his subject matter. Misunderstandings can, in time, be reduced; but, to limit oneself to clearly understandable verbal forms (even though the latter do not fit the case) is, in the clinicalist view, to betray the scientific goal and purpose for the sake of maintaining the scientific form. The scientismist would argue that, in such an instance, we are not ready for the effort; and the clinicalist would reply that we never will be if we do not make it.

Scientismist's modes of dealing with issues of fact (narrowing down connotational ranges, drawing literal implications, and testing the latter in a research process conforming to the requirements of experimental design) are not appropriate to clinicalist's statements as the latter are intended. But the latter are, nevertheless, testable in the crucible of experience with their use as guides to observation; and, in this repect, they must, in the long run, meet the competition of alternative formulations. Even so, clinicalists do not duly appreciate the value of efforts to test their statements, taken literally, from the viewpoint of highlighting avoidable ambiguities and pointing up untenable implications that they might themselves accept but for the negative outcomes of such tests. They are also apt to overlook the possibility of assessing the guidance value of looking rules by more rigorous procedures than reliance on the vagaries of selective recall. But they must also be conservative in accepting revisions since the latter may conceal major changes in outlook with respect to which there is, from their viewpoint, far more at stake than the literal content of propositions.

When the scientismist and clinicalist get together, then, regardless of how often and intimately they interact socially and of the absence of rivalry, one may expect a clash if they get to talking about substantive issues. Though the clash seems to be about specific issues, it is almost always better understood in terms of the inarticulated differences between the two subcultures. Even so, and assuming that the basic differences remain, it seems to me that each represents the maximum challenge to the other to show that his way is best. Insofar as the scientismist remains a scientist, he should welcome having around one to whom the uniqueness of the individual event is precious; for, in the latter's passionate regard for the unique, there is a protection for the former against smug complacency in oversimplification, and there is a challenge to richer theorizing and hypothesizing that can cope with the complexities of psychological phenomena. As a scientist, let him, if he will, maintain a suspicious attitude toward the clinicalist's data, weighing it for the possible admixture of observation and interpretation and for selective reporting; but there is still challenge in its scope and bearing on the complexities of behavior. Moreover, insofar as he is truly a scientist and not merely a faddist, the responsibility particularly devolves on him to be open to the manifold approaches to the accumulation and development of knowledge.

And the clinicalist, insofar as he is genuinely concerned with comprehension, should welcome the fact that there are others around testing other approaches to comprehension. Science does not aim at impoverishing reality, but at comprehending it. The oft apparent lack of concern with the unique is not at all what it seems. The great challenge of science is to be able to account for every unique event and to generate the possibility of new ones in terms that involve a maximum of order and a minimum number of concepts and principles. The clinicalist, unless he is to be as if reborn in every encounter, needs a base of parsimoniously ordered concepts as much as does the scientismist. Let him, if he will, be skeptical and critical of the wares displayed by the scientismist, but let him also be grateful for the challenge of the latter's passion for order and discipline.

As for the great majority of us who, perhaps without realizing it, have found a congenial integration of or compromise between the two subcultures or who comfortably move from one to the other, our problem is not to be overwhelmed by the hysteria generated by extremists. The enterprises of science, technology, and welfare—individually, in paired combinations, and collectively—are all big enough to have a place even for extremists, provided the latter are not endowed with the power to control or exclude others. These enterprises have all known their bigots; and, in many instances, the latter have made significant contributions. Even a Lysenko had something to offer—until, that is, he became the boss.

Let there be free competition of ideas, of methodologies, and even of doctrinaire views. But let us also beware of permitting, if only by default, extremists to curtail the competition or to build walls that block channels of free communication. Let us be mature enough to recognize our interdependence and consequent responsibility, within our means, to provide to each the conditions that will optimize his potential and maximize his contribution.

Live, let live, be glad that there are differences, enjoy them, and profit from them. All of this may be sage advice, but it does not settle the issue of what the scientist is seeking when he searches for knowledge. Nor does it point to the criteria by which he can measure the success he achieves in his quest.

16

VERITY *vs.* TRUTH
IN THE SCIENTIFIC
ENTERPRISE

When the authors of the American Declaration of Independence wrote, "We hold these truths to be self-evident," they did not realize that a future generation of philosophers would lay down rules of usage in accordance with which self-evident truths can have no truth value. By these later rules, a statement can have truth value only if one can judge its truth or falsity on the basis of empirical evidence; and the statement itself must be of an order that lends itself to either verdict. A declaration of human rights is not subject to the verdict of empirical evidence and, by the rules, cannot meaningfully be said to be true.

I have a hunch that the signers of the Declaration would have felt themselves rather put upon by these later rules. I suspect that they thought they were enunciating real truths, and not merely personal commitments. I think they felt they had gotten hold of an essence of human reality.

Indeed, to shift from the authors of the Declaration to the later philosophers, what is the status of the dictum that propositions in the syntactical form of statements of fact are meaningless if they do not lend themselves to empirical testing?

Most of you, I imagine, would agree that the rules are not, and are not intended to be, private conventions of a somewhat esoteric linguistic community. They are advanced for more general use. You will also agree that these rules are intended to sell themselves by their virtues and not to serve as constraints on academic freedom.

If these rules are promulgated and supported, it must be because of their wisdom—their utility in avoiding endless and profitless argument, their success in eliminating language maladapted for communication, and the time they free for activities more worthwhile than wrestling with pseudoproblems.

How do we know that these rules are so wise? Is wisdom immune to empirical test, to the judgment of fact? Why has no one compared probability samples of statements made by observers and nonobservers of the rules for univocality of reference and ease of comprehension? Why have not such samples been compared for their freedom from entanglement with so-called pseudoproblems? And if you were to carry out such tests with the finding that the new rules are not superior to the old, would the positivists and operationalists lay down their arms and passively accept the verdict? Or would they not rather challenge your evidence, the relevance of your criteria, the adequacy of your measurements? What I am trying to suggest is that the proponents of the new rules of truth are convinced of the wisdom of their rules, that wisdom goes beyond rules of syntax to issues of fact, and that the conviction of the wisdom of the rules rests on some foundation other than tests of fact. In other words, the proponents of the new rules hold out a brand of truth that is immune to the rules—a kind of truth that cannot be falsified by empirical data.

I want to discuss the two kinds of truth and their bearing on the scientific enterprise. Let me, in this chapter, reserve the word "truth" for the kind that supposedly can be contradicted by data, and the word "verity" for the kind that cannot be so contradicted. My main thesis will be that verities are far more fundamental to the scientific enterprise than are truths and that we, as scientists, spend an inordinate amount of time in trying to establish truths when we should be seeking verities.

In developing this thesis, I shall first argue that the pursuit of truth, as I have just limited the term, is futile. I shall then consider what I think the scientific enterprise to be really about and deal with the role of verities in this enterprise.

Let me, for the purpose of the first argument, stipulate that, if there is any way of establishing truth, experimentation (in the narrowest sense of the term, that is, with deliberately manipulated independent variables under conditions of random assignment, with control variables, and with observed dependent variables) will do it. Other than experimental research methods are, as modes of truth-seeking, compromises with practical necessity. However convincing the outcomes of a quasi-

experimental study or other marshalling of evidence may be in supporting some truth, one can always think of an experimental design that
would reduce some remaining sources of doubt if the design could be
implemented.

Let me, in passing, mention certain technicalities. I will not build
my case on these matters, but it is well to remember how shaky some
of our best research is in the context of truth-seeking. Consider:

1. The timing of the measures of dependent variables in relation to
the manipulation of the independent variables. It is well known, for
instance, that immediate effects may differ from long-range effects and
that changes in effects over time may go in either direction, toward
intensification (for example, sleeper effects) as well as diminution.
Unless, therefore, possible effects are sampled over time, one may be
seriously deceived by the experimental outcomes.

2. The disregard of psychometric considerations and related technology of measurement by many experimenters. Many psychologists
become obsessed with issues of reliability and validity in the measurement of personality, but they treat these same issues most cavalierly
when it comes to criteria of learning or the *ad hoc* measurements used
in so many experiments.

3. The effect of the nonpublication of negative results on the meaning of published significance levels.

4. The unknown bias introduced by pilot studies. In screening out
research designs (or features of such designs) that one has thought of
as appropriate, they introduce an alien selective factor between the
conceptualization of a problem and its translation into a research design. The effect is compounded by the frequent censorship of the actual
history of the implemented design as a result of journal pressures for
condensed reportage and/or blindness to the issue.

5. How our premium on originality discourages replication of studies.

6. The use of probability statistics on nonprobability samples of undefined populations selected by happenstance from a universe of conceivable populations.

7. The naïveté of assuming that operational definitions are unambiguous.

8. The assumption that operationally defined concepts necessarily
bear some relation to the concepts for which the hypotheses were
derived.

All these, and many more, are matters that bear on our present
standards of truth-seeking. For my immediate purposes, I will stipulate

that standards can be so perfected that the research flow can meet any internal criticism. But it would not be beyond question whether the perfected research can reveal and establish truth. I am arguing that, in principle, experimental method cannot establish truth, that is, confirm disconfirmable propositions.

1. We can design more than one experiment with bearing on any issue. We must, therefore, think, not in terms of one experiment, but in terms of a universe of possible experiments. Unless, however, we can specify the properties of the universe, any experiment or set of experiments is a nonprobability sample of the universe of possible experiments bearing on the issue. As such, it is subject to uncontrolled biases. Without some way of specifying the bounds and structure of the universe of possible experiments, no issue can be subjected to a program of experimentation with assured freedom from bias at whatever confidence level of assurance we may choose.

2. It may be suspected that any experimental outcome depends on an interaction between the experiment and history. That is, the obtained relationships between independent and dependent variables may be subject to peculiarities of time and place. We can, of course, repeat the same experiment within some time span, in different climates, different cultures, and so on. Can anyone pretend, however, that a decade, or a century, or a millennium, or the existing variations in culture and in local conditions exhaust the possibilities of history? There must always remain the possibility that our truths are true only within the frame of reference of some unknown qualification. But a statement that does not carry its necessary qualifications is, in principle, false; the experiment done under conditions that violate these qualifications would prove it false.

Not knowing all the necessary qualifications makes it, in principle, impossible to know whether we have hold of a truth or an approximation thereof. For millennia, man was in no position to observe any contradiction of the proposition that certain kinds of rocks have a downward-falling propensity. Note that this erroneous proposition is not an approximate truth. Nor can it be falsified by observation without access to gravity-free fields. That it could be rejected long before this point in history testifies to the role of verities as against truths in the scientific enterprise. The proposition itself is a verity, and it has been displaced by better verities. What Galileo's observations attacked was not the proposition as such, but an orientation from which it drew its strength, namely, the assumption that physical objects differ from one another in their downward falling propensities. The formula, $s = \frac{1}{2} gt^2$ does not contain an individual difference parameter. Even so, the full implications of Galileo's discovery could not be perceived until some seemingly unrelated notions emerged, namely, that an object such as a feather, falling in an atmosphere or against friction, is not in free fall. My point is that, even what one looks for, to say nothing of the technology of looking, involves an interaction with history. The *Zeitgeist* stands as a mute critic of the feasibility of truth-testing.

There is another point in the example I have just used that I can only make in passing. Implicit in the notion of truth is the assumption that isolated propositions with empirical reference have truth value. Note, however, that the acceptability of the downward falling propensity of objects rests not on directly relevant observations, but on a set of interlocking propositions some of which are not empirical at all. Roll hollow balls filled with feathers or with rocks down inclined planes; the rocks do not hasten and the feathers do not retard the descent. Is this critical? Not if sensible persons can assume that outer material over-whelms inner. Drop feathers and rocks in a vacuum. Is this critical? Not if you assume that vacuums can disorient objects. After all, if you were put, unprotected, into a vacuum, would you know down from up? Carve rocks into the shape of feathers and drop matched pairs in the ordinary atmosphere. But what has been done to a rock when it is forced into the shape of a feather? What would happen to your inner spirit if you were treated likewise? Propositions are never isolated. They come in sets that contain other members, all or some of which are implicit. They do not have individual, private truth values. To speak of the truth value of a proposition or set of propositions one must deal with all of the propositions (positive, negative, and defini-tional) that are hidden in it, a likely impossibility. Unfortunately, I cannot take the time to explore this point. Let me return to the basic point I have been making.

The logic of experimentation does not permit the confirmation of hypotheses. An experiment has the logical structure of a hypothetical proposition, "If A then B." To assert the truth of the proposition merely because, given A we find B, is to commit the fallacy of affirming the consequent. Denying the consequent, however, given the antecedent, denies the proposition.

Accordingly, it seems that science advances knowledge through its disconfirmations. The great concern with experimental or, more gen-erally, observational controls represents effort to deny the consequents in hypothetical propositions. Suppose we have exhausted all of the controls we can think of and that the relationship "If *A* then *B*" still holds. We cannot say that the proposition has been confirmed—merely that we have not been able to figure out a way to disconfirm it. Our definition of truth says nothing about our state of witlessness. A truth is something that can be upset by data, and it retains this property even while we are unable to think of what new kinds of data might upset it. What seems firm, however, is that a hypothetical proposition can be falsified by denying the consequent. Assuming a finite number of possible statements that are false, the advancement of assured knowledge moves inexorably with the elimination of false statements. Note that the assumption of a finite number of false statements may be quite an assumption; but, even if we do make it, the argument turns out to be specious: The denial of consequents does not offer a sure route to knowledge.

3. Thus, there is, in principle, no way of demonstrating with assurance that a statement is false in more than a trivial sense. This became clear with the introduction of the concept of suppressor variables. Suppose, for instance, that *B* varies directly with *A* but inversely with *C*. Suppose, further, that your method of varying *A* induces, unbeknownst to you, covariance of *C*. The variation in *B* will then be suppressed because *C* neutralizes the effects of *A*. Hence, the statement "If *A* then *B*" may be true subject to the qualification that *C* does not covary with *A*. On this basis, however, the disconfirmation of "If *A* then *B*" stands in the same relation of a possible interaction with history or other unknown as does its nondisconfirmation in the face of assiduous effort. The issue I am raising is not mitigated by changing our required significance level. Unless we can exclude the possibility of some unsuspected suppressor variable, no disconfirmation can be taken at face value regardless of how we place the required significance level.

4. Finally, for this line of argument, every experiment, in principle, has the properties of a black box with an interior that cannot be explored in truth. We know what independent and control variables we think we put into an experiment, but we do not know what we carry into the experiment along with these variables. We may have suspicions, hunches, hypotheses (and we can test for these), but beyond them lurk unsuspected possibilities.

It seems only yesterday that Bertrand Russell's quip about German rats sitting, thinking, surveying the situation while American rats run helter skelter in blind trial and error was but a clever joke. Germans were not then experimenting with rats, and American learning experiments precluded inference, reasoning, insight. Since then, however, it has been found that experimental outcomes can depend on interaction with the experimenter.[1] We may try to get around the problem by insisting on replications by different experimenters in different laboratories. But what can we do about the possibility of interactions with traits that currently run across the necessarily relatively homogeneous population of experimenters and laboratories? How many other as yet unsuspected interactions influence our outcomes?

And what of the dependent variables? Not so long ago all of us would probably have been quite content with measures of high reliability and face validity. Then components of reliable variance were discovered that were independent of the manifest content of the measures. Then came the realization that such face-irrelevant reliable components of variance could also constitute components of valid variance. These developments took place mainly in the context of personality and attitude measurement; but the issue of response sets or response styles cuts across the entire domain of psychological measurement, and had been reported earlier on tests of intelligence (for example, speed *vs.* accuracy in test-taking attitudes) and syllogistic reasoning (for example, the atmosphere effect). My point is that these developments should have shattered any confidence that with measures of sufficiently high reliability and validity, in whatever domain, we have any assured knowledge of what we are measuring. Nor can factor analytic technology, multitrait multimethod matrices, and so on do more than push back the boundaries of doubt. There must always remain the possibility that beyond those boundaries there lurk unsuspected variables that could revise entirely our notions of what we are measuring. So long as the suspicion remains abstract, we cannot test for their effects.

And what of the processes that intervene between the input and output variables of an experiment? Again, with some notion of their nature and experimental ingenuity, we can test for them. We can do nothing, however, about the abstract unparticularized suspicion that must remain as a matter of principle.

By now, you must be exceedingly impatient with me. I have been

[1] This issue is itself not resolvable by experimental tests precisely because of the already cited limitations of experiments. One may, of course, in every variety of instance, do one's best to figure out whether to take the possibility of experimenter effect seriously, but a negative outcome is not conclusive. Once the issue has been raised, it remains to haunt us.

building a case on the vaguest of possibilities, on might be's, on suspicions that something may be going on beyond anything we specifically suspect. Have I not been overlooking principles like parsimony and insufficient reason? Scientists do not take vague might be's seriously. What bearing do these principles have, however, on truth values and on the concept of truth as defined? They are principles of conduct, not of epistemology. They have bearing on what we do, not on properties of propositions. As guides to conduct, they must be evaluated in terms of why we are acting. But what logical connection do they have to truth?

What, then, becomes of a truth-seeking science when you cannot rely on confirmation as confirming or on disconfirmation as falsifying, when you have no assurance of what your inputs and outcomes are nor of the processes in between, and when you have no way of establishing the conditions on which your observations depend? Truth-seeking science is a delusion. Should you therefore become an utter uncompromising skeptic, abandoning all hope of science? Should you fall back on blind trust that the powers that be will not mislead you, sternly refusing to contemplate that you have done so and seeking distraction from self-confrontation in the scientific trappings of scientific busy work? What a schizoid existence you must then lead. Or must you not conclude that the nature of the scientific enterprise has been misconstrued?

What, then, is the scientific enterprise about?

Let us begin by considering why we perform experiments. We do so when we confront arbitrariness, either the ultimate arbitrariness of the universe in being as it is or the apparent arbitrariness that stems from the inadequacy of our comprehension. An experiment is critical only if we accept the possibility of an outcome that goes either way.[2] It deals with matters that are to us, at least as yet, arbitrary, that is, it deals with issues of fact. But would not science have reached its intended destination when the only source of arbitrariness left is in the ultimate arbitrarinesses of the universe? Let us assume that this is indeed the intended destination.

---

[2] There is another function for experimentation with respect to which the specific experimental outcome is irrelevant. An experiment or any other research design is a foray into the world on our terms and from our vantage point. When this function is salient, the goal is to get a better "feel" for the subject matter and often the principal outcome is the realizaion that we had asked a silly or naïve question. For reasons that should become apparent below, I myself consider the foray function of far greater significance than the function of ascertaining fact. This value, however, is irrelevant to the immediate argument.

If we keep the intended destination in view, some rather startling inferences may be drawn:

1. Any experimental test of an issue of fact is doomed to become trivial if it does not touch on some ultimate arbitrariness. Once we know the ultimate arbitrarinesses, the experimental issue that does not bear on establishing them must drop out as an issue of fact.

2. The purer the scientific concern, that is, the more detached it is from problems of immediate application, the less impetuously can it afford to pursue issues of fact. The number of ultimate arbitrarinesses must be assumed to be limited or the scientific enterprise itself must be assumed to be hopeless. Correspondingly, the number of issues of fact that must in the long run be resolved as issues of fact must also be assumed to be limited.

3. Assuming the feasibility of the scientific enterprise, its immediate concerns ought not to be with issues of fact, however these issues present themselves, whether as issues of isolated fact or in the guise of theories of relatively narrow factual scope. What we most need to be doing is to think things through so that we can recognize those issues of fact that have some reasonable prospect of turning out to have bearing on the ultimate arbitrarinesses. The more open we remain to the peer status of all issues of fact, the greater the risk of so cluttering up the scene that we become desensitized to issues of fundamental fact when they come along.

The last mentioned inference will obviously be most offensive to those among us who still rally to the banner of the antirationalism of eighteenth- and nineteenth-century science. There was good reason for giving up the hopeless aspirations of the Age of Reason. There are matters that cannot be established by reason—the ultimate arbitrarinesses—and our chances of discovering them are nil if we do not keep testing our formulations against experience. But the antirationalism of eighteenth- and nineteenth-century science was not even faithful to the significant scientific developments of its own day. The Copernican revolution that marked the birth of the Age of Science was literally a revolution in orientation and not a massive revelation of hitherto unrevealed fact. The momentous advance achieved by Newton was a masterpiece of reason resting on a series of incontrovertible tautologies. The transition of chemistry from a collection of recipes to a systematic science was made possible by the conceptual ordering introduced in Mendeleev's periodic table. The impact of Darwin's infinitely patient observations would have been negligible were it not for the set of concepts he introduced that could give his observations conceptual order.

In emphasizing the conceptual side of the scientific enterprise, however, I intend no comfort to those among us who espouse the hypotheticodeductive method as the basic model of psychological science. What this breed of psychologists has persistently overlooked is that the great triumphs of the hypotheticodeductive method in the physical sciences were not achieved in conjunction with theories of very narrow scope. The most narrow-gauged contribution had a place in a conceptualization that covered the cosmos; it did not stand off by itself indifferent to the rest of the known physical universe. Physical theory did not develop as a mosaic of narrow-gauged, low-level theories. Who would have taken the theory of relativity seriously if it did no more than set up some definitions and postulates that could account for the Fitzgerald contraction[3] and a few other odds and ends—and offered some sect of physicists opportunities for mutual reinforcement and recognition through the pursuit of a narrow band of experimental inquiries? What made relativity impressive was that it confronted the total Newtonian universe and went beyond the Newtonian horizons.

I know of no reason and can think of no precedent to justify an expectation that shutting out most of the world is a way of discovering it, or that any isolated hypotheticodeductive theory will ever amount to more than an intellectual game—a passing fad. There is reason, as I have already indicated, to suspect that most will, at best, turn out to be trivia.

We may be a long way from the kind of theory that parallels in the domains of the behavioral sciences the deductive scope achieved by the physical sciences in their domains. All the more is the reason for concern about a reward system that encourages endless blundering and thrashing about and adding to the clutter that fills the pages of our journals. All the more is the reason for concern about the tendency to mistake research volume or technical virtuosity for substantive accomplishment. All the more is the reason to give the utmost encouragement to the examination and reexamination—in the widest variety of contexts and perspectives and in the full panoply of their conceptual as well as empirical interrelationships—of our concepts of what we take to be significant psychological phenomena. And all the more is the reason for constant effort to provide an overall map of the psychological terrain in which a more detailed map of a particular sector has a definite place.

I am not suggesting that the broad concerns preclude attention to odds and ends that do not seem to fit any place. Most emphatically, the

[3] Which, incidentally, was not a factual observation. See note 5.

contrary! Odds and ends can play an important role in the evolution of concepts.

One can experience a datum as falling within the bounds of a concept and yet not meeting its specifications; or the datum may clearly meet the specifications yet be experienced as somehow not fitting. In either case, we are moved to reexamine the concept and its relation to other concepts. Not having a place for some datum may similarly challenge and generate discontent with the whole conceptual structure.

One loose end may as seriously challenge our concepts as a whole series of discordant observations or an experiment with an unexpected outcome. Indeed, loose odds and ends often offer the most serious challenges. Moreover, so little is truth at stake, that even a bad observation may instigate valuable deconceptualization by revealing a possibility that needs to be considered but that might otherwise have been overlooked. By contrast, a serious misconstruction of the nature of reality may be carried through an extravagant program of innumerable experimental studies so long as the scope of the program is kept narrow enough. It may be impossible to reveal the violence to reality within that narrow frame.

Here one discerns one of the most disabling effects of the truth-seeking mission on the scientific enterprise. Odds and ends do entail considerable risk of being rooted in errors of observation. Not even repeated observation of a particular loose end offers much reassurance since errors of observation have been known to persist. Bear in mind that truth-seeking science is a delusional enterprise in the first place and that potentially erroneous observations constitute the prime anxiety source in which the delusion is centered. Truth-seeking science must perforce treat odds and ends as informational noise that can be safely disregarded. Yet attention to them may hold the key to scientific progress, and, if it is not truth we are after, we can afford the risk.

I do not know what led Newton to such remarkable uncontradictable verities as that any change in direction or rate of motion of a material body implies the intrusion of an outside force or that every such intrusion involves an equal and opposite reaction. It is likely that aberrations in the movements of heavenly bodies had more to do with it than did the legendary falling apple. If it was the latter, the falling apple could have been dismissed as a trivium.[4] As to the aberrations, remember that

---

[4] The story of the literal and metaphorical impact of that famous apple has at least this much to support it: It dates back to Newton's own time and was publicized by Voltaire who heard it from Newton's niece, a Mrs. Conduitt. If true, one would suspect some dream preoccupations that were given resolution

the crucial observations leading to the law of gravitation had been made about a century earlier by Tycho Brahe who was not even impelled by them to join the Copernican revolution. The next important step came some thirty years later when Kepler, struggling with these observations, calculated that the planets were in elliptical orbits and not acting the way respectable heavenly bodies should, and then got the heretical notion that an ellipse is no less perfect a geometric curve than a circle. But it was not better or more extensive observations of the planetary motions that resolved the furor over Kepler's laws; and the oddity that did not fit Man's image of his universe—the oddity of planets seemingly following elliptical orbits when there was no good reason why they should not be going in circles—continued to generate controversy until, almost seventy-five years after Kepler announced his first two laws of planetary motion, Newton felt challenged by it as something that demanded explanation. It was at this point that Newton's genius recognized that the controversy over how the planets were moving was ignoring what was moving, namely, massive bodies. In the spelling out of the bearing and implications of this recognition, a new image of the universe was born, to remain unchallenged until various odds and ends began to gnaw at Einstein's conceptual vitals.[5]

---

by the startled contextual apprehension of the apple's impact; on this basis, the episode instanced one of those remarkable creative surges of primary-process thinking that have from time to time revolutionized the scientific and mathematical world. Maybe, we need to devote as much attention to training skills in harnessing primary process to the service of the ego as we do to developing scientific rigor. But forgive the idle speculation.

[5] According to Polanyi (see Michael Polanyi, *Personal Knowledge; Towards a Post-Critical Philosophy* [New York: Harper 1964], pp. 9–15), Einstein has explicitly and unequivocally denied any role of the findings of the Michelson-Morley experiment in the development of his thinking about relativity. Polanyi goes on to say, "The usual textbook account of relativity as a theoretical response to the Michelson-Morley experiment is an invention . . . the product of a philosophical prejudice. When Einstein discovered rationality in nature, unaided by any observation that had not been available for at least fifty years before, our positivistic textbooks promptly covered up the scandal by an appropriately embellished account of his discovery" (p. 11).

Although widely accepted as a "fact," the Fitzgerald contraction was a hypothetical concept advanced in 1893 as an explanation of the null results of the Michelson-Morley experiment. Fitzgerald attributed the contraction to the movement of a body through the ether. Relativity theory yielded an identical result, but on another basis.

From Polanyi's discussion of the evolution of Einstein's thought (including a detailed statement authorized for publication by Einstein himself in 1954), Einstein's initial impetus came when, at age 16, he was struck by a paradox in the then current theory of light. If one could travel along with a beam of light,

Note, in all this, that it was the overarching concepts that were at issue and that concepts are verities, not truths. Like a definition, which is an effort to encompass a concept in words, concepts may have empirical reference and, as already noted, they may be challenged by data; but they cannot be contradicted by data.

No data can contradict Newton's laws, for instance. A change in motion implies the intrusion of a force, by definition, and provides the measure of the latter. We can determine a measure of the mass of an object in some contexts and of the force associated with a generating procedure in other contexts. Thus, we determine independent values of a mass and of a force. When we bring the two together, we find that the acceleration is what would be expected from the relation $F = Ma$. The latter is still a conceptual circle, but it is a useful one. Suppose the acceleration differed from expectation. Would this disprove the relation? Not at all. We could question our measures. We could assume the random intrusion of undetected forces. We could assume that the mass of an object is not invariant or that forces generated in particular ways are variable. No matter how often our expectations were disappointed, $F = Ma$ would still remain a definitional verity. But we would have

the latter should appear as a spatially oscillatory electromagnetic field at rest. This seemed to Einstein to be inconsistent with both experience and the Maxwell equations. The second major anomaly ("oddity") that led to the theory was a lack of symmetry in the treatment of electric current in a wire in a magnetic field, depending on whether it is the wire or the magnet that is at rest. Note the intrusion of an aesthetic consideration, symmetry.

As a minor aside, though the lapse of time in the availability of relevant fact helps to make the role of conceptualization in scientific revolutions more dramatic, it is not at all critical in principle. Whatever the motivation of the positivistic textbooks may have been, I cannot see that the point would have been essentially altered if, in fact, the theory of relativity had been instigated as a specific response to the Michelson-Morley findings.

It is also worth noting another point in Polanyi's discussion of the Michelson-Morley issue. He points out that it was recognized as early as 1902 (the Michelson-Morley experiment was done in 1887) that the results of the experiment were not null; there was a calculable ether drift of 8–9 kilometers per second, and thousands of replications with better apparatus by D. C. Miller and collaborators, from 1902–1926, obtained the same result. Thus, the theory of relativity (which demanded the null result) was in conflict with available "fact" until at least 1927; and, in this case, the fact had to yield to the theory. A series of studies, starting in 1927, using methods and rationales other than that used in the Michelson-Morley 1897 experiment, have established the absence of ether drift. The original Michelson-Morley and subsequent findings have been explained in a variety of ways, so that, if the explanations are valid, the replication of the experiment millennia from now should yield the same result, that is, it is not the facts (the measured outcome) that have been challenged but the meaning of the facts.

little use for it either as a guide to conduct or in comprehending our world.

Experience may lead us to give up Newton's laws, but not by proving them false. If we give them up, it is because we find another set of definitions and concepts more helpful. And if we do give them up, we may eventually find it advisable to return to them, possibly in somewhat modified form.

Suppose you grant, if only for the moment, that the production of conceptual verities constitutes the primary and major task of the scientific enterprise. There are still some matters that cannot be settled by reason, namely, issues of fact that constitute the ultimate arbitrarinesses of the universe and other issues of fact the resolution of which may help us to grasp needed tasks of conceptualization. But if truth is beyond our reach, how can we deal with issues of fact? I must obviously reinterpret the scientific enterprise as something other than truth-seeking.

I have been careful to speak of the scientific enterprise rather than of some abstract impersonal science. It is a human enterprise and can only be comprehended as such. It meets human needs. It is one of the enterprises in which human beings seek to come to terms and to grips with, and to master the world in which they find themselves. A helpful metaphoric description of the scientific enterprise is that it seeks to accomplish its mission by working at the preparation of an efficient master chart or mapping of this world, a chart designed to be helpful in negotiating passage through this world, whether the passage is also to serve other utilitarian or merely sightseeing interests.

The map is worked and reworked, drawn and redrawn, to make it ever more comprehensive and efficient, efficiency being understood in the sense of minimizing the amount of redundant information that is entered as well as in relation to the pragmatic function of guiding the negotiation of the pathways of the real world.

The entries in the map, the propositions that are charted, tell us what to expect as we go from here to there, the significant features to look for in order to identify what is here and what is there, what needs to be done to achieve particular transitions, and, in the event that the expectations are not fulfilled, they direct attention to factors that could account for the failure. The primary function of the map is pragmatic, though the charting principles involve considerations that are not primarily practical. It is devoted to what works in finding one's way about the universe. Occam's razor is a charting principle that follows directly from the map's primary function: We do not make entries that correspond to things we have no positive reason to believe are actually there or that do not facilitate dealings with what seems to be actually there, for the same reason that no mariner would enter imaginary islands or nonfunctional scribblings on his navigation charts. The concept of truth, as defined, does not apply to the scientific map because at no point do we enter truths. What we enter are beliefs about what the world is like, the best beliefs we can come to on the basis of available data, repeated revisions, critical thought, and judgments of the expected worth of conceptual and factual alternatives. The main entries and the charting principles are verities just as are the latitudes and longitudes on a navigational map. The issues of fact are resolved as best we know how and no one assumes that the factual entries correspond to the truth, the whole truth, and nothing but the truth. There are deliberate omissions from the map in order to avoid unnecessary clutter and because we know the omissions can be inferred from the master chart.

In preparing the map, what we take to be fact is so imbedded in verities as to have no clearly distinguishable status. Some of the verities in which our facts are imbedded describe conditions of trustworthy observation, but there are others that relate to definition, classification, and prescriptions like the law of parsimony. Where, for instance, is the fact in the relation of the tubercle bacillus to pulmonary tuberculosis? In our day, it is in a circular definition, an incontrovertible verity; the diagnosis calls for positive laboratory findings. It was Robert Koch's good fortune, and ours, that he confronted a biased sample of cases that did not include clinically indistinguishable cases lacking the bacillus. Note that neither the circularity of the contemporary definition nor the faulty observation that led to the discovery lessens the pragmatic significance of the distinction: The bacillus-infected cases respond to certain kinds of treatment that do not affect the others.

At any rate, the test of the validity of the factual entries is not necessarily different than that applied to the verities because it is primarily the map that is being tested and not the entries. If the map fails us, it needs revision, sometimes in a particular sector, sometimes in its entirety. Experience and a reason I will cite shortly suggest that the issue is generally quite trivial if there is nothing more than a fact at stake. On the other hand, endlessly wasted effort is likely to ensue when a verity, for example, subconscious awareness, is treated as a factual issue. The concept of subconscious awareness is primarily a matter of definition and its empirical content is so general that to challenge the latter is to challenge the possibility of any knowledge. There simply is no factual issue. There must be subconscious awareness or there can be no awareness at all, not even a questioning of its existence.

I am not preaching a simple-minded pragmatism. The validity of propositions cannot be sufficiently tested for the scientific enterprise—as it can be for the technological enterprise—by how well they work. When you are building a bridge, you can take advantage of practical lore and know-how that has not yet been fitted into the framework of physical knowledge. In the scientific enterprise, we are concerned with the master map and demand a maximum of information value with a minimum of clutter in this map. The validity of the map is therefore tested, not merely by its pragmatic utility, but by its internal coherence, implicative structure, freedom from clutter, and comprehensiveness. We regard some of the entries with greater confidence than others, but we do so on the basis of how radically the map would have to be changed if we were to challenge them. This is why purely factual issues are apt to be trivial even in the short run; one can change the factual entry without changing anything else. Moreover, since our universe is still so largely, so to say, *terra incognita*, we prefer, the other factors being more or less equal, the kind of map that most facilitates exploration of the unknown, that is, one that points to places from which to take off and alerts us to what we ought to be looking for. The faith that we come to better and better approximations of reality is justified by the progressively increasing efficiency of our master map, both with respect to pragmatic validity and internal order.

In this enterprise, the well-designed experiment offers, when applicable, the most effective single device that has yet been invented for testing the validity of our map or of sectors thereof. Its main advantage is that, as noted earlier, it permits a foray into the world on our own terms, from our particular vantage point, and with the sharpest focus we can bring to bear on the issues that strike us as important in choosing among possible alternative ways of drawing some sector of our map. At best, however, it cannot test for truth; it can only test our comprehension of our world as achieved through past encounters by generating critical new encounters. It cannot tell us that we are right. It can only tell us that our map is still pragmatically sound or that it seems to require some emendation for it to meet the criterion of pragmatic validity. But it can never tell us with certainty what in the existing map needs change. At its best, too, it is a device in which we have more confidence than any other for resolving issues of fact and, as such, it is as relevant to the technological as to the scientific enterprise. For neither enterprise, however, can it tell us which are the most important factual issues that demand resolution. In other words, an experiment is not self-justifying, no matter how beautifully designed. Science is not for experimentation; the experiment is for the purposes of the scientific enterprise and must be governed by the latter.

Nor is the experiment the only device for testing the pragmatic validity of our map. If, as so often happens, we cannot think of any feasible way to design an experiment that is relevant and nondistorting or if it is not considered worth the investment, we fall back on other devices for testing the pragmatic validity of our map. Multivariate correlational techniques, for instance, permit a simultaneous examination of a greater number of variables than is generally feasible in an experiment, and they can help reduce apparent ambiguity when random assignment is impossible. It also seems to me to be a truism—a verity, if you will—that one critical case study can be worth more than a thousand badly designed or irrelevant experiments.

Indeed it may be added that, in a very fundamental sense, every empirical research study carried out for scientific purposes is actually a single case study. Let me illustrate the point by referring to a study in which I was able to cover every case in a defined population. This population could not be regarded as a probability sample of a larger population because of unique features of time and place.

"Heavens to Betsy," cried one statistician. "Don't you want to make some generalizations on the basis of your research? How can you do that if you disregard the logic of sampling?" My statistician friend, it seems, in common with a great many behavioral scientists, could only comprehend one kind of scientific generalization—from the statistics of a sample to the parameters of a statistical universe. But he has never asked himself why, in his role as scientist (as distinguished from the role of a quality-control engineer or some other technological role), he should want to know about this statistical universe. In effect, he is saying that science stops at the point when one has eliminated the possibility of sampling error. Perfect measurement spells the death of science! "Well," say I in reply, "just imagine that you have measured the performance of every sophomore in the country after administrations of drug A and drug B. What generalizations can you then make? To nonsophomores in Southwest Asia? When and if you can contemplate measuring every element in your statistical universe, you will discover that you are dealing with a single case, limited in time and space—your universe—and that it is at that point that you confront the real concerns of scientific (as distinguished from technological) generalization, that is, not so much the identification of isolated things and events as the mapping of relationships among all things and events in the universe of universes. I hope you will not be offended if I suggest that your generalization processes at that point will depend on the nonstatistical insights and understandings you will have achieved rather than on confidence intervals, *t* tests, and *F* ratios. You will want to study more cases, that is, more statistical universes, but your thinking will be more akin to that of the clinician than to that of the statistician.

My main thesis, however, is that while pragmatic validity is a necessary condition of the acceptability of the map in the scientific enterprise, it is not the only condition; and the bulk of the map-making activity should be going into working on these other requirements. The deflation of the experimental method as a basis for assured knowledge, speaks to this conclusion. Moreover, at any point in the history of our knowledge of the world, there are probably innumerable maps that can be drawn which are pragmatically equally valid, and we can doubtless be far more effective from a pragmatic point of view if we were to concentrate on map segments without concern about how they will fit together. The latter, appropriate to technology, seems to be increasingly what we are doing as scientists. Behavioral science—the "pure" variety, that is—is acquiring more and more of the accouterments of technology, but, paradoxically, with more and more disdain for and less and less to offer to technology. It is not, however, what I take the scientific enterprise to be about or for.

What I have been saying is subversive of established ways of doing things. Intellectual and emotional defense will doubtless be mobilized against my thesis. I hardly expect this book to change the face of psychology. I do hope it will loosen some rigidities and thereby ease the constraints on nonexperimental, nonstatistical inquiry for those who are so inclined. I do hope our students will be exposed to the notion that thought can be as scholarly as empirical research and may have at least as much to contribute to psychology. I do hope this book will contribute to a climate in which a thoughtful nonresearch doctoral thesis will be possible, using "research" in the indefensibly narrow sense that psychologists have assigned to the term. Most fundamentally, I do hope that those who are so inclined and appropriately gifted will be encouraged to pursue long-range programs of conceptual analysis, freed from obsessional hounding and badgering to produce premature and inappropriate empirical validation of their work.

At any rate, it is in the spirit of this chapter that I have written this book.

INDEX

abstract, meaning of, 148–149

abstractions and imaginal representations, 206–207

act(s), brief, 68, 255; initiation of, 255; and overshooting the mark, 255. *See also* action, blocked act, spontaneous act, unfinished business

action(s), and constraint, 296; and executive apparatus, 296; and external cause, 75–77; initiation of, 255; Janet's general theory of, 256; mobilization and demobilization of, 256. *See also* directed action, nonbehavioral action, reinforced action, spontaneous action

active image of man, and attention catchers, 110; described, 6; and determinism, 22, 38; and freedom, 292–298 *passim*; and motivation, 268

activity, in progress, 23. *See also* diffuse activity, directed activity, interrupted activity, quasirandom activity, scanning activity, spontaneous activity

actuality, and imagination, 181–183

acute motivation, 268–271

affectless motivation, 272, 275–276

aesthetic considerations, in science, 223, 330n

affect(s), 271–277; described, 272; and enduring concerns, 276; and feedback, 276; and motives, 274–276; normatization of, 276; and signification, 274; and society, 276

affective vs. affectless situational assessment, 275–276

Allport, Gordon W., 164n, 164–166, 165n

animistic orientation, 211

anthropomorphic fallacy, 229

antinomy of psychology and humanities, 3–9

antirationalism, scientists', 327

anxiety, existential, 211–212

appetitive drives, 244, 251–258 *passim*, 270–271; described, 254–255; and emotions, 271; and impulse, 254–255; and perpetuated motives, 254–255; quasi-, 257, 257n. *See also* drives

arbitrariness(es), ultimate, 327. *See also* law, ultimate

Aristotle, 176, 179

attention, and degrees of awareness, 109; as explanatory concept, 109; as mental faculty, 109–110; three meanings of, 111–112

attributive clearness, 112n

authentication vs. confirmation of hypotheses, 100n

authority and ego, 243

authority figure. *See* primal authority figure

awareness(es), and behavior, 81–85, 89–91, 95, 136; and behaviorists, 121; of behaviors, 104–106; defined, 83, 95; degrees of, 109, 112; and directed acts, 84; and Huxley, 177; and motivation, 84; as object of awareness, 119; objects of, 137; postulates about, 84–85; qualities of as discriminanda, 137; structure of and self, 197–199; spontaneity of, 85; and succession of subjects, 195–196, 198; and Titchener, 118–119; of unconscious motives, 102–103. *See also* conscious awareness, dual awareness, subconscious awareness, qualities of awareness

basic personality, 224

271; latent, 268; and manic excitement, 33; as master integrative concept, 29; and mediating interactions, 26; and motivated act, 79; and object self, 218–219; and omnipotence, 31; paradigm of, 23; prevalent concepts of, 259; and psychological processes, 28–29; and purpose, 80–81; and responsibility, 38; and scanning activity, 86; self-preservative, enhancing, determining, 219; self-related, 218–219; and situational assessment, 275; and superordinate event, 80–81; systemic structure of, 218; and transactions, 85. *See also* perpetuated motives

multiple personality, 291
Murphy, Gardner, 165

natural science, and psychology, 306n
naturalism, and freedom, 30n
nature, and mind, 50–54
necessity, and freedom, 32
neobehaviorism, 306
Newton, Sir Isaac, 171, 327–332 *passim*
nirvana principle, 249n, 250, 264
nonbehavioral action, 64, 77–79
noncognitive learning, 13
nonexperimental inquiry, 336
neurosis, and traumatic episodes, 244–249; and transference, 245–246, 248
nursing period, 247

object(s), constancy, 86–88; defined, 69–70; experiences as scientific, 121; identity of, 86–88; and relational network, 86–87; and things, 86–87
object self, 199–201; appearance of as actor, 210–211; and motives, 218–219
observables, exclusion of, 8
Occam, William of, 13, 332
occasionalists, 172–173
odds and ends, 329–330, 330n
oedipal period, 247, 252–254
omnipotence, 31–32
O'Neill, Eugene, 205
operational definition. *See* definition
operationalism, and behavioral sciences, 47; and behaviorism, 133; and intellectual climate, 53–55; philosophical roots of, 50–56; and positivism, 50, 53–55; and research, 49–50; and science, 54, 56; and scientism, 309; spread of, 47–56 *passim*; and terminology, 47–50, 53; and trait theorists, 281

organism, 165–167, 185–186, 190
overdetermination, principle of, 247n, 253n

pain, 79n, 203–204, 265
panmentalism, 175
parsimony, principle of (Occam's razor), 84, 156, 185, 243, 247n, 247–248, 309–310, 326, 332, 333; and Freud, 247–248; and intelligence, 233; justification of, 8; explained, 12–13; and qualities, 121–122; and reductionism, 162n
particularity, and clinicalism, 307, 313–317 *passim*
passive image of man, and attention, 109–110; and behaviorists, 6; and Burke, 240–242; and conditioning model, 14; described, 6; and determinants of behavior, 22; and drive, 6, 25n; and individual dignity and worth, 8, 11n; and motives, 25; and psychologists, 294; philosophical commitments to, 9
passive resistance, as active adaptation, 242
passivity, cases of, 241–242; and external givens, 241; and Greek tragedies, 242
Penfield, W., 167n, 167–168
perpetuated motives, 35–36, 218–221 *passim*, 225–229; and appetitive drive, 254–255; and behavior, 87; and enduring concerns, 36; meaning of, 87; re superego, 243
perseveration, 257
personality, changes in, 287, 288; characterization of, 280, 287; as motivational system, 37, 280, 287; nature of persisting, 183; of scientist in science, 302; and traits, 279–286
person system, 166, 180, 182–183
phenomenalism, 133–134
phenomenology, 117
philosophy, and psychology, 301–302, 305; and realities, 146–151
physiological psychology, 163
physiology and behavior, 126
Pickwick, Mr., and realities, 143–144
plans, and computers, 27–28
Platonic ideals, 149
pleasantness, 272–274
pleasure, 272–277 *passim*; and behaviorism, 261–262; and commitments, 273–274; dimensions of, 273; and effort, 272–273; and ego, 277; and Freud, 249n, 250, 254–255, 262–264;